Egypt: An Economic Geography

Egypt: An Economic Geography

FOUAD AND BARBARA IBRAHIM

I.B. TAURIS

LONDON · NEW YORK

Published in 2003 by I.B.Tauris & Co. Ltd
6 Salem Road, London W2 4BU
175 Fifth Avenue, New York NY 10010
www.ibtauris.com

In the United States of America and in Canada distributed by Palgrave
Macmillan, a division of St Martin's Press, 175 Fifth Avenue, New York
NY 10010

International Library of Human Geography 1

ISBN 1 86064 547 X hbk ISBN 1 86064 548 8 pbk

A full CIP record for this book is available from the British Library
A full CIP record for this book is available from the Library of Congress
Library of Congress catalog card: available

Set in Monotype Dante by Ewan Smith, London
Printed and bound in Great Britain by MPG Books, Bodmin

Contents

Tables

Figures

Illustrations

CHAPTER I

The State of Egypt at the Beginning of the Third Millennium

§ THE ancient Egyptians established a unique culture and an unprecedented advanced civilization thousands of years ago. Before industrialization started in Europe, Egypt was well equipped to compete with its neighbours beyond the Mediterranean, but its current state of development is not easy to assess. In modern times it has fallen behind countries in other parts of the world in terms of development. It fits neither into the category of a developing country, nor into that of an industrialized one. Egypt's economic and social characteristics provide contradictory indicators, some showing advancement, others the opposite:

- Egypt has reached a relatively high standard of technological development, though a large part of Egyptian society has no access to modern technology.
- Industrialization began in Egypt as early as in 1815, but in 2000/01 agriculture still employed 28.2 per cent of the total working population – more than the industrial, mining and construction sectors put together (see Table 9.2).
- The country has a remarkably well-qualified workforce and in recent decades has exported between 2 and 4 million skilled labourers and university graduates, mainly to the Arab states where they play a significant role in the development of these countries. In the USA, in Canada and in Australia, Egyptians rank among the best-qualified immigrants. However, illiteracy rates are still very high in the country.
- Egyptian agricultural statistics show per acre yields comparable to those of highly developed countries; this is partly due to the Green Revolution. However, Egypt's agricultural production depends to a considerable extent still on man and animal power.
- In the second half of the twentieth century Egypt developed a fast-growing energy sector based on its mineral oil and gas resources as well as on its potential for hydropower, but the competitiveness of its industrial products is decreasing year by year.

- Egypt has a relatively well-developed infrastructure and a vast expanding tourist industry.
- Egypt can look back upon a long tradition in building a politically mature civil society, in spite of all present setbacks. The revolution of 1919 against the British colonial power as well as the subsequent establishment of a parliamentary democracy with a multi-party system are evidences of this political maturity.

This list of indicators could be continued. Seen as a whole, it provides plausible reasons for classifying Egypt as 'a country in transition' with an emerging economy, like many other countries of what was formerly called the 'Third World'. The achievements mentioned can be considered important steps towards building a modern state. However, they have been brought about partly by importing Western concepts and technologies into a pre-modern society, and are a result of two centuries of developmental strife, which began with the reign of Mohammed Ali (1805–48). He cherished the ambition of developing Egypt, so as to enable it to take its place as a major world power following French ideals, and he ultimately challenged the Ottoman Empire.

Notwithstanding its many achievements, Egypt is still plagued by many ailments and shortcomings today, and shows disparities that are typical of developing countries. The deplorable social and economic conditions cannot be concealed behind the magnificent façades of the tall steel and glass buildings in Cairo, Alexandria and elsewhere, the modern metro in the country's capital, the gigantic structure of the Aswan High Dam, and the luxurious holiday resorts and the gated communities on the Red Sea and Mediterranean coasts. Critical voices in the country have openly drawn people's attention to the paradoxical state of development in Egypt (Heikal 1995; Ismail 1988; Zaki 1993). Among the economic problems most heatedly discussed in the country itself are the following:

Egypt's diminishing food production In spite of the continued efforts undertaken by the government to strengthen the country's food production by means of land reclamation in desert areas, and to protect it from too much stress by propagating birth control, the increase in arable land has not fulfilled expectations and population growth is still considerable (see Figure 1.2). From the mid-1940s to 2000, the per capita harvested area diminished to one-third. Whereas the total of Egypt's agricultural land remained more or less the same, the area harvested increased greatly owing to repeated cultivation of land in the same year, made possible through the availability of more irrigation water. But this success was undermined by the enormous population increase. During this time, Egypt turned from a food-exporting country into a food-importing one, although 29 per cent of the working population were still employed in agriculture in the year 2000. In 2001 the country had to import 5.1 million tons of wheat (see Figure 8.5), which is the staple food of the Egyptians. Cereal imports are laying a heavy burden on the nation's economy. In 2000, for instance, Egypt imported wheat, wheat flour and maize at a cost of about US$1.1 billion, a sum which constituted 9 per cent of the total value of the country's imports (CAPMAS 2001b).

External factors threatening the national economy The fact that Egyptian agriculture fails to supply the food requirements of the country's population would have no serious economic consequences if the deficits were balanced by a respective growth in other economic sectors, leading to equivalent exports. But the total growth rate of the Egyptian economy has shown a steep decline since the 1980s (see Figure 1.1). While official sources boast of the achievements made in the areas of land reclamation and industrial development, many people see a steady deterioration in the overall economy taking place. All economic sectors suffered considerably after the withdrawal of the financial aid from oil-rich Arab countries after the 1979 Camp David Agreement with Israel, but structural problems also ensued after the socialist regime came to an end, when economic liberalization measures were introduced and the Structural Adjustment Programmes of the World Bank were implemented. All these external factors coming into effect within only three decades changed the framework of Egypt's macroeconomic conditions decisively, making consistent planning of the country's economy impossible for the Egyptian government.

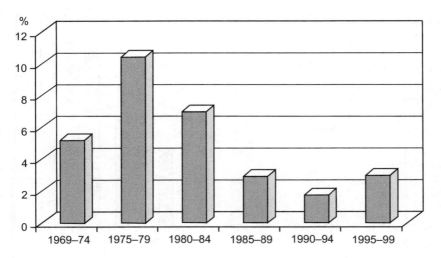

Figure 1.1 Per capita GDP in Egypt: growth rates 1969–99 (Author: F. Ibrahim 2002; cartography: J. Feilner; sources of data: Heikal 1995: 14-16; <http://www.sis.gov.eg/egyptinf/economy/html/ecoind1.htm>)

The heavy burden of external debt Egypt's external debt reached its highest peak of US$55 billion in 1989 (Muselhi 1993: 112), when the state was scarcely able to fulfil its debt servicing, which consumed more than 50 per cent of the country's hard currency reserves. The external debt decreased to US$32 billion in the year 2000 (World Bank 2001). The persistence of external debt is caused mainly by the chronic deficit in the foreign trade balance, which increased by 190 per cent from 1991 to 2000/01 (CAPMAS 1994a: 282; Ministry of Information 2002b).

The changing role of the public sector in Egypt's economy The socialist policies adopted by Nasser (1954–71) led to an enormous inflation of in the public sector and to a drastic diminution of the private one. Today, the public sector is still over-dimensioned, despite Sadat's and Mubarak's efforts to effect a transformation in the economy, which started in 1971. In 1989/90, parastatal firms working in the areas of manufacturing and trade still accounted for

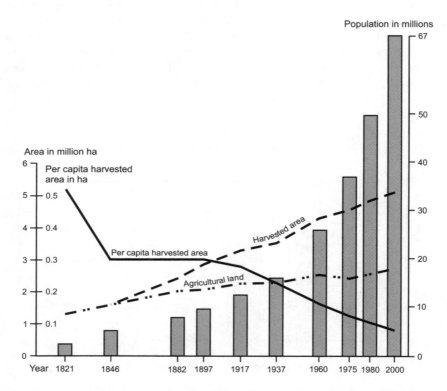

Figure 1.2 Population increase and availability of agrarian land in Egypt (Author: F. Ibrahim 2002; cartography: J. Feilner; sources of data: after Said 1993: 217; CAPMAS 2001b; UNDP 2002: 143)

more than two-thirds of the value of production and for three-quarters of employment (Giugale and Mobarak 1996: 141f). Up to now the greater part of the country's employed labour force has been engaged in the public sector, including parastatals. As was the case in other socialist countries with state-controlled economies, the Egyptian public sector was characterized by weak performance.

The first attempts at economic liberalization in Egypt consisted of the establishment of new private companies with strong state capital sharing, or of joint ventures, both of which soon proved to be failures (Ismail 1988: 25). Participating private entrepreneurs were usually politically influential persons whose primary interest was to gain profit by making use of the state's corrupt administrative apparatus. They exploited the subsidies and the privileges granted by the state and finally either sold their businesses at low prices when they had been ruined, or handed them back to the state, making it responsible for the welfare of the dismissed employees.

Deregulation of the economy and the labour market Between 1975 and 1999, Egypt's rate of unemployment increased from 2.5 per cent to more than ten times that figure (ILO 2001; World Bank 2001: 278; Ministry of Information 2001a). The latter source states that the total number of employed persons in the country was 17.434 million in 1999/2000. According to the World Development Report 2000/2001, the labour force in Egypt was 24 million in 1999 (World Bank 2001: 278). This means that the employment/labour force ratio was 72.6 per cent, so the unemployment rate was 27.4 per cent in that year. As the issue of unemployment was hotly politicized by the opposition, the government discarded the standard definition ratified by international conventions and calculated the unemployment rate down to 8 per cent in 2000/01 (Ministry of Information 2002a). According to a study by R. Assaad of the University of Minnesota, only one-third of new entrants to the labour market in 1998 found employment (Farag 2000). The desperate situation of the labour market was exacerbated by the application of the Structural Adjustment Programmes, intended, among other things, to privatize parts of the public sector and eliminate redundancy in the civil service. The implementation of both policies resulted in large numbers of employees losing their jobs. It was estimated that in the year 2000 the civil service required only 1.2 million of the 5.9 million persons actually employed in it (Kazim 2001; Internet 2001b).

Although reform is direly needed in the public sector, short- and medium-term measures have to be taken to solve the problems of the reform victims.

Rising prices, poverty and social inequity Consumer prices in Egypt started to rise dramatically after the 1970s. Based on 1987 prices (= 100 per cent), the 1995 index was 338.2 per cent in urban areas and 325.6 per cent in rural ones

(CAPMAS, annually 1988–95). This consumer price increase of about 230 per cent was accompanied by a per capita GNP increase of only 47 per cent. If one takes into account the fact that the per capita GNP of the great majority of Egyptians is less than one-third of the country's average, one recognizes that the real effect of consumer price inflation is even greater. In 1998, for instance, per capita GNP in Egypt was calculated to be US$1,290 on average. But 86 per cent of the population shared only 26 per cent of the country's GNP, while 74 per cent was enjoyed by only 14 per cent of Egyptians. This means that 86 per cent of the people had an average per capita GNP of only US$392, while 14 per cent had an average of US$6,863 per capita (*Al-Wafd*, 30 December 1999: 6), as one Egyptian economist has pointed out. According to the same source, 8.5 million households, i.e. about 55 per cent of the Egyptian population, had a monthly income of LE100–500 (= US$28–140; LE = Egyptian pound) and came under the absolute poverty line of US$1/day per capita. An official survey conducted by CAPMAS in 1999/2000 showed that the daily per capita income was distributed as follows: 20 per cent of the Egyptian population earned less than US$1, while 50 per cent earned US$1–2, and 30 per cent earned more than US$2. The overall average was US$2, which indicates a highly inequitable income distribution (Gamal-el-Din 2001). Heikal (1995) cites an international study of income distribution in Egypt according to which some 74,000 citizens possess wealth totalling about US$650 billion (see Table 1.1). He remarks that Egyptian experts consider this result to be a stark underestimate of the real state of wealth concentration in Egypt. Besides, the study left out real estate, such as the skyscrapers on the Nile, and also neglected Egyptian multimillionaires living abroad. Heikal stresses the fact that nine-tenths of this wealth was generated by corrupt and unlawful means – the use of political influence when granting commercial concessions for strategic commodities like weapons, iron, cement, sugar and meat (including the import of cheap meat, whose permitted date of consump-

Table 1.1 Egyptian multimillionaires: Egyptians with wealth equivalent to US$5 million or more (*c.* 1990)

Number of persons	Wealth in million US$
70,000	5–10
2,800	10–15
350	15–30
220	30–50
150	50–80
100	80–100
50	>100

Source: after Heikal 1995: 20

1. *Weathered rock in the South Sinai desert*: In Central and South Sinai one finds the contact zone between the old Precambrian metamorphic and effusive rocks and the younger Mesozoic sandstones. The canyons and bizarre weathering forms of the latter have of late become a tourist attraction. (Photo: F. Ibrahim)

tion has already expired). He laments tax evasion, misuse of influence and exploitation of the poor.

Problem number one: corruption This brief overview of the most acute problems hampering Egypt's development may have made it clear that the country still has a long way to go and that its future will depend not only on how its natural and human resources are utilized but much more on whether it will be possible to reform an ailing economic structure, adopt appropriate social policies and, last but not least, eradicate corruption. In 1998, Egypt was ascribed a deplorable Corruption Perceptions Index (CPI) of 2.9, which ranked it at 66 worldwide, while the 'cleanest' country, Denmark, had a CPI of 10, and the most corrupt country, Cameroon, with a CPI of 1.4, was ranked 85 (Internet 1999b).

CHAPTER 2

The People of Egypt

1. The complexity of Egyptian identity

The image Europeans and Americans usually have of Egyptians is rather stereotyped. In their minds, they classify them as Arab Muslims who were recently entangled in a war with Israel, and associate their country with hot desert, the Pyramids, the Pharaohs, the Nile and the Red Sea.

The Egyptians' own perception of themselves and of their country is different. Until quite recently, most did not consider the desert as part of their environment, although it covers 96.5 per cent of Egypt. Their traditional living spaces were on the one hand the intensively cultivated arable land and, on the other, the densely populated, commercially active towns. Only in recent times, after intensive political propaganda through the media, did the common citizen begin to be aware – without being actually convinced – that the desert could serve as a habitat, too.

The great majority of Egyptians are *fellaheen*, i.e. peasants or people living in rural areas, for whom the Nile valley has always signified the domain of life and the desert that of death. For them, the people of the desert are not Egyptians. They call the Bedouin *'arab*, using a term that has negative connotations for them. Such an unfavourable perception is reciprocated by the Bedouin, e.g. by those living on Sinai or along the country's north-western coast.

Like other peoples all over the world, Egyptians have complex identities. According to a given situation they can stress one or other facet. However, they always differentiate between the rural *fellaheen* (singular *fellah*) and the people of the *madina*, i.e. the town, the latter being associated with *madaniyya*, i.e. civilization. Urban people further define their identity according to the town they belong to; e.g. a *masrawi* is a man from Cairo (*masr* = Cairo), an *iskandarani* a man from Alexandria. Egyptians also differentiate regionally, between the people of Lower Egypt (see Illustration 13), who are called *baharwa* (singular *bahrawi*), and the Upper Egyptians, who are called *sa'ayda* (singular *sa'idi*) and considered by the *baharwa* as slow of understanding, tradition bound and less developed. The geographical border of the *sa'iid* (south) has been pushed further southward owing to the impact of the urban sprawl around Greater Cairo since the mid-twentieth century. Today the dialect border lies at about 200 km south of the country's capital in El-Minya Governorate, while the other *sa'idi* traits become dominant about 400 km south of Cairo from Asyut Governorate. On another level one differentiates between three categories of local population: the actual Egyptians, the Bedouin, with their characteristic way of dressing, and the dark-skinned Egyptian Nubians, who are often confused in Egyptian perceptions with the Sudanese immigrants. At the beginning of the twenty-first century the languages and dialects of the marginal groups are quickly disappearing owing to the assimilation of these groups into the main bulk of the Egyptian population. This process has been accelerated by rural–urban migration, formal education and more importantly also by the impact of television. The Cairene dialect, which used to be the language of a minority a century ago, has become the standard language of the country. Though Egyptian Arabic with all its various dialects is a language of its own, it is not perceived as such by Egyptians, who use classical Arabic at school and in the mosque, and consider this the real Arabic language. Literature produced by Egyptian writers of international renown, like Naguib Mahfouz, the winner of the 1988 Nobel Prize for literature, which is written in classical Arabic, is irrelevant to the local population. However, local groups of musicians and poets who use the vernacular language enjoy great popularity at a regional level, though they do not enjoy high esteem among the more educated. It is one of the dilemmas of the country that the people's spoken language finds no real acceptance in formal education, so that a person must necessarily be at least bilingual to belong to the educated class.

Egyptian identity is to a great extent also defined by religious affiliation. Differentiation is made between the *muslimeen* (singular *muslim*), the Muslims and the *aqbat* (singular *qibti*), the Christian Copts. The state itself underlines this difference by demanding a corresponding record in citizens' identity cards.

The fact that many Egyptians today claim to have an Arab identity is mainly due to the propaganda spread during the era of Nasser. Throughout the 1950s he called for pan-Arabism to serve his political ends, trying to legitimize himself as the leader of the Arab world. According to Nasser pan-Arab nationalism is based on a unity of language, of religion and of history. For some years Nasser was successful in creating a feeling among the Arabs that they should be united and stand together against Israel. Up until the revolution that brought Nasser to power, however, Egypt was still ruled by a king and a group of pashas who were of Ottoman descent and culture and who spoke Turkish in their daily lives. Moreover, the two most important political parties of that time, El-Wafd and Es-Sa'ad, did not derive their names from Islamic-Arabic history but from the struggle of the Egyptian people against British colonialism. Furthermore the names of the biggest banks in the country, Banque Misr (Egyptian Bank) and National Bank of Egypt, as well as that of the most important Egyptian newspaper, *Al-Ahram* (the pyramids), do not pay homage to any Arab elements in the country. The forced introduction of 'Arab nationalism' at the time as a compulsory school subject resulted in the systematic brainwashing of more than one generation of Egyptians. It was not until 1967, when Egypt was defeated in the war against Israel, that the ideology of pan-Arabism started to crumble, leaving in its wake a vacuum in which people could not find an orientation for their political identity.

With the beginning of Sadat's rule in 1970 Egyptians started to shift back to their previous Egyptian nationalism. Clear evidence of this could be seen in the change in the name of the state from 'United Arab Republic' to 'Arab Republic of Egypt', as well as in the change in the name of the country's only political party from 'Arab Socialist Union' to 'National Democratic Party'. This policy of de-Arabization culminated in Sadat's signing of the Camp David Agreement and in the official recognition of Israel as a state. Sadat paid for this with his life, and Egypt with the political breach with the Arab countries, which accused its government of treason against Palestine and dismissed it from the Arab League for more than ten years, during which the headquarters of the organization were shifted from Cairo to Tunis. In the 1991 Gulf War, Egypt played a key role by taking sides with the USA against the Arab leader Saddam Hussein of Iraq. The Egyptian people's opinion was divided upon this issue. M. H. Heikal (1992) was one of those who criticized the behaviour of the USA and their Arab allies, among whom was Saudi Arabia. Relations between the Egyptians and the Arabs were pungently expressed in a comedy titled *Putting It in Classical Arabic*, which lashed the Arabs of the Gulf countries in biting satire for despising the Egyptian migrant labourers and treating them like slaves. The play ran successfully for more than two years with full houses in a theatre in Cairo in the early 1990s.

In 1967 the Egyptian historian Namat A. Fouad (1973) already recognized the identity crisis her people were undergoing after Arab nationalism had received a severe blow through defeat in the war against Israel. She called for the country's history to be rewritten from an Egyptian perspective, eliminating the Arab one, since the latter gave a purely external point of view. Her book *Egypt's Character* conveys a significant message which was still considered of vital importance twenty-seven years after it was first published, when the Egyptian government celebrated it with a review in its publication *Egypt Magazine* (no. 21, autumn 2000), citing Fouad's claim that the country's civilization was a purely Egyptian one and that the majority of Muslims are the descendants of indigenous Copts and not of Arab invaders of the country. Arab nationalism was also denounced in the 1999 Arab Strategic Report, issued by the Al-Ahram Centre of Political and Strategic Studies in Cairo, on which Ezzat (2000) commented as follows: 'The plea of the report against Arab nationalism is based on an argument that accuses the founders and followers of this movement of a disinterest in democracy and a preoccupation, if not an obsession, with Israel's increasing power.' Such an attitude frees Egyptians to seek peace with their neighbour Israel, which is of vital importance to them.

2. *White Desert*: The White Desert north of El-Farafra Oasis in the Western Desert is famous for its fascinating mushroom-like white rock formations. Tourists looking for adventure come here on their four-wheel-drive or camel safaris. (Photo: F. Ibrahim)

The Egyptian geographer Gamal Hamdan, in his four-volume work *Egypt's Character* (1980–84), claims that Egyptian identity is built of four components: an African, an Asian, a Mediterranean and a Nile-related one. He speaks of the 'Arabization' of the Egyptians on the one hand and of the 'Egyptianization' of the Arabs on the other. Milad Hanna, a renowned Coptic writer, published a book on the same subject which he called *The Seven Pillars of Egyptian Identity* (1989). Four of the pillars he mentions are of a more or less historical nature: the Pharaonic, the Greco-Roman, the Coptic-Christian and the Islamic; the other three are geographic or cultural: the fact of belonging to the Arab world, to the Mediterranean region and to Africa. By using his pillar theory, and by avoiding any weighting according to importance or to sustainability, Hanna tries to give a picture of a people that has preserved its unity despite its internal cultural diversity.

According to Hamdan, the strongest of all influences on contemporary Egyptians is what he calls 'Europeanization' (see also Wirth and Mensching 1989). This influence had already begun in the nineteenth century with Mohammed Ali's orientation towards Europe and continued under British colonial rule over Egypt from 1882. As in the Arab countries, the European educational system was introduced and became the only one to enjoy official recognition. Owing to the activities of different European and American Christian missions, the French and the English (and American) educational systems existed side by side in Egypt, so that at the beginning of the twentieth century there were in Cairo, for example, the British Victoria College, the American College and the French École de Notre Dame. Native types of schools that had formerly played a role were completely marginalized and ultimately became almost extinct. Foreign Christian missionaries played an active role in the alienation of the Egyptians from their own culture, particularly by helping to replace an ancient form of Christianity, which had survived centuries of persecution, with a Christianity of a European type. Since converting a Muslim is a crime punishable by death in Islamic countries, the missionaries' work was concentrated exclusively on the Egyptian Copts. Despite British rule over Egypt the whole of the cultural sector was dominated by French influence, to the extent that the programmes offered by theatres, cinemas and radio stations were often direct takeovers of their French equivalents.

According to the general perception of the local population there exist two different cultures in Egypt. One is what they call *baladi* (local), which can be described as traditional and is considered by many to be backward; the other represents what is called *afrangi* (foreign) and is the 'progressive' Western one. The two cultures are considered by most people to be incompatible, and many Egyptians are unable to accept their own original cultural identity. Witness the following tragic event, which took place in Cairo after the Second World War. A young man who had successfully completed his studies abroad and was working in a good position in one of the ministries in Cairo was visited in his office by his father, a *fellah*, who came from the village in his kaftan, the traditional Egyptian dress. The young man felt so exposed before his colleagues that he was unable to bear the shame, and shot himself. The feeling of inferiority *vis-à-vis* the West, which is called the '*khawaga* [white man] complex' by the Egyptians, was exacerbated in the twentieth century owing to the rapid technological development in America and Europe with which Egypt as a whole could not keep pace. So Egyptians today see themselves confronted in their daily lives by a world full of the imported technology of TV sets, video recorders, CDs, mobile phones, computers and cars of the latest models from all over the world. The urban youth, brought up in the Western-type schools described above, today make up a constantly growing social class that has developed a strong taste for the consumption of Western material culture. This development has been accompanied by estrangement from their own culture, on which they turn their backs. In an effort to stress the relevance of the country's ancient culture, the beginning of the new millennium was celebrated in Egypt under the title '7,000 years of Egyptian culture'. But as yet no proper esteem of native culture can be observed even among educated Egyptians. For them, the ancient local culture seems to supply no point of reference or source of pride, though in fact, as is generally acknowledged by others today, it was of vital importance in the formation of European culture. Historically the science of Egyptology was founded by Europeans who appreciated whatever they found remaining of the old culture. For the man in the street in Egypt, however, the ancient monuments are merely something that attracts the tourists, just like the nightclubs or the floating hotels on the Nile.

If Egyptians cherish modern Western culture and simultaneously look down upon their own traditional oriental culture, they have simply adopted the European viewpoint of, among others, Napoleon's staff, who claimed to be doing scientific research in Egypt but, as their writings clearly show, despised the culture of the indigenous population of the country, which they were unable to understand. Egyptians internalized the image created by foreigners to such an extent that their identity became determined by it. The general feeling of inferiority continued when Egypt came under European rule. At the beginning of the twentieth century nationalism arose and Egyptians started fighting for independence, which they won in 1922. However, the newly born state copied European models in its structure and in the constitution formulated. Thus Egypt adopted a constitutional monarchy and a bicameral legislature consisting of an Assembly of Elders and an Assembly of Representatives, following the model of the British House of Lords and House of Commons, and the constitution proclaimed by King Fouad in 1923 followed the principles of the Belgian constitution of 1830/31 (Kramer 1977: 212). Years after the termination of British colonial rule, English and to some extent French remained the languages of science and of culture in the country, as well as being the languages spoken in everyday life in the houses of the Egyptian upper class.

The foundation of Israel in 1948 was considered as a threat to the Arab world's existence. When in later years the lost wars against Israel and quarrels among the Arab states led to disillusionment concerning the Arab issue among most Egyptians, an identity vacuum was created, and the soil was prepared for a resurgence of Islam, which had already begun in Egypt in the 1920s. This Islamic renaissance laid the foundations for a new global identity for most Egyptians. It is political in character and today embraces not only the Arab world but also Iran, Afghanistan, Pakistan, Bangladesh, Indonesia, Malaysia, Turkey, several African states and of late also Bosnia and the southern states of the former Soviet Union. And while the moral values of the Islamic religion were being rediscovered, a decisive change took place in the Egyptian people's attitudes towards Western culture, leading to a rejection of its system of values, or rather to criticism of what is understood as a total lack of moral values. Religious leaders call on the masses for a return to the basics of Islam as the intended foundation of a common culture. This movement is usually called Islamic fundamentalism today. Under the influence of the Islamists, the People's Assembly – the Egyptian parliament – introduced Article 2 into the currently valid constitution, declaring Islam to be the state religion and stipulating Islamic law, the *shari'a*, as the first source of all legislation

3. Anba Pola Monastery: The monasteries of the early Desert Fathers, especially those of St Antony and St Paul, are frequently visited by the Christian Coptic pilgrims who go there for retreats. (Photo: F. Ibrahim)

in the country. A series of changes followed thereafter to harmonize the legislation with these constitutional changes. Paradoxically, though, despite the widespread and to some extent aggressively expressed rejection of Western influence, no noticeable separation from Western material culture and civilization accompanied this. Rather, the opposite has been the case since the liberalization of the economy, as is clearly illustrated by the great number of luxury motor cars in the streets of Egyptian towns, TV dishes on roofs, the regular flights of the rich to Paris and London for shopping trips, the ready acceptance of the dictates of Western fashion, and the adoption of high-tech entertainment equipment. Thus the situation of Egyptians today is characterized by their internal conflict between, on the one hand, a wish to return to their cultural roots and, on the other, a continued dependence on Western material culture and civilization, which only a few in fact abandon in spite of the frequently uttered criticism of them. A study of the naming of children since the beginning of the twentieth century, carried out by the authors (1992, unpublished manuscript), reveals a phase during the colonial era in which European names were preferred, while some Copts chose Pharaonic names for their children. Today there is a clear preference for outspokenly Islamic names among Egyptian Muslims, and a revival of the traditional Coptic names among the Christians.

2 Women in Egyptian society

2.1 The early champions of the women's liberation movement

The beginning of the struggle of Egypt's women for their emancipation may be dated back to the following incident. In 1798, during Napoleon's conquest of Egypt, General Minou, the commander of the French troops, married an Egyptian after converting to Islam. He treated her very politely in public, according to French etiquette. This persuaded a group of other Egyptian women who lived in seclusion in their harems to send a petition to the 'Great Sultan' Napoleon, asking him to talk to their husbands and demand that they be treated similarly. As the French reports have it, many Egyptian women were later to suffer seriously for this audacity, after the French troops had left the country.

The concept of the liberation of women was indeed brought to Egypt from outside. Before the turn of the twentieth century awareness had been growing among women of the educated classes that theirs was an underprivileged role and that they did not receive an equal share of the blessings of modernity, since their own lives were mostly confined to the domestic sphere. They raised the issue of equal education for girls at all levels and formed secular philanthropic societies to help poor women and children. Gradually the first Egyptian women activists entered the public sphere and raised their voices, legitimizing their demands within the nationalist movement. However, when in October 1999 numerous distinguished guests from Egypt and abroad convened in Cairo to celebrate the hundredth anniversary of the 'Arab Woman's Emancipation' under the auspices of the country's First Lady, it was not to commemorate what the early defenders of women's rights had achieved but rather to commemorate the publication of a man's work considered the most important milestone on the way to women's emancipation, the classic of feminist literature *The Liberation of Women* by Qasim Amin (1863–1908). In this book the author, who was a judge at the Supreme Court of Justice at the time, offered a comprehensive concept of the emancipation of Egyptian women. His ideas about the 'New Woman' were vehemently criticized by some of his prominent contemporaries for potentially leading to immorality and decadence in Egyptian society. When women took up the cause a few years later, addressing the Egyptian Congress with a set of fairly modest demands, these were refused by that all-male institution.

In 1919, twenty years after the publication of Amin's book, Hoda Sha'rawi (1879–1947), the first woman to publicly demand female political and social enfranchisement, organized a protest march of a group of women in the course of which they demonstratively took off their veils, which they considered the symbols of their suppression, and threw them into the Nile. Her movement, which was limited to the upper social classes, was closely connected with the men's struggle against the colonial power, just as later in Algeria feminism and nationalism went hand in hand. Thus the women's ideas mostly conformed with those of the male fighters for national independence who wanted to modernize the whole of Egyptian society and considered the education of women as a precondition, while the situation of the women as such was not an issue. At the time the Arab world was on the defensive, trying to catch up with the industrialized countries, and it was believed that women should play their role in this struggle for progress. But after quasi-independence had been achieved in 1922 and a new constitution had been introduced a year later, declaring all Egyptians equal, Egyptian women were not granted the right to vote. In 1923 the Egyptian Feminist Union (EFU), a local section of the International Feminist Union, was founded by Hoda Sha'rawi. Its programme aimed at full political rights for women, at social reform as well as a reform of the laws regulating marriage, divorce and the custody of children, and also at female literacy. Egyptian women's cause was boosted at the time by their leaders' frequent participation in international women's conferences. Many improvements were achieved. The 1940s saw the beginnings of a pan-Arab feminism, but this has never really gained impetus to this day, in spite of efforts from various sides. In 1948 Doriya Shafiq (Doria Shafik, 1908–75; see her biography by Cynthia Nelson 1996) founded the Ittihad Bint Al-Nil, the Daughter-of-the-Nile Union, a feminist organization broadly based all over the country, focusing on literacy campaigns and hygiene programmes for lower-class women, with universal suffrage at the top of the agenda. When Doriya Shafiq saw that argument brought about no change, she resorted to more militant ways. In February 1951 she stormed Parliament together with more than a thousand women, demanding an end to the exclusion of 'half the nation' from politics, organized a sit-in and went on hunger strike. The *ulama*, the Islamic establishment, stated in various fatwas that suffrage was 'degrading to women and against their nature', a judgment that the Prime Minister felt obliged to respect. When the Islamists submitted a petition to the King asking him 'to keep the women within bounds', he assured them that women would have no political rights as long as he remained king. In 1953, one year after Gamal Abdel Nasser's revolution, Doriya Shafiq founded a political party, since the Egyptian Feminist Union, like all other independent organizations, had been declared unlawful. The new constitution of 1956 made voting obligatory for men, while women had to give proof of their literacy if they wanted to go to the polls. When Doriya Shafiq tried to put pressure on the government, she was placed under house arrest under the pretext that she was an agitator working for the Americans. Under Nasser's dictatorial rule, two of the journals she edited were banned, and many women activists withdrew their support for the cause for fear of their own safety. The new socialist government claimed to bring about gender equity and did in fact create educational programmes and employment for all, but it did not help women to meet their childcare needs, so that a double burden was laid on them.

2.2 Egyptian women today – between tradition and a shrinking economy

The role of the great majority of women in Egyptian society today is by and large still defined primarily by the traditional values of a patriarchal society. This is certainly true for the great number of women living in villages all over the country who are primarily occupied in taking care of their households and raising the children, as well as securing their families' livelihoods. In spite of numerous governmental campaigns propagating birth control, which have been to a certain extent successful, family size in rural areas is still large, as measured by European standards. Since the methods used in agriculture by the peasants are labour intensive, additional helpers are always welcome. It is estimated that about 60 per cent of all Egyptian women are either *fellahat* (singular *fellaha* = peasant woman) or have recently moved from villages to town. What they can watch on TV, which today is present also in the rural areas of the Nile valley, has little to do with their own reality. Women in the villages are exposed to strong social and economic pressure and so far only a few behavioural changes can be observed among them.

Under Nasser forced integration of women into the industrial labour force took place. Women worked side by side with men both in the newly erected and the older factories, all of which were run by the state. The women profited to a certain extent from the socialist programmes alleviating their situation. Today many of the poorer women living in Egyptian towns, especially those working in the informal sector, carry the greatest burden of domestic work and contribute most to household budgets without effective support from government programmes. Like rural women they are controlled by the patriarchal social norms in both the private and public spheres. Owing to their role in the family economy, some of them enjoy a relative degree of self-determination. Traditionally the Egyptian *fellahat* have always been free to sell their produce in the local markets, getting there on foot carrying their vegetables and live fowl in baskets on their heads, usually unveiled and unaccompanied by males. Nobody prevented them from staying in the markets for hours until they had sold most of their goods. And since the small farmers were poor, these women were usually their husbands' only wives, though Islam allows polygyny. And since most Egyptians are very fond of children, these women enjoyed positive acceptance by their husbands as the mothers of their children. The aforesaid does not mean, however, that the negative picture of the situation of women living in the Egyptian villages as drawn by the Western-influenced defenders of women's rights (e.g. El-Sa'adawi) is wrong. The traditional role of women can mean complete subjugation, leaving little room for women to decide for themselves and offering ample scope for conflict, especially if violence occurs. Differences between Muslim and Christian rural societies were probably negligible until the resurgence of Islam thirty years ago, but so far no research exists concerning this question.

4. *Sand dune encroachment in Ed-Dakhla Oasis*: Ed-Dakhla Oasis lies at the foot of a cretaceous escarpment of the Western Desert. Like most oases in that region it suffers from waterlogging and soil salinity resulting from bad drainage within the oasis depression. Sand dune encroachment is also a major threat here. (Photo: F. Ibrahim)

Educated women in towns who usually work in offices or as teachers are more exposed to Western influence. At the same time, religious leaders call on them to respect the principles of their religion. With growing Islamization, most Egyptian women started about thirty years ago to don Islamic dress, either through social pressure or in order to demonstrate an inner attitude, or a combination of both. In 1994, the government forbade the wearing of the Islamic headscarf by young girls in public primary schools, but in all other schools and the country's universities Islamic dress is worn by the great majority of girls, especially so in Upper Egypt, where hardly any Muslim woman not wearing Islamic dress and head cover can be found. More than eighty years after Hoda Sha'rawi led the protest march in the course of which the early feminists threw their veils into the Nile, her granddaughter complained that the whole of the Arab world today accepts the socio-religious order established on the Arabian Peninsula and tries to imitate it. Women in Saudi Arabia, with its theocracy of orthodox Islam, are denied basic human rights, but they are mostly rich and have the chance of a life of luxury, while Egyptian women are often dependent on husbands who can hardly feed their families (see Höber-Kamel 1995: 57). In terms of the challenges of modernity and the high educational standard many Egyptian women have attained, and for the sake of the complex development of the country, it seems necessary to revise the concept of gender segregation and other quasi-medieval structures which have been introduced in the socio-economic sphere on the Arabian Peninsula, and not to introduce them in Egypt and elsewhere where progress in overcoming the gender gap has been made. After graduating from university many Egyptian women today combine a career with founding a family, but in general Egyptian society still expects them to neglect neither their families nor their housework. Staying single to follow a career, or being married without the intention of having children soon, is not accepted by society, whether Muslim or Christian. The behaviour of emancipated Western women is generally disapproved of, and seen as the cause of the disintegration of families and of the problems of the youth.

Egyptian women of all social classes often appear to be surprisingly strong and self-confident. Widespread male labour migration made many women temporarily heads of their households. Poor women are often very creative in inventing means of securing the survival of their families. Many female university graduates are efficient in their work and play important roles in their spheres of influence, though they usually refrain from political activity. However, the present situation, with the introduction of a capitalist economic system based on an export-oriented rationalized productive sector, undermines women's access to economic resources. When formerly husband and wife were working in the civil service, their incomes were about equal if they had the same qualifications. Today, however, a man has a better chance of finding a job in the private sector, where he may receive a salary ten times that of his wife, who has to remain a civil servant. In the economic crisis that has characterized the beginning of the twenty-first century in Egypt, the situation is bad for all, but worse for the women, since the unemployment rate is particularly high among them. Not every job they are qualified for is considered acceptable for women, and generally they are less mobile than the men because of their greater family obligations. So only few women can work in the tourist business, especially in the new tourist ghettos on the Red Sea, where many men find employment today. Christian or Muslim daughters, fiancées or wives are often not allowed by male family members to work in places where they may have contact with men, be they colleagues or customers. This limits the radius of women's activities. What makes life harder for many women is that, for economic reasons and because of the dire state of the housing market, often young families are forced to share a flat with their parents-in-law. At the same time possibilities for individual recreation outside the house are not comparable to those enjoyed by women in Europe. Spending a weekend away from home and from the rest of the extended family is a habit only just being adopted by the affluent new middle class. The discrepancies between the lifestyles of women of the different social classes and locations in Egypt are as great today as they have ever been.

Recent changes in the country's agrarian structure brought about by projects of substantial capital investment have also led to a deterioration of the situation of the *fellahat*. Where formerly they contributed considerably to the household economy by selling the vegetables they had grown or the poultry they had raised, they find that today they have to compete with products from the highly subsidized capital-intensive modern agricultural enterprises that come up with new products, often of improved or hybrid types, at any time of the year thanks to new technologies. Some authors speak of 'a feminization of poverty' which results from the existing inequities in education and access to assets and from the growing number of women-headed households among the poor (Farag 2000). It is clear that at present social as well as economic developments are not favourable for women in Egypt. It is only to be hoped that this trend will not last and that a decisive change will be brought about in this respect, since women represent a great potential for the country that should not be underestimated.

2.3 Egyptian women in the modern age – equal rights under the law?

In the socialist era several new laws were passed securing women's rights, in particular in the labour force with such benefits as paid maternity leave, and during the 1970s some laws were changed alleviating the constraints placed on women by the personal status laws. In the current climate of Islamization a reversal is taking place. The women's movement in Egypt has lost its impetus even though gender inequity prevails in many spheres, for example in the inheritance laws. Considering secular viewpoints has become unacceptable. The terms 'emancipation' and 'feminism' have fallen out of favour for being related to a Westernization that it is feared might lead Egyptian women to a betrayal of their own culture. During the 1995 UN World Conference on Population, held in Cairo, there was a strong polarization of views between Western and Islamic representatives. However, the various groups unanimously demanded equal voting rights for all women, the abolition of all kinds of discrimination against women and of FGM (Female Genital Mutilation = circumcision), which is widely practised in Egypt and receives the support of Muslim religious leaders in spite of the fact that as such it is not Quranic. Various speakers at the conference stressed that it is not Islam which is hostile to women but the conservative male establishment, and attacked the representatives of the Al-Azhar University, considered to be the guardians of orthodox Islam.

On the whole, political apathy prevails among the women of Egypt today, exemplified by the fact that their presence at the polls is extremely weak. For the People's Assembly or the *shura* council, female members have to be appointed according to a quota system to overcome at least in part gender imbalance. At the same time women who run in the elections have a small chance of success. What a politically active women's movement might aim

5. Water pumping station in Bawiti Oasis: The ancient Bawiti Oasis in El-Bahariya in the Libyan Desert is today dependent on water from boreholes which reach down to depths of 1,400 m. The main products of the oases are high-quality dates which can be easily marketed in Cairo. (Photo: F. Ibrahim)

at today is a dialogue with the legislators and the religious leaders to prevent discriminatory laws and jurisdiction. In spite of the fact that Egypt signed the Convention on the Elimination of All Forms of Discrimination against Women in 1981, the UN identified various areas of concern for Egyptian women, among them the high rate of female school drop-outs, early marriages of girls in rural areas and, above all, legal issues. In 1999 the Court of Appeal of the People's Assembly confirmed that the Minister of the Interior was right to forbid a female university professor from travelling to Lebanon for three weeks to lecture at a university there against her husband's will (Mushira Musa, *Al-Ahram*, 18 February 1999, p. 12). Legislation in force in Egypt today allows a woman to be a minister, but her husband can prevent her from attending a conference. This is based on the *shari'a*, according to which a wife has to obey her husband in return for proper treatment. If she disobeys, he can divorce her and she loses her right to alimony, in spite of the fact that the Egyptian constitution stipulates equal rights for men and women and freedom of movement as a fundamental right of every citizen. It is likewise discriminatory for a woman that, according to a new law, a married woman must have her husband's name documented in her identity card, whereas the wife's name is not mentioned in the husband's. Certain amendments to the Personal Status Law implemented in 1979 which improved a woman's situation in case of divorce were declared unconstitutional and repealed during the 1980s. Generally, all laws dating from pre-colonial, colonial and post-colonial times are being amended to accord with the *shari'a*, as it is interpreted by the religious leaders. In the present climate one tends to forget that while the Prophet himself allowed his own wives various freedoms, women today are denied these on the pretext that they are against either 'Islam' or their 'cultural identity'. So some Muslim feminists are demanding a new interpretation of the Quranic texts and a consideration of the role of women in early Islamic times. In 2000, after years of heated controversy over social, religious and legal aspects, the Egyptian Ministry of Justice issued a new Personal Status Law called *khul'* (Law No. 1 of 2000), which is based on a rarely used Islamic practice. The law allows women to claim a divorce without justifying their reasons before a court on condition that they renounce their rights to all financial provision and that they also repay the dowry. The fact that the law was applied only 1,300 times during its first nine months in force, out of about 250,000 divorce suits annually, shows that it has to be considered in context. It is by no means a step in the right direction since it is financially discriminating for women. Only wealthy women can make use of it, and they may not be the ones who tend to suffer most. The majority of Egyptian women are not economically in a position to renounce their financial rights. On the other hand most religious leaders do not believe that the new law is in conformity with Islam, since in matters of marriage it is always the man who has to decide. Notwithstanding this, the law would still be problematic, since in a conservative society it carries a strong social stigma bearing in opposite directions: the attitude of a woman who leaves her husband is generally disapproved of, and at the same time it is absolutely degrading for a man to be left by his wife. Most probably he will retaliate and in the end the whole family, including the children, will suffer. The new law also allows for a premarital agreement known as *'isma*, regulating procedure in the case of divorce. It is laid down in a marriage contract between the two parties. Many men still refuse to accept such a clause in the marriage contract, considering it a great humiliation for them to renounce their rights.

It demands particular courage to defend women's rights in Egyptian society. Nawal El-Sa'adawi, one of the few contemporary women activists, lost her job in the public health administration years ago for speaking out against rural women's suppression by men, and lived in self-imposed exile for several years for fear of being targeted by Islamists. She cannot voice her protest in the country any longer. Three books she had published abroad and wanted to present at the Cairo Book Fair were confiscated in February 2001 at the port of Alexandria (<http://www.alahali.com/27-2-2001/sub6-3.html>). The Arab Women's Solidarity Association (AWSA), of which she was chairwoman and which had a consultative status with the United Nations Economic and Social Council, was dissolved by the government without explanation. Such censorship of intellectuals shows a discrepancy between what is laid down in the country's constitution and reality. It does not make sense in an age of free-flowing information around the globe through the Internet and the satellite dish. Having invested her hopes in democratization in Egypt, in 2001, after an interview in which the seventy-year-old woman activist spoke of a deep-rooted exploitation and oppression in class, patriarchal, national and religious systems, and described certain practices as contradictory to the true spirit of Islam and to a correct interpretation of the Quranic text, El-Sa'adawi was brought before the Shari'a Court in Cairo by which she was accused of apostasy. The judiciary was urged by the Mufti of Egypt to separate her from her husband since she was unfit to be the wife of a Muslim (see Chapter 3).

When the authors carried out a survey among a number of Egyptian university graduates, male and female, living in different towns in both the north and south of the country, about a women's movement or women's demands in the country, it became quite clear that no awareness of such matters existed among them. The only thing they understood was that women could get involved in some types of welfare work, as encouraged by the government through the First Lady and also carried out by a number of mosque-based organizations.

3 The Copts – the descendants of the Pharaohs as a minority today

As described above, the Egyptian population consists of a Muslim majority and a Christian minority, comprised mainly of Orthodox Copts. Fewer than 250,000 people belong to other Christian denominations. The ancestors of the contemporary Egyptians were by and large Coptic Christians. In the course of an Islamic rule lasting almost fourteen centuries the Christians were exposed to alternating treatment. Times of relative religious tolerance or more or less severe economic discrimination were followed by times during which they suffered physical violence. One feature of economic discrimination which inflicted extreme suffering on the Christians was the *djizya* (from *djazaa* – penalty), a tax every non-Muslim had to pay. This tax was vital for the state budget, with the result that the rulers were not interested in converting the whole population into Muslims. During the recurrent outbreaks of famine in Egypt many Christians were unable to pay the tax and saw no alternative but to convert to Islam. Several big *fellaheen* revolts against the imposition of *djizya* were recorded in the Nile delta during the eighth and the ninth centuries. They were brutally crushed and the churches of the rebelling people destroyed. Similarly today, conversion to Islam not infrequently takes place under economic and social pressure, which has increased since the deterioration of the economic situation in the country on the one hand and the resurgence of Islam on the other.

Since Egyptian Muslims and Copts have largely the same ethnic origin, they cannot be differentiated according to physiognomy. However, the ancestors of the Egyptian Muslims may have intermarried with other Muslims who came to their country, like Arabs, Turks and Mameluks who migrated from Asia to Egypt. The Copts, on the other hand, remained by and large ethnically unmixed. So, neglecting the minor influences of the Greeks and the Romans who ruled over Egypt from 332 BC to AD 641, one may consider them the direct descendants of the ancient Egyptians.

The Arab invaders called the Egyptian population *qibt*, which is derived from the Greek word *aigyptos* and means 'Egypt'. In the course of time the term became narrower in meaning so that finally it was used only for the native Christians of Egypt. The Coptic language is the demotic old Egyptian language, mostly written in the Greek alphabet. Today it is still used in church liturgy, but already by the tenth century the Copts were forced to use Arabic in the mass. As a spoken language Coptic was gradually dropped and was nearly completely replaced by Arabic by the fifteenth century. The Egyptian popular art of the Roman and the early Arabic eras is defined as Coptic art today. It influenced the style in which the mosques of the early Islamic era in Egypt were built. In fact the architects of many mosques of that period, for example the famous Ibn Tulun mosque in Cairo, were Copts. Granite or alabaster pillars in some mosques on which Christian motifs are found show that often churches were destroyed to acquire the valuable building material.

The schism between the Coptic Church and the Church of Rome took place in AD 451 at the Council of Chalcedon under the pretext of differences in perception of the human and divine nature of Jesus. In truth the matter was purely political and resulted from the hostile relationship between Byzantium and its Egyptian colony. The Coptic Orthodox Church, which has many common traits with the Roman Catholic Church as well as with the other orthodox churches, has preserved many early Christian elements, such as priests who are committed to matrimony, and a flourishing monasticism. Early Christianity owed much to the Coptic Church, whose theologians and philosophers at Alexandria often clarified difficult theological questions. The creed of St Athanasius the Apostolic, Pope of Alexandria in the fourth century, is still used worldwide. Egypt is considered the cradle of Christian monasticism since between the third and the fifth centuries St Paul of Thebes (Anba Pola; see Illustration 3), St Antony the Great, St Pachomius, St Shenute and others, who became known as the 'desert fathers', led their ascetic lives in Egypt and attracted many followers. During the second half of the twentieth century the Coptic Church experienced a spiritual revival which was brought about especially by the efforts of three Church leaders of that time: Pope Kyrillos VI (1959–71), an ascetic to whom many miracles are ascribed, his successor Pope Shenute III (from 1971), who improved the organization of the Church, and Metropolitan Athanasius of Beni Suef (1962–2000), who

6. Date-packing at El-Kharga Oasis: The packing of dates is the most important industry in the oases of the Western Desert. It takes place for about two months after the date harvest. At the El-Kharga factory about fifty persons are employed seasonally. (Photo: F. Ibrahim)

founded a religious order of nuns devoted to social welfare, thus reviving an old tradition of the Coptic Church.

The actual number of Copts living in Egypt is not known, but as a rough estimate, one may consider about 13 per cent of the total population as realistic. The Coptic Church puts the figure at 20 per cent while in its official publications the government mentions a proportion of less than 6 per cent of the Egyptian population. The latter figure is obviously too low. It serves the purpose, however, of minimizing the Christian minority, so as not to jeopardize the country's role as a leading Islamic country. Another sad consequence is that it reduces the chances of the Copts of gaining a fair proportion of seats in parliament and of higher positions in the state apparatus, as well as places for students in universities. The admittance quota for Christians to popular institutes such as the Police, Marine and Military Academies is very low at 2 per cent and from the biggest university in the country (184,501 students in 1999/2000), the famous Al-Azhar University, Christians are completely excluded, though secular subjects such as medicine and geosciences have been taught there since 1961. The same applies to more than 5,760 Al-Azhar schools, which are spread all over the country, although like the universities all these institutions are being constructed, maintained and run by the tax revenues paid by Christians and Muslims alike.

The geographical distribution of the Coptic population reflects their centuries-long discrimination and persecution. Quite early in their history they took refuge in Upper Egypt, when the Nile delta was plagued with recurrent persecution. Thus the number of Copts in the Nile delta is only 1 per cent today, according to official statistics, in El-Minya 20 per cent, in Asyut 10 per cent and in the other Upper Egyptian governorates about 5 per cent. Since the nineteenth century, the Coptic *fellaheen* have participated strongly in the migration to Cairo and Alexandria, where they have sought protection in anonymity, for the Christian minorities in the villages have been ever since targets of fanatical Muslims and at the mercy of despotic local administrators. The middle-class district of Shubra, in the northern part of Cairo, constitutes the strongest concentration of Christians in the capital. Its landscape is dominated by a great number of churches, as well as by shops with their owners' Christian names on the sign boards and with pictures of saints on the inside walls.

Formerly the Copts had a special reputation for their skills as craftsmen and for their abilities as tax collectors and as scribes in the state service, and thanks to the efficiency of the schools run by the Coptic Church many of them were able to qualify as finance administrators in the public service. But that is a thing of the past. The professional structure of urban Copts today is barely different from that of urban Muslims. There is, however, a relatively high proportion of Copts in middle-level positions in the civil service today, owing to the fact that these are low paid and unattractive, whereas securing a livelihood in the more lucrative private sector requires good connections to the state apparatus, which is still controlling it through regulations, licences and concessions. As a minority the Copts are largely lacking the required connections.

Although, thanks to their religion, the Copts have a certain affinity with the Western world, they participated in leading the fight against the British colonial power at the beginning of the twentieth century. At that time they were proportionally over-represented in the El-Wafd Party, which laid the foundations of the parliamentary system in Egypt. During the Nasser era, beginning in 1952, they were, however, systematically removed from the political scene. The appointment of a few Coptic members of parliament and one or two ministers, usually in insignificant ministries, by the President of the state serves merely as a sop to show that there is no discrimination. This also applies in the case of the candidateship of Botros Ghali for the post of UN Secretary-General in the 1990s, when the government actively made use of international recognition of his expertise in order to promote an Egyptian candidate.

4 The Nubians – a people without a homeland

Nubia was once a mighty kingdom and a country of a high culture. It saw 4,000 years of history before it gradually sank under the rising waters of the Sadd el-Ali (High Dam) reservoir during the 1960s, while the Nubian people as a whole suffered compulsory evacuation. The 50,000 Nubians who were living in that part of Nubia which lies in the Sudan and so were of Sudanese nationality were resettled at Khashm el-Girba on the Atbara river in the Sudan, while the 70,000 Egyptian Nubians were given new land at Kom Ombo, 50 km north of Aswan (see Chapter 6). The expulsion of the Nubian people from their homeland had already begun with the construction of the first Aswan Dam in 1902 and its heightening in 1930.

The Nubians are of a darker complexion than most Egyptians and belong to the Ethiopic (formerly so-called Hamitic) race, forming two groups speaking different Kushitic languages. The Egyptian Nubians belong to the Kenuz group and were called *barabra* (singular *barbari*) by the Egyptians, indicating by this name that they were unable to understand them. Since the gradual submersion of their homeland due to the construction of the first Aswan Dam at the beginning of the twentieth century Nubian men have been migrating, mainly to Cairo and Alexandria, in search of a livelihood. The majority of them initially worked as servants and as cooks in the villas of the pashas and beys, of diplomats and other foreigners, for the Nubians were highly appreciated for their cleanliness and honesty. Many of them also held jobs as uniformed waiters and janitors at renowned tourist hotels. Today the educational standard of the Nubians is higher than that of the rest of the population, so that they can find employment in a variety of specializations, though a high percentage of them, especially in Aswan, are active in the tourist industry. Even after their resettlement in Kom Ombo, migration to Cairo continued. So many of them employed landless *fellaheen* from the Nile valley to cultivate the land they had been given, in order to be able to take up employment in town, although usually leaving their wives behind to manage the farms and look after the families. Since evacuation from their homeland the Nubians have been trying to secure rights of occupancy on the banks of the Aswan water reservoir. However, owing to the hazard of water pollution, the resettlement of human communities there has become a highly controversial issue.

5 The Bedouin of the marginal deserts

It is difficult to calculate the numbers of the Egyptian Bedouin because statistically they are not differentiated from the rest of the population. The people of the Nile valley apply to them the term *'arab*, but besides the semi-nomads who traditionally live in the deserts raising sheep, goats and camels, this denotes also members of communities of Arab origin who, after migrating, settled on the fringes of the Nile valley, preserving their tribal traditions and their organizational systems. Even the approximately 15,000 inhabitants of the Siwa Oasis who are of Berber origin and identify themselves neither with the Arabs nor with the Bedouin are considered as *'arab* by the Nile valley Egyptians.

Full nomads with no specific place of residence are not found in Egypt any more. In 1907 635,000 persons, i.e. 5.6 per cent of the Egyptian population, identified themselves as *'arab*. Of these 100,000 were mobile Bedouin, either full nomads or semi-nomads (Schamp 1977: 403). Two or three centuries ago the numbers of the Bedouin population were much higher. The Bedouin were the feared pirates of the desert and used to wage armed raids against the *fellaheen* in their villages and against the monks in the desert monasteries, robbing and murdering. In Upper Egypt, far away from the central administration in Cairo, they were especially powerful. Today their descendants' settlements lie usually on the outer margins of the Nile valley, where they struggle hard to gain access to land for cultivation. The initial words of the names of these places are often 'Beni' or 'Awlad', both of which mean 'sons of', as in Beni Hilal or Awlad Ali (Girga), or 'Nag'', which means 'hair tent', as in Nag' El-Deir near Girga (Müller-Mahn 1998a: 263). However, similar names may also occur for old settlements on the Nile, as in the cases of Beni Suef and Nag' Hammadi.

After the integration and assimilation of the majority of the descendants of the nomads into the Egyptian population, the current number of those who can be classified as Bedouin and who still practise mobile livestock herding is to be estimated at 50,000 at most. The majority of them migrated from the Arab peninsula in the course of history, such as the Bedouin groups of Sinai, and the Awlad Ali who live along the western strip of the Egyptian Mediterranean coast and across the border into Libya. Others are African ethnic groups like the Ababda and the Bishariyiin, who speak Kushitic languages and live in the Eastern Desert on the borders with the Sudan.

The policy of the Egyptian administration has for a long time been that of pacification of the desert inhabitants, of their assimilation and of a partly forced sedentariness. Today the government is undertaking intensive efforts to create a loyalty to Egypt among the Bedouin in the border areas with Israel, Libya and the Sudan. Thus the Bedouin on Sinai are granted newly reclaimed agricultural land, and for the Awlad Ali in Marsa Matruh Governorate the state is implementing development projects, providing schools and fresh water as well as support for land reclamation. After the armed border conflict between Egypt and the Sudan about the Halayeb area on the Red Sea, which broke out after mineral resources had been discovered there in the 1990s, Egypt started building schools, hospitals and roads for the Bishariyiin population there. However, the old reciprocal animosity between the Bedouin and the rest of the

Egyptian population still exists, and the *'arab* are not recognized as Egyptians by the people of the Nile valley, while many Bedouin who have relations across the political borders have never really developed a strong sense of belonging to Egypt. The fact that the Bedouin's tribal borders extend across political ones accounts for their relatively free movement in those regions and for their generally fairly good economic situation, especially in the border zones with Libya and Israel, where they have ample opportunities for weapons and drug trafficking as well as for smuggling diverse other goods. Recently the Bedouin have begun to engage to a growing extent in Egyptian desert tourism, which has developed in particular in areas close to major tourist centres.

6 Dynamics of growth, spatial distribution and migration of the Egyptian population

The size of Egypt's population has changed considerably over time, reflecting the frequently changing political and economic conditions in the country. It is estimated that it reached an early maximum in 1300 BC, two centuries before the end of the Pharaonic era, with about 9 million inhabitants living in *circa* 20,000 settlements (Schamp 1977: 409), a figure matched for the first time again 3,200 years later in 1900 under British colonial rule. By 450 BC, during the time of the Persian colonization, the population had dropped to about 3.5 million, while in Ptolemaic times it rose again, so that it reached 7.5 million at the beginning of Roman rule. However, towards its end in AD 600, it was only 6 million.

During the era of Arab-Mameluk-Ottoman rule, Egypt was swept by wars and plagued by repeated economic crises and famines, so much so that when Napoleon's scientists wrote their *Déscription de l'Égypte* in 1798–1801 they estimated the size of the country's population at only 2.46 million. The reign of Mohammed Ali brought an end to the chaotic conditions and introduced a time of political stability. By 1846 the population had nearly doubled and was estimated at 4.476 million. The growth rate increased during the British colonial period, when in the thirty-five years between 1882 and 1917 the population rose from 6.804 million to 12.751 million. The next doubling took forty years, so that Egypt had a population of 26.1 million in 1960, after which the doubling of the figure gained further impetus and subsequently took less than thirty years. In 1990 Egypt had about 55 million inhabitants, in the year 2003 nearly 70 million. During the 1980s the population growth rate was 2.8 per cent annually, dropping to 2 per cent in the 1990s. This was partly as a result of decades of intensive governmental campaigns propagating birth control, but must also be attributed to other factors like increasing urbanization, growing female employment, the deterioration of housing conditions, the high rate of inflation and the increase in poverty among the majority of the population. A review of the birth and mortality rates since the 1960s gives the following picture. From 1965/70 to 1995/2000 the birth rate dropped from 41.8 per cent to 26.4 per cent annually per 1,000 inhabitants. In the same time span the mortality rate declined from 15 per cent to 6.4 per cent annually per 1,000 inhabitants. Despite this positive development Egypt will be confronted with serious problems in the coming twenty to thirty years for demographic reasons, for the population pyramid of the 1996 population census shows that at the time 37.8 per cent of Egyptians were younger than 15 and that the proportion of women of reproductive age (15–49) was rather high at 50.3 per cent of the total female population, while the proportion of persons over 60 years of age was only 5.8 per cent. Between 1960/65 and 1995/2000 the life expectancy at birth increased from 46 to 66 years for men and from 49 to 70 years for women, while the fertility rate per woman dropped, and was 3.4 children in 1996/98 as compared to 4.41 ten years earlier (CAPMAS 2000).

Most Egyptians live congested in the narrow Nile valley. Only 1 per cent of the population lives concentrated on the oases, which are dispersed over the desert areas that constitute 96.5 per cent of the country's total surface. With a population of 68 million inhabitants distributed over an area of 35,000 km², the actual average population density for 2003 can be calculated at 1,940 inhabitants/km², which is an unusual figure for an agricultural country of this size. The more the number of people living in the country increases, the smaller the per capita nutritional area becomes (see Figure 1.2). Between 1821 and 2001 the cropping area, which thanks to an all-year-round favourable climate and availability of irrigation water was 1.9 times as large as the agricultural area in Egypt today, decreased from 5,280 m² to 865 m² per capita.

In order to be able to compare the population densities of the various governorates correctly, one must take into account the different shares of desert land. Considering this factor one recognizes that the governorates of the central Nile delta are extremely densely populated: El-Qalyubiya with 3,301 inhabitants/km², El-Minufiya with 1,802 inhabitants/km² and El-Gharbiya with 1,754 inhabitants/km², according to the 1996 census. On the other hand the marginal delta governorates of Kafr-esh-Sheikh and El-Beheira with 647 inhabitants/km² and 394 inhabitants/km² respectively are much less densely populated. In Upper Egypt the governorates of Sohag with 2,019 inhabitants/km² and Asyut with 1,804 inhabitants/km² are those with the greatest population density.

Urbanization is steadily increasing in Egypt. In 1897 the proportion of urban inhabitants was only 13.6 per cent. A hundred years later, in 1997, it had risen to 43 per cent. In the two largest urban agglomerations of Cairo and Alexandria alone reside about 66 per cent of Egypt's urban population today. The current high urbanization rate is mainly the result of decades of accelerated rural–urban migration since the beginning of the twentieth century. While the increase in the rate of urbanization was only 0.1 per cent between 1897 and 1907, it rose to 6.3 per cent in the following decade. Migra-

7. *Fig plantation west of Alexandria*: Along the Mediterranean coast in north-west Egypt one finds orchards of fig trees which depend on the winter rainfall (200 mm). The orchards were established not only for the production of the fruit, which is eaten fresh or used for making jam, but also serve the local Bedouin of the Aulad Ali ethnic group in demonstrating their claim to the land. (Photo: F. Ibrahim)

tion from all parts of the country was directed towards Cairo and Alexandria. The Suez Canal Zone has not received any greater numbers of migrants from rural areas, although the government has been trying to upgrade the war-ridden region as an economic pole within the country, for which it possesses an excellent infrastructure. During the thirty years from 1966 to 1996 the proportion of inhabitants of the three governorates of Port Said, Ismailiya and Suez as a percentage of the total population of Egypt declined from 3 per cent to 2.7 per cent. On the other hand the fast-growing tourist industry in the governorates of South Sinai, Red Sea and Marsa Matruh has been attracting migrant labourers and caused a growth in the population there of about 58 per cent in the ten years between 1986 and 1996. However, the total population of these three governorates amounted to only 424,000 persons in 1996. The only governorate of Upper Egypt that was able to strike a balance between emigration and immigration was Aswan, by virtue of the construction of the High Dam and subsequent industrial development as well as flourishing tourism through which jobs were created. In general, however, Upper Egypt is the traditional emigration area, where apart from agriculture employment opportunities are limited.

For decades the government has been trying to counteract the ever-increasing population pressure on Greater Cairo by decentralizing industry, administration, tourism and higher education. So far, however, these endeavours have had little effect. This is partly due to the concurrent economic policy of privatization which embraced these sectors. Regional planning is none of the private investors' concern. They are more interested in securing the largest possible market, which lies undoubtedly in Greater Cairo. As a consequence many young people come to the capital from all over the country in search of a livelihood. For highly qualified labour market entrants especially the mega-city offers a wide array of employment opportunities, which cannot be found in any of the other towns, including Alexandria. Besides, for the medium-qualified employment-seekers both Cairo and Alexandria offer not only greater opportunities but also higher wages than the other regional capitals. And though the latter are large cities, most of them are still of a rural character in terms of their supply of goods and services as well as of cultural and recreational facilities.

Since 1976 the migration stream to the Cairo Metropolitan Area has slowed down. Table 11.1 shows that Cairo's share of the country's total population increased steadily between 1937 and 1976, but has remained constant at 20 per cent since then. The situation of Alexandria is similar. There are various reasons for this current stagnation of migration. In the first place, employment opportunities have been dwindling in these big cities too, while housing has become almost unaffordable there. For young people wishing to start a family today the most serious problem is securing a place to live. While formerly the bride's father used to ask about the possessions and the profession of the suitor, today the availability of housing has become the crux of the matter. Another reason for the stabilization is the relatively strong migration from Cairo out of the country. Both the qualificational level and the financial status of employees living in Egypt's capital are above average, which facilitates their migration abroad. The presently accelerating wave of emigration began in the 1960s. At that time several hundred thousand university graduates migrated, in particular to the USA, Canada and Australia. The number of Copts in the migration to these countries was over-proportional. According to Coptic sources 1–2 million permanent Coptic immigrants lived in these countries in 2001. In parallel, labour migration was also enhanced to the Arab oil-producing countries.

The total number of Egyptians living abroad is difficult to calculate. According to a government source it was 1.9 million in 2001 (CAPMAS 2001b). Less official estimates indicate 2.5 to 4 million Egyptian emigrants. Underlying the figures, however, are considerable fluctuations in the political and economic situation in the region. The Gulf War of 1991 alone resulted in the return of almost 1 million Egyptian labour migrants from Iraq, and similarly the economic crisis in the Gulf States in the 1980s and the deterioration in relations between Egypt and Libya compelled thousands of Egyptian labour migrants to return home. Although the Egyptian labour force working abroad is an important asset for the country's economy owing to their high remittances, which amounted to US$3.02 billion in 2000/01, the problem of unemployment in the country is exacerbated if remigration sets in suddenly, as happened in the 1990s. A great proportion of the emigrants are *fellaheen*, like those who worked in agriculture in Iraq. On their return they not only bring money but also technical innovations which they introduce in their home villages. However, those who had to flee from Iraq in 1991 came penniless, since they had not been allowed to change their savings into hard currency and the local currency became practically worthless overnight.

In 2003, according to the Egyptian Minister of Labour Force and Migration (cited in *Al-Ahram Ektesady*, 10 March 2003: 36), there were 1.9 million Egyptians working in the Arab countries, including 900,000 in Saudi Arabia, 300,000 in Jordan, 250,000 in Kuwait, 70,000 in the Emirates, 55,000 in Iraq and 20,000 in Qatar.

CHAPTER 3

From Foreign Rule to Self-determination

1 Egypt's history seen from an Egyptian perspective

The fact that the majority of present-day Egyptians reveal an identity which hardly relates to their indigenous Pharaonic past and take no particular pride in their ancestors' ancient culture unless they are taught to do so at school, while at the same time they show great willingness to respect and to adopt what is foreign, be it Western-European or Oriental-Arab, may be a result of more than 3,000 years of history during which the native Egyptian people were subjugated by foreign powers who invaded their country, despising, discriminating and exploiting them. It is time to see Egyptian history from a perspective that focuses on these facts.

As early as during the nineteenth dynasty (1306–1224 BC) Asian groups dominated the country (Helck 1977: 116), and soon after the Libyans took power. They were followed by the Nubians (713–636 BC), after whom came the Assyrians. From 525 to 332 BC, with a short interruption when the Libyans usurped power again, the Persians ruled over the country on the Nile. After the invasion of Egypt by Alexander the Great in 332 BC, the Ptolemies reigned, maintaining their own language and culture, so that the ancient Egyptian culture fell into insignificance. After the defeat of Cleopatra and the victory of Augustus in 30 BC Egypt was a Roman, and later a Byzantine, colony. Becoming Rome's granary meant for Egypt another era of exploitation during which the *fellaheen* suffered under the merciless practices of the tax collectors and the arbitrariness of the administrators. The Egyptians who had been Christianized very early by the apostle St Mark were exposed to severe persecution by the Roman emperors. Under Diocletian (AD 284–305) alone, 144,000 Egyptian Christians died as martyrs, according to Coptic sources. After the church schism of Chalcedon in AD 451 the Christian rulers of the Byzantine Empire also persecuted the Egyptians, who retained their allegiance to the Church of Alexandria. When the Arabs conquered Egypt in AD 640 many Egyptians thought that this would free them from the Byzantine yoke. However, the country then had to serve as a granary for the Muslim world, first for the caliphs of El-Madina, then for the Umayyad dynasty of Damascus and the Abbasid dynasty of Baghdad, while subsequently Egypt was ruled by a succession of dynasties of Tunisian, Turkish, Kurdish and Syrian origin between the ninth and the thirteenth centuries.

The inequality between the ruling classes and the Egyptian people was especially flagrant in Mameluk times, when the country was ruled by former slaves of Asian origin who were mostly unable to speak Arabic. Two big revolts against Arab foreign rule are recorded, one in 725–33, the other in 832, which were both bloodily crushed, after which the cruelties of the Abbasids against the people were exacerbated.

The conquest of Egypt by Sultan Selim I in 1517 was a prelude to a 400-year-long Turkish rule over Egypt, which proved a disaster. When Napoleon invaded Egypt in 1798 the country was economically in ruins and the number of its inhabitants had dropped to a long-term minimum. In their pursuit of the Mameluks all over the country the French inflicted torture upon the *fellaheen*, raped their women and burnt their villages. The subsequent era of the Mohammed Ali dynasty brought Egypt a limited degree of independence, but the rulers were despotic and imposed their alien Ottoman culture upon the Egyptians in all spheres of life. So by the time Egypt came under British hegemony it had experienced a long period of foreign domination, and the situation appeared more bearable than during the preceding eras.

The year 1922 brought about the country's nominal independence. For the first time in history Egyptians could determine their own fate. In fact it was the people's rising of 1919 and not Nasser's revolution of 1952 which marked the historical turning point, bringing about the beginning of self-determination for Egyptians. Significantly enough the symbol of that rising was a crescent and a cross, which stood for the incorporated union of the Egyptian people, of Muslims and Christians. Under the constitutional monarchy a politically mature system started to flourish, the better of which Egypt has not seen to this day. But since Great Britain's legal privileges over Egypt remained largely untouched, some historians consider the termination of the British protectorate as a farce. It has to be admitted that the constitution introduced by King Fouad and the parliamentary government system based on it did not guarantee true democracy, but it cannot be denied that a hitherto unknown process of democratization began at that time for the good of the Egyptian people, while the presence of British troops by the Suez Canal was of lesser relevance for their immediate interests. For the *fellaheen*, i.e. for the bulk of the population, after 3,000 years of foreign domination, an era of peace, security and sovereignty of the law had begun, even though the feudal structures were still unbroken. It is the merit of Nasser's socialism to have opened the way for feudalism to be overcome in the countryside and capitalism in the towns. But the price paid was the loss of the hard-won democracy and the introduction of a party dictatorship supported by the military. The state-directed economic system proved to be a failure in Egypt, as it did elsewhere, and the wars with Yemen and Israel eroded Egypt's meagre resources.

8. *Water buffalo employed in fieldwork*: Although most *fellaheen* today keep water
buffalo primarily for milk and meat production, some still use them for pulling the
hook plough, for threshing or for lifting water. (Photo: F. Ibrahim)

Under Sadat (1970–81) the multi-party system was restored, and with the
support of the USA a peace treaty with Israel signed. This president played a
distinguished role in the country's economy by adopting the *infitah* (opening)
policy, by which he encouraged private Egyptian and foreign capital investment. However, this resulted in uncontrolled capitalism, which brought no
benefit to the country owing to the spread of corruption. Sadat, who under
Nasser had been a commissioner for the promotion of cooperation with
other Islamic countries, encouraged the revival of Islamism in the country,
so that the Muslim Brotherhood (Al-Ikhwan al-Muslimun), which had been
systematically persecuted and almost dissolved under Nasser, regained its
strength. Many of the Brotherhood's members returned to Egypt from exile
and were able to build up new, more radical groups, Al-Gama'at al-Islamiya
among them. Although still officially prohibited, they were able to extend
their activities over the whole country and invade the trade unions in the
industrial plants as well as the schools and universities and propagate their
political agenda from the pulpits of the state mosques. In 1981 members
of the group murdered Sadat, whom they considered a traitor of the Arab-
Islamic cause.

Mubarak, Sadat's successor, continued the domestic and foreign political
course Sadat had adopted, while corruption continued and reached unprecedented dimensions. Initially Mubarak failed in appeasing the Islamists, in

spite of his display of tolerance towards them. When they started expressing their claim to power by assassinating tourists, Copts, members of the government and even by attempting to kill Mubarak himself, he arrested more than 25,000 of them (Ghanem 1999). On account of such internal political instability martial law remained in force during his presidency after the state of emergency had initially been declared under Sadat. Thus Egypt was reduced to a police state with curbed freedoms for the people and a staggering democratization process.

2 Civil society in Egypt – an agent of social and political change?

The question of whether a civil society exists in the Arab world is frequently discussed today, and it is a most sensitive issue. Some claim that it was already part and parcel of the early Islamic societies, but after thirteen centuries of despotic governments in the region this is more or less a matter of historic interest.

The concept of a civil society is closely linked to that of democracy, which is today considered by most people – though not by all – as a prerequisite of sustainable development and as the only way of attaining a lasting peace domestically as well as worldwide. While some radical Islamists, including in Egypt, consider democracy and pluralism as Western constructs that are not compatible with their political philosophy, other more moderate Islamists accept the concepts and integrate their activities into their framework. But civil society must necessarily be weak if the state is overwhelmingly strong, whereas a strong civil society can challenge an authoritarian state. If we consider the history of Egypt, we find that after centuries of suppression of the masses, towards the end of the nineteenth century various civil institutions existed in Egypt and became a driving force that finally led to the termination of colonial domination of the country and to nominal independence from Britain. The movement aimed at and partly achieved a pluralism with political and religious freedom, respecting minority rights as well as the rights of women, during the so-called 'liberal age' between 1922 and 1952, until a serious setback in the development of Egyptian civil society occurred in the middle of the twentieth century with the adoption of military rule, the abolition of the multi-party system and the political orientation towards the Soviet Union.

What is the state of civil society in Egypt today? Thousands of institutions claim to be its representatives. To what extent do they entertain political freedom? How far-reaching are the rights of an individual in the country?

The Egyptian constitution of 1970, which was amended in 1980, is for the most part a democratic one, if it were not for one article in it, which may be used to make all its democratic intentions futile. It is Article 2, which stipulates the Islamic *shari'a* as the primary source of all legislation. This means that non-Muslims as well as women are not granted full civil rights, and it

9. *The threshing sledge* (norag): The wheat-threshing sledge is one of the old agricultural tools still in use in Upper Egypt today. (Photo: F. Ibrahim)

opens the door for varied interpretations, which can be strong tools in the hands of fanatical and politically biased judges and violate the fundamental rights of the country's citizens. Besides, for more than twenty years Mubarak succeeded in obtaining from the People's Assembly a continued renewal of the emergency powers first granted in 1981.

According to the constitution the ruling system consists of three main instruments:

- The President of the Republic, in whose hands lies the executive authority, and who shapes public policy. He is also Supreme Commander of the Armed Forces, of the National Defence Council and of the Supreme Police Council. Hosni Mubarak became head of state in 1981. During the first twenty years of his rule he formed eleven cabinets which had an average lifetime of twenty months.
- The People's Assembly, which represents the legislative power. The incidents that took place before the elections for this institution in 2000 reveal much about the state of civil society in Egypt: hundreds of people were detained without charges and Saad Eddin Ibrahim, a professor of sociology and a prominent defender of civil society, was arrested, tried over a period of months and finally sentenced to seven years' imprisonment, being accused of damaging the national peace. The Ibn Khaldun Centre for Developmental Studies, which was officially registered as a civil com-

pany, whose founder and director he was, was closed. The institute had been supported by EU funds and had tried to promote political awareness and participation in national elections among the Egyptian population (see Khaled Dawoud, 'The State versus Ibrahim', *Al-Ahram* Weekly On-line, 22–28 February 2001, issue no. 522). After the opposition had forced the government to implement a law stipulating that only judges and not government officials should supervise the elections, supporters of the ruling National Democratic Party (NDP) tried to interfere in various towns. In spite of its unpopularity the party had formerly won around 90 per cent of the seats compared to only 38 per cent of the 454 seats in the elections of 2000, which were the first held under judicial supervision – though it may not have been complete. However, of the 256 'independent' candidates who had won seats, 218 joined the NDP immediately after the elections, so that the party's share rose to 85.5 per cent of all seats. Seventeen members of the outlawed Muslim Brotherhood managed to be elected as 'independents'. Only sixteen seats went to members of opposition parties (G. Essam El-Din, 'Rank-and-file dissenters', *Al-Ahram* Weekly On-line, 23–29 November 2000, issue no. 509).

- The *shura* (Consultative) Council. Its 264 members are partly elected and partly appointed by the head of the state. This council is concerned with issues of national unity and social peace.

The most popular opposition in the country is the Islamists, whose radical wing would like to see Egypt turned into an Islamic republic like Iran or the Sudan. Since parties based on religion are illegal, the Islamists cannot be officially represented in the People's Assembly. Some of the groups they form are responsible for terrorist strikes against government members, Western tourists and Copts. Their attempts to overthrow the government, which they believe comes too much under the influence of the West, made Mubarak crack down upon them repeatedly. Whether they are to be considered as part of a civil society is a matter of definition, since it is understood by most that civil society should be based on tolerance. Many Egyptian thinkers are of the opinion that the government's generally sceptical and often hostile attitude towards civil society can be considered a mixed blessing. Although on the one hand the government sets strict limits to the freedom of speech and of thought, on the other it has so far managed to prevent the country from falling into anarchism. However, some intellectuals also speak of McCarthyism, finding themselves caught between the limitations set for them by the government on the one hand and by the fundamentalist Islam that challenges Egypt as a modern state on the other.

The press in Egypt is nominally free, yet some opposition papers and many books are banned by the censorship authorities. Various writers are in jail or live in exile, like Abu Zeid, a professor of Arabic literature, who was tried and divorced from his wife against their will after he had published an analysis of the Islamist discourse. The recurrent accusation for intellectuals expressing critical views is that they are apostates, the punishment for which sanctioned by Islamic *shari'a* is death, to be carried out either by the government or by an individual Muslim where the government fails to act. The existence of autonomous associations representing the citizens' interests seems to indicate the presence of a civil society. But the lack of state respect for them and acts of intolerance are experienced again and again. Amnesty International identified over thirty 'prisoners of conscience' jailed in 2000 alone who had exercised their right to freedom of expression (see Tariq Hassan-Gordon, 'AI says rights are under attack', <http://metimes.com/2K1/issue2001–8/eg/ ai_says_rights.htm>).

The number of registered civil associations in Egypt, among which are professional syndicates, mosque- or church-based associations and development organizations, as well as political parties, grew considerably after political and economic liberalization. It stood at about 14,000 in the 1990s. The government considers this expansion as politically risky and fears that it may lead to a strengthening of the opposition, despite the fact that it tries to promote economic participation and to put an end to the economic centralization that had been characteristic of industrial technologies as well as of development strategies since independence. Some NGOs are not independent and have to be considered creations of the government. All of them come under the control of the Ministry of Social Affairs, through which their structures are supervised and which was given great power over them according to Law 32 of 1964, which was redrafted several times but not changed, although human rights organizations condemned it strongly, and Law 153, which was meant to replace it and which also gave the government strong control over the NGOs' activities, until it was finally found to be unconstitutional and made defunct in 2000.

Of the many NGOs represented in Egyptian civil society today, there are a great number of mosque- or church-based ones that have developed from traditional institutions. They provide social welfare and charity to the poor, acting as social networks where the government fails to give support. A new type of mostly foreign-funded professional NGOs that emerged generally act as advocates of social and political change and concentrate on democratization, the empowerment of women and human rights questions. They have been particularly provoking to Hosni Mubarak's administration, which in turn accused them of dangerous foreign interference in the country's affairs, of misunderstanding gender issues and lacking consideration for the Egyptian cultural context. The fact is that in the case of many of these NGOs their priorities are set by international donors who have their own perspectives and select the target communities. So women, landless peasants and other marginalized groups are encouraged to form interest groups, to practise self-help and to form safety nets, aiming at their integration into the formal sector. So far these organizations have mostly lacked popular support, as well as support from any other indigenous agents that might be interested in bringing about political change. But they have helped draw people's attention to some important issues, like the human rights question, growing social injustice and environmental problems.

In the long run Egypt's economy will only be able to survive *vis-à-vis* the highly competitive international economy if the country's society is granted a chance of full political participation, so that it can play an active role in development. The organizations for businessmen, for bankers and for importers and exporters have already voiced their interests and put pressure on the government to expand the private sector further. Finally, Egypt's economy will only flourish if the government starts rewarding competency rather than loyalty.

CHAPTER 4

Egypt's Natural Potential

1 Geological and morphological structures of the country

1.1 Outline of the geology of Egypt

Egypt and the African continent as a whole were once part of the old Gondwana continent, which started disintegrating in the Jurassic age. The Egyptian Basement Complex consists of two different blocks of Precambrian rocks: the southern part of Jebel Uweinat/Gilf Kebir belongs to the older pan-African Eastern Saharan Block, while the eastern mountain range is part of the Nubian Shield, which was joined to the continent later during the phase of pan-Africa's consolidation (Luger et al. 1990: 122). From the Cambrian to the Carboniferous period, marine and continental sedimentation took place in the west of the Libyan Desert, when the whole area sank and a fault trough formed which extended from the present Syrte Basin to Darfur (Sudan). During the Carboniferous period the area of present-day southern Egypt was vaulted up when the African continent collided with the northern continents. Following the prevailing gradient, the main direction of drainage was southward, unlike the direction in which the Nile runs today. It was not till the Jurassic age that the previous direction of drainage was restored, when the Gondwana continent fell apart. At the same time the East Saharan Block was tilted up to the north and the north-west. Owing to these tectonic activities the basins of Ed-Dakhla and Asyut were created, the former being an important precondition for the sedimentation of huge deposits of an excellent water-storing capacity.

From the Upper Jurassic to the Tertiary various transgressions took place which are responsible for the older marine and the younger continental sediments which can be found spread as far as southern Egypt today. In the north they reach a thickness of 4,000 m, while they thin out towards the south. When the huge block of the Basement Complex of the Nubian Shield was lifted up, the Late Mesozoic rock layers which consisted mainly of fluvio-lacustrine deposits in the south were more strongly eroded. Thus the old folded and metamorphous rocks of the Basement came to the surface in the present-day Red Sea Mountains. The granite intrusions in the area of Aswan were exposed and formed the first cataract, which has obstructed navigation since man has inhabited the area.

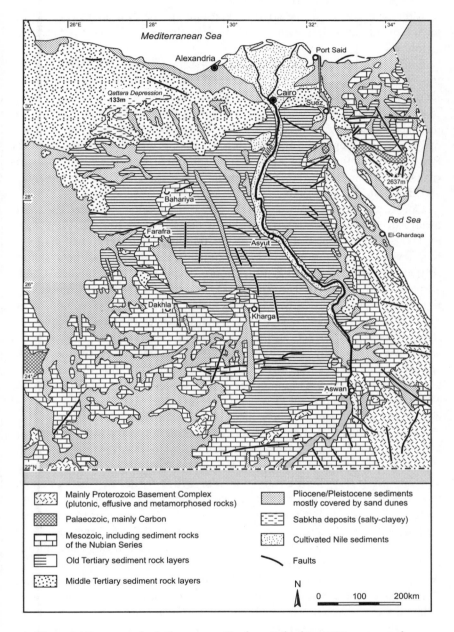

Figure 4.1 Egypt: geological structure (Author: F. Ibrahim 2002; cartography: J. Feilner; source: after Egyptian Geol. Survey n.d.)

1.2 Genesis of the lower Nile course

After Said (1993) the geological evolution of the Nile in Egypt and the formation of the river's various valleys over time can be described in short as follows.

During the Tertiary there were several marine transgressions which caused the northern parts of Egypt to be covered by oceans. During these times the sandstone and limestone deposits of the Muqattam Hills and today's steep rims of the Nile valley were formed. When during the Pliocene and the Miocene the ocean gradually receded to the north, and simultaneously the land was uplifted, Egypt's drainage systems were created, principally directed from the Red Sea Mountains in the south-east to the north-west. The corresponding rivers caused the formation of huge deltas, today the area between El-Faiyum and the Qattara Depression.

During the Pliocene an uplift in the Strait of Gibraltar separated the Mediterranean Sea from the ocean, so that it dried out. Its bottom, lying 3,000 to 4,000 m below the surface of the surrounding land, functioned as a new base level for the erosion, which was much lower than it had been before, so that the river valleys cut in much more deeply. The first Nile, the Eonile, was formed in a structural lineament between the old Basement Complex and the younger plateau in the west. It was mainly fed from the mountains along the Red Sea to the east, which were much higher at the time than they are today. The valleys formed during this more humid phase still exist as wadis which are periodically activated today. The incision caused by the Eonile, which reached 2,500 m in northern Egypt, equalled in dimension the Grand Canyon of the Rocky Mountains of today. When the passage between the Mediterranean and the ocean was opened up again, the Nile canyon turned into a gulf which was gradually filled up by sedimentation.

During the first half of the Pleistocene, about 1.8 to 0.8 million years BP, a desert climate prevailed in Egypt, which made the river dry out. When the climate became more humid again 800,000 to 400,000 years BP, the Prenile was formed. It was the first fluvial system in this region that had a connection to East Africa. It was made possible because the Ethiopian highland was tilted northward, so that the main drainage in Ethiopia was to the north and no longer to the Red Sea in the east, as had been the case previously. Thus the waters of the rivers that were the forerunners of the Blue Nile and the Atbara could break through the Nubian Shield and feed the main river. During the course of these events the six Nile cataracts existing today were formed. This Prenile had a much greater discharge than the later Neonile and its sediments were coarser. The discharge of the Neonile changed greatly during the 400,000 years of its existence. Repeatedly the connection to its southern catchment areas was interrupted when the Nubian Shield was uplifted. Also the alternation between dry phases and wet phases played an important role in both discharge and sedimentation.

During the Holocene, i.e. during the past 11,000 years, the Neonile went through a wetter phase with perennial drainage, followed by a relatively dry phase, during which drainage was reduced drastically.

1.3 Groundwater systems and mineral resources

The groundwater system of the Western Desert (see Figure 4.2)

About 69 per cent of Egypt's surface is covered by the Western (Libyan) Desert, which largely overlies the Nubian Aquifer System (formerly called Nubian Sandstone). This is a groundwater system of a complex structure which extends over a vast area of 2 million km² in Egypt, Sudan, Libya and Chad. The geological origin of the sediment layers dates mostly from the Mesozoic era, especially the Jurassic and the Cretaceous. Only a minor part originates from the Palaeozoic era (Thorweihe 1990: 601ff).

To the north, at the southern scarp of the Qattara Depression, the Egyptian Nubian Aquifer System is interfaced with saline groundwater, while in the east it borders the crystalline Basement Complex east of the Nile, which is poor in groundwater. In the south, the Jebel-Uweinat-Safsaf-Aswan Uplift Axis of the basement divides the Nubian Aquifer System between Egypt and the Sudan. The Misaha Graben, however, links the two sections of the Nubian Aquifer System. It is directed to the south and interrupts the uplift. This graben is of minor importance as regards the recharge of the Egyptian groundwater system from the wetter areas of the Sudan over a distance of 1,500 km, since the speed of the northward groundwater movement is only 3 cm/year. The groundwater of the Nubian System in Egypt, which is fossile and whose potential recharge must necessarily be of local origin, dates from the more humid climatic phases of the Late Pleistocene and the Holocene. The groundwater of Wadi el-Gedid (New Valley) has an estimated age of more than 20,000 years. It is difficult to measure its exact age with the 14C and 36CL methods which have been applied so far, since the water lifted from the boreholes does not usually originate from one single layer.

The groundwater system of the Western Desert of Egypt is divided into three units, which are interconnected:

- To the north there is the North-Western Basin with the Qattara Depression and Siwa Oasis. This basin is of subordinate relevance as regards human use, since its water is mostly salty.
- To the south, separated by the El-Bahariya-Cairo Arch of the basement, there is Ed-Dakhla Basin, the most important groundwater system in Egypt. Its northern part is dominated by mostly continental Cretaceous permeable sediments which cover the less permeable sediment layers of the Palaeozoic era. Over the layers of the Lower Cretaceous, which have a good water-storing capacity, lie the clayey and denser sediments of the Upper Cretaceous and the Tertiary. To the south are the continental Cretaceous

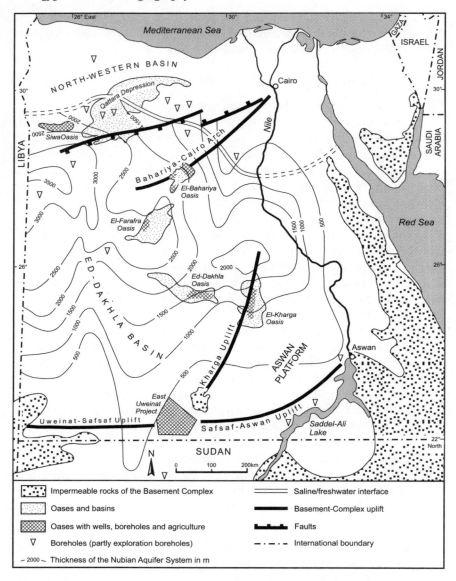

Figure 4.2 Egypt: hydro-geological situation (Author: F. Ibrahim 2002; cartography: J. Feilner; sources: after Thorweihe 1990; Heinl and Thorweihe 1993)

sediments, which are about 1,000 m thick and consist of very permeable coarse-grained sandstone. Among these deposits there are thin, less permeable layers.

• The third unit is to be found east of the El-Kharga Uplift of the Basement Complex, which can be described as the Upper Egyptian Plateau. This part, already uplifted during the Lower Cretaceous, was less influenced by the various marine transgressions of the Cretaceous period. The deposited layers found here are comparatively thin and less permeable, since they contain higher amounts of clay and silt.

The groundwater potential of El-Wadi el-Gedid

In 1958 President Gamal Abdel Nasser announced the El-Wadi el-Gedid, ('New Valley') project as an alternative to the densely populated 'old' Nile valley. According to the plans, millions of people were to be resettled there thanks to the deep-well drilling for groundwater. Instantly the cultivation of new land in the oasis depressions of El-Kharga, Ed-Dakhla, El-Farafra and El-Bahariya was started. Since the early 1960s the amount of groundwater extracted there has more than doubled. It is 500 million m^3 annually today. Recent estimates of the total amount of groundwater available in the Nubian Aquifer System amount to 150,000 km^3 (Heinl and Thorweihe 1993: 119). This equals the Nile run-off of 1,800 years or a water column of 75 m over the entire area of 2 million km^2 (Thorweihe and Heinl 1998: 5). If 1.5 m of this water were to be used for agricultural purposes annually, the water would be used up within only fifty years. Recent studies show that in the last 8,000 years the groundwater recharge has been negligible, so that experts call the extraction from the Nubian Aquifer System 'mining of an unrenewable resource' (ibid.: 21). Needless to say, the whole calculation is based on a purely theoretical model. In fact the situation is much more precarious, for if groundwater is pumped up, the water table around the borehole falls rapidly in the shape of an extraction cone. When this is the case, greater energy has to be used to extract the water. It is generally assumed that the profitability limit for pumping up water for agricultural purposes lies at a depth of 100 m. In Egypt, a depth of 50 m should not be exceeded, since so far neither the *fellaheen* nor the investors in agricultural projects pay for the water, and the resources of the state are limited. For more than forty years now, the irrigated agriculture of the El-Wadi el-Gedid project has been unprofitable. Nevertheless, hopes remain high and there are plans for extending it.

Egypt's mineral resources

Mining has a very long tradition in Egypt, and as early as the first dynasty turquoise and malachite quarries were active in Wadi Sidri on Sinai. More than 3,000 years ago gold was mined in the mountains of the Eastern Desert. The oldest known map showing mineral deposits dates back to the time of Ramses II (1290–24 BC). It is a papyrus on which the map of a gold mine in the area is drawn. At that time copper ore was mined at Gabal Gara and in different places on Sinai. Precious stones were actively produced during the times of the Romans and the Ptolemies. The output decreased gradually until it stopped completely in Ottoman times. The British tried to reactivate mining in the country, but soon gave up because of the strong international competition at the time. Forty-eight former gold mines are known in Egypt, three of which were still working in the 1960s. The gold-quartzite dykes are found in the Late Cambrian slates as well as in the younger granites of the Eastern Desert. Gold deposits are, however, also found in the eluvial and alluvial soaps (Schamp 1977: 20).

Today, iron ore, phosphate and salt are the most important mining products of Egypt after oil and gas. Until the 1970s the iron of the oolitic haematites in the sandstone layers of the Nubian Series at Aswan were transported by ship and rail to the furnaces at Helwan. Gradually they were replaced by the limonitic haematites from the oasis of El-Bahariya, which is situated closer to Helwan. The iron ore mined there is also of higher Fe content. In 2000/01 Managem in El-Bahariya produced 3.226 million tons of iron ore of a 50 per cent Fe content (CAPMAS 2002: 85). This does not meet the country's demand, however. So there are plans to exploit the newly found deposits near Aswan.

In 2000/01 1.292 million tons of phosphate were produced (ibid.), mainly from the Upper Cretaceous layers at Safaga and El-Quseir on the Red Sea, but in 2001 several of the quarries had to be closed there. Part of the Egyptian production of phosphates is exported, mainly to South and East Asia, through the port of Safaga, but most is used for the local production of agricultural fertilizers, for which there exists a rising demand in Egypt. For many years now, there have been plans to start production in Abu Tartur, which is situated in the Western Desert between El-Kharga and Ed-Dakhla. About US$3 billion have already been invested in this gigantic project, especially to establish the necessary infrastructure, e.g. a railway line over 650 km to Safaga, a high-voltage transmission line from Nag' Hammadi and an extension to the port of Safaga. Profitability will only be reached if 7 million tons of phosphate can be exported yearly from Abu Tartur. The government is currently trying to raise production to 600,000 tons annually with the help of 3,500 people employed there. The phosphate layers of the Upper Cretaceous are, however, not sufficiently thick, and the mining requires especially expensive techniques owing to the geological structure of the deposits, and the phosphate type is not very well suited to the production of fertilizers suitable to be used on Egyptian soils. Several foreign investors, to whom the government would have liked to sell the project, showed an interest, but no positive results have as yet been activated (oral communication March 2000).

The production of salt for local household consumption takes place around Lake Maryut, Lake El-Bardawil and Lake Mansala. In 2000/01 the production of table salt amounted to 2.578 million tons (ibid.). Because of severe pollution of the lakes by various industries and agricultural as well as household waste water, the quality of the salt is below the desirable standard and represents a serious health hazard for the Egyptian population.

The production of manganese on Sinai was interrupted by the Israeli–

10. *The Archimedean water screw* (tambur*)*: The picture shows members of a *fellaheen* family working together on their extremely small field to which they lift water from one of the irrigation canals with the help of a traditional water-lifting device, the Archimedean water screw. (Photo: F. Ibrahim)

Egyptian wars, but has been resumed. In 1964 production was 300,000 tons (Statistisches Bundesamt Wiesbaden 1993: 92). Coal mining at El-Maghara on Sinai was resumed in 1992, so that limited amounts of coal could be transported to the ferro-silicon factory at Idfu. The total reserves at El-Maghara are estimated at 27 million tons (ibid.: 82). However, coal mining there has proved uneconomic so far. Other important minerals mined in Egypt in 2000/ 01 were kaolin (226,000 tons), quartzite (69,000 tons) and gypsum (4 million tons) (CAPMAS 2002: 85f).

Most important of all the country's mineral resources is mineral oil. In 1992/93, the production reached its peak so far at 45 million tons, decreasing to 33.9 million tons in 2000/01. Most of it is used to meet the country's high demand for electric power (see Table 9.4). The production of natural gas and its derivatives reached 21.6 million tons (Ministry of Information 2002b). In 1999, Egypt gained more than US$1.3 billion from the export of petroleum and petroleum products (Internet 2000a). However, the net profit from the export/import of crude oil and related products fell drastically from US$1.5 billion to 0.6 billion between 1997 and 2002. Petroleum ranked in fourth place in providing hard currency for the country in 2000/01, after tourism (US$4.27 billion), the remittances of Egyptians working abroad (US$3.02 billion) and income gained from the Suez Canal (US$1.82 billion) (Ministry of Information 2002b). It is estimated, however, that if the country continues extracting mineral oil at the current rate, the reserves will last only until the year 2028. Crude oil reserves were estimated at 3.8 billion tons in 2001, those of natural gas at about 54 trillion ft³ (ibid.). At present Egypt is trying to reduce its output of crude oil and to use gas for the production of electricity. Gas and mineral oil were subsidized by US$3.8 million in 2002. The most important oil fields being exploited at present are along both coasts of the Gulf of Suez, a trough fault, in whose Tertiary and Cretaceous rock layers the oil is found. These oil fields were already known in Roman times, but systematic exploration and production started only at the beginning of the twentieth century. Since the 1960s production has increased considerably (see Illustration 21). Vast new oil fields have been explored in the country's west in the Libyan Desert between the Qattara Depression and the Mediterranean coast, in a fault running in an east–west direction. Egypt's hopes are presently concentrated on these. In 2000, new oil fields were discovered in Beni Suef, Wadi er-Raiyan, Qarun, Faiyum and El-Fors in the Qattara Depression.

Mineral gas production is of relatively recent origin in Egypt. Since the second half of the 1980s production figures have been rising fast. Production takes place mainly in the northern Nile delta at Abu Madi and at Balteem, and offshore near Abu Qir, Rosetta and Dumyat, as well as in the oil fields near Port Fouad and At-Timsah. There are strong hopes in Egypt for a lasting peace with its eastern neighbours, so that in future gas can be exported through a pipeline to Israel, Palestine and Syria. In 2001, before the escalation of the war in Palestine and the events of 11 September, Egypt, Jordan, Syria and Lebanon signed an agreement to transfer Egyptian gas from Al-Arish on the Mediterranean coast to Aqaba and later to Syria and Lebanon (Internet 2001k). In 1994 gas accounted for 80 per cent of electricity production in Egypt and 95 per cent of the energy used for the production of fertilizers, while in 2000 it accounted for 35 per cent of the total energy consumed in Egypt (A. Ibrahim 2001).

2 Climatic conditions (see Table 4.1)

In their perception of the climate prevailing in their country, most Egyptians differentiate between a cooler winter and a hot summer, while they consider spring and autumn of subordinate relevance. Although the main criterion thus seems to be temperature, Egyptians describe rain as *shita*, i.e. winter. *Fellaheen* engaged in agriculture have a much more sharply differentiated perception of climatic conditions during the course of the year. They use the old Coptic calendar, according to which each month is attributed special characteristics as regards the availability of Nile water, cooler or hotter phases, rainfall probability, fog and air humidity.

In fact temperatures during the course of the year are a less decisive factor

Table 4.1 The climate of Egypt: a north–south comparison

	Jan	Feb	Mar	Apr	May	June	July	Aug	Sept	Oct	Nov	Dec	Year
Alexandria (7m above sea level)													
T in °Celsius	14	14	16	18	21	24	25	26	25	23	20	16	20
Td max in °Celsius	18	19	21	24	27	28	30	31	29	28	24	20	25
Td min in °Celsius	9	9	11	13	16	20	23	23	21	18	15	11	16
R in mm	49	31	12	3	2	0	0	1	1	9	29	56	193
Cairo (20m above sea level)													
T in °Celsius	12	14	16	20	24	27	28	28	25	23	19	14	21
Td max in °Celsius	19	21	24	26	33	35	35	35	32	30	26	21	28
Td min in °Celsius	9	9	11	14	18	20	22	22	20	18	14	10	16
R in mm	4	5	3	1	1	0	0	0	0	1	1	8	24
Luxor (96m above sea level)													
T in °Celsius	13	15	19	25	30	31	32	32	30	27	21	15	24
Td max in °Celsius	23	25	29	35	39	41	41	41	38	35	30	25	34
Td min in °Celsius	6	7	11	16	20	23	24	24	21	16	12	8	16
R in mm	0.1	0.2	0	0	0.5	0	0	0	0	0.1	0.1	0.1	1
Quseir (10m above sea level)													
T in °Celsius	18	18	21	23	27	29	30	30	29	27	23	20	25
Td max in °Celsius	22	23	25	27	30	32	33	34	32	30	27	24	28
Td min in °Celsius	14	14	16	19	23	25	26	27	25	23	19	16	21
R in mm	0	0	0.4	0.2	0	0	0	0	0	1	2	0.2	4

T = mean monthly/annual temperature; Td max = mean daily maximum temperature; Td min = mean daily minimum temperature
R = mean monthly/annual precipitation
Source: after Schamp 1977: 26ff

than the annual or daily amplitude of the temperatures. This is why mean temperatures are not good indicators. Instead, mean maxima and mean minima should be considered. In the south, the annual amplitude of the temperatures is greater and the climate more continental. In winter the nights are colder in the south than in the north. On Sinai, where the mountains rise to a height of 2,637 m, the temperatures are much lower and the rainfall is higher than in other parts of the country of the same latitude. Snowfall can occur there, and frost in winter is normal.

Annual amounts of rainfall decrease rapidly from north to south (Alexandria: 193 mm; Cairo: 24 mm; Aswan: 3 mm). However, variability is great and increases with growing aridity. In Egypt rainfall as a rule occurs between October and April, December being the wettest month. Along the Mediterranean coast snowfall can occur but is a rare event, while hail is quite frequent.

From the above a simple climatic zonation can be derived. There is a narrow strip of a typical Mediterranean climate with rather cool, wet winters and dry, hot summers in the north. The remaining parts of the country – with the exception of Sinai – have a fully arid hot subtropical desert climate. A decisive factor for Egypt's climate is the location of the country between two great climatic regimes, the zone of the westerlies to the north, which in winter allow wet Atlantic air masses to enter the Mediterranean low-pressure area, and the high-pressure area of the horse latitudes to the south, which is responsible for the desert belt from the Atlantic coast of West Africa across Egypt and Arabia to Central Asia. Owing to a northward shift of the high-pressure area in summer, Egypt's climate is hot and lacks rainfall during that season. When the high-pressure area moves southward again, owing to the changed position of the sun in winter, Atlantic cyclones enter the area of the Mediterranean and cause rainfall there.

The winds prevailing in Egypt are the north-eastern trade winds. In winter they are interrupted by WNW winds from the Atlantic. In spring and in early summer there are spells of hot, dry dust storms called *khamaseen*, since they usually occur during the fifty (*khamseen*) days between Easter and Whitsuntide, according to the Coptic calendar.

3 Soils

Most soils in Egypt have the following characteristics which are typical of drylands:

- low humus content
- little biological activity
- coarse to medium-fine soil texture
- low field capacity.

Two main categories of soil can be found:

- Aridisols: mineral soils that have an aridic moisture regime. They are the soils that prevail in desert regions.
- Entisols: mineral soils with no distinctive horizons within 1 m of the soil surface. They are found on alluvial deposits as well as in sandy and rocky deserts.

While the Aridisols usually have a topsoil (A-horizon) consisting partly of crusts of carbonates and of soluble salts and clay, the Entisols are raw mineral soils with weakly developed profiles, since they were either formed by young accumulations or have already been capped. Often they are strongly saline, as, for example, in the northern parts of the Nile delta and in the Qattara Depression.

Topographical conditions are a decisive factor in the formation of soils. They influence the texture as well as the humidity of the soils, and the chemical processes they are exposed to. Roots of desert plants penetrate easily in wadis with deep soils, as well as in nebkas, the smaller sand dunes usually formed around shrubs in the desert, which in turn enhances their growth since they are favourable biotopes in the arid lands.

Of greatest importance for agriculture in Egypt are the Nile sediments of the Holocene, which to a large extent originate in the volcanic highlands of Ethiopia. These sediments are up to 8 m thick in the Nile valley and about 10 m thick in the Nile delta. The grain size of this mostly fine material decreases from south to north and from the valley scarps to the centre of the valley. In Wadi Halfa, for example, the relation between fine sand (grain size 0.02–0.2 mm), silt (grain size 0.002–0.02 mm) and clay (grain size < 0.002 mm) is 34 : 38 : 28, whereas it is 17.7 : 26.9 : 55.4 in Cairo (Schamp 1977: 18). A study of the change in soil texture from the middle to the outer parts of the Nile valley shows a drastic decrease in the content of silt and clay from 37.5 per cent to 20.8 per cent and from 32.1 per cent to 9 per cent respectively. Likewise, the nutrients that are important for the growth of plants and trace elements decrease: namely the organic matter N, Fe, Mn, Zn and Cu (Kishk 1985: 15–23). According to Kishk the deficiencies of the latter at the rims of the Nile valley are caused by the fact that no siltation has occurred there since the construction of the Aswan High Dam (see Chapter 6).

4 Vegetation, fauna and the processes of desertification

Owing to its climatic conditions Egypt has developed a desert flora throughout with forms more adapted to the Mediterranean influence in the north. As in other drylands of the world, this natural vegetation can tolerate extreme heat and dryness as well as great variation in rainfall, the so-called high rainfall variability. Among the adaptive mechanisms are reduced evapotranspiration, as, for example, through small leaves and thorns, as well as hairiness and a leathery leaf surface. Cushion plants and bulbous plants are such adapted forms. Trees and shrubs with these characteristics are concentrated in locations with deeper soils, i.e. in wadi beds, depressions and in the foot zone of escarpments. Seasonally and episodically growing grasses, herbs and bulbous plants also occur, covering patches of the soil surface. For the growth of the vegetation it is important which kind of surface run-off prevails. It can be linear or diffused, depending on the topographical conditions.

After Kassas (1971: 477ff) we can differentiate between three regional types of vegetation in Egypt:

- the type of the Mediterranean coastal zone, which spreads southward to 29° latitude
- the type of the coastal region of the Red Sea
- the type of the Western Desert, the Eastern Desert and the Nubian Desert.

On Sinai characteristics of all three vegetation types can be found. In Egypt's north the Mediterranean desert zone takes the form of a desert steppe with herbs and shrubs of the *Thymelaeaceae* and *Chenopodiacea* families. South of these, *Artemisia* species (vermouth) and caper trees (*Capparis*) occur. On the saline soils of the depressions and of the dried-up lagoons we find halophytes. In the brackish waters of the Natrun valley and in the outer parts of Lake Qarun in Faiyum there are cypress grass (*Cyperaceae*), bulrushes (*Juncaceae*) and tamarisks (*Tamarix*) (Schamp 1977: 77). In the south-east of the Mediterranean desert zone *Pennisetum* species occur on limey soils, and species of *Ephedra*, as well as of *Salicornia* on pebbly soils. In wadis we may find different types of acacia trees. Along the Red Sea coast a longitudinal strip of desert vegetation profits from the relatively high air humidity, the run-off from the mountain range and the wet saline soils in the coastal depressions. Here halophytes occur, around which nebkas tend to form. In the extreme south of Egypt's Red Sea coast in Ras Muhammad and along the Gulf of Aqaba, there are mangrove swamps, and around wadi mouths there are acacia trees and dum palms (*Hyphaene thebaica*) as well as ephemeral herbs and grasses.

In the deserts, which are described by some as lacking rainfall altogether, and which make up the largest part of the country, the topographical conditions, the occurrence of groundwater close to the soil surface and erratic rainfall are decisive for the location of the vegetation. One may find acacia, *Balanites aegyptiaca* or dum palms scattered or in small clusters here. Favourable for these are locations in wadis or depressions or in the foot zones of mountains. The drainage lakes of the oases of the Western Desert with their salty water are the places where plenty of bulrushes and reeds grow, which serve the local population for mat-weaving (see Illustration 14).

Among the trees found in the Nile valley today is the date palm (*Phoenix dactylifera*), which has been one of the most useful plants for man in the

11. The water wheel (sakya): The water wheel is widely used in Egypt for irrigation, as on this sugar cane field in Upper Egypt. (Photo: F. Ibrahim)

region for the past 6,500 years. There are also a number of trees growing wild, among them sycamore, mulberry, tamarisk, *Acacia nilotica, Acacia nubica,* the Lebbach tree and, in Upper Egypt, the dum palm.

In the Nile river itself, as well as in the many irrigation and drainage canals, there are large stands of aquatic plants of various kinds. The most widespread today are bulrushes and the water hyacinth (*Eichhornia crassipes*). The latter originates from America and was imported via India to the Nile as an ornamental plant, but has become an utterly undesired weed, which is hard to eradicate (see Chapter 6).

Egypt's varied flora is rich in medicinal ingredients which were well known to the ancient Egyptians and served them for many purposes. Of late they have been rediscovered as a potential means of producing modern phytopharmaceuticals. A bio-technology laboratory was established to investigate the therapeutical value of the plants in cooperation with several pharmacological centres in Egypt (see <http://www.businesstoday-eg.com/msurv1.html>). The ideal locations for growing the medicinal plants are the various oases with their relatively unpolluted environments.

A description of Egypt's vegetation would not be complete without mentioning the problem that has come to be called desertification. One has to differentiate, however, between the processes currently occurring and those that happened in ancient times. Little research exists on the latter, but it may be legitimate to draw comparisons with processes of desertification that happened in the desert steppes of Tunisia in Roman times (see Ibrahim and Mensching 1976). The rich fauna living here at that time – including lions, leopards and many kinds of antelopes – which had a considerable food demand that could only be satisfied if plenty of biomass and a greater number of smaller animals than exist there today were available, are indicative of a denser vegetation in northern Egypt in Roman times, especially in wadis. Of the bigger mammals merely a small number of red foxes (*Vulpes vulpes*), fennecs (*Fennecus zerda*), jackals (*Canis aureus*), hyenas (*Hyaenidae*), Dorcas gazelles, lynxes (*Lynx*), wildcats and hares are found today. They live either in deserts or close to villages. Since no considerable climatic change has taken place during the past 2,500 years, the cause of the degradation of flora and fauna can only be attributed to overuse of the natural potential, which in drylands inevitably leads to soil degradation, if not to desertification.

A special type of desertification in the extremely arid Western Desert is the encroachment of sand sheets and sand dunes on arable land, settlements and infrastructure, especially in the oases (see Illustration 4). These almost purely natural phenomena are hard to combat. Establishing living and non-living windbreaks may be helpful against blowing sand sheets, but is hardly effective in stopping the rapidly advancing barkhan dunes.

The soil degradation currently taking place is another special form of desertification. Precious agricultural land is being lost through processes of salinization and by drifting sand sheets. The losses are occurring in the Nile delta and the Nile valley, in the oases and on newly reclaimed land as well as on old agricultural land. Since the construction of the Aswan High Dam the soil degradation caused by these processes has increased enormously (see Chapter 6). Equally regrettable is the immense loss of fertile agricultural land through urban sprawl, which has taken place during the past decades in the Nile valley and Nile delta. According to some experts this is also to be considered as a type of desertification. It is estimated that more than 8,000 ha of the best land in the country fall prey to urban encroachment annually. The government has been fighting this problem for decades through restrictive laws and its new town planning strategies (see Chapter 11).

CHAPTER 5

The Regional Structure of Egypt

§ In the Egyptians' perception their country consists of three main parts:

- the land of the *fellaheen* in the Nile valley
- the urban areas
- the formerly almost uninhabited deserts.

Since this regional structure is adequately reflected in the chapters on agriculture and settlements, here we present a division of the country according to its physical-geographical structure, taking into consideration the various environmental qualities which make the specific areas favourable or unfavourable as human habitats.

1 The Western Desert

The Nile, winding its way in an S shape from south to north, divides Egypt in two big desert areas: the Western (Libyan) Desert, which covers 680,000 km², i.e. more than 68 per cent of the total area of the country (1,002,000 km²), and the Eastern (Arabian) Desert, which covers an area of 220,000 km², i.e. more than one-fifth of it. As has been mentioned before, the Western Desert consists mainly of Mesozoic and Tertiary nearly horizontal layers of limestone and of sandstone (see Figure 4.1). Geological structures and tectonic conditions caused the formation of vast plateaus and escarpments which formed glacis of debris on their steep slopes when arid morphodynamics prevailed for a longer period of time. On the plateaus we find hamadas, deserts of debris which developed through the weathering of the upper layers of sediment rocks. On the lower plains as well as in the basins, ergs with mobile crescent-shaped barkhan dunes were formed. The largest area of ergs is in the Great Sand Sea, which runs in a north-westerly–south-easterly direction over hundreds of miles in the western part of the Western Desert.

In the Western Desert there are three areas of potential economic use.

The coastal area along the Mediterranean from Alexandria to El-Alamein, Marsa Matruh and Es-Sallum at the Libyan border Here we find Tertiary limestone and sandstone formations and intermittently sheltered bays of

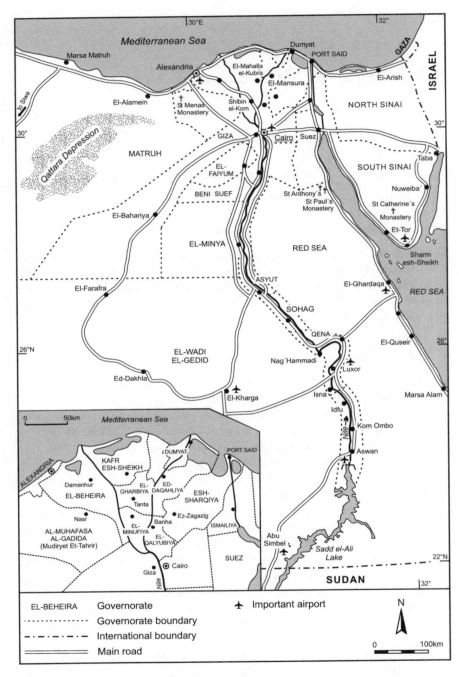

Figure 5.1 Egypt: administrative division (Author: F. Ibrahim 2002; cartography: J. Feilner; sources: various official publications)

white fine sands, forming the beaches that are the basis of existing domestic tourism as well as of projected international tourism. Between the present coastline and the plateau, and the Pleistocene marine terraces to the south of these, there are depressions running parallel to the coast separated from the sea by long stretches of limestone ridges and by sandy bars along the beaches, like the area of Lake Maryut south-west of Alexandria. The whole area is being developed rapidly at present. Holiday villages, often in the form of gated communities (see Illustration 28), cover the entire coastline, while to the south Bedouin have started cultivating figs during recent decades, thus making their claims to the land visible (see Illustration 7).

The Qattara Depression and Siwa Oasis The Qattara Depression, covering an area of nearly 20,000 km², lies 60–135 m below sea level and is surrounded by escarpments and steep ridges of the Miocene and the Eocene. In the depression itself we find salt lakes and clay plains, which are inhospitable to man. In the 1970s a gigantic project for the production of electric power using sea water that was to be diverted over 50 km into the depression with the help of a canal was envisaged here. Evaporation from the lake surface was to provide a constant gradient, so as to keep the artificial waterfall running (see Ibrahim 1982a). The project was first conceived by the German geographer Albrecht Penck in 1916. One of the main reasons why the idea never materialized was the expected high cost, estimated in 1980 at about US$5 billion, since two tunnels would have had to be built. It would have been much cheaper to have used nuclear explosives, but the international donors who had shown an interest in the project finally withdrew from it for environmental reasons.

In the oases around Siwa and in Siwa itself the traditional oasis economy still prevails, though agriculture here suffers from the extreme salinization of the soils. Water flows spontaneously or can easily be extracted from the many springs, and its overuse has led to a rise in the groundwater table and the constant growth of the lakes, in which the saline drainage water gathers. A huge dam was built recently in one of the three lakes to keep the water away from the agricultural land. Three factories in Siwa produce mineral water, for which there is a growing demand in Egypt with its flourishing tourism. The Siwan authorities make great efforts to attract more tourists to the oasis, but at the same time are aware of the possible negative effects of tourism on the indigenous culture. The historic pedigree of the oasis as well as its natural beauty offers great potential, but so far the infrastructure is not sufficient for international tourism on a greater scale.

The New Valley Depressions Over a distance of more than 1,000 km a chain of depressions winds in a north–south direction in the middle of the Western Desert from the oases of El-Bahariya, El-Farafra, Ed-Dakhla, El-Kharga and Baris to the depressions of Toshka and East Uweinat. The formation of these depressions is still a matter of conjecture. Figure 4.2 shows that some of them lie in geological basins, as in the case of Ed-Dakhla, and others on Old Basement arches, as in the case of El-Bahariya and El-Kharga, but the formation of the present-day depressions is not directly related to these geological structures of the Basement Complex. One plausible explanation for their existence given by Schamp (1977: 12f) is that the formation of the depressions of the Western Desert, including Qattara, Wadi en-Natrun, El-Faiyum and Wadi er-Raiyan, went hand in hand with the formation of the escarpments in the sedimentary rock layers. Tertiary faults helped expose these layers to weathering and erosion. The geomorphologically hard layers formed the escarpments, while those easily erodable formed the foreland basins. The erosion processes in the forelands came to a standstill when the erosion-base level reached the groundwater table.

The agricultural exploitation of these vast depressions based on tapping the Nubian Aquifer System is dealt with in the chapters on groundwater (see Chapter 6) and land reclamation (see Chapter 8). Since the 1950s the government has been cherishing ambitious plans for reclaiming several million acres of land for agricultural purposes, hoping to settle more than three million people from the congested Nile valley there. In 1996, however, only about 150,000 persons lived in El-Wadi el-Gedid, and the arable area did not exceed 40,000 acres.

2 The Eastern Desert

The Eastern (Arabian) Desert, which in its southern extension is known as the Nubian Desert, consists in large part of the Red Sea Hills. These reach their maximum elevation in Gabal Shayeb el-Banat (2,187 m), while the northern parts are less high and consist mostly of Tertiary and Mesozoic rock formations. The escarpments formed here are interrupted by the fault of Wadi Araba. To the south the overlying layers were mostly eroded owing to an uplift, so that the Basement Complex forms the surface in nearly all parts between the Nile valley and the Red Sea. Unlike in the Western Desert, deep valleys are incised in the Eastern Desert. This is due partly to the greater relief dynamics and partly to the lesser permeability of the Basement Complex, which mostly consists of crystalline rock. The deeply cut old wadis, which are reactivated whenever erratic rainfall occurs, have steep slopes, and many of them are filled mainly with fluvial and aeolian sands. They are used by the few Bedouin living in the Eastern Desert for grazing their herds.

The Red Sea coast saw great economic changes during the last decades of the twentieth century, one reason being the enormous increase in oil extraction there, the other the international tourism boom in the area between El-Ghardaqa and Safaga and southward to El-Quseir and Marsa Alam. At the turn of the millennium the most active development was taking place north

12. Harvesting in Upper Egypt: Children are an indispensable part of Egypt's agricultural labour force. The picture shows young *fellaheen* taking part in the harvest of potatoes (foreground) and of sugar cane (background). (Photo: F. Ibrahim)

of El-Ghardaqa at El-Gouna, and farther to the north at Ain Sukhna. In the latter, hotels and camps built mostly for domestic tourism, as well as gated communities for the well-to-do people of Cairo for weekend use, compete for space with the new port, constructed here because the port facilities at Suez were no longer sufficient. A new, fast road was built along the coast, and the road through the desert to Qena and Luxor in the Nile valley was improved, so that these two important centres of tourism could be reached more easily. A day trip to Luxor is now possible from the Red Sea coast.

3 The Sinai Peninsula and the Suez Canal Zone

The granite horst of Sinai divides the northern part of the Red Sea graben along two lines: the Gulf of Aqaba and the Gulf of Suez, with the Sinai Peninsula, which covers an area of 61,000 km², in between. In its southern part (see Illustration 1), which consists of the Basement Complex, we find Gabal Katharina (2,635 m), Egypt's highest mountain. In the sixth century Emperor Justinian had St Catherine's Monastery built at its foot. Today it belongs to the Greek Orthodox Church and is inhabited exclusively by Greek monks. It has been a place of pilgrimage throughout history, especially for believers of the Orthodox Churches. The northern part of the peninsula, covering about two-thirds of Sinai, consists of Tertiary and Mesozoic sedimentary rock layers. They form a series of escarpments tilted steeply to the south and to the east. Northern Sinai's drainage takes place through the Wadi-el-Arish system northwards into the Mediterranean.

Since Egypt's peace agreement with Israel in 1979 the development of Sinai has been one of the foremost aims of the Egyptian government, which hopes that in the near future at least three million Egyptians will live on the presently still thinly populated peninsula. Many new communities have been established along the coast between Suez and Et-Tor, mainly concerned with the exploitation of oil at the Gulf of Suez. The Salam Canal, which is to bring Nile water to the northern part of Sinai for irrigation purposes in desert land reclamation projects, is presently under construction. There have also been efforts at land reclamation east of the Suez Canal (see Ibrahim 1985b), and a long-term project supported by the UN World Food Programme (WFP) for the sedentarization of the Sinai Bedouin is going on. By providing them with food, wells and building materials for houses, the intention is to encourage this group to start engaging in agricultural activities. The Bedouin's response has not been too positive so far. Their integration into the country's formal economy may take time. Presently their cultivation of drugs in the remote valleys of Sinai is a serious problem, against which the government has had to take severe measures repeatedly.

Administration-wise, Sinai has been divided into two governorates since 1979: North Sinai, in which agriculture is to be promoted, with its capital of El-Arish, and South Sinai, with Et-Tor as a capital. For the southern governorate the aim is to develop tourism further. Sharm esh-Sheikh, with its international airport, has already become a great attraction for mostly younger people from all over the world who want to enjoy scuba-diving or snorkelling in some of the world's most spectacular coral reefs, and also the nightlife and golfing.

Development on the Sinai peninsula was until recently impeded by the difficulty of communication with the rest of the country across the Suez Canal, the small ferries being inadequate. The situation improved greatly when in 1982 the 160-m-long Ahmed-Hamdi Tunnel under the canal was opened. In 2001, two new bridges were inaugurated, the Qantara bridge for motor cars and the Ferdan iron bridge for trains.

The Suez Canal Zone forms a marked border area between the thinly populated Sinai deserts and the green Nile delta in which the population is concentrated. Three urban centres have developed in this zone since the construction of the canal in the mid-nineteenth century. They are the capitals of the governorates of the same names: Port Said, Ismailiya and Suez. The Suez Canal Zone suffered severely during the Israeli bombardments in 1967 and 1973. Since the 1980s it has seen strong economic development. Suez is today the third-most important location for the petrochemical industries after Cairo and Alexandria. Ismailiya, with its historical colonial town and green alleys, is a centre for recreation, but also for agricultural development, and is home to

13. Fellaheen *of the Nile delta*: This *fellah* and his wife are standing in the courtyard of their house. The containers for the wheat harvested on their fields (right) as well as the oven for baking bread (left) are made of Nile silt mixed with cow dung and straw. (Photo: F. Ibrahim)

the new Suez Canal University. To attract foreign investors a free trade zone was established at Port Said. Though import rates are high, industries have not yet developed here to the extent expected in spite of exemption from high customs duties.

During Pharaonic times an artificial waterway already connected the Red Sea and the Mediterranean. It is reported that in 1850 BC a canal linked an eastern Nile arm near Ez-Zagazig with the Bitter Lakes, which at that time were not yet separated from the Gulf of Suez. This waterway between the two seas, which passed through the area where we find Cairo today, was silted up at times, but reconstructed again. Between 1859 and 1869 the Suez Canal, which runs for over 171 km without locks, was built under the supervision of Ferdinand de Lesseps. The Egyptian Vice-King had promised to contribute 20,000 workers to the construction. He recruited the men among the *fellaheen* population by force. In the hostile deserts thousands died from hunger, thirst or cholera. The canal exclusively served Europeans in their trade with Asia by shortening the sea journey by about 40 per cent. It has been continuously deepened and widened. Today its fairway is about 180–205 m, while its navigable depth is 21 m. This allows fully loaded tankers of 170,000 gross register tons and unloaded tankers of 400,000 gross register tons to pass through it. However, the maximum capacity of the canal is eighty ships daily, since except

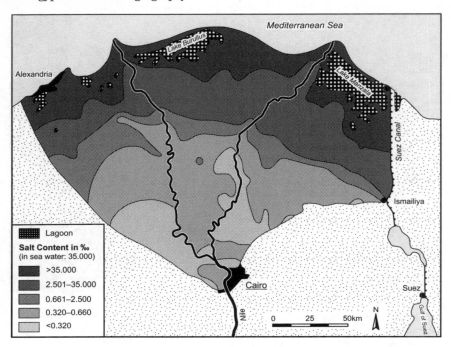

Figure 5.2 Soil water salinity in the Nile delta (Author: F. Ibrahim 2002; cartography: J. Feilner; source: after Abu-Zeid 1987: 187)

for that part in the Great Bitter Lake, it permits only single-lane traffic (see Illustration 30). The government's apprehension that the canal might be used less frequently after the first supertankers had been built proved vain. It is true that the number of ships that passed through the canal decreased from 21,250 to 13,490 between 1966 and 1999; however, the net tonnage transported increased from over 274 million tons to almost 385 million tons, and the revenues from the dues paid increased from US$95 million to US$1,700 million in the same time span (CAPMAS 1986: 107 and 2001: 104). This made the Suez Canal the third-most important hard currency source for the state after the remittances of Egyptians working abroad and tourism. However, the dues had to be reduced for reasons of competitiveness.

4 The Nile Valley

In the narrow Nile valley 48 per cent (2002) of the Egyptian population are concentrated. Here lie the governorates of Cairo and of Middle Egypt: El-Giza, Beni Suef, El-Faiyum and El-Minya, as well as the governorates of Upper Egypt: Asyut, Sohag, Qena, Luxor and Aswan. As a rule, all nine governorates south of Cairo are subsumed under the term 'Upper Egypt' (see Chapter 11).

In Upper Egypt the Nile valley is steep sided and deeply incised into the Tertiary limestone and limey sandstone layers. In the area of Nubia it is very narrow. At Aswan, not far north of the First Cataract, it is only about 1 km wide and there is practically no alluvial plain. On both sides of the valley there are layers of reddish-brownish sandstone, and granite blocks and inselbergs come to the surface. Between Isna and Sohag the river starts meandering in the gradually widening valley. In Middle Egypt the Nile valley is 15–20 km wide and the present river bed is situated close to the steep eastern rim of the valley. In many places Pleistocene Nile terraces can be found between the Holocene river plain and the scarps of the valley sides, which consist of Tertiary and Cretaceous layers. Unlike the valley bed, which consists of the fertile black soils, the older Nile terraces are formed by gravel and coarse sands. The most expansive Pleistocene Nile terrace is situated in the Kom Ombo plain, where in the 1960s many Nubians who had lost their land in the south when the Sadd el-Ali was constructed were resettled.

El-Faiyum Oasis lies in a former part of the Nile valley, later cut off from the main valley. Today it is fed with Nile water through Bahr Yousif, a Nile arm. The oasis covers an area of 1,800 km² and drains off into Lake Qarun, which has grown considerably during recent decades owing to increasing irrigation and drainage.

5 The Nile Delta

At approximately 22,000 km² the area of the Nile delta is nearly twice as large as that of the Nile valley; 43.5 per cent of the population of Egypt lived here in the governorates of Dumyat, Ed-Daqahliya, Esh-Sharqiya, El-Qalyubiya, Kafr esh-Sheikh, El-Gharbiya, El-Minufiya, El-Beheira and Ismailiya in 2002 (CAPMAS 2002: 3).

At the beginning of historical times in Egypt there existed many lakes and swamps in the region, and the Nile delta was covered by a number of Nile branches which were constantly changing their courses. Just like the alluvial plain of the Nile valley, the Nile delta was amphibious in character. Today there are seven Nile branches and two major canals in the extremely flat plain of the Nile delta. The gradient towards the Mediterranean is very small at about only 0.01 per cent, and the difference in altitude over the distance of 160 km between Cairo and the Mediterranean coast is only 20 m. There are no natural elevations in the Nile delta. The few minor places that may seem to be such are the remains of former settlements covered by mud or sand. Several settlements here were destroyed by earthquakes in historical times, like the old part of the town of Damanhour.

The Nile delta, just like the Nile valley, is suffering severely from urban encroachment. The network of settlements of all sizes has grown denser and denser over recent decades, so that the land under cultivation has decreased drastically. The north, where soil salinization is extreme (see Figure 5.2), as around the coastal lagoons of Lake Idku, Lake Burullus and Lake Manzala, is less densely populated.

From the western and the eastern rims of the Nile delta human activities were extended considerably into the adjacent desert areas in the twentieth century. On the one hand, new areas were brought under cultivation with the help of several land reclamation projects; on the other, new towns were established there like Madinet es-Sadat, Gharb en-Nubariya and Borg el-Arab el-Gedida in the west, and Madinet es-Salam, Al-Ubur, Esh-Sheruq, Heliopolis el-Gedida, Er-Rihab, Badr, Madinet el-Ashir min Ramadan and Madinet es-Salhiya el-Gedida in the east (see Chapter 11).

CHAPTER 6

Egypt's Water Resources and Water Demand

§ THE backbone of Egypt's agrarian economy today – just as in ancient times – is the availability of sufficient amounts of cheap water for irrigation purposes. In this respect Nile water is still of prime relevance in spite of the discovery of the Eastern Sahara Basin with its huge groundwater reservoir. So the government's master plan for the use of water for the year 2000 shows a near-complete dependency on Nile water for its great land reclamation projects (Ministry of Information 2000: 70ff).

Table 6.1 shows the country's water needs for the last quarter of the twentieth century calculated according to two different models. Here the unreliability of the data and the fact that the subject is more or less a matter of speculation and of political manipulation become obvious. There is relative accordance in the two models only concerning the water loss caused by seepage in the irrigation system, as of 17 billion m^3 and 25 billion m^3 respectively. The fact that such a great amount of water is available in cultivated areas but cannot be utilized by the crops grown shows the low degree of efficiency of the irrigation which, according to the official statistics, is 51 per cent (CAPMAS 1987: 46). As its first aim, therefore, the master plan aims

Table 6.1 Egypt's annual water requirements 1974–2000/01 (in bn m^3)

	USAID calculation 1974	Egyptian calculation 1974	Egyptian calculation 1982–87	Egyptian calculation 2000/01
Irrigation	26.0	39.9		
Losses in the canal system	11.2	8.0	49.7	50.7
Losses by seepage in soil	14.0	9.3		
Domestic and industrial use	1.0	1.0	6.7	12.0
Navigation and hydro-energy*	3.0	2.5	4.0	2.4
Total	55.2	60.7	60.4	65.1

* For purposes of navigation and power generation more water is discharged through the High Dam in winter than is required for irrigation during that season.

Sources: after CAPMAS 1987: 145 and 171; El-Kharbutl and Abdal-Ati 1998: 67ff; Ministry of Information 2002b

Table 6.2 Egypt's water resources 1974–2001 (in bn m³)

	1974	1982–87	1997	2000/01
Nile discharge through the Aswan High Dam	56.2	55.5*	55.5*	55.5*
Groundwater and return flow to the Nile	2.7	2.9	4.6	5.4
Recycled drainage water	2.5	3.5	3.8	5.2
Total	61.4	61.9	63.9	66.1

* This is the official figure for the Nile water Egypt is entitled to. The actual discharge is much higher

Sources: after CAPMAS 1987: 171; Barth and Shata 1987: 57; Ministry of Information 1998; Ministry of Information 2002b

at raising efficiency in irrigation to 70 per cent. If this materialized, several billion cubic metres of water could be saved and used for the forthcoming land reclamation projects.

Table 6.2 shows that the government's optimistic plans to reduce water loss and to make more intensive use of recycled drainage water have been of little success. According to even more optimistic models of calculation, in future 9 billion m³ can be gained through hydrologic projects on the upper Nile course, and a further 4.5 billion m³ through the exploitation of groundwater resources in desert areas. The example of the Jonglei Canal (see below), through construction of which it was hoped to gain 10 billion m³ of water annually, shows that no high-flying hopes should be raised by such projects as long as the civil war raging in the Upper Nile region of the Sudan is allowed to continue. Plans to use the deep groundwater aquifers in desert areas cannot be economically viable for agrarian production owing to the high energy costs of extracting the water.

The following gives an outline of the overall situation concerning Egypt's water resources.

1 Rainfall in Egypt – an under-used potential

Egypt is situated in the subtropical dry belt. Rainfall constitutes an important factor in agriculture only in the narrow strip along the Mediterranean coast and on the Sinai peninsula. Barth and Shata (1987: 51f) give the following picture of rainfall and surface run-off for this area taking into consideration high rainfall variability:

- During an average winter season rainfall amounts to 10 billion m³, which leads to a surface run-off of 0.5–1 billion m³ of water.
- In particularly wet years, i.e. about 20 per cent of all years, rainfall may be about 15 billion m³, accounting for 1.5 billion m³ of surface run-off.
- In about 10 per cent of all years the water available rises to more than

20 billion m³ thanks to the influence of the seasonal winds, so that the surface run-off may reach 5 billion m³.

So far these amounts of water have remained largely unutilized. Through the implementation of suitable measures for collecting and diverting this surface water, for example with the help of low earth dams (water harvesting and water spreading) and water-saving methods of irrigation, however, large areas could be cultivated in Egypt's north, and thus contribute considerably to the country's economy. The Bedouin of the Mediterranean coastal areas have for a long time made good use of such rainfall as well as of the relatively high humidity of the air there by cultivating olives, figs (see Illustration 7) and the Indian fig (*Opuntia ficus indica*).

2 Groundwater – a limited resource

Barth and Shata (1987: 52ff) divide the groundwater regimes of Egypt according to their productivity into the following five main categories.

The huge aquifer of the Nubian System

This has a depth ranging from 100 m to 3,000 m and lies on the Basement, the north-eastern part of which is situated in the area of the Western Desert and belongs to the great North-East–East African Artesian Basin. It contains fossil water of the pluvial times of 20,000–40,000 years ago whose salt content is relatively low (< 500 ppm). After long-term use these resources will be exhausted, since recharge from the Nile valley or from tropical Africa is negligible.

Discharge of the Western Desert, whether natural or anthropogenic, takes place in three main areas:

- in the Qattara Depression, in which more than 3 million m³/day are discharged; in Siwa Oasis alone, there are more than 200 springs with a total discharge of 200,000 m³ daily, the number rising because of new boreholes being drilled
- in the Farafra-Bahariya Depression in which the discharge is at present 400,000 m³ daily; according to government plans it will be increased to a total of 1 million m³ daily
- in the Kharga-Dakhla Depression with its more than 900 shallow wells and deep boreholes and a total extraction of 3 million m³ daily, allowing an area of 40,000 ha to be irrigated.

In the area of the Eastern Desert the groundwater aquifer in the sandstone of the Nubian Series is much less rich, since the layers are rather thin and the underlying Basement is not favourably shaped. This is similar to the conditions in Sinai, although here the depth of the Nubian Sandstone aquifer reaches about 500 m. However, its water has a relatively high salinity of 1,500 ppm.

The groundwater body in the sands and gravels of the Pleistocene Nilotic deposits

This aquifer is about 350 m deep and here the underlying Pliocene clay layer acts as an impermeable front. About 350 billion m^3 of water of a salt content of 500 ppm are available, with a constant recharge from the Nile system. Discharge or extraction from this groundwater takes place in the following areas:

- west of the Nile delta in Wadi en-Natrun and in the Qattara Depression
- east of the Nile delta in Wadi et-Tumeilat, along the Bitter Lakes and the Suez Canal
- in the lagoons of the northern Nile delta
- in countless wells in the Nile valley and the Nile delta which are used for irrigation and for drinking-water purposes by households.

In the northern part of the Nile delta severe intrusion of the salty Mediterranean water into this aquifer is taking place due to over-exploitation. On the newly reclaimed land of Gharb en-Nubariya north of the Natron valley, a vast saline lake has developed owing to both over-pumping and insufficient drainage.

The fissure limestone (karstic) aquifers

To these belong many wells and springs in different parts of Egypt in the Western as well as in the Eastern Desert, on Sinai and in the Nile valley, as for example the springs of Deir Anba Pola and Deir Anba Antonius, the desert monasteries near the Red Sea, and the mineral springs of Siwa and at Helwan south of Cairo.

The shallow groundwater body in the Mediterranean Calcarenites

The water stored in these marine and terrestrial deposits is rather saline (1,000 ppm) and is found on top of an intruding wedge of more saline sea water. This groundwater is used by most of the population settling along the 1,000-km-long Mediterranean coast to the west and to the east of the Nile delta. Local rainfall provides a limited amount of recharge here.

The groundwater aquifers in the valley beds and in mobile sand sheets, especially on Sinai and at the Red Sea

These are useful to the local population and are mostly exploited by them with the help of shallow wells.

3 The Nile (see Figure 6.1)

3.1 The natural hydrological system of the Nile

The Nile, which is known to be the longest river on earth, has its catchment area in the mountains and plateaus of the inner and marginal tropical

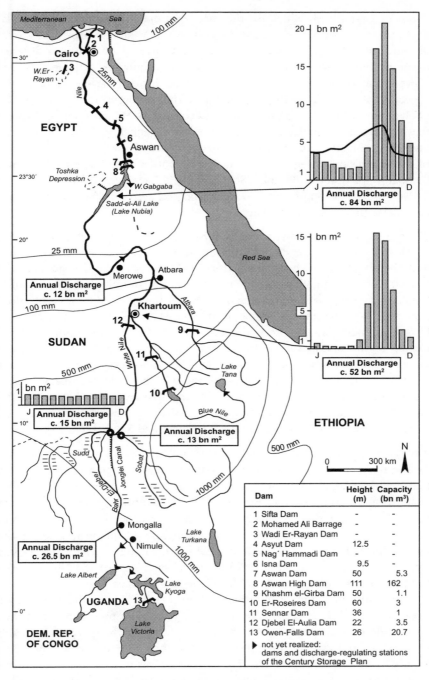

Figure 6.1 Mean Nile water discharge (Author: F. Ibrahim 2002; cartography: J. Feilner; sources of data: Schamp 1977 and others)

zones of East Africa, which for the most part are in Uganda and Ethiopia. From there it takes its course northwards to the Mediterranean over a total distance of 6,671 km. In northern Sudan and Egypt it flows over a distance of more than 2,700 km without receiving any tributaries, since in this area a hyper-arid climate prevails. The Nile passes through various climatic and vegetational zones from tropical rainforest and mountain forest with ten to twelve humid months and more than 1,600 mm of annual rainfall, through the high-rainfall woodland savannah, the dry savannah and the thorn-scrub savannah, until it finally reaches the eastern part of the Sahara Desert, one of the world's driest regions, for which evaporation rates between 2,078 mm (Fentzloff 1961) and 9,300 mm (Schendel 1967) have been calculated.

Nile sources belong to two main hydrological systems which characteristically determine the Nile discharge.

The system of tributaries with an all-year-round constant run-off

This lies in the areas close to the equator in the East African Highlands with their big lakes, such as Lake Victoria, Lake Albert, Lake Edward and Lake Kyoga. Here the rainfall peaks are in spring and in autumn, but the run-off is levelled by the big lakes, so that the discharge of the Nile tributaries is balanced over the year. The annual discharge of Bahr el-Djebel, which runs through Juba in southern Sudan, is 26.5 billion m^3. North of it the Nile enters the large swamp region of the Sudd in which the river loses about half of its water through evapotranspiration. Bahr el-Ghazal, a south-western tributary of Bahr el-Djebel, loses about 95 per cent of its water in the Sudd swamps, so that it discharges merely 0.6 billion m^3 annually into that river. The balance of the annual discharge from this southern part of the river basin is 14.9 billion m^3, measured south of the Sobat mouth (El Saiyad and Saudi 1966: 64).

The system of tributaries under monsoonal influence

The main catchment area of this system is the Ethiopian Highlands with their high rainfall in summer. The Sobat, which receives three-quarters of its water from the south-western Ethiopian Highlands and only one-quarter from the south, discharges 13.3 billion m^3 of water into the White Nile annually, the Blue Nile about 52 billion m^3, and the Atbara 12 billion m^3. Before the construction of the Sadd el-Ali the annual mean run-off of the Nile at Aswan was 84 billion m^3. Calculations of the annual discharge of the Nile into the Sadd el-Ali storage lake today are based on this amount.

The monsoonal climate of Ethiopia is responsible for the high degree of seasonality of the run-off of the three Nile tributaries mentioned, and thus also of the Nile: 63 per cent of this water, which is discharged into the High Dam reservoir today, is concentrated in the three months from August to October. This flood carries 130 million tons of silt of volcanic origin from Ethiopian soils. It was responsible for the creation of the fertile black soils of the Nile valley, which are the reason why the ancient Egyptians named their land 'Kemet', i.e. 'black land', in contrast to the infertile desert, the 'red land' (Schoske et al. 1992: 15). Since in Ethiopia today state control of deforestation is less strict than formerly, erosion in the Ethiopian Highlands has increased, so that the amount of silt transported by the Nile should have become greater in recent decades. The seasonality of the Nile discharge due to the monsoonal rains was the reason why formerly the Nile run-off at Aswan in September was usually about thirteen times as great as in April. The variability was not only seasonal but annual, corresponding with the high rainfall variability in Ethiopia. Extreme discharges measured at Aswan were 141.6 billion m³ in 1878/79 (Said 1993: 140) and 34.8 billion m³ in 1983/84 (El-Naggar 1999: 119).

3.2 The use of Nile water in Egypt before the construction of Es-Sadd el-Ali

In Egypt the cultivation of grain was already known 9,000 or 10,000 years ago (Schoske et al. 1992: 15). With the increasing aridification of the Sahara during the Holocene the Egyptians started settling permanently in the Nile valley and cultivating there, tilling the soils of the alluvial plain. When the land was still wet after the annual flood had receded, the farmers planted their crops. The earliest mention of basin irrigation dates back to the Ninth/Tenth Dynasties (2234–2040 BC). The topography of the Nile valley was well suited to the construction of large irrigation basins: long natural dams on both sides of the river separated it from the lower parts of the alluvial plain which in normal years was completely flooded seasonally. After the recession of the

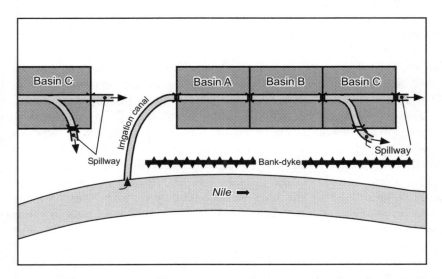

Figure 6.2 Historical irrigation system of Egypt: seasonal basin irrigation (Author: F. Ibrahim 2002; cartography: J. Feilner; source: after Willcocks 1913)

flood some of the water remained behind in the depressions of the alluvial plain. This natural system was transformed into a highly elaborate man-made system of basins, dykes, outlets and canals in Pharaonic times. The technology developed allowed the water to remain in the basins for forty to fifty days and then to flow back into the Nile or into other basins situated downstream (see Figure 6.2). The *fellaheen* sowed into the still-wet soil, and for most of the crops they cultivated no further irrigation was needed. In certain areas they applied additional methods of water-lifting with the help of the *sakya*, a water wheel (see Illustration 11), the *shaduf*, a lever, and the *tambur*, a spiral pump (Archimedean water screw; see Illustration 10).

The techniques of construction of canals with weirs and locks were developed in very early times, too, so that already Senostris II and his grandson Amenemhet III of the Twelfth Dynasty (1991–1786 BC) were able to lower the water table of Lake Qarun in Faiyum so as to be able to carry out land reclamation measures in the oasis. Until the second half of the nineteenth century basin irrigation remained the prevalent form of irrigation in Egypt. As a rule it allowed only one harvest annually; however, the noxious salts were washed out of the soils regularly. Moreover, the fields received annually fresh layers of Nile silt containing numerous nutrients, which were of great importance for the crops planted and at the same time improved the soil structure. The sedimentation that took place annually is estimated at 19–21 tons/ha on average (Anhoury 1941: 503).

After 1861 all-year-round irrigation increased rapidly in Egypt for economic as well as for political reasons after the completion of the great delta weir of Al-Qanatir al-Khayriya at the Nile fork north of Cairo. Its construction was started during the reign of Mohammed Ali (1805–48) with the intention of extending the area cultivated with cotton, for which there existed a great demand in England at the time, imports from America having stopped owing to the Civil War there. The construction of the first big dam at Aswan in 1902, however, was decisive for the introduction of all-year-round irrigation. The dam was heightened in 1912 and 1933, so that a storage capacity of 5.3 billion m^3 was finally reached. The water stored annually in autumn served for irrigation purposes in spring and summer, when the Nile water level was low. During the main Nile swell from August to October the 180 floodgates of the dam were opened. They were closed only after the water level had fallen again. In this way the main Nile flood, which is heavily laden with the silt introduced by the Blue Nile, could pass through, thus preventing siltation of the reservoir. Simultaneously further dams were built in various other parts of the Nile course. Their main purpose was to lift the water locally, so that it could be led into the corresponding irrigation canals, as, for example, the Ibrahimiya Canal, or the Bahr Yusif Canal, which branches off from it. Mainly on the basis of the dams described, irrigation took place on 83.2 per cent of Egypt's arable land all year round in the 1960s before the

Sadd el-Ali was constructed. Only one-sixth of the arable land, i.e. 1 million acres, exclusively in upper and middle Egypt, was still under the system of basin irrigation.

3.3 Efforts towards total control of the Nile discharge

Since Nile water is essential not only for Egypt, but also for its southern neighbour the Sudan among others, various agreements have been made between these two states during the past century, and also with other states sharing the Nile basin, to secure the water requirements of the two countries. Two official Nile water agreements between Egypt and the Sudan were signed (see Table 6.3):

- The first was signed in 1929 under colonial influence in connection with the construction of the Sennar Dam in the Sudan with the help of which the British wanted to develop the irrigation scheme of the Gezira. The heightening of the old Aswan Dam was also part of this agreement. According to its terms the Sudan was to fulfil its Nile water requirements mainly during the time of the Nile flood when Egypt had a surplus of water. When the water level was low, i.e. at the time of water shortage downstream, Egypt was to have priority over the water. To make this possible Egypt constructed the Djebel-el-Aulia Dam with a storage capacity of 3.5 billion m³ on Sudanese territory on the White Nile south of Khartoum in 1937. Its water was released in spring at the time of a low water level, to serve Egypt's needs.
- The second agreement was concluded in 1959 in connection with the planning of the Sadd el-Ali, the High Dam of Aswan. It allows Egypt to use 55.5 billion m³ of Nile water annually, while the Sudan is entitled to 18.5 billion m³. The annual water loss in the storage lake through evaporation and seepage was calculated to be 10 billion m³.

Already in colonial times in 1940 the so-called 'Century Storage Plan', a comprehensive concept of Nile water management within the river basin,

Table 6.3 Nile water distribution between Egypt and the Sudan (in bn m³)

	Egypt	Sudan	Total
Before the construction of the Aswan High Dam*	48.0	4.0	52.0
After the construction of the Aswan High Dam**	55.5	18.5	74.0
Increase through construction of the Aswan High Dam	7.5	14.5	22.0
Estimated loss in the storage lake through evaporation and seepage			10.0

* According to the agreement of 1929 ; ** according to the agreement of 1959
Source: after Said 1993: 237ff

had been devised. According to this plan, a cascade-like system of weirs was to be constructed along the Nile course from its source to the delta to make the best use of the water. Parts of this plan had already been realized when Nasser began the construction of the Aswan High Dam, which he favoured for political reasons. So in 1954 the Owen-Falls Dam at the exit of the Nile from Lake Victoria was completed. The construction of similar dams at Lake Albert and Lake Tana was to follow. According to the plan, dams were also to be built at Nimule, Merowe and Wadi Halfa in the Sudan, as well as in Wadi er-Rayan, south of Faiyum in Egypt. The Sennar Dam built in 1925 and the Roseires Dam built in 1966, as well as the Jonglei Canal project, were also part of the plan for the Sudan. It was hoped that the latter bypass canal would avoid the considerable water losses of the Nile and its tributaries in the Sudd area, and it had already been largely constructed, when in 1983 its completion was made impossible by the resurgence of the civil war in the Sudan. Discussions about the canal had, however, also been controversial for ecological reasons, since it would have utterly changed the habitat of the local southern Sudanese population. After CAPMAS (1987: 59), the realization of the Century Storage Plan would have rendered the construction of the Sadd el-Ali superfluous.

3.4 Egypt's mega-project of the 1960s: Es-Sadd el-Ali, the High Dam of Aswan

With the Aswan High Dam, inaugurated in 1971 after eleven years of construction, control of the Nile water discharge reached a new level. The event marked the beginning of the era of long-term water storage in which near-total control of Nile water was achieved: 32 billion m^3 of precious Nile water, which until then had flowed into the Mediterranean without being of any practical value to Egypt's economy, were now to be made good use of. While the old Aswan Dam merely stored the Nile water seasonally, the High Dam of Aswan, 3,600 m long and 111 m high, allows storage for more than one year so that the extremes of the Nile discharge between wet and dry years can be levelled out. The reservoir created south of Aswan has at present reached a length of 500–600 km across the Egyptian–Sudanese border, with a water surface of about 5,500 km². It was at first called Lake Nasser in Egypt, although it is known as Es-Sadd el-Ali Lake there now, while it is called the Nubian Lake in the Sudan. Its storage capacity is about 160 billion m^3, of which 30 billion m^3 were intended for the expected sedimentation of Nile silt in the next 300 years.

Planning and construction

The plan to build a high dam (*sadd ali*) at Aswan dates back to 1949. When Nasser came to power after the revolution of 1952, he made the dam the object of his own life fulfilment, raising high hopes among his people.

As in other developing countries of the world at the time, the dam was a prestige project, demonstrating the nation's greatness. Egyptian singers hailed the Sadd el-Ali as 'the fourth pyramid' and Nasser cherished being likened to his predecessors, the Pharaohs. Such mega-dams were in full accordance with the Zeitgeist of superlatives in the middle of the twentieth century. Nasser prepared a detailed plan based on the studies of Western, especially German, experts, with the help of German companies. The World Bank signalled readiness to finance the project with US$1,610 million (Shibl 1971: 81), but later succumbed to pressure from the USA and withdrew the promises given. In order to be able to carry out the project in spite of this setback, Nasser was forced to nationalize the Suez Canal in 1956, which brought about the tripartite attack of Israel, Great Britain and France. The three considered Nasser's act as an infringement on their spheres of influence. The conflict, which came to be known as the Suez Crisis, was terminated after a Soviet ultimatum and US intervention. Israeli troops had to evacuate Sinai, which they had occupied in the course of events. When finally the Soviet Union stepped in as a financer of Egypt's High Dam project, this led to the long-standing presence of thousands of Russian experts, especially engineers, in the country, and made it politically as well as economically totally dependent on the Soviet Union for about fifteen years. However, President Gamal Abdel Nasser's ambitious plan now had a chance of success.

Objectives declared – objectives fulfilled

Nasser's foremost goal was to realize a project that could be the backbone of Egypt's development, to make it one of the most modern and economically powerful countries in the world. Among other things national income was to be doubled within ten years.

The following gives a short overview of the particular objectives to be realized:

- An additional 7.5 billion m³ of Nile water were to be gained for irrigation purposes, with the help of which agricultural land was to be extended by 456,000 ha, i.e. by 22 per cent. In Upper Egypt 395,000 ha of agricultural land were to be managed under all-year-round irrigation instead of under seasonal basin irrigation, so that there could be two harvests annually.
- The area of cultivation of summer crops, such as rice and maize as well as sugar cane, was to be extended. Hitherto the limiting factor had been water, since the main period of growth was the time when the Nile level was low.
- The overall water requirements of Egypt were to be secured. Thus far, when rainfall deficits occurred in the monsoonal catchment areas of the Nile sources, the discharge in Egypt could fall to below 50 per cent of the mean, causing famines there.
- The dam was also to prevent extreme Nile floods, which in particularly wet

years could increase the discharge by up to 80 per cent above the mean, leading to flood disasters in many parts of Egypt.

- The High Dam should serve to produce hydro-energy as a basis for the industrialization of the country. Twelve turbines to be installed in lateral outlets of the dam together with others at the old Aswan Dam were to produce 10 billion kWh of electric energy annually. As part of the strategy a huge industrial complex was to be created in the region of Aswan.

The gigantic project was not only of great importance for international politics, as shown above, but also for Egyptian domestic politics during the time of Nasser. In the course of the sixteen years of his rule, Nasser created, through intensive propaganda for the Sadd el-Ali among his people, the vision of a new Egypt of great agrarian productivity which would catch up with the industrialized countries – thanks to plenty of cheap energy produced at the High Dam.

The current picture as regards the realization of Nasser's goals is as follows.

Land reclamation In spite of the fact that more water is available for irrigation the extension of the area under cultivation hoped for did not materialize. According to a UNDP publication (2002: 150) the cultivated area grew by 457,000 ha between 1970 and 1998, while according to CAPMAS (2000: 68) 743,000 ha were reclaimed during this period. This means that 286,000 ha of the fertile old land must have been lost through salinization, waterlogging, alkalinization or drifting sands, as well as through urban sprawl. The quality of the soils in the newly reclaimed areas that were to be irrigated with the help of Nile water is by no means as high as that of the fertile soils of the alluvial plains in the Nile valley. This means that greater amounts of fertilizers have to be used, which causes ecological hazards and moreover makes the profitability of such great projects in the deserts doubtful.

How far has the main target of the construction of the High Dam, namely the strengthening of Egypt's food basis, been realized? The answers to this question are controversial, since reliable data do not exist. Though the politicians speak of the great successes of the land reclamation projects that followed the construction of the High Dam whenever they have a chance, the total area of the reclaimed land did not practically increase during the first fifteen years after construction, as the figures in Table 8.9, which are all based on official sources, show. In the calculations mentioned here, land reclamation on the basis of groundwater was disregarded, for its share was negligible at the time. It is symptomatic that even the ministers do not quote the official government publications, according to which, in 1985, the area of reclaimed land was much greater than mentioned in Table 8.9. In fact the data are sometimes misleading, since it is not always clear whether 'reclaimed land' is equivalent to 'land under cultivation'. As a rule a great part of the

14. Fellaheen family weaving mats: In spite of the fact that the agriculture of the *fellaheen* is very labour intensive, many of them engage in the weaving of mats from the leaves of palm trees in order to generate additional income. (Photo: F. Ibrahim)

newly reclaimed land is not tilled at all and will never be so. There are various reasons for this. Often the necessary water for irrigation is lacking. This is particularly the case at the end of canals if the off-take of water at their beginning is too great. There are also often problems of management by the authorities in charge – lack of competence or of interest on the part of the new landowners who are as a rule not farmers but high-ranking state officials, war veterans, urbanites who have become rich or Egyptians who have returned home after working abroad and who consider the acquisition of land a worthwhile investment.

The extension of permanent irrigation The goal of using the increase in Nile water to introduce permanent irrigation instead of the basin irrigation that was still practised in some areas of the Nile valley was achieved. The natural annual amelioration of the soils, however, which had been considered the cause of their fertility for thousands of years, does not take place any more (see Chapter 4).

Drought and flood disaster prevention Since the completion of the Aswan High Dam Egypt has suffered neither from detrimental Nile floods nor from crop failure due to low Nile levels. It has been estimated that the harvest losses during the dry phase of the early 1980s would have been the equivalent of about US$600 million had not water stored by the Sadd el-Ali been available. This fact is taken for granted, but it should not make us paint too sinister a picture to justify the construction of the High Dam, as Hartung does when he writes (1991: 80), 'What would the *fellaheen* have done in the meagre years of 1966, 1968 and 1969, as well as in the drought years of 1972, and in particular from 1979 to 1988? Probably millions would have starved.' It is not legitimate to draw such a comparison with biblical times nowadays; first, the complete dependence of Egypt on its agriculture is a thing of the past, and second, there exist today numerous other storage basins along the Nile course. In 1991/92 agriculture contributed no more than 18 per cent to Egypt's GDP, and the country fulfilled 51.8 per cent of its wheat requirements through imports from abroad (CAPMAS 1993: 78 and 254).

Increased production of summer crops The area utilized for the cultivation of rice increased by about 23.5 per cent between 1960/64 and 1988/92. During the same time the area planted with maize shrank by 13.2 per cent (Simons 1977: 574; CAPMAS 1993: 43f). The per hectare yields of rice increased by 18.5 per cent and those of maize by 117 per cent, which can be partly attributed to the availability of more water for irrigation of the old agricultural land, but also to the Green Revolution in Egypt, which was made possible by it.

Production of hydro-energy The turbines first installed at the High Dam did not work effectively and soon had to be replaced by others with American and West German support. So at last in 1990/91 the electricity produced reached 86 per cent of the 10 billion kWh originally projected. Today, however, the Aswan High Dam has lost its former relevance as a power source, since petroleum and gas supply most of the country's energy needs. In 2000/01 the power stations at the two Aswan Dams together provided about 17 per cent of the 77 billion kWh of electricity produced in Egypt (Ministry of Information 2002b; see also Table 9.4).

Undesired consequences of the project

Besides the positive effects described here, negative consequences caused by the construction of the High Dam, foreseen by some whose voices remained unheard at the time, became clearly visible to everyone in the decades that followed. It had not been opportune during Nasser's time to voice doubts about the realization of the ambitious aims. Sadat, who was the first person to attack the policies of his predecessor in public, at times had to speak out against critics of the High Dam, since the Egyptian people identified themselves so much with the project then that anything negative said about the dam was unacceptable. When a drought phase occurred in East Africa between 1979 and 1984 during which the Nile discharge was less than half its mean amount, this enhanced support for those who had always been in favour of the High Dam. However, gradually the people's opinions changed when the negative ecological impact became obvious all over the inhabited parts of

15. Pigeon towers on a fellaheen *house*: Many *fellaheen* build pigeon towers of old earthen pots and Nile silt on the flat tops of their houses. Raising pigeons and other fowl is an important income-generating activity in rural Egypt. (Photo: F. Ibrahim)

the country, as well as the negative economic effects and the fact that many of the goals that had been pursued had not been achieved. The most critical consequences of the construction of the High Dam are as follows.

Sedimentation of Nile silt in the storage lake According to Hamdan (1981: 984) experts were not right when they expected Nile silt to be deposited in front of the dam; neither are the deposits evenly distributed all over the lake area. Sedimentation is in fact taking place in the southern third of the lake, where the velocity of the flow of the silt-laden flood is drastically reduced. This has already led to the gradual formation of a new delta. In 1996 Hamdy El-Tahir, President of the General Corporation of the High Dam, warned (Al-Mahdi 2000: 33): ' ... the deposited silt may build a delta in the south. The Nile can divert its course to the West into the desert. This can lead to a disaster.' It means that the hydrologists' calculations, according to which the provision of an extra storage capacity of 30 billion m³ would solve the problem of siltation for the next 300 years, are of little relevance. Egypt is confronted with a serious danger which threatens the lives of its entire population of 70 million people. Plans for the construction of a 500-km-long canal from the southern end of the lake to Aswan for diverting the silt-laden Nile water are neither technically feasible nor economically viable.

Soil degradation on the old agricultural land 1. <u>Decrease of nutrients</u> The fact that the Nile water discharged from the storage lake is extremely poor in silt became the subject of controversial discussions among experts as to what this meant. Wolff (Kreditanstalt für Wiederaufbau 1986: 91) holds that the Nile silt is of no practical relevance for the amelioration of soils and that also formerly there had been little sedimentation on the fields of the *fellaheen*. The other fact he stresses, that the nutrients contained in the deposits do not fulfil the requirements of the crops grown today, is of course true, especially since the Green Revolution has also had its effects in Egypt. The Egyptian soil scientist Kishk (1985; 1986; 1993), who studied the situation over many years, gives a more detailed picture and states that it is not its nitrogen content which makes the Nile silt so fertile, as some would have it, but the great variety and combination of particular trace elements it contains, such as iron, manganese, zinc and others. In 1974, only a few years after the High Dam had started functioning properly, the deficits of important micronutrients in Egyptian soils were first mentioned by the experts. To make up for them about 120 types of fertilizers of different compositions were put on the Egyptian market. This, however, was no solution to the problems arising from the low natural nutrient content of Egyptian soils today, for about 60 per cent of the landowners are peasants who cultivate 1 acre on average per household (CAPMAS 2002: 70) and have neither the financial resources nor the know-how to select from the many types of fertilizers available those that are suitable for their fields as well as for the crops they cultivate.

2. Damage through excessive use of chemical fertilizers   After the Aswan High Dam had been completed, the decisive phase of intensification of agriculture in Egypt began. Since there were no more seasonal limitations of cultivation caused by lack of water, more and more commercial fertilizers were applied to raise the productivity of the land. While the natural annual fertilization through river silt did not take place any more, the extraction of important minerals from the soils increased through perennial cultivation. Egypt ranks today among those states with the highest use of chemical fertilizers per hectare, the others being mostly industrial countries with highly developed agriculture. The main problem is that because of lack of knowledge or care, the application of chemical fertilizers is often not only ineffective but even counter-productive, so that already considerable ecological damage has been caused (Statistisches Bundesamt Wiesbaden 1988: 44). Since after 1994 the state stopped subsidizing fertilizers as part of the IMF Structural Adjustment Programmes, they became unaffordable for most *fellaheen*, who began to feel the loss of the Nile silt all the more acutely.

3. Salinization   Theoretically, the problem of increasing soil salinity in the Nile valley and in particular also in the Nile delta can be solved with the help of technical applications. However, the Egyptian reality makes these unfeasible.

The insufficient training of the *fellaheen* in the new techniques, the inadequacy of the measures taken by the state and in particular widespread corruption have so far rendered all projects to combat soil salinity futile. Kishk (1993: 83) gives a characteristic example. For years there was a national project to instal an underground tile pipe drainage system with the support of foreign donors. Its failure could be all too easily foreseen, for owing to corruption only half of the drainage pipes were in reality put in place. The system would, however, only work if the drainage net was complete. Also, the installation of the pipes at a certain depth and with a certain gradient was not carried out with the necessary precision, and through the negligence of the firms contracted the sand and mud filters to be installed at junctions were often not put in place at all. So this project, not lacking in good planning and expertise as well as financing, eventually failed (see also Table 6.1).

The causes of the accelerated salinization of soils since the construction of the Aswan High Dam have in the meantime not only raised a critical awareness among many *fellaheen*, but have also been described in scientific (among others Barth and Shata 1987: 2) as well as in official Egyptian (CAPMAS 1987: 79 and 87) publications. They can be summarized as follows:

1. Presently Egypt suffers from excessive irrigation since unlimited amounts of water seem to be available. There exist neither attempts to control over-irrigation nor endeavours to sensitize farmers to its fatal consequences.
2. The cultivation of crops with a high water demand, like sugar cane and rice (see Table 8.5), increased owing partly to the greater water availability in the main season of plant growth and partly to the state's agrarian pricing policy which favoured these crops.
3. All-year irrigation was also introduced in the areas of former seasonal basin irrigation in Upper Egypt without constructing the necessary drainage net which permanent irrigation requires.
4. From the new land reclamation projects in the deserts on the higher Nile terraces saline drainage water seeps down and leads to additional salinization of the groundwater and of the best soils in the alluvial plain.
5. The salt content of Nile water doubled as a consequence of the high rate of evaporation in the Sadd el-Ali storage lake (see Table 6.3) and due to the annual passing of several billion cubic metres of highly saline drainage water into the river from the cultivated land.
6. Owing to excessive irrigation about 10–15 billion m^3 of drainage water seep into the soils annually and mix with the groundwater, especially in the Nile delta, which today has a salt content ten times as high as that of Nile water (CAPMAS 1987: 87; see Figure 5.2). Through the rise of the groundwater table, coupled with the elimination of the former fluctuation of the Nile water level, large areas in the Nile valley and the Nile delta are suffering from waterlogging, which leads among other things to insufficient airing

of the soils and to reduced biological activity. High summer evaporation rates make the salts rise to the surface and concentrate in the topsoil.

7. Parallel to the construction of the High Dam a well-functioning drainage system should have been established, as was projected in the earliest plans. To this day it does not exist, so that irreversible ecological damage has been caused in the meantime.

Other adverse ecological consequences 1. <u>Increased lateral erosion in the river</u> Erosive activities in the Nile course increased owing to the river's greater velocity of flow, which was enhanced by the reduced amounts of sediments transported. Formerly the deposited silt had continuously smoothed out the surface of the river bed, thus reducing the water turbulence and the river's erosivity. Great damage occurred particularly to the dams and locks downstream, so that some of them had to be replaced by stronger ones.

2. <u>Deepening of the river bed and sedimentation within the Nile course</u> The changed run-off in the Nile and in the irrigation canals not only caused stronger lateral erosion but also led to a deepening of the river bed in some places and to the formation of islands in others. The latter enhanced the growth of aquatic plants, such as the fast-growing water hyacinth and various reeds. This is particularly adverse to Nile navigation, especially during low water levels in winter. To make navigation in that season possible, about 2.5 billion m³ of water which cannot be used for irrigation purposes in winter have to be discharged additionally from the High Dam Lake. Moreover, the water plants, which also spread in the irrigation canals, cause greater water loss through increased evapotranspiration. Thousands of *fellaheen* are today occupied all year in eradicating the water hyacinth, once introduced in Africa for the sake of amenity but harmful in the course of time. Needless to say, during the eradication of the plants the *fellaheen* wade in the water, thus exposing themselves to the risk of infection with bilharzia (see below).

3. <u>Increased littoral erosion at the Nile mouth</u> Since only little sedimentation of Nile silt takes place today along the Mediterranean at the northern coast of the Nile delta, much stronger littoral erosion is taking place there now. Thus in many parts the sandy beaches of former summer resorts, like Gimsa and Ras el-Barr, have disappeared. Before the construction of the High Dam annual sedimentation had protected the coast against gradual marine transgression, which is probably also partly caused by land subsidence.

4. <u>Ecological and economic effects along the delta coast and in the lagoons</u> Fishery on the Mediterranean coast, which had formerly been an important economic activity in the area and provided the population with cheap animal proteins, experienced a serious downturn after the High Dam began functioning. The lack of Nile silt led to a decrease in plankton on which the fish used to feed in the Mediterranean waters. The amounts of fish caught in the

grounds along the delta coast fell from 38,000 tons in 1962 (Simons 1968: 184) to barely 12,000 tons in 1985 (CAPMAS 1992: 62).

Owing to the rise of the groundwater table in the Nile delta the discharge of fresh water into the brackish waters of the lagoons increased. As a consequence their salt content dropped to 1,400 ppm in the south and to 2,800 ppm in the north (CAPMAS 1987: 59). This led to a decrease in the fish population of the lagoons, so that the catch there also decreased from 60,000 tons in 1966 (CAPMAS 1987: 89) to 14,000 tons in 1975 (CAPMAS 1992: 62).

The losses for the fishing industry in the delta and at the Mediterranean coast could only partly be compensated by the fish caught in the reservoir at the dam which amounted to 25 tons in 1985 (CAPMAS 1992: 62). This catch is taking place far from consumer markets. It should be noted, however, that owing to a much bigger and more modern fishery fleet, and to an improvement in fishing technology and rearing of fish in fish farms, the catches in the Mediterranean and in the coastal lagoons have recovered over the years and reached 199,400 tons in 2000 (CAPMAS 2002: 63) (see Chapter 8).

High water losses If the calculations of some Egyptian experts are correct, the High Dam led to Egypt losing water instead of gaining it. The following are the most important causes of the heavy water losses that are occurring:

1. <u>Evaporation and seepage in the storage lake</u> According to reliable Egyptian sources (e.g. Shalash 1977) the annual loss in the lake itself is not 10 billion m³, as formerly believed, but should rather be calculated at 16 billion m³. The calculations are based on the assumption that the annual evaporation is 2,754 mm/m³, which means that if the average size of the lake surface is 5,500 km², the loss of water through evaporation alone must be 15.147 billion m³ per year. According to official Egyptian publications the water surface in the 1980s was 6,000 km² (CAPMAS 1987: 64) and the water loss through seepage alone into the coarse-grained Nubian Sandstone at the oscillation line along the banks of the lake was 1 billion m³ (CAPMAS 1987: 72).

2. <u>Water loss in the discharge system</u> The amount of water lost through seepage in the new run-off and drainage system increased from 2 billion m³ to 16 billion m³ annually between 1964 and 1972 (CAPMAS 1987: 144ff). There are two main reasons for this, the first of them being the fact that, unlike formerly, when there was a water shortage, people now do not use water economically but irrigate excessively, because they have free access to it. The second reason is that frequently water is let out through the dam merely because it is required for the production of hydroelectric power, or because it is necessary to raise the water table for purposes of navigation. This is particularly so in winter, when less water is needed on the fields. The amount of water lost in this way since the construction of the High Dam is calculated at 2.4 billion m³ annually (see Table 6.1). One has to come to the

conclusion that all these losses cannot be outbalanced by the 7.5 billion m³ of water gained. The fact that this negative balance has not yet been fully felt in Egypt is due to two different factors:

- The Sudan is not yet fully able to utilize its share of the Nile water of 18.5 billion m³ annually, so that Egypt can make use of a proportion of it.
- In the 1980s a climatic dry phase was prevailing in Africa, which caused the Nile run-off to fall under its mean for several years and reduced the surface of Lake Sadd el-Ali, so that evaporation and seepage rates were relatively low.

The uncontrollable rise of the storage-lake water table (see Figure 6.3) When in 1975 the water table of the Sadd el-Ali storage lake reached 175 m above sea level, while the maximum permissible level is 182 m above sea level, the situation was considered alarming and the construction of the Toshka Canal (see Figure 6.1) as a spillway was started in great haste and without the necessary preliminary studies. It was completed in 1980 and connected to a natural reservoir with a storage capacity of 120 billion m³. Through this canal water should be conducted in an emergency from a bay in the west of Lake Sadd el-Ali, about 250 km south of the dam, over a distance of about 25 km to the Toshka Depression in the Western Desert, some 100 km south of the New Valley oases. After the Toshka Canal had been buried under the

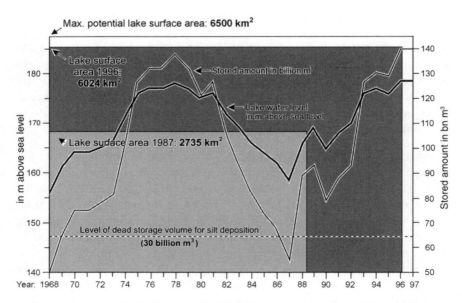

Figure 6.3 Aswan High Dam storage lake: fluctuation of the water table 1968–97 (Author: F. Ibrahim 2002; cartography: J. Feilner; sources of data: Al-Kharbutli and Abdel-Ati 1998: 274; CAPMAS 1998: 33; Said 1993: 237)

sand for years the idea of creating a gigantic project there was revived in 1997 (see Chapter 12).

The increased bilharzia hazard Through the construction of the Aswan High Dam the risk of contracting bilharzia, a dangerous disease caused by certain worms (*Schistosoma*), increased for all those Egyptians who have direct contact with Nile water. In the life cycle of the worm a freshwater snail that makes its habitat in the aquatic plants of the Nile plays a decisive role as an intermediate host. Through direct contact with contaminated water the larvae enter the human body through the skin, affecting different vital organs, which can cause years of illness or even death. In spite of improved methods of treatment, bilharzia has been on the increase in the tropical and subtropical countries of Africa and Asia since dams were built, allowing an expansion of irrigation, which brought about favourable conditions for the pathogenic agents in the stagnant waters. The fact that bilharzia still exists as a serious danger can be seen from the fact that in 1999 the government had 1,980 centres, units and inspectorates devoted to combating the disease. Between 1986 and 1999 the number of institutions for the treatment of bilharzia was increased by 42 per cent (CAPMAS 1995: 168; CAPMAS 2001b: 127). Today, unlike in former years, the Egyptian authorities admit frankly that the increase in bilharzia in Upper Egypt has to be attributed to the dam:

> The rate of the persons affected with bilharzia has increased after the system of basin irrigation was replaced by the system of permanent irrigation. The reasons for this are:
>
> 1. Formerly the canals fell dry seasonally, which made the snails die. This does not take place today.
> 2. There are more stagnant waters and more water plants today, which form the habitat of the snails.
>
> So it is not amazing that in the areas of Sohag, Qena and Asyut, bilharzia increased after the method of irrigation of 336,000 ha of agricultural land there was converted from basin irrigation to permanent irrigation after the construction of the Sadd el-Ali. Bilharzia can be combated, if the *fellaheen* protect themselves against it. That solution is, however, merely theoretical and can never be of any practical relevance unless their way of life changed and became more urban. (CAPMAS 1987: 90)

Since they are aware that most of the methods suggested for avoiding infection with bilharzia are hardly practicable for the *fellaheen*, the health authorities sometimes put insecticides, mainly copper sulphate, in the Nile water to kill the snails so as to interrupt the infestation cycle. For the Egyptian people this entails another health hazard. For the method to work, the chemicals would have to be applied countrywide in the Nile as well as in the canals. This is impossible, since the Nile provides the drinking water for the majority of the

Egyptian people. In a report by the German Kreditanstalt für Wiederaufbau (1986: 109), which finances rehabilitation projects carried out since the construction of the Aswan High Dam, it is stated as a positive development that between 1955 and 1976 the infection rate of people living in the Nile delta fell from 31 per cent to 27 per cent. The authors seem to have overlooked the fact that during the same time the percentage of those living under the risk of contracting the disease decreased much more owing to the rapid urbanization process that took place in the country. At the same time hygiene in Egyptian villages and the supply of clean drinking water improved greatly, so the percentage of people suffering from bilharzia should have decreased much more significantly. A decrease in the number of people affected of only 4 per cent must be considered a failure in combating the disease. According to the daily paper *Al-Wafd* the rate of infection in Egypt in 1999 was still 20 per cent (*Al-Wafd*, 11 April 1999: 6). Moreover, most statistics do not show that there are two different types of bilharzia, namely the less serious form affecting the bladder and the mostly fatal one affecting the intestines and eventually destroying the liver. Today this latter, dangerous type is on the increase (Kreditanstalt für Wiederaufbau 1986: 106). In Upper Egypt this type of bilharzia was completely unknown until the construction of the High Dam. The snail hosting the worm that causes the disease was able to migrate upstream only after the seasonal Nile swell with its torrential flood ceased to take place.

Safety hazards 'In times of danger, the water table of the storage lake should be lowered to less than 150 metres to limit the consequences of a possible destruction of the upper part of the Dam and of the resulting inundation, if e.g. bombs should be dropped on it, such as were used in World War II.' (Arafa, Minister of Affairs of the Sadd el-Ali, 1965: 119)

Hartung (1991: 80) considers this measure absurd and completely unsuitable for really precarious situations, since only a maximum of 605 million m³ of water daily can be let out, so that it would take up to 200 days for the water table to drop from 170 or 183 m to below 150 m. According to him the dam is not safe from military attack, and the power station, which is an open construction, is particularly easy to destroy. Egypt, situated in the centre of the Near East trouble spot, is especially vulnerable here, as could be observed during the Gulf War of 1991, when it was reported that Iraqi rockets stationed in the Sudan were targeted at the High Dam since Egypt had sided with the USA in that conflict. The dam might also be a target for terrorists. Since what happened to the Twin Towers in New York on 11 September 2001, it has become clear that Egypt, too, is vulnerable to such an attack.

After the Egyptian authorities had insisted for years that the dam was earthquake proof, they admitted in October 1992 that they were concerned about the dam and that already in November 1981 it had been damaged by an earthquake for which an intensity of 5.5 on the Richter scale had been recorded. Egypt is an earthquake-prone area, situated within the seismic focus of the East African Rift Valley System. Damage was caused in Egypt by the earthquakes recorded in 1964 (6.9 on the Richter scale), 1981, 1983, 1985, 1987 and 1992. Egyptian geologists assume that the reason why more severe earthquakes have occurred relatively frequently during the recent past is the enormous compressive load of the storage-lake water on the earth's crust. Hamdan (1981: 1,016) compares the danger posed by the gigantic amount of water stored here (up to 120 billion m³) to that of an atomic bomb that may explode at any time. Wüst (1983: 768) describes the situation in the following way:

> If a bomb hit the top of the Dam, the water pouring out uncontrolled would make the Dam burst in its complete breadth within a few hours. The masses of water sweeping across the whole of Egypt (they would be at least the discharge of two years within hours or days) would cause utter devastation from Aswan to Damietta, destroy all cultivated land, and most probably about 99 per cent of the total population would lose their lives. Cracks in the Dam, as they have already been discovered, can lead to disastrous effects, even in case of minor earthquakes. It is hard to say if and to what extent the enormous weight of the water masses of the lake of 164 billion tons will have its effects on the tectonics of the area. It is for sure, however, that only 200 km E of the lake, there is one of the most active faults of the earth surface: the Red-Sea Fault, along which earthquakes occur quite often.

Destruction of World Heritage The constant rise of the groundwater table and the increasing salinization of the water have caused great damage to most of Egypt's ancient monuments between Luxor and Alexandria, remnants of unique cultures. In many cases the groundwater today reaches their foundations, so that the salts concentrated in the stones activate the processes of chemical weathering that make the masterpieces of ancient masonry and architecture that have survived for thousands of years in Egypt's desert climate crumble away. This means a loss for the whole world. For Egypt it means also an economic loss that the whole nation will feel one day, for tourism still depends to a considerable extent on these monuments. Costly repairs have had to be carried out and special techniques developed to solve the problem. The dismantling of parts of the Luxor Temple alone and its reconstruction on a plate of concrete and steel cost several million US$. Already work has begun to create replicas of some of the ancient tombs that have suffered from the rising groundwater level. In the long run this will not satisfy the people who come to Egypt to see authentic examples of the Pharaonic culture.

Expulsion of the Nubians – destruction of an ancient culture An exodus of 120,000 Nubians had to take place before the High Dam could be built.

Their land was inundated by the waters of the new lake. The Nubian people had lived in this border area between Egypt and the Sudan for thousands of years, retaining their own language and culture. The Nubian nation that had produced this unique culture, inseparably connected with the Nile and the land in its narrow valley, was expunged within a few years when the dam was built. Seventy thousand Nubians living in Egypt were resettled at Kom Ombo, north of Aswan, where they were given land away from the Nile, by the banks of which they had traditionally lived. For the 50,000 Nubians living in the Sudan the irrigation scheme of Khashm el-Girba was established. Some of the stone monuments of the Nubian culture were saved at enormous financial expense before Nubia and other examples of the Nubian culture vanished in the floods of the reservoir. The world viewed with great interest as twenty-four Nubian temples were saved, among them Abu Simbel (see Illustration 18) and some remains of the early Christian Nubian kingdoms. Far more money was spent on this than on the resettling of the Nubian people. Although they were the ones most directly affected, nobody asked their opinion when the agreement for the construction of the High Dam was signed by the heads of state of Egypt and the Sudan. After they had been evacuated many of the displaced Nubians were completely uprooted and disorientated in their new environments, suffering physically as well as mentally. Some never gave up and tried to settle again on land close to their own, which they had lost. However, the considerable fluctuations in the surface area of the reservoir, dependent on the varying Nile discharge between dry and wet phases in the river's catchment areas, make it difficult for them to settle on its shores. The establishment of floating settlements has been discussed, but the technical problems have not been solved so far. FAO, the UN organization, sponsored a project for resettling people along the lake in villages that were named after the old Nubian places, most of which were drowned in the waters of the lake, like Jerf Hussein, Toshka, Kalabsha, Abu Simbel, Qostol, Adendan, El-Allaqi and Es-Sayala. *Al-Ahram*, the semi-official Egyptian newspaper (6 January 1993: 3), reported under the heading, 'Migration to the south – cultivation at the lake is our only way to solve the problem of unemployment' on the successful reclamation of 1 million *feddans* (420,000 ha) of land by the shores of the lake, and the fact that about 1,800 families from the Nile valley had received land free of cost to settle there. In addition, they were said to have received starting capital of LE 500 (*c.* £100 sterling), as well as long-term interest-free loans for buying tractors, water pumps and pipes. The government promised, among other things, the construction of roads, schools and hospitals, and a guaranteed supply of food. The project was not aimed at the Nubians who had lost their land; on the contrary, they had to see it being given away to strangers. If the project were successful, it would lead to the pollution of the storage lake, for example with bilharzia and other water-borne diseases.

Since the lake is practically the only source of drinking water for the entire country, the whole lake environment should be a protected area.

Most of the Nubians in the Sudan who were resettled in Halfa el-Gadida, north of the newly constructed Khashm el-Girba dam, found it hard to adjust to their new situation. They complained of tropical diseases like malaria and bilharzia that formerly had been unknown to them. There were also animosities with the nomadic tribes of the Shukriya and the Hadandawa, whose tribal land they had been given. Similar problems occurred also with the Ababda, who held customary land rights in the areas given to the Nubians. In the Sudan, the nomads look with mistrust upon the Nubian invaders with their organized settlements and their individual land ownership, which are unknown to them, while the Nubians consider the nomads as uncivilized. Both groups blame the state – the nomads since it gave the Nubians land and housing as well as a relatively good infrastructure, the Nubians since it did not keep its promise of admitting only a few nomads into the area (Salem-Murdock 1984: 359). In a country like the Sudan, in which traditional land rights still play an important role and where tribalism exists, it is practically impossible for a group to survive in another tribe's territory.

Recommendations for the future of Es-Sadd el-Ali

We cannot yet assess the advantages and disadvantages of the construction of the Aswan High Dam in full, since many of them depend on long-term factors that are not yet operative. For the same reason no economist is in a position to carry out a balanced cost-benefit analysis valid for a longer period of time. Moreover, abstract but invaluable factors like culture, people's self-determination and safety as well as their human rights can hardly be assessed in terms of figures. No matter whether the benefits are ultimately found to outweigh the disadvantages or vice versa, the most critical question remains unanswered: what will be the fate of the Egyptian people once the southern section of the Sadd el-Ali Lake is silted up? Some of the solutions that have been suggested are discussed here:

- Smith (1986) recommends clearing away the deposits forming the delta at the southern tip of the storage lake and using the fertile silt for land reclamation elsewhere. It has to be remembered, however, that the delta is located on Sudanese territory and that Egypt cannot act as it would like here. That Egypt will in future have to observe the Sudan's rights if it does not want to run the risk of political consequences was already strongly underlined by the Sudan's former Prime Minister Al-Mahdi in his book (2000) *The Nile Waters. The Promise and the Threat.* What Smith suggests may be technically feasible but is not economically viable. Such measures were not considered elsewhere, for example for the Khashm el-Girba dam on the

River Atbara, though it was 70 per cent silted up within only thirty-four years.

- Hartung (1991: 80) suggests the construction of a new dam at Wadi Gab-gaba, to the east of the present lake. Studies should be initiated immediately to ascertain whether this new project would be not only technically feasible but could also be carried out in a way that is ecologically, economically and socially justifiable. It should not be left until the danger is imminent.
- Hamdan (1981: 1,017) quotes Fathi (1981: 29), who suggests turning the Sadd el-Ali into a one-year storage dam. It would thus be similar to the old Aswan Dam, but have twice its storage capacity.

A combination of the three suggestions listed here might be the best solution. It seems advisable to study the old Century Storage Plan again, and to see whether such measures can be integrated into it. This would mean that the Sadd el-Ali would lose its present paramount function as a long-term storage dam, and that the water would be stored in various locations along the southern parts of the Nile course.

CHAPTER 7

Development and Features of the Egyptian Economy

1 From socialism to capitalism – fifty years of changing economic policies

After the revolution of 1952, which brought about the end of the monarchy in the country and forced the ruling family that had its roots outside Egypt into exile, there followed three phases of extremely diverse economic policies which are closely associated with three different state presidents. As much as their personalities, the changing international political and economic environment played a decisive role in the economic policies they tried to adopt in Egypt.

1.1 The state-controlled economy under Nasser (1952–70)

Several changes occurred during the time of Gamal Abdel Nasser's presidency and have to be attributed partly to him:

- the introduction of socialism as a national policy, following the pattern of the communist states existing at the time
- the strengthening of the public sector as the main plank of a planned economy
- the socialist land reform
- the construction of the Aswan High Dam
- the two Egyptian–Israeli wars of 1956 and 1967.

Twice Egypt was defeated by Israel during this time, and in the 1960s it interfered unsuccessfully in the civil war in Yemen. These wars exhausted the country's meagre resources and weakened its waning economy further. After the Soviet Union had provided the necessary capital as well as the technical support and qualified manpower for the construction of the Aswan High Dam, Egypt was completely dependent economically on that superpower for years.

Egyptian agriculture experienced its greatest change in decades through Nasser's socialist land reform. Feudal land ownership, usually in the form of absenteeism, was abolished and land ownership limited to 100 *feddans* (42 ha) per nuclear family. Simultaneously the legal position of small farmers and landless *fellaheen* who worked on rented land was strengthened. But the state was unable to make swift progress in the distribution of land among the landless, so the expected positive results did not materialize. In most cases mismanagement by the administration had adverse consequences, namely the degradation of the former feudal farms, which had earlier worked with considerable economic efficiency. After the land had been redistributed among smallholders, its extreme partitioning proved a drawback in terms of production. Moreover, owing to the frozen land rents, a situation comparable to that in the housing market occurred. It was not until 1992 that this problem was finally tackled and a new land rent law passed which was enforced as from 1997.

The most serious adverse effects of Nasser's socialist policy on the present-day structures of Egypt's economy are the inflation of the public sector, which persists to this day, and the weakening of the private sector. The foreign and Egyptian companies that were nationalized in Nasser's time were controlled by parastatal organizations managed in the same way as the public sector. Owing to corruption and mismanagement they did not work efficiently.

Two major merits of Nasser's policy should, however, be borne in mind: one being the special consideration paid to the poorer sections of the population, i.e. the *fellaheen* and the workers, in terms of strengthening their position *vis-à-vis* the big landowners and the owners of industrial companies, and by improving social laws; the other being a policy of industrialization that served the needs of the people, based on long-term planning and the encouragement of local production through limiting imports. Furthermore, neither Nasser nor his ministers were corrupt.

1.2 Sadat's Open Door Policy (1971–81)

President Sadat's era brought great political and economic changes to the country. He initiated an orientation towards the West which stood in sharp contrast to Nasser's socialism. Moreover, after Egypt's partial victory in 1973, Sadat acted as the leading force in the peace process with Israel, which culminated in the signing of the Camp David Agreement in 1979. The latter brought about the termination of a thirty-year-long war with Israel – though it also sparked the animosity of some Arab states towards Egypt, which resulted in their withdrawal of economic support. Sinai was returned after Egypt had paid considerable sums to Israel as compensation for the infrastructure it had established on the peninsula during its occupation since the war of 1967.

Sadat's peace policy was accompanied by two seemingly contradictory strategies: a policy of economic liberalization, following the example of the Western capitalist countries, and a policy of strengthening the Islamic character of the country and of allowing the return of members of the Muslim Brotherhood, which had been forced into exile under his predecessor, and of tolerance if not outright support for right-wing Islamist groups like Al-Jama'at al-Islamiya, which later proved fatal for the President himself. In terms of the country's economy, Islamization under Sadat brought about an increase in the number of Islamic banks and investment companies whose ethos was based on the principle of profit-sharing instead of paying interest, which contradicts the rules of Islam. About 300 Islamic institutions managed a total capital of US$8–12 billion at the time, equalling the state's entire annual budget. Four of these companies alone had 375,000 shareholders whose invested capital amounted to US$4.3 billion. The great euphoria this engendered was undermined, when later, during Mubarak's presidency, several of these companies were found to have adopted fraudulent practices. Many Egyptians lost all the money they had saved while working abroad, which they had invested in these companies hoping for good returns.

Sadat's decision to liberalize the country's economy was of great and far-reaching significance for Egypt. His aim was in the first place to promote the investment of foreign as well as of Egyptian capital in the country. By helping to create an atmosphere conducive to investment he brought about an end to the flight of capital Egypt had experienced in the preceding years. But it also led to the establishment of many ultra-modern factories, mostly backed by foreign investors, which caused serious problems for existing local industries that had offered better chances of employment for the local population. And massive imports led to the Egyptian market being flooded with foreign goods. Only the 'fat cats', a limited number of persons among the richer class, could profit immediately, often through corruption and illegal transactions, while the disparities between the social classes, which Nasser had tried to wipe out as far as possible, grew. When Sadat tried to raise the price of hitherto highly subsidized bread, there was a people's revolt. Hunger spread among the growing numbers of the poor, and the general lack of long-term planning proved detrimental, especially for the industrial sector of the economy. The huge sums spent on the construction of new towns and other housing communities had no positive effects, as will be described in Chapter 11.

1.3 Economic liberalization and the implementation of the Structural Adjustment Programmes under Mubarak (since 1981)

Mubarak, unlike his predecessors, introduced no spectacular new concepts in foreign or home affairs or in the economy. He continued what had proved successful under them, but he also had to bear the burden of the problems brought about by the policies they had propagated. He followed Sadat's policy of good relations with the Western countries, on whom Egypt now depended economically. He liquidated those Islamic banks and investment companies that had been engaged in fraud. He dealt cautiously with the Islamists at first, but started cracking down on them after they tried to kill him and members of his government. Within the two first decades of his rule, four Five-Year Plans for restructuring the economy were introduced. Some of their aims have been fulfilled.

Under IMF (International Monetary Fund) pressure, the Structural Adjustment Programmes were implemented from 1991. The government committed itself to applying strict measures for the liberalization of the economy, and privatization of many state-directed companies was carried out. In 1994 the GATT Agreement was signed. State control over the price of certain agrarian products that had formerly been declared of strategic importance, like wheat, rice and cotton, was lifted, and the high customs tariffs on imported goods reduced. All this went hand in hand with a strong devaluation of the Egyptian pound. State subsidies were by and large stopped, with the exception of those for bread, edible oil and sugar as well as mineral oil and gas.

Privatization of public sector enterprises proved difficult at the beginning,

Table 7.1 Balance of foreign exchange payments: exports 1996–2001

	Million US$			Relative importance (%)		
	96/97	98/99	00/01	96/97	98/99	00/01
Commodity exports						
Agricultural exports	330	550	582	1.6	2.7	2.6
Industrial exports	2,022	3,440	3,771	9.9	16.7	16.7
Energy exports						
(petroleum, gas, electricity)	2,578	1,150	2,562	12.7	5.6	11.3
Subtotal commodity exports	4,930	5,140	6,915	24.2	25.0	30.6
Service exports						
Transport	686	715	881	3.4	3.5	3.9
Suez Canal tolls	1,850	1,800	1,816	9.1	8.7	8.0
Tourism	3,646	3,200	4,268	17.9	15.5	18.9
Governmental receipts	216	355	197	1.1	1.7	0.9
Other services receipts	2,719	2,900	2,616	13.4	14.0	11.6
Total services exports	9,117	8,970	9,778	44.9	43.4	43.3
Total commodity and services exports	14,047	14,110	16,693	69.1	68.4	73.9
Production factor returns collected						
Investment returns collected	2,052	1,890	1,802	10.1	9.1	8.0
Expatriates' remittances	3,256	3,500	3,021	16.0	17.0	13.4
Total returns collected	5,308	5,390	4,823	26.1	26.1	21.4
Current transfers collected						
Governmental transfers	890	1,000	987	4.4	4.8	4.4
Private and institutional transfers	73	135	69	0.4	0.7	0.3
Total current transfers	963	1,135	1,056	4.8	5.5	4.7
Total current revenues	20,318	20,635	22,572	100.0	100.0	100.0

Source: after Ministry of Information 2000: 118; Ministry of Information 2002b

since investors were exclusively interested in economically successful businesses. So the state looked for forms of privatization other than complete sale, for example leasing state-owned hotels to private companies or selling companies' shares to their employees.

Tables 7.1 and 7.2 give a general picture of the performance of Egypt's foreign trade from 1996/97 to 2000/01.

Significant points concerning the development of exports as shown in Table 7.1 are:

- Exports in both the commodity and service sectors increased, while the remittances of expatriates declined in relative importance.
- Tourism has the greatest relative importance in the foreign trade balance, but a drop in its revenues in 1998/99 shows its vulnerability to incidents of terrorism in the country.
- The Suez Canal tolls remained stable as regards the absolute figures, but were slightly declining in their relative importance.
- In 1998/99 a serious drop in petroleum exports was experienced owing to international market conditions. However, they recovered their relative importance in 2000/01 when the net revenue was US$355 million.
- There was steady growth in the relative importance of service exports, which reached 74 per cent in 2000/01.

Table 7.2 shows the development of imports and the trade balance in that period:

- Commodity imports accounted for more than three-quarters of all imports, while those of services constituted less than a quarter.
- Intermediate commodities imports took pride of place, constituting one-half of the commodities imports, while consumer goods made up 28 per cent. Imports of investment goods declined to 22 per cent in 2000/01, which signifies a weakening in the investment sector.
- The trade balance deficit increased from US$9.8 billion to US$11.8 billion within two years. The reason was the increase in commodities imports, while at the same time the export values remained almost stagnant. In 2000/01, however, the trade balance deficit decreased slightly to US$10.36 billion.
- If it were not for the revenues from foreign tourism and from the Suez Canal tolls, the balance of payments would show an increase in deficits of about 40 per cent.

Other figures that characterize the state of the Egyptian economy under Mubarak are, according to the World Development Report 2003 (World Bank 2003) and other sources:

- Gross international reserves dropped to US$13.5 billion in 2001.

- Foreign debts were calculated at US$29 billion. However, according to the estimate of the former Prime Minister, Mohy-ed-Din, foreign and domestic debts amounted to US$110 billion (Internet 2001g).
- From 1990 to 1999 the average annual growth in GDP was 4.4 per cent. Growth in the value-added of agriculture was 3.1 per cent, of industry 4.7 per cent, and of services 4.3 per cent. The GDP growth rate dropped to 2 per cent in 2002.
- Per capita GNP rose to US$1,400.
- Government expenditure for social services dropped from 32.1 per cent to 23.6 per cent between 1990 and 1998.

Table 7.2 Balance of foreign exchange payments: imports 1996–2001

	Million US$			Rel. importance (%)		
	96/97	98/99	00/01	96/97	98/99	00/01
*Payments – commodity imports**						
Consumer imports	4,047	4,690	4,837	20.5	20.6	20.5
Intermediate imports	6,687	7,570	8,588	33.8	33.3	36.5
Investment imports	3,985	4,641	3,850	20.2	20.4	16.3
Total commodity imports	14,719	16,901	17,275	74.5	74.3	73.3
Services payments						
Transport	242	380	472	1.2	1.7	2.0
Tourism	1,333	1,350	1,086	6.7	5.9	4.6
Governmental expenditures	511	550	405	2.6	2.4	1.7
Other services payments**	1,863	2,500	3,421	9.4	11.0	14.6
Total services payments	3,949	4,780	5,384	19.9	21.0	22.9
Total services and commodity payments	18,668	21,681	22,659	94.4	95.3	96.2
Production factor returns payable						
Investment returns paid	106	320	150	0.5	1.4	0.6
Interest on loans and liabilities	980	755	729	5.0	3.2	3.1
Total returns payable	1,086	1,075	879	5.5	4.6	3.7
Current transfers payable	14	20	20	0.1	0.1	0.1
Total current payments	19,758	22,776	23,558	100	100	100
Trade balance	-9,788	-11,760	-10,360			
Service balance	5,168	4,190	4,394			
Balance of commodities and services	-4,620	-7,570	-5,966			
Balance of production returns	4,223	4,315	3,944			
Balance of transfers	948	1,115	1,035			
Current account and transfers	550	-2,140	–			

* Commodity imports in the form of donations included; ** Trade payments included
Source: after Ministry of Information 2000: 119j and 2002b

- The share of the subsidies of total government expenditure dropped from 26 per cent to 15 per cent between 1990 and 1997.

The last two items show the impact of the Structural Adjustment policy aimed at reducing subsidies and the government share in social services. One of the great problems resulting from Nasser's economic policy was the enormously inflated number of people employed in the public sector. Millions would have been left unemployed if the Structural Adjustment Programmes had been put into practice immediately. So the transformation was carried out gradually; for example, the state guarantee of employment for all university graduates, which had existed for forty years, was progressively eroded. The low salaries the state pays today make jobs in the public sector less attractive. A state-employed engineer, who formerly would have received a relatively respectable salary, is nowadays paid so little that he would normally prefer to look for employment in a private business or work as a waiter in a tourist hotel.

From the start, and also following IMF pressure, Mubarak and his government had seen it as one of their most important tasks to reduce the external trade balance deficit. Although the GATT agreement imposes painful limitations on the country's economy, Egypt tries to increase its exports of industrial as well as agrarian products, and to reduce its imports at the same time. During recent years the quality of Egyptian industrial products has improved considerably and many firms apply international quality standards, hoping to enhance their export chances. However, competition on the international markets is tough, so that Egypt has to struggle hard to compete.

2 Deregulation of the economy and the problems of unemployment and migration

According to the World Bank the total labour force in Egypt was 24 million persons in 1999, 30 per cent of whom were women (World Bank 2001: 278). As the number of those employed in that year was 17.434 million (Ministry of Information 2001a), the employment/labour force ratio was 72.6 per cent, which means that the unemployment rate was 27.4 per cent. It has to be noted in this context that the unemployment rate among women is 2.5 times that of men, and that in general unemployment is greater among high school and university graduates than among the rest of the population. Vocational training and manual work being of low social prestige among certain sectors of Egyptian society, many young people in the country find themselves in a dilemma. Unemployment, one of the country's great problems, is a consequence especially of the change from the long-established state-controlled economy, in which every university graduate had to be employed by the state.

Besides the unemployment referred to in the official statistics there is the hidden unemployment, which exists in various forms in Egypt. It had still not been eradicated in public administration and other parts of the public sector at the beginning of the twenty-first century. In 2003, 7 million persons were employed in the civil service and parastatals of the productive and service sectors (*Al-Ahram Ektesady*, 6 January 2003: 25). This means that about 40 per cent of the country's active labour force was employed and paid for by the state. It is estimated that only one-fifth of the civil servants in Egypt were actually needed (Internet 2001b).

Such over-employment results in various problems:

- Over-staffing in the public sector leads to a situation in which nobody feels responsible for the work that has to be done, so that efficiency is generally low.
- Many laws introduced in the socialist era under Nasser are still in force, making it next to impossible to dismiss employees who do not fulfil their obligations. So many civil servants in fact have two or three jobs, neglecting their official work, which secures them certain privileges as well as a pension when they retire, and working much more devotedly in their other jobs as taxi drivers, hotel employees or craftsmen. So there exist side by side a weak public sector and a highly productive informal sector.
- Since the state has to pay enormous sums of money amounting to one-third of its public budget (ibid.) to its huge number of employees, salaries must necessarily be kept low. In 2003 a young state-employed university graduate received a monthly salary of about US$25. If he wanted to buy 1 kg of meat, he had to spend one-sixth of it. Such conditions inevitably lead to corruption, dishonesty and negligence in the public service.
- The process of economic transformation is extremely difficult because of the situation described. To make privatized businesses function effectively and to reduce their production costs great numbers of employees have to be dismissed at the outset.

Changes in the employment structure in Egypt also contribute to unemployment in the country. As Table 7.3 shows, the proportion of those employed

Table 7.3 Agriculture in Egypt: its role in the national economy 1970/71 and 2000/01

	1970/71	2000/01
Proportion of total employment (%)	53	28.2
Contribution to GDP (%)	29	16.5
Share of total value of commodities exports (%)	63	8.4

Sources: after Ministry of Agriculture and Land Reclamation 1992: 4; Ministry of Information 2002a in agriculture decreased rapidly between the years 1970 and 2001. With the tractorization of Egyptian agriculture, manual labour became more and more redundant. The surplus manpower migrated not only to the services and trade sector (48.6 per cent in 2000/01) but also to the production and construction sector (23.2 per cent in 2000/01; see Table 9.2). As a rule Egyptians prefer to invest in the tertiary sector rather than in manufacturing. Capital invested in trade and in real estate has brought quick and secure returns during recent decades, but unfortunately has created hardly any job opportunities. In Egypt, as in many developing countries, the informal sector is of great importance. It responds very sensitively to changing economic conditions. The retail trade as well as the crafts industry depend on it. It gives millions of people in the big cities, especially women and children, who have no other sources of income, an opportunity to earn a livelihood through their own work. The exact number of people employed in this sector is not known. It should, however, be no less than the number of those employed in the formal sector. People can earn more in the informal sector, but payment is usually related to performance, unlike in the formal sector. As a rule there is no social security and the conditions under which people work may be catastrophic, with child labour a common trait. Without the existence of the informal sector, however, the infrastructure of the big cities would collapse totally. This is shown very clearly by the example of the 50,000 *zabbaleen* (garbage collectors; see Illustration 25) working in Greater Cairo. They have so far saved the 17 million or more inhabitants of the capital from suffocating in their own garbage. In 2002/03 the state replaced most of them with Spanish and Italian companies which do not recycle the solid waste.

As already mentioned, the lack of sufficient employment opportunities in the country forces many young Egyptians to consider engaging in labour migration for a limited time or perhaps leaving the country for good. This is very harmful for the country's economy, for those who leave have often received an expensive university education in their home country as medical doctors, engineers, mathematicians, etc. But the remittances of the Egyptian labour force abroad are an important pillar of Egypt's economy. In 2000/01 they constituted Egypt's second-largest source of foreign currency at US$ 3,021 million (see Table 7.1). The exact size of the emigrant labour force is unknown. Official sources mention 1.9 million persons, while others make them up to 5 million (Internet 1999a). In 1999 Egyptians constituted 35 per cent of the Arabic-speaking employees in Saudi Arabia and 18 per cent of all foreign ones (ibid.). Before the Gulf War of 1991 nearly 1 million Egyptians were working in Iraq alone. When the war broke out they had to leave the country overnight. These events, and the economic crisis in some Arab states caused by the deterioration in the price of oil after the mid-1980s, created a strong wave of remigration of Egyptian foreign workers back to their home country. This caused additional problems on the Egyptian labour market, in particular since the better-qualified workers stayed abroad. With the economic depression in the country at the beginning of the twenty-first century many are trying to leave Egypt for good and settle down with their families in countries like the USA, Canada or Australia, especially since emigration to Europe has become extremely difficult for Egyptians. In particular, many Egyptian Christians try to escape from the increasingly hostile atmosphere created by certain sectors of Egyptian society and seek refuge where they hope to be met with greater tolerance. The Coptic diaspora outside Egypt has been estimated at more than 1 million by the Coptic Church of Egypt.

The trend towards emigration, to which an end cannot yet be foreseen, brings about a number of serious economic and social consequences, such as the following:

- Egypt is suffering a 'brain drain', since often the best and most active people leave the country.
- The mass migration means a great economic loss for the Egyptian state, because it has invested enormous sums in every single qualified labour migrant or emigrant.
- The labour migrants spend part of the money earned abroad on housing in Egypt, for which the state grants high subsidies. However, usually the flats remain unoccupied until the owners return home for good. This undermines all the efforts of the Egyptian government to solve the housing problem.
- Relying on the remittances of labour migrants as a main source of foreign currency, the Egyptian government neglects the development of the country's industries, which have in fact lost their competitiveness on the world market (see below).
- The remittances of Egyptian foreign workers abroad sometimes help to raise the purchasing power of their families and relatives. This leads to inflation, which negatively affects above all the poor.
- Labour migration to the Arab countries is a factor of instability for the Egyptian economy. In the past political or economic crises in neighbouring countries sometimes led to a mass remigration of Egyptian workers, as happened when they were forced to flee from Iraq, Kuwait, Yemen, Libya and the Sudan. These events made the unemployment figures in Egypt rise dramatically.
- Remigrants may experience problems of reintegration. Often they enjoyed a much higher economic status abroad and find it difficult to adapt when they are back in their home country. This is particularly so for many *fellaheen* who migrated to the oil-producing Arab countries and did not work in agriculture there. It is hard for them to face the difficulties of everyday life in Egypt after their return, to reintegrate into the society of their small home villages with its patriarchal structures and to resume

the hard work in the fields or face unemployment. Most of them turn into workless white-collars oriented towards the possession of consumer goods.

3 Education and the labour force

The UN Human Development Report 2000 ranked Egypt at 119, far behind other Middle Eastern countries, such as Israel (23), Lebanon (82) and Iran (97). This was mainly on account of Egypt's deficiencies in primary education. The adult illiteracy rate is also relatively high (see below). Undoubtedly, the government will have to exert greater efforts to ensure primary education for all children of school age. If Egypt is to take part in the process of economic globalization, the quality of school education has to be raised. At present there exists an imbalance in the distribution of budget resources between primary and university education, with the latter being inflated at the expense of the former. With 1.72 million students enrolled in higher and university education in 2000/01 (Ministry of Information 2002a) and about 300,000 new university graduates annually, the first two decades of the new millennium will witness a huge increase in the number of university graduates, most of whom will either not find jobs or will be absorbed by the civil service, contributing further to disguised unemployment. If its well-qualified manpower is to make Egypt competitive in the region, especially in the areas of medicine and pharmacology, banking, tourism, law, engineering and information technology, this requires greater attention to the quality rather than to the quantity of higher education.

3.1 Historical development and the present state of education in Egypt

Until the nineteenth century education in Egypt was in the hands of the religious institutions. The Muslim sheikhs had their Quran schools (*kuttab*, plural *katatib*), in which children mainly memorized the Muslim holy book. By writing the different verses on little boards they learnt the classical Arabic language. The Coptic Church had its own schools in which, besides religion, the children were also taught mathematics, so that the Copts who had attended such schools were often employed in the public administration of the country because of their particular skills in bookkeeping. Al-Azhar Mosque, founded in the tenth century by the Fatimids, was, with its university, for centuries the most important institution of higher education not only in Egypt, but also in the whole Arab world. In the nineteenth century Mohammed Ali introduced a modern European-style educational system, which was later extended by Ismail. During the British colonial period this system was further developed. However, the British were primarily interested in the education of a local class able to work in their administration of the country. At the same time Christian missionaries, mainly from Italy, France, England and North America, came into the country and founded their own schools. These were attended by the children of the Europeans living in Egypt, but also by those of the Egyptian upper class. No missionary work as such took place, since according to the Quran, a Muslim who betrays his faith, as well as the person who induces him to do so, is to be punished by death. This is why converts to Catholicism and Protestantism were primarily the Egyptian Christians. As a reaction to this the Copts founded their own secular modern schools, which were open to Muslims and Christians alike.

The public school system was expanded further in the twentieth century. Today primary school education comprises five years, followed by three years of preparatory school and another three years of secondary school. A pupil can enter the secondary general school only if he has received good marks in the centralized exams which take place in the country annually. Those who are not admitted may enter the professional schools, which are specialized in various branches – technical, agricultural, commercial or those qualifying students for work in the tourism business. Graduates of the professional schools may enter the higher technical institutes, while admission to one of the country's many public universities is granted only to students who have received excellent marks in the annual countrywide *as-sanawiya el-'ama* final exams. There is a quota system according to which the students are admitted to the various areas of study. The highest marks are required for admission to the faculties of engineering, architecture and pharmacy, as well as human and veterinary medicine. There are no fewer than thirteen public universities and about as many higher technical institutes in Egypt. Cairo alone has four public universities, with branches in other parts of the country: Al-Azhar, which originally consisted solely of a faculty of Islamic theology but was turned into a modern university offering all other areas of study in the 1960s; Cairo University, which was founded in 1908 as a private university; Ain Shams University, founded in 1950; and the University of Helwan, founded in 1975. The University of Alexandria was founded in 1942. New universities were founded after 1957 in Asyut, Qena, El-Minya, Es-Zagazig, El-Mansura, Tanta, Shebin el-Kom and Ismailiya.

Of the 1.72 million students enrolled in Egyptian universities and higher institutes in 2000/01, about 44 per cent were women (Ministry of Information 2002a). In 1999/2000 the technical (i.e. vocational) secondary schools had 1.91 million full-time students, 46 per cent of whom were female. As regards the general schools there were 7.93 million pupils in primary schools, 4.66 million in preparatory schools and 1.31 million in secondary schools; of the latter about 47 per cent were girls (CAPMAS 2001b: 175ff). Since the 1980s the percentage of female pupils and students has increased steadily, since many girls today try to qualify for later employment. From 1980 to 1997 the enrolment ratio improved from 72 to 95 per cent of the relevant groups in

16. Palm-tree roots stripped of topsoil: After the construction of the Aswan High Dam no more Nile silt, which had for thousands of years been used for brick-making in Egypt, was deposited along the river. Nevertheless, many farmers who were in need of money sold the fertile, but now unrenewable, topsoil of their fields to the brick factories. The picture shows the result of this harmful practice through which the upper roots of the palm trees have been stripped naked. The making of bricks from Nile silt has been illegal in Egypt since the 1980s. (Photo: F. Ibrahim)

primary education and from 43 to 75 per cent in preparatory and secondary education (World Bank 2001: 284).

The problems of public education in Egypt today can be summarized as follows:

- Although school attendance has been compulsory in Egypt for decades, the adult (fifteen years and older) illiteracy rate is relatively high, particularly among women (1998: total – 46.5 per cent; women – 58 per cent; men – 35 per cent; ibid.: 274). According to a 1992 UNICEF study one-fifth of all Egyptian children had never attended school and about 30 per cent of the rest were drop-outs. The most frequent reason why children stayed away from school was the poverty of the parents, who could not afford the costs of school uniforms and textbooks. Moreover, children from the poorer population usually help support their families with some kind of work in the informal sector and are therefore unable to attend school. Although children under fourteen years of age are not allowed to work regularly in Egypt, 10 per cent of children aged ten to fourteen did so in 1999 (World Bank 2001: 278).

- The quality of school education has to be improved. Though in primary schools the average number of pupils per class was forty-two in 1999/2000 (CAPMAS 2001b: 175), classes of sixty pupils are not uncommon, but owing to the methods the teachers apply discipline is generally good. However, since the percentage of children of compulsory school age is high at 17 per cent of the total population, the state is confronted with a great financial problem in having to provide the corresponding infrastructure for 12 million young people. In Egypt public education is free at all levels up to university. Although public expenditure on education decreased from 5.7 to 4.8 per cent of GNP between 1980 and 1997 (ibid.), education consumed 14.7 per cent of the state budget in 1999/2000. However, in the years 2000–2010 the government needs to build 27,000 new schools, which would cost about US$60 billion, while the state can afford only 25 per cent to 30 per cent of this sum. Therefore, other – possibly private – sources will have to be tapped (Tadros 2001).

- Egyptian teachers in public schools are seriously under-paid. This makes them neglect their work and look for additional sources of income to feed their own families. Many parents pay high sums for private lessons for their children because they want them to succeed in the annual exams. Organized private lessons have come to form a parallel institution to the public school system. Some teachers earn more from private lessons than from their work in school. The state tried to stop this, applying drastic measures. However, without an increase in teachers' salaries the problem cannot be solved. Good Egyptian teachers find work easily in the Arab countries.

- Education in the professional schools is neither up to date nor adapted to the labour market. This is why job opportunities for the graduates are not good and businesses have to train their own personnel.

- For financial reasons the state is unable to offer the necessary number of places in universities for high-school graduates. So new specialized private professional training colleges have been opened, but relatively high fees have to be paid to enter them.

- The fact that the country produces more university graduates than can find work leads to dissatisfaction among young people and enhances their readiness to migrate under the economic conditions prevailing. This is an option which as a rule young educated women cannot avail themselves of, unless they migrate with their families or marry men who already live abroad.

- Standards of education offered in Egyptian universities have deteriorated during recent years. There are too many students and inadequate finance. Corruption is rife here, too, so that sometimes university professors who, like their colleagues in state schools, receive low salaries are open to bribery.

3.2 Privatization of education – a chance for the elite to qualify for the modern labour market

Up to the 1970s more than 97 per cent of schools in Egypt were in the public sector. Since then, however, the private educational sector has experienced a boom. The reasons are varied:

- After the era of Nasser's socialism had come to an end and private investment was encouraged by the state, fear of the nationalization of private schools, such as had already been experienced by some famous institutions like the English Mission School in Cairo and St Mark's College in Alexandria, was no longer a factor.
- Since Egypt's defeat in the war against Israel in 1967 the country's economic situation has deteriorated. The adverse effects of this were felt most severely in the public service sector, especially in education and healthcare.
- The oil boom in some of the Arab countries since the 1960s has caused a severe economic imbalance in the MENA region and triggered an influx of thousands of well-qualified teachers from Egypt. This has led to a further deterioration in Egypt's public school education where good teachers are lacking.
- To increase their income the remaining teachers depended on giving private lessons to their pupils in their own homes, neglecting their official work at school. Today, parents who want to make sure that their children succeed in their school careers have to pay so much for private lessons that it has become economically more appropriate for them to send their children to private schools, where they are better taken care of.
- Both Sadat's and Mubarak's policies of economic liberalization strengthened the upper middle class economically. Together with the upper class it constitutes about 7–10 per cent of the country's population, thus forming a substantial market for private schools. There may be up to another 7 per cent of the population who are ready to spend a great proportion of their income to offer their children a chance of a good education, which is of high social prestige in Egypt, where children's results in the annual school exams are a topic of discussion for everyone for weeks after they have appeared.
- The trend among the upper middle class of pulling out from state-run schools has widened the social gap between the economic classes of the population and in turn made private schools all the more indispensable to the higher classes.
- Since 1991 implementation of the Structural Adjustment Programmes has forced the Egyptian government to impose drastic cuts in the national educational budget. Thus the already desperate conditions in state-run schools have been exacerbated.

The above-mentioned factors have led to the different private education institutions flourishing, especially in Cairo and in Alexandria, because in these two mega-cities income levels are much higher than in the rest of the country. In other large cities, growth in the private educational sector is much slower, and in purely rural areas it is almost absent. Private education has become a lucrative business for investors. This is why shareholder companies have started gaining ground in this sector, too. According to *Al-Ahram Weekly* (15–22 February 2001) the Minister of Education declared the government's intention of encouraging private cooperatives to establish schools which the state might then rent from them.

The most widespread private educational institutions are still kindergartens and pre-schools, which became increasingly popular among the growing number of working middle-class mothers. Both Muslim and Christian societies are active in the field. The standards as well as the fees vary greatly. In crowded urban areas the spaces rented for schools of this type are very limited and often completely unsuitable for children. Private schools at the primary and preparatory stages are markedly more expensive, which leads to a more pronounced social selection of pupils. The most expensive schools in the country are the American School in Cairo, with annual fees reaching US$10,000, and the Showaifat School in Cairo, for which the fees amount to about US$6,000. The latter belongs to a chain of elite schools also found in Lebanon and the Gulf States. Cheaper private schools charge fees of about US$400 annually. These fees, too, are far beyond the means of a graduate civil servant who has worked in the state service for twenty years and receives a salary of about US$800 annually. The majority of the schools belonging to Christian churches, especially those run by nuns or monks, usually charge lower fees than other private schools and are also attended by Muslims since they have a good reputation. The boom in private secondary schools was strongly enhanced by the sharpening of competition for admittance to universities. Many private schools have specialized in the two top grades of secondary education to prepare students for the final state examination so that they can attain the highest marks possible. In this way an affluent elite that can profit from the new private educational system has considerable advantages over those who are dependent on the public system.

What is characteristic about the majority of the new private schools is that the English language is used in teaching all subjects, and that this is an element used in advertising. The reasons behind this are:

- The managers of these schools want to underline the elitist status of their institutions by giving them an international character and by imitating the upper-class British colonial culture.
- Owing to the poor state of foreign language teaching in public schools, secondary school graduates are normally completely unable to read English

17. *Nile barges* (falukas): Nile barges are used for transporting pottery, bricks and other building materials. Since a new law forbade brick-making from Nile silt, the Nile banks have lost their former importance as favourable locations for the brick industry. (Photo: F. Ibrahim)

or French when they attend university later. After graduating their chances of finding well-paid employment in the tourism industry, in one of the branches of the many international import-export companies or in the newly founded multinationals in Egypt are thus very poor. Here private schools fill a gap by producing graduates who have had a chance to acquire valuable skills qualifying them to work in a globalized world.

Privatization in higher education is proceeding at a slower pace, due mainly to the great expense involved in establishing technical or medical faculties. Some private universities also suffer from the government's reluctance to acknowledge the certificates they give to graduates. It is hard to believe today that in the middle of the twentieth century the American University in Cairo (AUC) also had to struggle a long time for full recognition. Today it is the most renowned university in the country, but exclusively reserved for the young generation of the upper classes. In 2001 the construction of new buildings for this university began on a campus situated north-east of the Muqattam mountain in El-Qahira el-Gedida (New Cairo), following a general trend of establishing private universities in the new communities around the big cities. The cost of the new structures will amount to US$290 million, and the university will have additional new faculties for natural sciences and engineering (Internet 2001e), for which there exists a great demand in Egypt. The private Sitta October University in Giza was established in the 1980s. It is relatively well equipped, but its reputation at a scientific level is affected by the fact that it admits students of lower standards of learning as well as drop-outs from other universities. The private section of the Marine Academy of Alexandria, in contrast, enjoys an excellent reputation. Further private universities, which are partly still lacking fully fledged programmes, are the University of Al-Ashir min Ramadan in the satellite town of the same name, the Misr University of Science and Technology at Sitta October, the Modern Academy at Maadi, Sadat's Academy at Madinet es-Sadat, and a German University in Cairo which is in the planning stage. The recent establishment of several open universities is an attempt to introduce fees in the public higher education sector, too. Here the facilities of existing state universities are being used, but less strict admittance regulations applied. Courses are offered for about US$60 per subject/term. The numerous private higher institutes, which have appeared also in the provincial cities, teaching mostly computer science, tourism and in some cases also social sciences, still have to be evaluated. In 2000/01 there existed thirty-four faculties in private universities in Egypt, in which a total of 17,311 students were enrolled, of whom about 5,800 had been newly admitted in that academic year (Ministry of Information 2002a). One of the reasons for the establishment of the numerous new higher institutes for paying students is the acute lack of employment opportunities for secondary school graduates. However, since the employment chances of university graduates are also very low given the state of the Egyptian economy at the beginning of the third millennium, young people are actually postponing confronting the problem.

4 Egypt as a rentier state

Wurzel (2000 and 2001) and others describe Egypt as a rentier state which as such is largely dependent both on economic rents as well as on politically motivated external financial flows. In their definitions of rent Wurzel (2000: 102ff) and Schmidt (1991: 78 and 67) give various shades of meaning. According to them a basic rent is the income gained out of a title possession, for example a land rent. A rent differs from profit in that it is not reinvested to promote production. Rents are revenues that are appropriated without the implementation of production factors or direct payments. The difference between the ideal competitive price and the actual market price can also be described as a rent. In the Egyptian economy Wurzel (2000: 121ff) identifies the following economic characteristics which make him classify the country as a rentier state:

- The country's economy depends largely on three types of rents:
  1) international economic rents
  2) external political (geopolitical) rents
  3) domestic economic rents.

- Both external and domestic economic rents are being appropriated by the state, which holds various other monopolies, especially in the trade sector. The state monopolies in internal economic activities are partly responsible for the inflation of the public sector. Through another significant area of state monopoly, the foreign exchange market, the state gains considerably by compelling foreign investors, tourists and Egyptian workers living abroad to exchange their hard currencies at state-controlled banks at artificially inflated rates. From the early 1990s Egypt had started to devalue its local currency under pressure from the World Bank and the IMF. In 2001 alone, the Egyptian pound was devalued by 25 per cent and even more drastically in 2003.

- Relying largely on external rents, the Egyptian state became independent of the domestic economy, apart from the internal rent-generating sectors. This led to neglect of the domestic economy, so that little investment was made for modernization of the old industries to render their products competitive on the world market. This applies in particular to the textile industry, in which Egypt possesses comparative advantages (high-quality cotton, cheap skilled labour, a huge inland market). As a rentier state Egypt follows a policy of import and consumption rather than of investment and development, which requires greater effort.

- The consequences of the rentier economic system for Egyptian domestic politics are disastrous. The allocation of income from rents is directed mainly towards the privileged groups that support the political regime in power. Among these groups are parts of the civil service, especially the higher ranks of the police and the army, as well as those employed in the rent-generating sectors, for example export and import, tourism and the petroleum industry. Domestic taxes, which should be the backbone of the state budget, play a subordinate role in Egypt. In democratic systems taxation is the basis of representation rights. As the various rents it receives make the Egyptian government almost independent of taxation, it is not in need of the people's consent, and democracy becomes unnecessary. Besides, the state monopoly in the acquisition of international rents has consolidated the pre-existing centralistic and bureaucratic state structure. The state monopoly on rent allocation has also strengthened the paternalistic, patriarchal and authoritarian behaviour of the government towards its people.

- In a rentier state with otherwise meagre economic resources competition over privileged access to rents has come to determine the relationships among the different social groups, and between these and the state. This has led to the formation on the one hand of strongly privileged groups which are loyal to the ruling system, and of discriminated groups on the other. The latter constitute the largest proportion of the population and are highly responsive to the political ideas of radical Islamists.

- The economy of the rentier state is vulnerable, for it is at the mercy of

18. *Temple of Ramses II at Abu Simbel*: The Ramses Temple at Abu Simbel was one of the few ancient Nubian monuments that were dismantled and reconstructed again on a higher elevation before the floods of the storage lake of the Aswan High Dam started to submerge the land of the Nubian people and the rest of the temples, old churches and other monuments there. (Photo: F. Ibrahim)

international fluctuations over which it has no control. International political rents that flow into Egypt on account of its geopolitical importance in the Near East amounted to US$2.5–3 billion in the form of routine payments from the USA and the EU states in 1996/97. If one adds to them US$2 billion from the Suez Canal revenues, US$2.5 billion from the export of petroleum, US$3.7 billion from foreign tourism and US$4 billion from the remittances of Egyptian workers abroad, one gets a figure of about US$15 billion, which constituted 65 per cent of the state budget in that year (see Wurzel 2001: 13).

Nearly all the rents on which Egypt is presently dependent may be jeopardized if the political situation in the Near East changes. The geopolitical importance of Egypt may be reduced if the conflict between Israel and the Arab states is resolved. The revenues gained from the Suez Canal are at risk if the war with Israel flares up again, as happened between 1967 and 1975. Similarly vulnerable to war situations are the remittances of Egyptians working abroad and income from tourism, as was demonstrated by the situation during the wars against Iraq in 1991 and 2003, after the massacre of tourists in Luxor in 1997 and during the Second Intifada after 2000. Petroleum is a non-renewable resource and due to be depleted within a foreseeable span of time; already the government has had to limit its exploitation. In 2002 the USA threatened to freeze the capital development aid of US$2 billion which it used to grant Egypt annually, if it did not stop persecuting intellectuals, and US$130 million which had already been promised were withdrawn immediately (see Internet 2002b). In short, the rentier economic system of Egypt is anything but sustainable. It has rendered the country highly vulnerable to recurrent economic crises, hindered the development of the domestic economy and strengthened an undemocratic political system.

CHAPTER 8

Egypt's Agriculture under Stress

1 Foreign currency versus food security

After having been the backbone of the country's economy for thousands of years, agriculture in Egypt has lost its prominent position rapidly during recent decades, beginning in the 1960s. Nevertheless, this sector of the economy is still considered an important source of Egypt's hard currency revenue, and at the same time is expected to guarantee relative food security for a constantly growing population. This means that Egypt's agriculture has to provide high-quality products for export, and at the same time large amounts of staple crops to feed the nation. However, as Table 7.3 shows, the contribution of agriculture to national income fell between 1970/71 and 2000/01 from 29 per cent to 16.5 per cent. During the same period agrarian production's proportion of total export value decreased dramatically from 63 per cent to only 8.4 per cent, while the numbers of people employed in agriculture, which had been 72 per cent of the working population in 1947, dropped from 53 per cent to 28.2 per cent of all persons employed in the country during that span of time. Egypt's degree of self-sufficiency in the most important food items, shown in Table 8.6, is discussed below.

2 Land tenure and land distribution in Egypt

From the beginning of Ottoman rule over Egypt in 1517 to the time of Mohammed Ali (1805–48) agricultural land in the country was divided into revenue areas for taxation purposes. The tax creditors were obliged to pay fixed sums to the Turkish sultan, but were free to demand much higher tax payments in turn from the *fellaheen* tenants who cultivated their land. Within this system of fiscal administration and land rent there were 300 Grand Mamelukes who controlled huge estates that made up two-thirds of the agricultural land under irrigation in Egypt. When in the eighteenth century, owing to inadequate maintenance, most irrigation mechanisms on the land in the hands of these feudal lords no longer functioned properly, large areas of the land, especially in Upper Egypt, could no longer be irrigated. At the time 80 per cent of the cultivated land was under the system of tax farming, while the rest was considered privately owned and was administered by the *waqf* or *habus* system, meaning that it belonged to religious foundations. According to official rules it could be used by the descendants of those who had donated it without their paying taxes, but they did not have the right to sell it.

Mohammed Ali dispossessed the Mamelukes and abolished the old system of taxation of landed property. However, subsequently he had to impose a similar system again to secure the necessary revenues for his treasury. This led to the development of a new social class of tax collectors, mostly Turkish nobles who were endowed with numerous privileges. Among others, they had the right to use part of the land belonging to the state as private property and could have it tilled by forced labour, while they themselves were exempted from paying taxes. The private estates owned by the princes of Mohammed Ali's dynasty were also tax free. It was not until the time of British colonial rule that a general liability to pay taxes for agricultural land was introduced.

The most decisive change concerning land tenure was brought about by the Land Reform Laws of 1952, 1961 and 1969 under President Nasser. Land ownership was successively limited to 200 *feddans*, 100 *feddans* and finally to 50 *feddans* (1 *feddan* = 1.038 acre) per individual and to 100 *feddans* per nuclear family. Tables 8.1 and 8.2 show the effects of this redistribution of feudal land. The reforms meant that between 1952 and 1970 about 817,500 *feddans* (848,600 acres) of agricultural land, i.e. 12.5 per cent of total arable land, were sold cheaply to about 342,000 landless *fellaheen*, which then constituted about 9 per cent of all rural families (Abdel-Fadil 1975: 10).

The structure of land ownership before the First Land Reform in 1952, and in 1995 before implementation of the new land rent law in 1997, was as shown in Tables 8.2 and 8.3 and in Figures 8.1 and 8.2.

Table 8.1 Distribution of land ownership in Egypt 1896–1995*

Land owned in *feddans***	1896		1952**		1995	
	Owners (%)	Area (%)	Owners (%)	Area (%)	Owners (%)	Area (%)
50 and more	1.0	45.2	0.4	34.2	0.2	14.5
10–< 50	5.1	20.8	2.5	21.6	1.6	18.8
5–< 10	6.7	9.5	2.8	8.8	2.3	9.6
< 5	87.2	24.5	94.3	35.4	95.9	57.1
Total	100.0	100.0	100.0	100.0	100.0	100.0
Total in 1,000	1,153	5,299 f.	2,800	5,922 f.	3,908	5,887 f.
Average ownership	4.6 *feddans*		2.1 *feddans*		1.5 *feddans*	

* The large number of landless *fellaheen* are not considered here;
** before the socialist land reform; *** 1 *feddan* = 1.038 acre

Sources: after Waterbury 1984: 268; CAPMAS 2000: 65–7

Table 8.2 Sizes of landholdings* in Egypt 1950 and 1985–87

Sizes of land-holdings in feddans**	1950		1985–87	
	Share of landholdings (%)	Share of agricultural land (%)	Share of landholdings (%)	Share of agricultural land (%)
100 and more	0.7	29.7	0.03	9.8
50–< 100	3.4	22.3	0.12	3.0
10–< 50	5.2	11.5	2.72	18.2
5–< 10	12.2	13.3	7.0	16.6
3–< 5	16.2	9.8	13.4	17.8
1–< 3	40.9	11.6	44.43	28.6
< 1	21.4	1.8	32.3	6.0
Total	100.0	100.0	100.0	100.0
Total number/ area	1.003 m holdings	6.144 m *fed.*	2.468 m holdings	6.562 m *fed.*

*Landholding = owned land + leased-in land minus leased-out land
** 1 *feddan* = 1.038 acre

Sources: after Abdel-Fadil 1975: 14; Ministry of Agriculture and Land Reclamation 1991: 24

Table 8.3 Distribution of land ownership by size of holding in Egypt 2000*

Land owned in feddans**	Share of owners (%)	Share of agricultural land (%)
100 and more	0.7	8.6
50–< 100	0.9	6.4
20–< 50	1.4	9.4
10–< 20	2.8	9.7
5–< 10	4.3	10.4
4–< 5	3.7	8.4
3–< 4	5.0	9.1
2–< 3	8.4	10.5
1–< 2	14.3	11.1
< 1 (ø: 0.4)	58.5	16.4
Total	100.0	100.0
Total number / area	4,056,800 owners	6,108,400 feddans

* The large number of landless *fellaheen* are not considered here
** 1 *feddan* = 1.038 acre

Source: after CAPMAS 2002: 70f

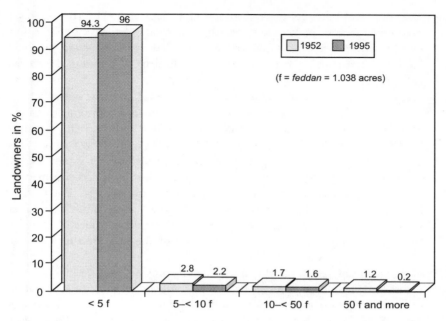

Figure 8.1 Agricultural land ownership in Egypt 1952 (before the land reforms) and 1995 (Author: F. Ibrahim 2002; cartography: J. Feilner; sources of data: after CAPMAS 1994a: 76; 1999c: 68–70)

Proportion of the agricultural
area of Egypt in %

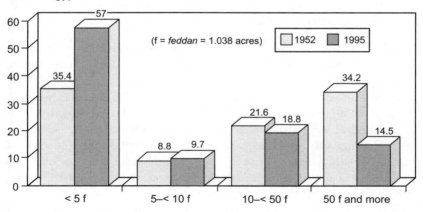

Figure 8.2 Farm sizes in Egypt 1952 (before the land reforms) and 1995 (Author: F. Ibrahim 2002; cartography: J. Feilner; sources of data: after CAPMAS 1994a: 76; 1999c: 68–70)

- The situation both before and after the socialist land reforms shows a predominance of smallholders (owning less than 5 *feddans*). In 1995 they constituted 96 per cent of all landowners. The area cultivated by them increased considerably from just over one-third to 57 per cent. However, for a realistic assessment of the reform measures one must consider the actual size of the land owned by the smallholders. This increased only from an average of 0.8 *feddans* to 0.9 *feddans*, so that the economic situation of single households was still critical. In Figure 8.3 the Lorenz curve of land ownership distribution before 1952, in 1965 and in 1995 shows that the land reforms had brought about considerably greater equity in the 1960s. A serious setback occurred in the 1990s, however, accompanied by a dramatic increase in the number of minute landholdings. The reasons for the extreme fragmentation of the holdings are the Islamic inheritance laws prescribing partitioning, coupled with the great number of children the *fellaheen* have. After the implementation of the new land rent laws in 1997, the situation improved slightly.
- 64.6 per cent of agricultural land was held by only 5.7 per cent of landowners in 1952, namely by those who owned 5 *feddans* or more. The situation did not change greatly during the following four decades, so that 42.9 per cent of the land belonged to 4.1 per cent of landowners in 1995. More equity could be seen, however, in 2000.
- In 1952 and in 1995 those who owned 100 *feddans* or more comprised 0.2 per cent and 0.06 per cent of landowners respectively.

Dispossessing the feudal class and redistributing the land among landless peasants was in fact a revolutionary act and remains one of Nasser's great achievements. However, the success of the land reform was not as great as government propaganda at the time claimed. The reform, which had been overdue for social reasons, was impaired by the following factors:

- It led to extreme partitioning of feudal land, which later proved unfavourable when attempts were made to modernize agriculture and introduce mechanization.
- State bureaucracy, with all its deficiencies, meant that in some cases years elapsed before the confiscated estates were assigned to new owners. Many farms, and especially the irrigation constructions and assets which have to be continuously well maintained, were neglected during this period, so that eventually they could not be operated any more. Also, in many cases the land was not assigned to landless *fellaheen*, as had been the original intention, but to members of the military.
- Some influential feudalists managed to get around the reforms and distributed their land nominally among relatives in order to keep it for themselves.

The least spectacular but most important part of Nasser's land reform, which was also of long-lasting effect, was the introduction of laws strengthening the rights of tenants *vis-à-vis* landlords. Up to that time absenteeism had generally prevailed in Egypt's rural areas. Only once a year, after the cotton harvest, did the lessors, who normally lived in town, visit their lessees to collect the land rent. According to Nasser's laws, rack-rents were forbidden and the landlords' gains were not to exceed seven times the amount of the tax they themselves had to pay. Moreover, the new leasehold conditions generally were more in favour of the tenants. They made it almost impossible to cancel a lease, and if a landlord wanted to sell his land the tenant had the right of pre-emption. As a negative consequence of this, however, no landowner wanted to make a long-term tenancy contract any more, preferring to let the land informally for one season only and then demand a rent that was about ten times as high as it should normally have been. The government reacted to this situation and in 1992 raised rents officially to more than three times the amount they had been before, following the principles of a free market economy.

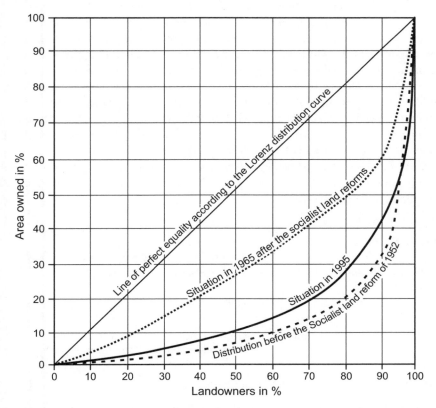

Figure 8.3 Distribution of land ownership in Egypt 1950–95 (Author: F. Ibrahim 2002; cartography: J. Feilner; sources of data: Abdel-Fadil 1975: 13; CAPMAS 2000: 65–7)

The new policy was to close the gap between the rents paid and the market prices for landed property. This hit the small landholders, who were already struggling to make a living, hard. They are not able to pay the LE1,500–2,300 rent required per *feddan* yearly. This is why today agricultural land is gradually reverting into the hands of richer people, who usually gain their main income from other sources. Müller-Mahn (2001c) speaks of 'the return of the Pashas' in this context. This is, of course, only meant to be figurative, because most of the 'returning' landowners own less than 5 acres. However, it is estimated that after the application of the new land law in 1997 about one million tenants lost the land that their fathers and grandfathers used to rent for cultivation before them. Landowners took it away, sometimes with the support of the police, under the pretext that they wanted to farm themselves. In most cases, however, they let it to other tenants, not only because in this way they could get a higher rent but also because they wanted to prevent the old tenants from acquiring customary occupancy rights. For the same reason, they made the new renting contracts valid only for one year. Now they usually change tenants annually. This practice will ultimately lead to adverse consequences, because under such insecure conditions tenants will not invest in soil improvement, but will rather practise strip mining. Both the new tenants and the old ones, if they are able to pay the inflated land rents, are hardly able to make ends meet. To illustrate this, we give the example of a tenant from Abu Qurqas, El Minya Governorate. He was able to keep his 1 *feddan* after agreeing to pay LE1,800 annual rent. In 2000 he grew wheat in winter, followed by maize in summer. His harvest was 2.5 tons of wheat and 2.7 tons of maize. He sold about 80 per cent of it for LE2,300 and kept the rest to be consumed by his family. After paying rent and deducting the costs of seeds, fertilizers and pesticides, hardly any cash profit was made, while he and his family had worked hard all year without pay. However, he did make the following subsidiary gains:

A tenant's subsidiary gains

Food for family consumption	1 ton of wheat and maize various vegetables grown around the fields
Fodder for two sheep, a donkey and a cow:	straw from the wheat harvested
Fuel:	stalks and inner cones of the maize harvested
Occasional small cash income:	from selling sheep from time to time from selling butter made from the cow's milk

Source: Fieldwork F. Ibrahim 2000, Abu Qurqas, El Minya Governorate

It is certain, however, that the same *fellaheen* family fared much better before 1997 when the land rent was less than one-third of what it is now.

For Egypt's agriculture not only the structure of land ownership, but also the structure of landholdings is of great relevance. A landholding is the operational unit of farming. It consists of the land owned and the additionally rented land, minus the leased-out land. In 1977/78 there were in Egypt 3.38 million landowners with 3 million landholdings divided between 14 million land parcels (Commander 1987: 9; CAPMAS 1988a: 64ff; Hamdan 1984a: 405). Only 14.3 per cent of all landholdings consisted of an undivided land parcel, while 45 per cent of landholdings consisted of four land parcels or more. Besides the reasons for extreme land partitioning already mentioned, absenteeism is also responsible, while at the same time much land is being let because of the small size of the different parcels. Land leasing has a tradition in Egypt. It started in the nineteenth century when large estates were given to members of the ruling class of Ottoman descent. These landlords were no farmers but stood at the top of a hierarchy that had developed over time and consisted of a system of tenants and sub-tenants by which the latifundia were divided into operational sizes. The smallholders at the bottom of this hierarchical system were usually left in a dreary economic situation with less than 25 per cent of the gains made through their work to keep as their own. Even after the land reform of 1961 had been carried out, only 43 per cent of the agricultural land consisted of purely owned holdings; 19.5 per cent consisted of purely leased holdings and 37.5 per cent of mixed (partly owned and partly leased) holdings; 88 per cent of tenants paid rent in cash. In the remaining cases payments were made with parts of the harvest, if no other arrangements had been agreed on (Abdel-Fadil 1975: 20f).

In spite of the small sizes of their plots the *fellaheen* working on rented land are not the poorest among the rural population. Indeed, the absolutely poor are the landless *fellaheen*, who are hardly ever mentioned in the statistics. According to El-Khyar (1982, cited in Abdel-Moiti and Kishk 1992: 223) their number amounted to 59.3 per cent of the rural population in 1950 before the first land reform, and decreased to 37.8 per cent in 1976. Their proportion is likely to be at least 30 per cent today, although according to official data they constituted only 14 per cent in 1985–87 (Ministry of Agriculture and Land Reclamation 1991: 24). The majority of them procure a living for the families by working as farm labourers. Renting land is completely out of their reach, especially since 1997, when rents were raised all over the country with the effects described above.

3 Historical development of Egypt's agricultural production (see Table 8.4)

Wheat and barley were the main field crops in ancient Egypt. They were cultivated in irrigated basins in autumn and winter after the Nile swell had receded. Besides these, beans, lentils, lupins, onions and garlic were grown to a great extent. Also, cultivation of flax as well as of plants used in the production of dyes was of considerable importance. Well-known permanent cultivations of Pharaonic times were the olive tree, the date palm and the vine. The most important fodder plant was *bersim* (*Trifolium alexandrinum*), the Egyptian clover. Also cotton, sorghum and sesame were known in early times. During the Middle Ages the Arabs introduced cultivation of rice and sugar cane, as well as various fruit trees, among which apricots, peaches, plums and citrus were the most important. Maize was first cultivated in Egypt in Ottoman times.

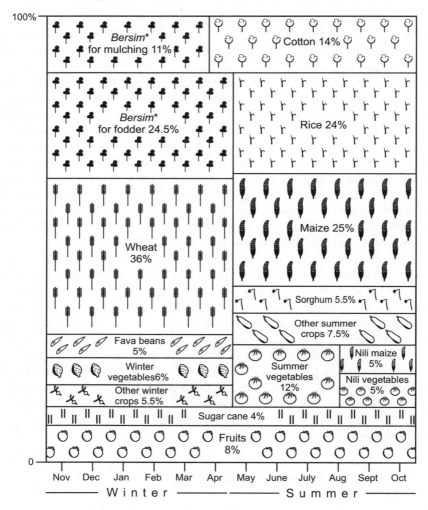

Bersim (Trifolium alexandrinum) = fodder plant

Figure 8.4 The crop pattern in Egypt 1997 (1.9 crops annually) (Author: F. Ibrahim 2002; cartography: J. Feilner; source: altered after Said 1993: 255)

After permanent irrigation had been introduced, and partly replaced the former basin irrigation under Mohammed Ali, there was a decisive change in the structure of agricultural production. Some crops lost their importance or disappeared completely, like barley, leguminous plants, flax and dye-providing plants. The areas on which crops like maize, *bersim*, cotton, rice and vegetables were grown were greatly expanded.

Various factors determine the times at which crops are grown, or crop rotation, such as availability of irrigation water, farm size, profit margins, the

Table 8.4 Agriculture in Egypt: most important field crops 1950–2001 by share of harvested area (%)

Crop	1950–54	1960–64	1970–74	1978–81	1988–91	1998–2001
*bersim**	23.2	23.8	25.8	24.9	21.5	17.5
Maize	18.5	16.8	14.7	17.1	16.6	13.7
Wheat	16.7	13.5	11.7	12.4	14.8	17.3
Rice	5.4	7.7	10.1	9.0	8.2	10.4
Cotton	18.8	17.0	14.3	10.7	8.0	4.7
Sorghum and barley	5.4	5.2	5.0	4.5	3.6	4.3
Leguminous plants	4.7	5.0	3.8	3.0	3.4	3.3
Vegetables**	2.4	4.3	7.0	9.0	9.7	12.9
Fruits in orchards	1.0	1.4	2.3	3.1	6.4	8.2
Sugar: cane and beet	1.0	1.2	1.5	2.3	2.6	3.1
Others	2.9	4.1	3.8	4.0	5.2	4.6
Total harvested area	100	100	100	100	100	100

* *Trifolium alexandrinum*, Egyptian clover ; ** Partly including potatoes

Sources: after Commander 1987: 60; CAPMAS 1993: 42ff; Ministry of Agriculture and Land Reclamation 1992: 101f; CAPMAS 2001b: 39ff; Ministry of Information 2002a

Table 8.5 Agriculture in Egypt: water requirements of the major field crops

Crop	Water requirement per cropping period per *feddan** (cubic metres)
Wheat	1,000–1,500
*bersim***	2,500
Maize	2,500
Cotton	2,500–4,200
Rice	10,000
Sugar cane	16,800
Average	8,000

* 1 *feddan* = 1.038 acre; ** *Trifolium alexandrinum*, Egyptian clover

Sources: after Simons 1977: 577; CAPMAS 1987: 145ff

availability of capital, machines or labour, and last but not least the state's agrarian policy.

Until the construction of the Sadd el-Ali the cultivation calendar depended mainly upon the seasonal Nile swell. The agrarian year traditionally started on 11 September, like the ancient Coptic year. The interaction between the regular fluctuations of the Nile discharge and the climatic seasons brought about the following characteristic cultivation periods:

The Coptic agrarian year (starting 11 September)

nili	July to November:
	The time of the Nile swell in autumn, i.e. the time when the land was formerly partly flooded, sedimentation of silt took place and the irrigation basins were filled
shitwi (winter)	November to May:
	The time of low temperatures and high air humidity, i.e. the time of low evapotranspiration, when winter crops can grow
seifi (summer)	March to August:
	The time of high temperatures and low Nile water level, i.e. the time of plants' greatest water demand; historically cultivation took place during this season only on small parts of the land to which the water could be raised with the help of various technical devices

Figure 8.4 shows the present cultivation calendar, which is adapted to the situation existing today. The cultivation of cotton extends over three normal cultivation periods because of its long vegetation period. Quite frequently, prior to the cultivation of cotton, *bersim* or beans are grown since these improve the soil through nitrogen fixation. The water requirements of the different crops grown in Egypt today vary greatly (see Table 8.5). The Egyptian Ministry of Irrigation's planning is based on them. The annual water demand for irrigation in the Nile valley is currently calculated at about 50 billion m³, giving each *feddan* on average about 7,000 m³ of water for that purpose.

4 The country's agricultural production today

4.1 Cotton – raw material and source of foreign currency

With the introduction of permanent irrigation in Egypt during the nineteenth century ideal conditions pertained for growing cotton. There were relatively heavy soils, high temperatures, low air humidity, and sufficient soil moisture through irrigation. The period of cultivation from March to October is moreover the best time for plant growth because of the long duration of sunshine. In the middle of the nineteenth century Mohammed Ali had seized the opportunity offered by the obstruction of cotton exports from America during the Civil War and tried to open up the British market for Egyptian cotton. For this purpose he built the Delta Dam, which was completed in 1861. After their occupation of Egypt in 1882 the British continued the policy and expanded the cotton cultivation area. To secure enough water for the irrigation of the cotton fields in summer they built three dams on the Nile, which were completed in 1902: one at Aswan, another at Asyut and the third at Sifta (see Figure 6.1). Further dams followed at Isna, Nag' Hammadi and Jebel el-Aulia (Sudan). Towards the end of British hegemony over Egypt, in 1938, cotton constituted 91 per cent of the total value of exports.

The main areas of cotton cultivation are in the Nile delta, where permanent irrigation was introduced first. In 1961 the area of cultivation reached its maximum at 2,000,000 *feddans*. Since that time it has decreased steadily. In 2001 it was only 720,000 *feddans*. There are four main reasons for the decline of cotton cultivation in Egypt, which continues today:

- International demand for cotton, especially for the long-stapled type grown in Egypt, is in decline. The new cotton-spinning and weaving machines no longer depend on this high-quality cotton.
- Cotton is available on the world market at low prices from the cheap-labour countries in Asia with which Egypt cannot compete.
- The Egyptian government adopted a policy of self-sufficiency as regards the country's staple foods, and thus tried to reduce the area cultivated with cotton in favour of food crops.
- The time during which Egypt depended totally on the Soviet Union economically after the construction of the Sadd el-Ali, during which the *fellaheen* were forced to cultivate cotton so that the country could pay back its debts, is over. Cotton production had been very unpopular then, because it is labour intensive and, since the state held the monopoly as the only buyer of cotton, prices paid to the producers were extremely low.

In 2001 the government tried to encourage farmers to grow cotton again by contributing around LE176 per *feddan* to cultivation costs, in addition to LE100 to fight cotton pests, especially the boll-worm, which had devastated the harvest of previous years. In 1998/99 the per-*feddan* yields reached an unprecedented low of 199 kg of ginned cotton. In 1981/82, the yield had been 578 kg/*feddan* (Ministry of Information 2000: 66f). It is to be expected that the production of cotton will decline further, especially when government measures to liberalize the economy become fully effective.

Cotton was not only the raw material that Egypt supplied to the British cotton industry in colonial times and the country's first source of hard currency (and thus also relevant in terms of foreign politics later), it also played a most important role in the home economy until the end of the 1970s. Hamdan (1984a: 236f) described the situation at that time as follows:

- One-quarter of Egyptian production was related to cotton.

- 25 per cent of the Egyptian labour force were engaged in the cultivation of cotton or employed in the cotton industry. The cultivation of cotton, which has not been mechanized to this day, is extremely labour intensive. It requires 95 labour days/ha and another 214 labour days/ha for the harvest, which is usually carried out by young people.
* Egypt's textile industry employed 300,000 workers, i.e. 25 per cent of all industrial workers in the country.
- The oil produced from the cotton seeds fulfilled 30 per cent of Egypt's demand for edible oil, while the residues from the seeds provided *c.* 800,000 tons of first-class animal feed.

4.2 Grain production and food security (see Tables 8.6 and 8.7)

Before the First World War Egypt ranked among the food-exporting countries. Up to the early 1960s the country was self-sufficient. Since the 1970s grain consumption has increased drastically, while grain production has increased only very slowly. The production and significance of the main grain types are analysed below.

Wheat (see Figure 8.5)

Annual per capita consumption of wheat and maize in Egypt was 290.5 kg in 1998. Egypt has the highest wheat consumption rate in the world. Bread is taken with every meal and is the staple food of the poorer population today. There are three main types of bread in Egypt, differing according to the grain they are made of and to the areas of consumption:

1. The first is very thin and flat and consists of a mixture of wheat and maize; it is produced by women in rural areas for domestic consumption. In middle Egypt a certain type of this bread, called *bettau*, is made of maize with the addition of *helba* (fenugreek) as a spice.
2. *Eesh baladi* (local bread) is a flat bread which is sold in towns and in bigger villages. The state provides the bakeries with subsidized wheat flour for its production. In 1980 consumers of this bread paid only 36.6 per cent of the world market price for wheat (Hamdan 1984a: 267). In 2001, the government allocated US$2.1 billion to subsidize basic commodities, mainly bread (Internet 2001a).
3. Besides these two, another type of bread can be bought in the bigger towns, the more expensive *eesh fino*, a white baguette-type bread which is produced in special bakeries and consumed by the upper and middle classes.

The change in food habits in recent times from maize bread to wheat bread was brought about by urbanization and by the rapid growth of Egyptian villages, where today commercial bakeries satisfy the great demand. The reasons why in many villages women still bake their own bread, even though state

Table 8.6 Egypt's most important food items: per capita consumption (1998) and national self-sufficiency (2000/01)

Food item	Annual per capita consumption (kg)	Self-sufficiency (%)
Wheat	174.5	58.8
Maize	116.0	56.6*
Rice	52.9	100.0
Fava beans	6.1	94.0
Vegetables	168.4	100.0
Fruit	93.5	99.0
Meat	11.7	80.4
Poultry	7.0	100.0
Fish	11.1	76.0
Milk	79.2	35.0**
Eggs (number)	41.0	99.9
Edible oil	15.4	34.8
Sugar	26.9	56.6

* This figure gives the country's overall self-sufficiency in maize and takes into consideration high imports of fodder maize.

Sources: after CAPMAS 2000: 70–2; Gamal-el-Din 2001 (*); Internet 2001c (**); Ministry of Information 2002b

Table 8.7 Grain – Egypt's production and degree of self-sufficiency 2000/01

Type	Area cultivated in 1,000 *feddans**	Production in 1,000 tons	Yield in tons/*feddan*	Self-sufficiency (%)
Wheat	2,395	7,017	2.93	58.8
Maize	1,839	6,474	3.52	56.6**
Rice	1,567	6,002	3.83	100
Sorghum	468	1,328	2.84	***
Barley	172	350	2.03	***
Total	6,441	21,171	–	–

* 1 *feddan* = 1.038 acre; ** This figure gives the country's overall self-sufficiency in maize and takes into consideration the country's high imports of fodder maize; *** No figures available

Sources: after Ministry of Information 2001b and 2002a; Gamal-el-Din 2001 (**)

subsidies make the wheat bread from the bakeries relatively cheap, are the following:

• Consumption depends on the food habits of the people.
• In many villages there are no bakeries.

- Experience has taught the *fellaheen* that the production of the local bakeries is unreliable, so they prefer to depend on their own produce.
- In some areas, especially in the oases, it is considered shameful for a household to buy bread in the market.
- Home-made bread consisting of maize flour is still cheaper than the subsidized wheat bread bought at the bakeries.
- The state-controlled bakeries often sell bread of inferior quality, since the good flour is sold in the black market. Some bakeries offer a better-quality bread of the same type at a higher price, but this is too expensive for most people.

When the government tried to raise the bread price radically in the 1970s, this led to political unrest. However, pressured by the World Bank to stop the subsidies, the state reduced them gradually. Considering the country's food consumption statistics, we should remember that a great proportion of the cheap wheat flour delivered to the bakeries is used illegally as chicken feed. Table 8.6 shows that during 1998 Egypt had to import more than 40 per cent of the wheat consumed in the country, which cost more than 4.4 per cent of the country's total imports, about US$554 million (CAPMAS 2001b: 274ff). At the same time the value of the export of cotton and cotton yarn, Egypt's main agricultural export goods, reached only US$309 million. The decreasing self-sufficiency of the country in terms of staple foods is a topic of discussion among economics experts. As regards the huge wheat gap (see Figure 8.5) the question is being raised as to whether efforts should be made to produce greater amounts of wheat for domestic consumption, or whether it would be more profitable, since Egypt has excellent soils and a favourable climate, to produce agrarian goods of a higher value, like early vegetables or fruits, for

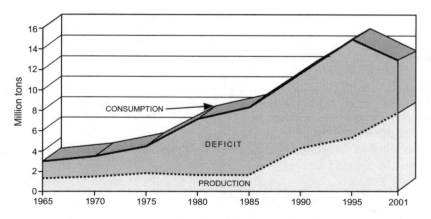

Figure 8.5 The wheat gap in Egypt (Author: F. Ibrahim 2002; cartography: J. Feilner; sources of data: Sadowski 1991; CAPMAS, Statistical Year Books for the years 1989–2001; Ministry of Information 2001b)

export. The GATT agreements, however, make it difficult for Egypt to sell its produce on the European markets.

Wheat production is of special relevance for Egypt for various reasons:

- If the country is dependent on wheat imports to a considerable extent, this might be used as a political weapon against it.
- Water requirements for growing wheat are relatively low (see Table 8.5). If other field crops with a greater water demand were to be cultivated instead, this might create problems, as there is already a water shortage in Egypt today.

From the point of view of the farmers, some other aspects are relevant:

- The cultivation of wheat is less labour intensive than that of most other crops, e.g. cotton.
- Wheat straw is an important fodder in Egypt, where animal feed is scarce. In the 1980s the price of straw was sometimes higher than that of the wheat itself. When the state tried to introduce a Mexican type of high-yielding wheat as part of the Green Revolution, the farmers refused to grow it although its yields of grain were higher than those of the local types of wheat. The reason they gave for this was that the stalks were short and not suitable as animal fodder.
- After the liberalization of Egyptian agriculture the cultivation of wheat started being profitable, while during the 1980s the farmers grew wheat unwillingly since the state, as the only buyer, paid very low prices. At the time they were only 68 per cent of the world market price which the state had to pay for the wheat it imported from abroad (Hamdan 1984a: 267).

Maize and rice (see Table 8.8)

Maize and rice have a comparatively high water requirement as compared to the traditional Egyptian staple grain of wheat (see Table 8.5). That is why formerly they were mostly cultivated in the *nili* season. The yields, especially of rice with its extreme water demand, were subject to great fluctuations depending on the amounts of water then available through the Nile flood. When after the construction of the Aswan High Dam more water was available for irrigation, cultivation of maize and of rice shifted in the main to the *seifi* season.

Table 8.8 shows the development of the cultivation of maize and rice between 1952 and 2000/01. During this time, the Green Revolution took place, so that the per acre yields increased drastically. Since the 1970s, and especially since the 1980s, high-yielding hybrid seeds have been introduced. This has meant that farmers cannot replant part of their own harvest but have to buy new seeds annually, which formerly had not been the case. The high-yielding crop types have a high water demand and usually also require the application of large amounts of fertilizers and pesticides, so that today Egypt ranks among the countries with the highest input rates of these. In 1994 the Egyptian parliament passed the first comprehensive law for the protection of the environment. Some now speak quite frankly about the contamination of soils with high loads of fertilizers and pesticides.

As Table 8.8 also shows, the area on which maize was cultivated increased slightly from 1952 to 2000/01, while the area on which rice was cultivated increased more than threefold. In the same span of time the per acre yields of maize tripled, while those of rice almost doubled. The total production of maize more than tripled and that of rice increased more than tenfold during the same period. In 1998/99 Egypt exported 350,000 tons of rice (Ministry of Information 2000: 114). The value of rice exports in 2000 was about US$94 million (CAPMAS 2001b: 279). Thus rice became the country's second-largest agricultural export commodity after cotton. However, Egypt could only export such great amounts of rice by importing cheap lower-quality rice from South-East Asia to cover local demand. As already mentioned, the maize harvested in Egypt plays an important role in the production of bread, but it is also used as animal feed. This explains why Egypt imported maize costing US$500 million in 2000 (CAPMAS 2001b: 280), but was self-sufficient in the maize required for its population's food. The overall degree of self-sufficiency in maize was 56.6 per cent in 2000/01.

Because of its high water requirement and its relative salt tolerance, rice is almost exclusively grown in the Nile delta and in Faiyum, while maize is grown all over the Nile valley and the Nile delta with a more or less equal distribution. In order to save water for irrigation in Toshka, the government

Table 8.8 Maize and rice – Egypt's production and degree of self-sufficiency before and after the Green Revolution (1952 and 2000/01)

	Area cultivated (*feddans*)*	Yield (kg/*feddan*)	Production (tons)	Self-sufficiency (%)
Maize:				
1952	1,704,000	880	1,506,000	c.100
2000/01	1,839,000	3,520	6,474,000	56.6**
Change (%)	+8	+300	+330	−43.4
Rice:				
1952	374,000	1,380	517,000	c. 100
2000/01	1,567,000	3,830	6,002,000	100
Increase (%)	+319	+178	+1,061	+/−0

* 1 *feddan* = 1.038 acre; ** This figure gives the country's overall self-sufficiency in maize and takes into consideration the high imports of fodder maize.

Sources: after CAPMAS 1993: 43ff; Ministry of Information 2002a; Gamal-el-Din 2001 (**)

plans to reduce the area of rice cultivation in the Nile delta by more than half. This is, however, a highly controversial issue, especially given that agronomists maintain that rice is highly suitable for the salty soils of the northern delta. According to the Ministry of Information (2002b) the area targeted for rice cultivation was 600,000 acres less than the year before.

Sorghum

For several decades, Egypt has been among the leading countries with respect to the per acre yields of sorghum (2.74 tons/acre in 2000/01; Ministry of Information 2002a). The area under cultivation, however, was subject to great fluctuations because of competition with maize. Between 1980 and 1989 alone, the area planted with sorghum decreased by 25.4 per cent in favour of maize. From 1990 it increased gradually, so that it reached 468,000 *feddans* (486,000 acres) in 2000/01 (ibid.). The reason was that those responsible had come to understand, particularly after the low water level of the Nile in the second half of the 1980s had led to a decline in maize yields, that sorghum is more drought resistant and more salt tolerant than maize. At present the government encourages the cultivation of sorghum on saline soils as well as at the ends of irrigation canals that do not receive enough water when the water level is low.

Sorghum serves as food for the people and as animal feed. Its nutrient content is higher than that of the maize with which it competes: it contains 30 per cent more calories, and the protein and fat production per acre is higher than for all other types of grain grown in Egypt (Simons 1968: 124). Among the different types of grain produced in Egypt, sorghum ranked in fourth place after maize, wheat and rice with a production of 1,328,000 tons in 2000/01 (Ministry of Information 2002a). Since it requires relatively high temperatures it is mainly cultivated in Upper Egypt. In 1985–87 the areas on which sorghum was grown were in the governorates of Sohag (40 per cent), Asyut (33.9 per cent), and El-Faiyum (12.5 per cent), as well as El-Minya, Beni Suef and Giza (together 13.6 per cent). Before the construction of the Aswan High Dam more sorghum was cultivated in the *nili* period (August to December) than today (1960–63: 11.5 per cent; Simons 1968: 134); it is now mostly cultivated in the *seifi* period (March to July) (1996–99: 97.1 per cent; CAPMAS 2000: 40ff).

Barley

When Napoleon conquered Egypt in 1798 the scientists who accompanied his army described barley as the most common field crop in the country. From then the area on which it was cultivated shrank drastically, reaching its minimum at only 88,100 *feddans* in 1988. During the following years it increased again and was at 172,000 *feddans* in 2000/01. The cultivation of barley has been shifted to desert areas, where it is grown as a pioneer cultivation plant on newly reclaimed land which has sandy saline soils lacking in humus, so that the production of barley now takes place mostly in governorates with a high percentage of soils of inferior quality. In 1985–87 the largest areas of barley cultivation were in the governorates of El-Beheira, including the desert land reclamation project of Tahrir-Province (26 per cent), in Esh-Sharqiya (17 per cent), El-Faiyum (11 per cent) and Ismailiya (9 per cent). Cultivation of barley in Upper Egypt is negligible. There are two main reasons for the decline in the cultivation of barley in Egypt in the twentieth century. The first and most important is that the food habits of the people changed. They developed a preference for maize and wheat, so that barley is used mainly as animal feed now, especially for poultry. The second reason is that barley as a winter crop has been replaced by *bersim*, which is of dual use: as animal feed (see below) and as a means of soil improvement through nitrogen fixation before the cultivation of cotton.

4.3 Leguminous crops and oil-producing plants

Leguminous crops, such as fava beans (*Vicia faba*; *ful*), lentils, chickpeas, lupins and fenugreek (*Trigonella foenum-graecum*; *helba*), are mainly cultivated in Middle and Upper Egypt as winter crops. Because of their high protein content, legumes, and especially fava beans, have always played an important role in Egypt as a meat substitute, especially for the poorer population. The fava bean, in Egypt known as *ful*, is a staple food in the country. Most Egyptians, especially those in towns, eat *ful* and flat bread for breakfast practically daily. The beans are cooked overnight on a very small flame and can be prepared in many ways. Usually they are consumed warm with salt, oil, lemon and cumin. The traditional food stands and the hawkers with pots on their carts offer *ful* and *ta'miya* (falafel) made of ground fava beans as a cheap hot meal at all times of the day. The production of fava beans in Egypt cannot fulfil the demand. In 1980 the self-sufficiency rate was 86 per cent; in 2000/01 it had increased to 94 per cent, by which time the area on which the beans were grown covered 413,000 *feddans* (Ministry of Information 2002a).

The self-sufficiency rate of lentils is much lower and was only 8.8 per cent of the country's requirements in 1998 (CAPMAS 2001b: 70). This is why lentils, another Egyptian staple food, and also once very important for the poorer population, are today relatively expensive. Chickpeas, fenugreek (*helba*) and lupins are today among the traditional foods which are less frequently consumed in Egypt. Chickpeas are usually eaten roasted like nuts, while fenugreek is mostly consumed in germinated form. *Helba* seeds are prepared like tea in case of stomach pain or for lactating mothers, but are also one of the ingredients of the traditional pastry-like bread called *bettau*, which the rural women of Middle Egypt bake to this day. The production of lentils, chickpeas and lupins is shrinking and stood at about 23,100 tons in total in 1999 (ibid.: 45f).

The vegetable oil produced in the country is mostly cottonseed oil. It is

19. *Sphinx and Pyramids of Giza*: The 4,500-year-old Sphinx and the Pyramids of Giza are the ancient monuments visited most frequently by tourists in Egypt. (Photo: F. Ibrahim)

produced all over the Nile valley and the Nile delta. In 2000/01 Egypt had to import 65.2 per cent of its requirements of edible oil (see Table 8.6), while annual production in 1999/2000 was 403,000 tons. Other oil-producing plants accounted for a cultivation area of 267,000 *feddans* (CAPMAS 2001b: 82; Ministry of Information 2002b). The following oil-producing plants are cultivated, listed here according to size of cultivation area:

- groundnuts (summer crop): preferably grown on the sandy soils of the eastern delta
- sesame (summer crop): mainly grown in Qena
- soybeans (summer crop): mainly grown in Beni Suef, El-Gharbiya and El-Minufiya
- flax (linen; winter crop): grown almost exclusively in the governorate of Ismailiya
- sunflowers (summer crop): grown mostly in El-Faiyum and Beni Suef; the cultivation area of this important plant could easily be extended
- olives: mostly grown in Marsa Matruh, including Siwa Oasis, El-Faiyum and on northern Sinai; recently large areas of newly reclaimed land were planted with olive trees.

The cultivation of soybeans and sunflowers was introduced in Egypt only in the 1960s. It was hoped that the soybean especially, with its high content of protein and of fat, would make a significant contribution to feeding the people as well as animals. So far, however, soy products are not consumed by Egyptians at all. Most groundnuts harvested are sold roasted for direct consumption or used as ingredients for sweets, biscuits or cakes. Sesame is consumed as *halawa tehiniya* in sweet form with bread, or as a salad with salt, spices and lemon as a side dish. The production of olive oil is rare and takes place only in desert areas, such as Siwa Oasis. However, green or black olives are frequently consumed after having been preserved in salt.

4.4 The most important field crops in Egypt: fodder plants

There are few natural pastures for the country's animal population in Egypt's desert climate. Therefore fodder has to be produced by the *fellaheen* on irrigated fields to feed their more than 18 million head of livestock, as well as about 31 million domestically raised rabbits (2000; after CAPMAS 2001b: 52ff). The most widespread fodder plant, *bersim* (*Trifolium alexandrinum*), an Egyptian variety of clover, has accounted for more than 95 per cent of all fodder cultivation areas recently (e.g. 1980 and 1991; Ministry of Agriculture 1992: 104f). However, this primary source of animal feed in Egypt can stand neither heat nor aridity and so is not grown in summer. It was cultivated on 50 per cent of the whole area planted with winter crops in 1989, but this decreased to 39 per cent in 1999. The common type of *bersim* is grown for one season from December to May, during which time it can be cut three to four times, but about one-third of it is cut only once and then mulched (*bersim tahrish*). The soils improved in this way are planted the following summer either with cotton or maize, which require good soils and profit from the nitrogen fixation supplied by the roots of *bersim* and through the creation of humus by mulching. In summer there is a shortage of green fodder, so that dry feed must be used, such as maize, barley, dried *bersim* (*daris*), and wheat straw (*tibn*), as well as the high-quality feed of the residues (*kusb*) of the cotton seeds remaining after the production of cottonseed oil. Among the few fodder plants available in summer are soybeans, *lubya* (*Dolichos lablab*; hyacinth beans), Sudan grass (*Sorghum sudanensis*), elephant grass (*Pennisetum benthamii*) and fodder beet. These mostly introduced fodder crops help to solve the problem of lack of feed in summer and are not liable to endanger cotton production by hosting the cotton boll-worm. Other fodder plants such as the fava bean, the meadow pea (*Lathyrus pratensis*), fenugreek (*Trigonella foenum-graecum*) and barley are not available in summer, since they, too, are winter crops. An extension of the cultivation of *bersim higazi* (Spanish trefoil; *Medicago sativa*), a clover of superior quality, is not possible since like the common type of *bersim* it enhances the spread of the cotton boll-worm. Therefore its cultivation is limited to peripheral, mainly desert areas, far away from the cotton-growing areas. *Bersim higazi* remains on the field for five to six years and can be cut about nine times annually. So far no real solution has been found for the seasonal fodder scarcity problem, with the result that many farmers feed their animals on the green leaves of still-growing maize plants, although the grain yields can be reduced by about 40 per cent through this practice (Hamdan 1984a: 326).

The question is whether it is really desirable given the land shortage in the country to turn plant production into animal production. From the point of view of the *fellaheen*, this form of processing of biomass seems to be worthwhile, otherwise they would be unlikely to practise it. In terms of the macro-economy, other factors have to be taken into consideration. It was discovered that the production of one hundred calories through the meat of the water buffalo is fifty-five times as costly as the same amount produced through maize or sorghum, and twenty-one times as costly as through fava beans, which are also of high nutritional value for other reasons (Abdel-Fadil 1975: 75). Until the 1990s price relations in Egypt were extremely distorted through state subsidies for bread and the control of prices for agrarian goods, so that often prices for animal feed were higher than those for food for the people. When, in the 1980s, the price of wheat straw was six times as high as that of wheat, the *fellaheen* naturally tried to sell their wheat unthreshed, though this was illegal. The competition between the cultivation of fodder plants and of crops for human consumption will lead to a critical situation in Egypt in the very near future, since demand for meat is growing steadily in the country. This is due not only to the population explosion, but also to changing food habits in certain sectors of Egyptian society. Between 1972 and 1998 the annual per capita consumption of meat, including poultry, nearly tripled (CAPMAS 1980: 218; CAPMAS 2000: 72). Three factors are mainly responsible for this:

- The high rate of urbanization: urban people in Egypt consume more meat than the rural population.
- The remittances of Egyptians working in the Arab countries to their relatives at home often lead to a rising standard of living among the latter and especially to their consuming higher-quality food.
- Structural changes in the economy during recent decades have led to the rise of a newly rich social class which has higher demands, not least concerning food.

Today Egyptian agriculture planners unanimously wish to see the cultivation area of *bersim* reduced in favour of that of wheat. But since farmers gain about 52 per cent more if they cultivate *bersim* rather than wheat (Ministry of Agriculture 1991: 553ff), their plans must remain unrealistic. The interests of the different groups differ greatly in one other point: Egyptian agronomists would like to see a change from traditional animal husbandry to a more rationalized fattening of the animals, as well as to specialized dairy farming.

For the *fellaheen*, however, their animals are also very important as beasts of burden, which they depend on for turning the water wheel and for pulling the hook plough (see Illustration 8) and thresher (see Illustration 9), as well as for transport. Experts whose aim is modernization of Egyptian agriculture consider these things a waste of valuable energy, which should rather be diverted into producing meat and milk. They want to replace animal power and see more engines and tractors employed. In doing so, they overlook the fact that the *fellaheen* cannot afford agricultural machines and that for them they are not suitable, since they own only very small plots: 82 per cent of them possess farms of less than 2 acres (see Table 8.3). Models for development imported from Europe or the USA cannot simply be transferred since they do not suit the particular conditions of Egyptian agriculture. But a solution to one of Egypt's greatest challenges today will have to be found very soon: namely, the best possible distribution of scarce agrarian land among the different field crops.

4.5 Fruits and vegetables

The situation concerning the production of fruits and vegetables in Egypt is not unlike that pertaining in the production of fodder. Table 8.4 shows that during the last five decades, the area cultivated with fruits as a proportion of the total area of agrarian land increased more than eightfold. If we consider that the cultivation of fruits in orchards means that the land cannot be used for a second harvest in the same year, as would be possible if it were planted with other crops, the area should be considered to be double this. All kinds of fruits are consumed in Egypt, mainly by the better-off townspeople. The cultivation of fruit trees entails a long-term investment, and is therefore usually undertaken by the richer entrepreneurs in towns. For these reasons a further extension of fruit cultivation in Egypt at the cost of grain production will increase social injustice in the country. An example of this is the development of the area covered by apple plantations, which was insignificant once and then increased rapidly, so that it stood at 1,700 *feddans* in 1971 (Simons 1977: 597) and 76,000 *feddans* in 1995 (CAPMAS 1998: 47), with an upward trend. Apples are still very expensive in the country and are consumed only by richer people. Formerly, only imported apples from the USA, Iran, Lebanon or Cyprus were available on the Egyptian market. Today the amounts imported have been reduced after local production increased threefold between 1991 and 1995, so that it amounted to 438,000 tons (CAPMAS 1998: 53). The areas of cultivation are mainly on newly reclaimed land, 70 per cent of them in the desert province of Nubariya, west of the delta. The new types of apples cultivated were introduced from the USA in a campaign to make the desert green in the 1970s. The first apples can already be harvested one or two years after the planting of the trees, which makes them more profitable for investors than citrus, which can be harvested for the first time after

20. Pharaonic Island, Gulf of Aqaba: The Gulf of Aqaba is a favourite holiday area not only for foreign tourists, in particular visitors from Israel, but of late also for Egyptians of the higher income classes. However, at times tourism here suffers from political instability in the region. (Photo: F. Ibrahim)

about four years, or olive trees, which are harvested for the first time after about six years. The main harvest of the new espalier cultures is in summer, meaning that older schoolchildren can be employed in it during their long summer holidays. Egypt considers Libya, which imports great amounts of apples annually, Saudi Arabia and the United Arab Emirates as target markets. However, to succeed in these markets it will have to compete with products from Turkey and Lebanon. Further new types of fruit produced in Egypt and sold in the markets at relatively high prices are strawberries and cantaloupes, a particularly tasty type of melon.

The figures reported here do not include the 6.6 million date palms, which are grown all over the Nile valley and in the oases (see Illustration 6) on agrarian land. Dates are nutritious and also affordable to the poorer people, who like to consume them especially during the Ramadan season. Watermelons, which were grown on 10 per cent of the agricultural land cultivated with vegetables in 1995–97 according to the official data (CAPMAS 1998: 49), are also relatively cheap. The cultivation of fruits is mostly concentrated in northern and Middle Egypt for logistical reasons. For climatic reasons, however, we find a concentration of date and banana production in Upper Egypt. For hydro-economic reasons an extension of the cultivation area of fruits is not desirable, since about half of all the types grown in Egypt are tropical or subtropical species, like citrus and banana, and therefore have a high water demand.

The area planted with vegetables as a proportion of the whole cultivated area of Egypt increased fivefold in the five decades from 1950 to 1999, which has to be considered a positive development, since vegetables are an important component of the diet of all classes of Egyptian society. The development is also due to a change in people's nutritional habits, which accompanied the urbanization process. Townspeople consume more commercially produced vegetables and fruit, while rural people pick wild plants and grow their own vegetables. The favourable temperatures in Egypt at all times of the year allow the production of nearly all kinds of vegetables. So those of the temperate zone such as cabbage, carrots, potatoes and beetroots can be grown as well as those of the Mediterranean climate such as peppers, aubergines and artichokes, and those of the tropical zone such as *bamia* (okra; ladies' fingers; *Hibiscus esculentus*), *mulukhiya* (Jews' mallow; *Corchorius olitorius*), and *qulqas* (arrowroot; *Maranta*). The cultivation of vegetables takes place all over the Nile valley and in the Nile delta, where the biggest towns are. For climatic reasons, but also for easier marketing, the cultivation of some vegetables, for example potatoes, French beans, carrots, cauliflower and artichokes, is concentrated in the Nile delta as well as around Giza.

Among the various types of fruits and vegetables we find one prominent species each. For the fruits this is citrus. It was cultivated on 36 per cent of the total cultivated area of fruit, while the cultivation areas of the three types of fruit next in significance, grapes, peaches and apples, covered only 14 per cent, 9 per cent and 8 per cent respectively in 1995 (CAPMAS 1998: 47). As for vegetables, tomatoes rank in first place with 30 per cent of the whole cultivation area of vegetables in 1999 (CAPMAS 2001b: 43). The fava bean, which is normally grown on an area of similar size and sold dry, does not count as a vegetable in the statistics. It is grown all over the country, with a concentration on Upper Egypt.

Egyptians view the recent import regulations of the European Union with great concern, since they limit their chances of exporting fruits and vegetables radically. It is hoped to increase exports to the Arab states, although no striking success has been achieved so far. In 2000/01 Egypt exported agricultural products amounting to US$590 million, 8.4 per cent of the value of the country's total commodity exports (Ministry of Information 2002b). The main vegetables and fruits exported are onions, citrus, potatoes and garlic. Since the gains from fruit and vegetable production are two to three times as high for the producers as those from wheat, Egyptian economists would like to see an increase in the production of agrarian export goods of high value, maximizing use of scarce agrarian land. Hamdan (1984a: 338) calculated that Egypt could earn sufficient foreign currency to pay for its wheat imports if it found a way of exporting the strawberries grown on 27,500 *feddans*. However, the export of fresh products, such as citrus and potatoes, is suffering from costly, cumbersome and time-consuming regulations. Exporters complain of having to procure permits from three ministries and three Customs-related offices, and of the inefficiency of both the seaport of Alexandria and of Cairo airport. This is one reason why Egypt is unable to compete with other similar suppliers in the region such as Morocco, Turkey and Israel. To promote the export of manufactured agricultural products, new large entrepreneurs, such as Faragello at Borg el-Arab el-Gedida, have adopted international quality standards (ISO), observing ecological and health requirements, and thus have managed to gain a foothold in the European market. Since Egypt signed an international agreement for the production of organic food, for which there exists a rising demand in Europe and other parts of the world, great hopes have been placed on the introduction of organic farming in particular areas of the country, such as Siwa and other relatively unpolluted oases of the Western Desert.

4.6 Sugar cane and sugar beet

Until 1965 Egypt used to produce a surplus of sugar. In 2000/01 the country's total sugar production amounted to nearly 1.4 million tons, 1 million tons from sugar cane and 0.4 million tons from sugar beet, while in the same year sugar consumption in Egypt was about 2.2 million tons. This marked a deficit of about 0.8 million tons, which had to be imported at a cost of approximately US$240 million (El-Batriq et al. 2001). Per capita consumption of sugar was 33.8 kg in 1999/2000, which was 1.5 times as high as the average worldwide per capita consumption. In 2000/01 Egypt had to import more than 40 per cent of its sugar requirements (see Table 8.6). The question arises as to whether Egypt will ever be self-sufficient in sugar again. Potential growth in the country's sugar production is limited. It seems impossible to increase per acre yields, for with an average yield of 48 tons/acre in 2000/01 (Ministry of Information 2002a) a maximum seems to have been reached. Expansion into other cultivation areas is not advisable for the following reasons:

- The cultivation of sugar cane takes place mostly on relatively heavy soils, which are only to be found in the old irrigated land of the Nile valley. Newly reclaimed land in the desert areas is not suitable. In practical terms this means that the production of sugar cane can only be increased at the cost of other, more important field crops.
- Sugar cane is no seasonal plant. It remains in the ground for a period of three years and is cut annually during this time. An alternative use of the land would allow, for example, an annual harvest of wheat and one harvest of maize.
- Sugar cane requires *c.* 16,800 m³ of water per *feddan* annually, i.e. sixteen times as much as wheat and 6.7 times as much as maize (see Table 8.5). Since water is an extremely scarce resource in Egypt, this means that,

according to hydro-economic calculations, Egypt would have to give up 16 *feddans* of land cultivated with wheat or 6.7 *feddans* of land cultivated with maize for every additional *feddan* of land on which sugar cane might be grown. Moreover, it has to be considered that the price of sugar on the international markets is much lower than the production costs in Egypt.

- Sugar cane is known as 'the crop of crime'. Attacks perpetrated by Islamist terrorists have taken place repeatedly from the criminals' hiding places in the sugar cane fields. This is why the government wants to reduce the areas of cultivation of this crop. Nevertheless, in 2000/01 305,000 *feddans* in Upper Egypt were cultivated with sugar cane (Ministry of Information 2002a).

At present a possible way out of the dilemma lies in the cultivation of sugar beet, which started in Egypt in the 1970s. In 2000/01, the area of cultivation, which is situated nearly exclusively in the northern Nile delta, reached 151,000 *feddans*, with a per *feddan* yield of 23.5 tons on average. In the first sugar beet factory, a French-Egyptian company built in Kafr esh-Sheikh, 95,000 tons of sugar were produced in 1993, i.e. 9.4 per cent of total sugar production, which amounted to more than 1 million tons in that year. The plant's capacity was expanded to 250,000 tons annually. In Belgas, Ed-Dagahliya, a second sugar beet factory, a Saudi–Egyptian joint venture, was started in the mid-1990s with a capacity of 120,000 tons of sugar annually. A third sugar factory of this kind was constructed in Faiyum with an annual capacity of 120,000 tons of sugar from sugar beet planted on 50,000 *feddans* (Internet 2001d). It stopped production in 2003. Since sugar beet has a lesser water demand but requires good soils, like sugar cane, it is improbable that it will replace sugar cane in the country in the long run. For the farmers, cultivation of sugar cane is particularly profitable. Among the important by-products are fodder, syrup, raw materials for the production of paper and alcohol as well as fuel and fertilizers. A disadvantage of sugar beet as compared to sugar cane which should not be overlooked is the fact that it can be attacked by pests that endanger the cultivation of cotton (Hamdan 1984a: 354).

5 Land reclamation – Egypt's hope for the future (see Figure 8.6 and Table 8.9)

As described above, the greatest problem in Egypt's agricultural sector is scarcity of arable land. However, this could be overcome to a certain extent, if water for irrigation could be secured at reasonable cost. Since the era of Nasser the state has made great efforts, accompanied by intensive propaganda, to reclaim desert land (see Table 8.9) and to open up new water sources, for example through the construction of As-Sadd el-Ali. However, as Barth and Shata (1987: 10) stated in the late 1980s, of the 900,000 *feddans* (378,000 ha)

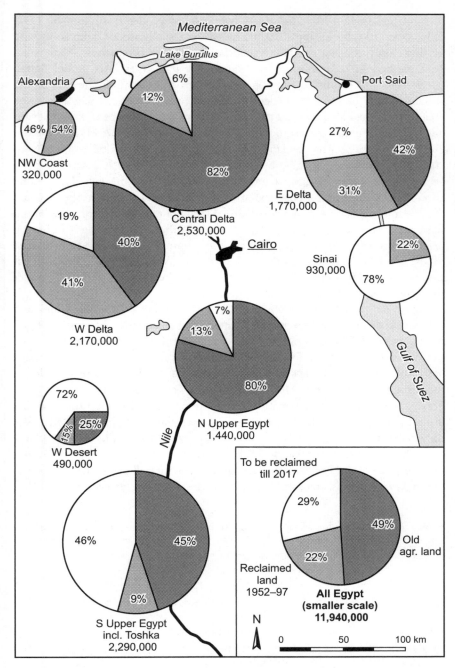

Figure 8.6 Old and new agricultural land in Egypt: regional distribution 1997–2017 (in *feddan*; 1 f = 1.038 acres) (Author: F. Ibrahim 2002; cartography: J. Feilner; sources: after CAPMAS 1999a; Ministry of Information 2000: 135ff)

of land reclaimed within the thirty-five years since the revolution of 1952, only about 500,000 *feddans* (210,000 ha) were actually under cultivation, and of these only 200,000 *feddans* (84,000 ha) were of a productivity that could be described as of minimum profitability. A few years later Abdel Fattah (1992: 100) also expressed the opinion that not more than about half of the reclaimed land had really reached productive capacity. Official data about the area of reclaimed land are, as mentioned, often exaggerated or lacking relevant detail. According to a government publication (CAPMAS 2002: 73) 3.17 million *feddans* (1.33 million ha) of land were reclaimed in the period from 1952 to 2000/2001. However, to give a realistic estimate of what has actually been achieved, we not only have to take into consideration the fact that merely about half of the areas mentioned are under cultivation, but also the fact that the average yields on the newly reclaimed land are extremely low, while at the same time input costs are very high. If a semi-official publication is right, the productivity of the newly reclaimed land amounts only to one-fifth of that of the old land in the Nile valley (*Al-Ahram*, 15 April 1995: 20). This is what makes land reclamation in desert areas a doubtful enterprise, especially under the economic conditions prevailing in Egypt.

Figure 8.6 shows that the share of the governorates of the Nile valley and the central delta in the government's future land reclamation programmes will be rather small. This is due to the fact that the gravel-covered high terraces of the Nile are not suitable for land reclamation, and also that the government has abandoned its old plans to continue drying out Lake Burullus in order to reclaim agricultural land. This figure also shows that from 1952 to 1997 the greatest share of land reclamation, i.e. 55 per cent of the land made arable in that period, was on the western and eastern flanks of the Nile delta. Not only were the topographical conditions and the soil quality advantageous there, but also the water was accessible. However, in the government's future programmes of land reclamation the greatest share will go to two peripheral regions, where it is envisaged that huge development projects will absorb

Table 8.9 Areas of land reclamation in Egypt since 1952 according to various sources

Period	Total area of reclaimed land	Source of information
1952–68/69	365,000 ha	Marei, Minister for Agriculture and Agrarian Reform 1970: 360
1952–78	391,000 ha	Samaha, Minister for Irrigation 1980: 36
1952–85	380,300 ha	Wali, Minister for Agriculture and Agrarian Reform 1985: 37

Source: F. Ibrahim 2003

several million Egyptians from the congested Nile valley. These regions, which are scheduled to constitute 65 per cent of the area to be reclaimed up to 2017, are on the one hand the south-western desert, embracing Toshka, East Uweinat and Darb el-Arbain, and on the other North Sinai together with the eastern bank of the Suez Canal. Whether these gigantic new projects, especially those in the south-western desert, will meet a better fate than their predecessor, El-Wadi el-Gedid project, is a matter of speculation. For the hopes raised by the great campaign launched by Gamal Abdel Nasser forty years earlier were by no means less than those raised today in connection with the Toshka mega-project. Nasser's dream to reclaim 5 million *feddans* of the Western Desert with the help of groundwater did not materialize, and up to the present day only 40,000 *feddans* have been reclaimed, constituting only 1 per cent of the targeted area.

5.1 Land reclamation in the Nile delta and at the Mediterranean coast

The western delta and the north-west coast

In this region, in the governorate of El-Beheira alone, lay 27 per cent of the total area of land reclaimed in Egypt up until 2001. Here we find the greatest of Nasser's land reclamation projects that actually materialized: Mudiriyet et-Tahrir (Liberation Province). The land was reclaimed originally for irrigation using Nile water and then given to small-scale farmers. The later development in the western delta, especially in West Nubariya and Natrun Valley, followed other principles. Since the times of Presidents Sadat and Mubarak, attempts had been made to distribute the land among graduates of the agrarian schools, but great tracts were taken by wealthy Cairenes and former high-ranking military personnel. They were able to invest great amounts of capital and established plantations on which grapes, apples, strawberries, potatoes and other types of fruit and vegetable were grown, for which they expected to find good markets in the country or abroad. Some established poultry farms, demand for the products of which is high in Egypt.

One of the new large-scale agricultural projects of the 1990s (see Chapter 12), for the irrigation of the country's north-western coastal strip, has been under way for several years now. Starting from the Rosetta Nile arm, the An-Nasr Canal is being built to the west at a length of 82 km for the irrigation of 318,000 *feddans*. A second section in the west, called the Al-Hammam Canal, is also under construction. It is 50 km long and is intended to irrigate 72,000 *feddans*. Its westward extension will be 75 km long and is to facilitate the irrigation of 148,000 *feddans*. Until 2000/01 infrastructure works for these two canals had been carried out over 186 km (Ministry of Information 2002b).

In December 2000 the Minister of Water Resources and Irrigation announced the launch of a new project for the reclamation of 200,000 *feddans* west of the Nile delta with the help of a 31-km-long canal branching off westwards from the Rosetta Nile arm and a water pumping station of a capacity of 12 million m³ daily. The project will take five years to implement and is to cost LE3 billion, to be paid in instalments by the owners of the land (Internet 2000c). Before the start of this project almost the entire desert strip along the road between Cairo and Alexandria was already occupied by rich people's farms with pretentious villas behind high walls and guarded gates: a new form of gated feudalism. Only a few of these farms are actually functioning economically. This is obviously a revival of the old spirit of 'rental capitalism' (see Chapter 7), for the urban-based owners are no farmers and, at most, spend their weekends here. Their main intention is to secure possession of cheap land for speculative purposes and to make full use of the privileges and concessions granted by the state. A state-owned weekly published a report on what is called 'the land mafia' in Wadi en-Natrun, according to which top officials and their relatives got hold of estates of up to 7,500 *feddans* each (*The Egyptian Gazette*, 14 March 2000: 7). Most of them made very small down payments without ever completing the instalments. Though they received the land from the state on condition that they should use it for farming or for industrial purposes, only 3 per cent did so. Most of the land was sold later at high prices to real-estate speculators.

The situation of the small-scale farms on the 'old new land', as the early generation of reclaimed land is called, is quite different. In the process of privatization and of diluting the public sector, the state-owned farms in these land reclamation areas were distributed among former employees of the farms on very generous terms. Other small-scale farmers are the young graduates of agricultural schools and colleges who were granted land by the state. Many of the small farms, however, suffer from serious problems: shortage of irrigation water, a permanent increase in the costs of power for the water pumps, transportation difficulties, a general increase in production costs, and failure in marketing the products. Thus, in early 2001, the oranges were left unpicked on the trees, because their off-farm prices, which were only one-seventh of the prices paid in Cairo, were far under the production costs (Al-Basil 2001). Al-Basil investigated the case of 500 graduates in the South Et-Tahrir reclamation area and described the situation as follows. After the state-run company had stopped marketing the products in 1998, the small-scale farmers were unable to manage this themselves owing to their lack of expertise. In addition, the products were unsuitable for export since the fruit trees were suffering from various pests. Also, the price of fertilizers had risen sixteenfold in only a few years, while off-farm prices had dropped by half. To meet the rising production costs the farmers had drawn bank credits at high interest rates, reaching 14 per cent annually. The average debt of these farmers climbed to LE60,000, and they were hardly in a position to pay the annual interest rates. The 'mother' of all problems, as one of the affected farmers put it, was the shortage of irrigation water. After the distribution of the land previously belonging to the local state farm among small farmers, they had shifted from growing field crops with low water requirements to growing fruit trees such as oranges and bananas, which have a high water demand. To combat the water shortage, they had dug more wells and extracted much more water than before. So they had reached the deeper aquifer, which contained saline water from the Mediterranean. Irrigation with saline water, together with the lack of a functioning drainage system, had made the soils deteriorate and destroyed many orchards (ibid.).

The eastern delta and Sinai

According to government plans, the greatest expansion of agrarian land in Egypt is in future to take place in the eastern Nile delta and on Sinai. Until 2001 about 690,000 *feddans* of desert land had been reclaimed there (CAPMAS 2003a: 23). Development on Sinai is to take place primarily along the Mediterranean coast between Dumyat and El-Arish and will be supported by the construction of the Salam ('peace') Canal. The canal was planned for a capacity of 4.45 billion m^3 annually, half of which will be taken from the Nile south of Dumyat, and the rest from recycled agricultural drainage water. The water is to be used for the irrigation of 220,000 *feddans* west of the Suez Canal and 400,000 *feddans* in northern Sinai, reclamation of which is still under way. Work on the first phase of this huge project is about to be completed, including construction of the Dumyat Dam, an 87-km-long canal and a water culvert underneath the Suez Canal. On Sinai about half of the infrastructure for the LE5.5 billion project had been completed by the beginning of 2001. This included the excavation of part of the 175-km-long Sheikh-Jaber Canal, the installation of two of the three projected water-pumping stations, as well as the construction of two of the thirty-five planned model villages. Owing to its location near the densely populated Nile delta and the country's economic centre of Greater Cairo, as well as its Mediterranean climate with the higher air humidity favourable to agriculture, this project seems to have a greater chance of success than the projects in the Western Desert. However, the major question, which has been left largely unanswered, is where Egypt is going to find the billions of cubic metres of water required for the project when the country is already suffering a water shortage.

Three of the land reclamation projects in this region are discussed below.

Draining the coastal lagoons One of the main areas of land reclamation in the northern and north-eastern Nile delta is the lagoons along the Mediterranean coast. Up to 1984 67,700 *feddans*, i.e. 13 per cent of the lakes area, had already been drained. According to the plans, 265,000 *feddans*, i.e. 63 per cent of the whole area of the lagoons, was to be drained by 2000 (*Al-Ahram* 1984: 3). In 2001 Lake Manzala had already lost 80 per cent of its former area.

The results so far, however, are not encouraging. Some of the drawbacks that became evident are:

- Agriculture is generally unprofitable here. The value of the fish catch extracted from the same areas had been greater than that of the agricultural produce grown on the saline soils after the draining of the lagoons.
- Much of the local population is deprived of the chance of earning a living here today. Owing to the low degree of productivity of the reclaimed land only a few former fishermen who lost their original jobs here can live off the newly introduced farming. This is why many of them started digging ponds in the fields to make fish farms. For the country's economy this meant a double loss. To get the project under way the state invested *c.* US$2,400/*feddan* for the drainage of the lakes. Then high costs arose in reversing the procedure (ibid.). Added to this, most of the reclaimed land was distributed among people of influence and not among the local fishermen who are the losers in the project (ibid.).
- Production of valuable animal protein, of which there is a deficit in Egypt, was reduced. For many years a large proportion of the country's requirements in meat, fish and dairy products had to be imported from abroad and substantial investments had to be made to produce these locally. Fish – formerly cheap and therefore consumed by those not so well off – is an expensive food item today, for the middle classes also.
- The lakes suffer additional pollution. The coastal lagoons, which had already been polluted through industrial and household waste water, are now under new stress through immissions of herbicides, pesticides and chemical fertilizers from the surrounding areas under agricultural use. Lake Manzala, for example, receives daily 11 million m^3 of pollutants: 2 million m^3 from Cairo's sewage and 9 million m^3 of drainage from agricultural land. The increase in organic matter in the water of the remaining parts of the lagoons has already led to severe eutrophy and to an increase in water weeds. Water hyacinths became a serious problem in Lake Manzala (ibid.).

The Bitter Lakes project (see Figure 8.7) The so-called Bitter Lakes project was the first enterprise of land reclamation on Sinai in which Nile water was used. It was started under Nasser, but completely destroyed in 1967 by the Israeli army. Under Sadat it was re-established. The Nile water used is diverted from the Ismailiya Canal and conducted through a system of pipes under the Suez Canal. Since there is a difference in height of 11 metres east and west of the canal, pumps had to be installed to raise the water. The areas reclaimed are part of the former beds of the Bitter Lakes but have in the meantime been covered by sheets of Aeolian sand. The weakly developed soils possess high contents of gypsum and soluble salts, especially sodium. Through irrigation

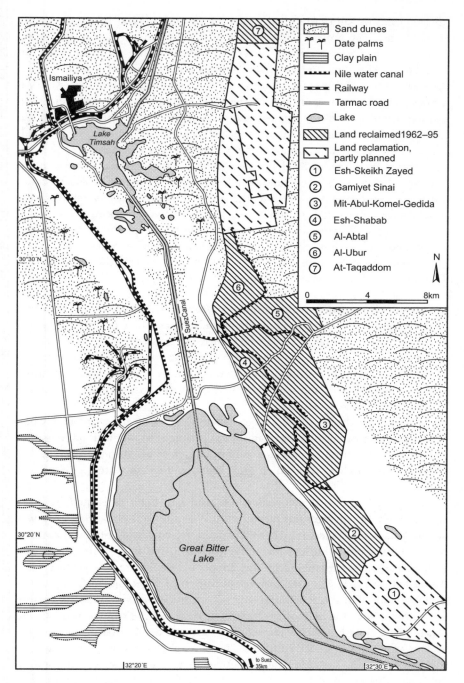

Figure 8.7 Land reclamation on the Great Bitter Lake, Sinai (Author: F. Ibrahim 2002; cartography: J. Feilner; sources: Israel Survey 1977 [map] and survey F. Ibrahim 1996)

the processes of salinization and formation of gypsum and calcareous crusts are enhanced. The project was originally meant for flood irrigation, but during the time of Sadat the drainage system was filled up and sprinkler irrigation introduced. After the land had been subdivided into plots of 5 *feddans* each, the new owners did not continue with the sprinkler irrigation system. Two factors were mainly responsible for this. The authorities in charge were slow and inefficient in carrying out routine maintenance as well as repairs to the technical infrastructure, so that this was frequently not functioning. Second, cooperation between the large number of landowners was lacking, in particular since many of them lived in town. Without such constant cooperation, however, the system's huge centre-pivot units of a diameter of 450 m could not work effectively. According to the project's plans about twenty farmers should have cooperated in running each unit. However, owing to technical problems, as well as to the users' failure fully to accept the system, it was abandoned after a short time. The farmers made their own decision and applied flood irrigation, with which they were more familiar, wherever possible. This led to serious negative consequences:

- Since flood irrigation requires much more water than sprinkler irrigation, the amount of water that could be provided was sufficient only for a small part of the land that had been reclaimed at such high cost.
- The land had been prepared for sprinkler irrigation, for which levelling of the ground is not necessary. When the farmers applied flood irrigation, the higher parts of the land remained dry while those lower down were waterlogged.
- As described above, the drainage canals were filled up with sand when introduction of sprinkler irrigation was planned. So when flood irrigation was later practised, a drainage system, which is an absolute prerequisite for it, was lacking. This led to great damage through waterlogging.

Up until 2001 about 30,000 *feddans* of land had been reclaimed here, of which about 50 per cent was farmed. Much of the land already utilized was at Mit-Abul-Kom el-Gedida, where a cooperative consisting of 400 members, mostly remigrants who had formerly worked in the Gulf States, had been formed: 160 active members of this cooperative cultivated 15 *feddans* each. About half the land was used for the cultivation of vegetables and fruit under drip irrigation. On the remaining land wheat, barley, groundnuts and sesame were grown with the help of sprinkler irrigation. Of the twenty-four existing centre-pivot units fourteen were working at the time. A total of about 2,400 *feddans* of land was under cultivation here. New extensions were located in the villages of Al-Taqaddom and Al-Amal in the north (Survey F. Ibrahim 2001; see also Figure 8.7).

The people who profited from the Bitter Lakes project were either army veterans, people who had worked abroad and owned capital, or graduates of certain professional colleges or universities who were given land, since it was believed that they possessed the necessary know-how to manage it profitably. Most of them, however, worked primarily in other professions and considered it an additional source of income or merely a worthwhile investment. The Bedouin of Sinai were barely represented among the owners; neither were the landless *fellaheen* from the Nile valley given a chance here. The distribution of the land, as elsewhere, did not follow social principles. Since the state owed great sums of money to the contractors who carried out the land reclamation work, it had to sell part of the land to those who owned the necessary capital in order to be able to pay the contractors. Former members of the military were exempted from paying for the land they received. In 1995 the project started to expand by about 40,000 *feddans* in a southward direction. The new project area bears the name of its sponsor, Esh-Sheikh Zayed, President of the United Arab Emirates. In 2001 work there had not yet been completed. In 2000 a new section of about 4,000 *feddans* in the north called Al-Amal was reclaimed and divided among young graduates of agricultural colleges (Survey F. Ibrahim 2001). The project may well profit from the construction of two new bridges across the Suez Canal, completed in 2001: the El-Ferdan railway bridge and the El-Qantara bridge for cars.

Es-Salhiya agricultural model project (see Figure 8.8) In 1978 the largest and technically most sophisticated land reclamation project of the era was launched at Es-Salhiya in the desert of the eastern delta margin. It was a joint-venture project among five investing companies, the most important of which were the Arab Contractors Company and Pepsi Cola International, which held 60 per cent and 15 per cent of the capital respectively. Modern centre-pivot and drip irrigation methods were used to cultivate 55,000 *feddans* which had been reclaimed from the desert. The main field products were vegetables and fodder. The latter was used to raise beef and dairy cattle of high-quality European breeds. A total of twenty-three chicken farms were also established within the project. In 1982/83 the project had revenue of about US$8 million, divided as follows: 36 per cent from fattened cattle, 10 per cent from milk, 30 per cent from eggs, and 24 per cent from field crops, mainly vegetables (Arab Contractors' Publication No. 40, 1983). By 1990, however, the project had almost come to a standstill. The running and production costs had been higher than the revenues from the beginning. The management could draw a veil over its economic fiasco as long as the project was profiting from state subsidies and enjoying exceptionally generous state facilities on account of the fact that Osman, the owner of Arab Contractors Co., was a relative of Sadat's. When the latter died in 1981, his successor curbed Osman's irregular-ities. In 2001 the project was slowly being rehabilitated under the control of the Ministry of Agriculture. The Arab Contractors Co. incurred a heavy debt burden of LE2 billion. However, the state itself was also indebted by LE3.5 billion to that company (*Middle East Times* 2001).

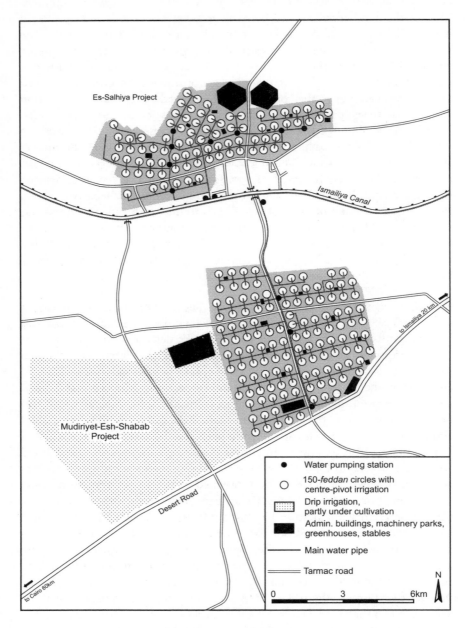

Figure 8.8 Agricultural model project of Es-Salhiya (Author: F. Ibrahim 2002; cartography: J. Feilner; source: after Arab Contractors' Publication No. 40, 1983)

The central delta

In the governorates of Kafr esh-Sheikh and Daqahliya in the northern part of the central Nile delta, attempts have been made for several decades to re-claim land through the drainage of coastal lagoons. Until 1999/2000 258,200 *feddans* of land had been reclaimed here in this way (CAPMAS 2003a: 23). The hazards are manifold, since the northern parts of the Nile delta are situated mostly below sea level and ever since have suffered drainage problems. The saline soils need great amounts of fresh water to wash out the salt. This leads to a further rise in the groundwater table and to a concentration of salt in the topsoil. Figure 5.2 shows that in the areas concerned the salt content is higher than in sea water.

5.2 Land reclamation in the Nile valley

The higher sand and gravel terraces of the Nile, as well as the old saline lake floors around Lake Qarun (Lake Moeres), are relatively unsuitable for cultivation. Nevertheless, the administrations of all governorates situated on the Nile try to follow the general trend of reclaiming land in these areas, accompanying their efforts with strong propaganda. The most serious con-sequence of this is the salinization of the fertile agricultural land in the Nile valley, since the drainage of newly reclaimed land situated on a higher level takes place at the expense of the old land, which is situated much lower.

5.3 Land reclamation in the Western Desert

In the Western Desert the ambitious project of El-Wadi el-Gedid (New Valley) was started in 1958. The plan was to turn more than 5 million *feddans* of desert into arable land (Schamp 1977: 69). The project area is a depression running in a north–south direction parallel to the Nile, in which the old oases of El-Bahariya, El-Farafra, Ed-Dakhla and El-Kharga are situated (see Figure 4.2). After more than forty years of great effort, enormous public investment and intensive political propaganda, the results are not at all impressive today. Besides 15,000 *feddans* of old land, only about 40,000 *feddans* of newly re-claimed land are under cultivation (Al-Kharbutli et al. 1998: 113). From these one has to deduct the *c.* 17,000 *feddans* of arable land that were lost once the traditional wells had dried up, through desertification (see Illustration 4) or through salinization as a consequence of excessive irrigation and insufficient drainage. Only if one considers all these factors can one assess the success of the project properly. According to Bliss (1989: 169ff) the oases of Dakhla and Kharga together held about 30,000 *feddans* of arable land at the begin-ning of the twentieth century. This means that traditional technologies for the production and use of groundwater were of no lesser efficiency than the modern ones, which depend on the deep aquifers. Moreover, the traditional technologies were cheaper, better adapted to the natural and social conditions of people in the oases, and environmentally favourable, guaranteeing sustainable use. The reasons why the El-Wadi el-Gedid project was not successful can be summarized as follows:

- The project was based on the idea that lack of water was the only obstacle for the development, so that a positive result could be achieved merely by providing water. This idea proved to be wrong.
- No proper coordination existed between the authorities in charge of water production and those responsible for planning the cultivation of the land.
- The centuries of experience of the indigenous population of the oases concerning water extraction and an economic use of precious groundwater were disregarded.
- The costs of lifting the water with the help of deep drilling were under-estimated. Politicians as well as technicians have high hopes for the use of the water resources of the huge Nubian Groundwater Basin (Hamida 1992) and do not consider that it is uneconomical to lift water from a depth of more than 50 m for agricultural use (Abulila, Director of the Agrarian Department at El-Kharga: oral communication 1989). The water used at Wadi el-Gedid is in most cases lifted from far greater depths.
- Owing to the ineffectiveness of the drainage system there is strong salinization.
- Since there is no effective control of the artesian springs, there is over-irrigation. For 1980 the amount of water wasted was estimated at 30 per cent of all the water produced (Lloyd 1992: 64). Also, the cultivation of rice, which takes place here, is not advisable under the conditions pertaining, because of its high water requirement. However, rice is relatively salt tolerant and the experts hold that the sandy soils are improved when the salt is washed out through irrigation by inundation.
- Little is done to avoid the problem of corrosion, which is a danger for the water pipes and the reservoirs. The systems have to be renewed at short intervals, which entails high costs.

All this means that the Egyptian oases, which formerly secured a living for their inhabitants and produced a food surplus, today depend totally on imports from the Nile valley. Almost all the fruit and vegetables, as well as the other food items offered on the market at El-Kharga, for example, are brought from Asyut or transported via Asyut to the oasis. From the early 1990s it was planned to use the water resources of the Nubian Aquifer System in Sharq-Uweinat (eastern Uweinat), which belongs to El-Wadi el-Gedid administratively but lies at a distance of more than 400 km from El-Kharga. It is to be expected that the problems which arose in El-Kharga and Ed-Dakhla will also hamper the development there (see Chapter 12). So far there are no greater land reclamation projects for Siwa Oasis, which is situated in the extreme west of the country, not far from the Libyan border. The development of tourism is favoured there, as well as of facilities for physiotherapy based on the traditional application of hot sand baths. Three mineral water bottling-factories have already been established. As regards agriculture, traditional irrigated cultivation is still dominant. Since the oasis is situated relatively far from larger towns (310 km from Marsa Matruh, 608 km from Alexandria), and since it could only be reached by gravel road through the desert until the mid-1980s, there is still a high degree of self-sufficiency there. However, far too many new springs have been opened up in recent years with an often uncontrolled discharge of water, since pumping is not necessary in most cases – at least at the beginning. This has already led to severe problems of soil salinization. The highly saline drainage water has formed huge lakes which are constantly growing and endangering the whole oasis, especially since it lies well below sea level. Further expansion of the cultivation would mean more lifting of underground water and an increase in drainage water, gradually submerging the whole oasis.

6 Animal husbandry and the fishing industry (see Tables 8.10 and 8.11)

The supply of animal protein, especially for the rural poor, is insufficient in Egypt. The price of 1 kg of meat or fish is the equivalent of about one-tenth or one-sixth of the salary of a young university graduate. The average consumption of meat, milk and eggs (see Table 8.6) in the country is about one-fifth of that of the average European. Although the animal stock is relatively high (see Table 8.10), local meat and milk production is low. This is partly due to the fodder problem in the summer months, which has been described above, and partly also to the fact that the working potential of the cattle is still very important to the *fellaheen* (see Illustrations 8 and 9) owing to the low degree of mechanization in their agriculture.

For several decades the government tried to establish special cattle-fattening and dairy farms and imported highly productive animals, above all Friesian

Table 8.10 Livestock in Egypt 1992 and 2000

Animals	1992	2000	Change (%)
Water buffalo	3,642,000	3,379,000	−7
Cows	2,478,000	3,930,000	+42
Camels	185,000	141,000	−24
Sheep	3,111,000	4,469,000	+44
Goats	2,865,000	3,424,000	+20
Pigs	27,000	40,000	+ 48

Sources: after CAPMAS 1998a: 59; CAPMAS 2002: 57

cattle, from abroad. These animals are usually cross-bred with local stock to achieve a better adaptation to existing environmental conditions. An example of efforts in this direction is the cattle farms in the Es-Salhiya project in the eastern Nile delta (see above): 4,200 dairy cows were kept there in a state-supported project which produced 1,786 litres of milk per animal on a yearly average in 1993. The average milk production of a local cow is only c. 700 litres annually with a fat content of 4 per cent; that of a water buffalo is c. 1,200 litres annually with a fat content of 7 per cent. Also, through the so-called 'Veal Project', the state tried to improve the supply of meat. In this project the owners of certain cattle-fattening farms were given interest-free credits. They could also buy subsidized fodder at about 10 per cent of the market price. In this project, too, only rich investors were supported by the state. And the produce did not help the poorer classes of the population, since about 90 per cent of them cannot buy veal, which costs four times as much as poultry (which many people also cannot afford).

The increase in the number of pigs raised in the country is not related to the local population's requirements – Muslims do not consume pork. It serves the rising demand of tourists. In Egypt pigs are kept exclusively by the mostly Christian garbage collectors who feed the animals on vegetable and fruit waste collected from households. The reorganization and modernization of garbage disposal in the country, which started during the late 1990s and in which Germany also had a share by providing a modern garbage combustion plant, might affect the production of pork.

In spite of a steady increase, the total amount of fish landed in Egypt was relatively small in 2000 at 724,000 tons (CAPMAS 2002). For most of the Egyptian population fish is a food item they favour but cannot afford. Although Egypt possesses more than 2,500 km of coastline, only about a quarter of

Table 8.11 Fishing in Egypt 1962–99

Fishing area	Share of total catch (%)		
	1962	1985	2000
Salt water:			
Mediterranean	31.4	7.5	7.6
Red Sea and Suez Canal	22.8	13.6	11.3
Fresh and brackish water:			
Mediterranean lagoons, Lake Qarun, Lake Er-Rayan	30.8	26.8	20.5
Nile and canals	15.0	14.1	11.1
Sadd el-Ali storage lake	0	15.7	2.6
Fish farms and rice fields	0	22.3	46.9
Total catch (tons)	120,318	159,945	724,400

Sources: after Simons 1968: 184; CAPMAS 1992: 62; CAPMAS 2002: 63

the fish catch comes from the sea. Table 8.11 shows that in the three decades that followed the construction of the Sadd el-Ali, great changes took place in terms of the origins of the fish landed. With its share dropping from 31.4 to 7.6 per cent of the country's total catch of fish within less than forty years, the Mediterranean coast, once the main fishing area of the country, lost its former importance. The reason is that no Nile silt reaches the area any more. This silt had been an important pre-condition for the development of plankton, which in turn led to the richness of the fish population there (see Chapter 6). Through the introduction of bigger ships and improved techno-logy in the industry, fishing on the Egyptian Mediterranean coast was able to recover, however, so that the absolute numbers of fish caught there today are higher than they were before the construction of the High Dam. In what was formerly the second-most important fishing area in Egypt, the lagoons of the northern Nile delta, fish production decreased relatively. However, from Lake Burullus and Lake Manzala alone, 17.4 per cent of the country's fish were caught in 2000. The fish farms established in recent years, primarily along the northern lagoons, contributed 44.7 per cent of the total fish caught in Egypt (CAPMAS 2002: 63). The reasons for the great increase in fishing in the Nile delta and the Nile valley are their favourable locations close to the big markets, the establishment of the new fish farms there, and the rise of a new affluent class which can afford the expensive fish. Neither Lake Sadd el-Ali nor the Red Sea is situated in such a favourable position. Transport in refrigerated railway wagons or other vehicles over long distances entails high costs in Egypt's hot climate.

The main problem in the fishing industry in the northern lagoons, in par-ticular Lake Manzala and Lake Maryut, is the severe pollution of the lakes through sewage water from industries and households. Tests revealed high rates of contamination of the fish from Lake Maryut with quicksilver and cadmium, which surpassed the values permitted by the World Health Organ-ization (WHO) nearly threefold. Consumption of such fish can cause various health problems. Thousands of local fishermen who are in constant contact with the water of the lakes suffer from kidney and liver diseases. Through sewage water and garbage dumped into Lake Maryut, the growth of reeds and aquatic plants has been enhanced, so that a rapid drying process is taking place there. The lake is shallower today than it used to be and its size is only about one-quarter of what it was forty years ago (Abdel-Hakim 1958: 23; *Al-Ahram Iktisadi*, 28 March 94: 21).

Lake Sadd el-Ali, according to official statements an important supplier of fish in the future, has so far not lived up to these hopes, not only because it is situated too far away from the markets, but for other reasons also. It could not even make good for the losses which occurred in the fish landed at the Mediterranean coast, closer to consumers, after the construction of the High Dam. The relative importance of the Sadd el-Ali reservoir as a fish supplier dropped from 15.7 per cent of the country's total fish catch in 1985 to one-sixth that value in 2000 (see Table 8.11).

At present, there are the following plans for the development of the fishing industry in Egypt:

- The water quality of the lagoons and the Nile is to be improved by reducing their contamination, partly with the support of international organizations for the protection of the environment.
- On land that is unsuitable for agricultural use fish farms are planned. At the end of the second millennium about 420,000 acres of land in the Nile delta were already being used as so-called 'fish farms and baskets gardens', contributing more than one-third of the country's fish production.
- There are plans to release spawn in the Egyptian lakes.
- The 'super male' of the Nile perch, which can produce 4,000 kg/ha of fish weight in only 145 days, is to be introduced.
- *Mabruk*, a fish species feeding mainly on freshwater snails that have so far resisted eradication through the application of chemicals, is to be introduced. If this succeeds, bilharzia could be reduced among the rural population and at the same time the fish supply would be enhanced.

CHAPTER 9

Old and New Industries in Egypt

1 The history of industrialization in Egypt

1.1 Traditional Egyptian industries

Technological standards in the productive sector in Egypt at the turn of the nineteenth century were excellently documented by Simon Gérard, a member of Napoleon's scientific expedition to Egypt in 1798–1801. At the time demand was mostly met by local craftsmen. Of major importance for the whole country was cotton manufacture, which was centred in Upper Egypt, particularly between Girga and Aswan, where cotton was grown. However, raw cotton was also imported from Syria. The wool industry had its centre in the oasis of El-Faiyum, where sheep with high-quality wool were bred. The Nile delta, on the other hand, especially the areas of Minuf, Shebin el-Kom and Tanta, specialized in growing flax and in the linen industry. Silk weaving was concentrated in El-Mahalla el-Kubra, where at the time about 900 weavers were working. Since no silk was produced in Egypt it was imported from Syria through the port of Dumyat. The finished product was partly exported back to Syria; most, however, was taken to Cairo for further processing. Beside the textile handicrafts, the production of dyes, mat-weaving, the grinding of grain, olive and sesame presses, the sugar industry, pottery and the production of gunpowder were the main branches of manufacture in Egypt. Besides these there existed in Cairo a great number of handicrafts organized by street according to type. The craftsmen, a great number of whom were Christian Copts, formed guilds.

1.2 The early phase of industrial modernization 1815–38

Mohammed Ali (1805–48), whose ambition was to make his country a leading and independent military power under his leadership, established in the first place a modern arms industry. He brought experts from England and France into the country and forced Egyptian craftsmen to work in his new factories after he had closed down their smaller workshops. The number of workers in Egypt's industrial sector at the time amounted to 40,000. In addition there were several thousand women producing semi-finished goods, mostly as home workers. Mohammed Ali's agents used cruel methods to force the women to work, with the result that some of them mutilated their limbs to escape the violence. Mohammed Ali also brought slaves from the Sudan as workers for his factories. Table 9.1 shows the structure of industries at the time. They comprise three major sectors: textiles, food and arms, with a distinct concentration on northern Egypt, especially Cairo and Alexandria. The sources do not mention the great number of small-scale industries satisfying the needs of the rural population, such as pottery, mat-weaving, woodwork, smithery and especially the production of agricultural tools.

1.3 The first recession 1838–82

The collapse of the industries established by Mohammed Ali started towards the end of his rule owing to external as well as to internal political factors. The Ottoman Sultan in Istanbul and the European powers forced Mohammed Ali to reduce his army and to open up the Egyptian market to goods from outside the country. This was a severe blow for the Egyptian weapons industry. Most other industries, too, characterized by mismanagement, forced labour and high production costs, could not survive under these conditions, so that in due course many Egyptian factories had to be closed down. Only during the time of the Khedive Ismail (1863–79), who, like Mohammed Ali, wanted to transform Egypt following the European model, was change brought about. At the cost of high external debt he promoted the industrialization of the country. However, unlike Mohammed Ali, he established a dependent economy, since he financed his projects and his extravagant lifestyle by incurring huge debts in England and France. In this economy the textile industry was pre-eminent, followed in second and third places by the sugar industry and the weapons industry. The whole crafts sector, which suffered under high direct and indirect taxation, deteriorated further.

1.4 Egyptian industries under colonial rule 1882–1927

The British conquest of Egypt led to a period of still greater dependence for the whole Egyptian economy. Being mainly interested in Egyptian cotton as a cheap raw material for their own textile industries, the English extended irrigation along the Nile, and an era of construction of new weirs, dams and canals began. During the first thirty-five years, from 1882 to 1917, the area under cultivation in Egypt expanded by nearly 70 per cent from 4.7 million acres to 7.9 million acres. At the same time the industries established under Mohammed Ali and the Khedive Ismail were systematically destroyed in order to prevent any competition for British industrial products on the Egyptian market. So most factories and wharves were closed down and private industries were submitted to taxation of 8 per cent.

1.5 Recovery of the industrial sector 1927–59

Recession in international trade during the First World War and later during the Great Economic Depression of 1929–32 offered Egypt a chance

Table 9.1 Industries in Egypt 1816–44

Branch	Location	Remarks
Cotton ginnery and pressing	Bulaq (Cairo)	partly with steam engines from America
Cotton weaving (32 plants)	Bulaq and other places	export to Syria, Asia Minor, Europe
Linen weaving	Nile delta	30,000 looms; annual production: 3 million cloths; export to Europe
Silk weaving	Cairo	Armenian workers
Wool weaving	Bulaq	Raw material from Tunisia
Production of *tarbush* (fez, a traditional cap)	Fuwa / Rashid (Rosetta)	wool from Spain; Tunisian workers
Production of indigo	Dispersed	Indian experts
Polishing of rice (3 plants)	Rashid	partly with steam engines
Production of sugar and rum	Cairo	about 300 employees; animal power
Production of edible oil	Cairo, Upper Egypt	from flax, sesame, lettuce seed
Leather processing	Rashid	Russian administration
Glass manufacture	Alexandria	for domestic demand
Printing press	Bulaq	for state demand, textbooks for schools
Production of paper	Cairo	from rags
Gunpowder production (7 plants)	Cairo	French experts
Iron founding	Bulaq	English experts
Shipbuilding	Alexandria	1,500 employees, French management
Production of arms (5 plants)	Bulaq	arsenal, warships

Source: after Kassem 1987: 46f

to break away from economic dependency on Great Britain. Since fewer goods from abroad were reaching the country, Egypt was forced to fulfil its demand for industrial products locally. Therefore numerous small factories were established all over the country. The recession in cotton exports made many feudalists invest in local industries instead of in cotton production. In 1920 Misr Bank, the first bank in Egypt, was founded with the aim of encouraging the establishment of new industries, and in 1930 there followed a reformation of the customs system, aiming at protection of local industries. Imported finished goods were subject to a higher taxation than raw materials. Through the discovery and production of petroleum in El-Ghardaqa in 1913 and Ras Gharib in 1938 Egypt was able to meet its energy demands independently. This positive trend in Egyptian industry continued during the Second World War, during which Egypt had to provide its own population as well as the Allied forces based in the region with staple food items. The strategy of self-sufficiency and of substituting local products for imports was continued during the years after the war, so that between 1945 and 1950 imported consumer goods decreased by 63 per cent (Kassem 1987: 310).

The revolution of 1952 at first brought no major change in industrial policy, but very soon state intervention in the industrial sector, and in particular in heavy industry, increased. By 1954 the state owned 50 per cent of the capital of the Iron and Steel Company at Helwan, and about as much of that of the railway supply company, as well as of the cement industry. Industrial production grew by 410 per cent between 1952 and 1965; however, its structure remained largely unchanged. Consumer goods constituted about two-thirds, and only 3 per cent were investment goods.

1.6 Nationalization and the expansion of state-controlled industries 1959–67

With a rigorously planned economy, and through the nationalization of banks and of all the major economic enterprises in the hands of Egyptian or foreign individuals, Nasser tried to make the Egyptian economy independent of Western hegemony. His era was characterized by a protective policy focused on import substitution and the establishment of a public industrial system that generated about 90 per cent of the value-added in industrial establishments (Soliman 1999: 11). The socialist laws of 1961 gave the state full control over the industrial sector in the country. The size of the plants established increased decisively, so that in 1961 only 2.5 per cent of the factories employed more than half of all industrial workers in Egypt and contributed 63.1 per cent to the country's industrial production value (Ismail 1988: 159). In spite of the generally adverse effects of a state-controlled economy, there was high growth in Egypt's industrial sector amounting to 8.9 per cent annually during this era, as compared to a mere 2 per cent in the preceding period. In 1965 Egypt's industry contributed 21.8 per cent to the national income. In the

21. Petroleum industry near Ras Gharib/Red Sea: The Red Sea coast is the location of two important but incompatible pillars of Egypt's economy: petroleum production and tourism. Strict laws exist for the protection of the environment, but much remains to be done. (Photo: F. Ibrahim)

preceding years it had contributed only between 8 and 10 per cent (Kassem 1987: 357ff). However, the growth rate declined sharply during the second half of the 1960s, owing not only to Egypt's involvement in wars with Israel and Yemen but also to the expansion of state bureaucracy and the pursuit of socialist rather than economic management principles.

1.7 The era of the Open Door policy

After Egypt's defeat in the war against Israel in June 1967 a time of neglect of the whole economic sector began. The greatest part of the government's investments were diverted into the arms industry. Only after the country's partial victory in the October War of 1973, when the chances of a lasting peace with Israel improved, was there a suitable climate for foreign and local investments. Parliament passed Law No. 43 in 1974 and Law No. 32 in 1977, aiming at liberalization of the Egyptian economy. This meant in the first place favourable conditions for Egyptian and foreign investors, who were granted the following privileges:

- complete or partial customs exemption
- unlimited transfer of foreign currency
- easing of import and export formalities

- exemption from taxation of profits gained from trade or industrial activities for ten or more years
- exemption from observation of labour laws
- official guarantees of no nationalization or confiscation, and numerous bilateral guarantees for investments made.

The generous facilities offered by the new Open Door policy led to a resurgence of industrial capitalism after it had been non-existent in Egypt for two decades. However, the rapid growth in GDP, reaching 9 per cent annually in the 1970s, was due not to industrial development but to the expansion in oil exports, the reopening of the Suez Canal and increasing remittances from Egyptian expatriates in the Arab Gulf states. In fact, industry's share in GDP dropped from 21.8 per cent in 1965 to 14.9 per cent in 1978 (Soliman 1999: 12), for the investment environment at that time encouraged growth in non-traded goods and the service sector of the economy at the expense of the traded commodities sector. This hampered growth in the production of export commodities and enhanced the import of consumer, intermediate and investment goods (ibid.). And although the private sector made big strides in the 1970s, these were made mainly in the trade and construction sectors, and not in the industrial sector. The reason for this was that private investors, still mistrustful of the state after Nasser's nationalization campaigns, opted for quick and sure returns rather than for investment in industry with long-term prospects. Soliman (ibid.: 13ff) gives the following explanation for this non-productive, non-industrial turn in the Egyptian economy:

- The taxation law of 1974 did not offer adequate incentives for Egyptian capital to be invested in industries. It was not until 1977 that discrimination against national investors ceased.
- Anarchic liberalization created insecurity for industrial producers, for the domestic market was invaded by imported goods. Consequently national production decreased and many enterprises went bankrupt.

Table 9.2 Egypt's national economy: sectors of employment and share of GDP 1989/ 90 and 2000/01

Year	Employment (%)		Value added as % of GDP	
	1989/90	2000/01	1990	2000/01
Agriculture	35.0	28.2	19	16.5
Industry, mining, energy and construction	20.8	23.2	29	32.8
Services and trade	44.2	48.6	52	50.7

Sources: after Statistisches Bundesamt Wiesbaden 1993: 53f; World Bank 2001: 296; CAPMAS 2001b: 267; Ministry of Information 2002a

1.8 Industrial growth under Mubarak and the implementation of the Structural Adjustment Programmes

Various indicators show that Egypt's industry experienced an upward trend under Mubarak. Some of these indicators are (ibid.):

- The share of industry, excluding petroleum and the construction sectors, in the country's GDP rose from 13.5 per cent in 1980/81 to 20.2 per cent in 2000/01 (Ministry of Information 2002b); including them, the industrial share reached 32.8 per cent in 2000/01 (see Table 9.2).
- The growth rate of industry 1990–99, value-added, was higher at 4.7 per cent than that of the GDP at 4.4 per cent, that of agriculture with 3.1 per cent and that of services at 4.3 per cent (World Bank 2001: 294).
- There is a steady and rapid increase in the share of the private sector in industrial output. In the six years between 1994/95 and 2000/01 alone, the share of the public sector in the value of industrial production dropped from 39.4 to 12 per cent (see Table 9.3).

These positive figures relating to the development of industry after its deterioration in the 1970s do not mean all is well with this sector of Egypt's economy. The following chapters will address some of its major problems.

Table 9.3 Egyptian industries: production values 1994/95 and 2000/01 (in m LE)

	1994/95*			2000/01**		
	Public	Private	Total (%)	Public	Private	Total (%)
Food	1,888	2,673	18.2	1,389	8,006	15.7
Textiles	2,074	5,751	31.2	360	18,011	30.8
Chemicals	3,362	3,281	26.5	3,555	13,253	28.2
Mineral and extracting	1,147	1,315	9.8	938	4,575	9.2
Engineering	1,409	2,188	14.3	908	8,680	16.1
Total	*9,880*	*15,207*	*25,087*	*7,150*	*52,525*	*59,675*
	39.4%	*60.6%*	*100%*	*12 %*	*82%*	*100%*

* 1 LE = US$0.28 in 1994/95; ** 1 LE = US$0.24 in 2000/01

Sources: after Ministry of Information 1996: 89; Ministry of Information 2002b

2 The economic and political background of Egyptian industries

In Egypt today the following types of industries are to be found:
- the old industries that already existed in the nineteenth century and which are based on local agrarian raw materials
- the small-scale industries that have traditional as well as modern elements and belong mostly to the informal sector

- the new industries founded in the earlier part of the second half of the twentieth century or which expanded strongly during that time
- the new modern capital-intensive industries working with advanced technology.

2.1 Old industries

As an agrarian country Egypt's traditional industry sectors are the agro-industries, in particular the textile and food industries. Since the 1970s, with the growing importance of petroleum production and, related to this, the chemical industry, the share of agriculture-based industries in the total value of industrial production has decreased considerably. The share of the food and textile industries was reduced from *c.* 63 to only 48 per cent between 1973 and 1999. During this period the share of the mining, petroleum and chemical industries increased from 20 to 36 per cent. However, the old industries are still of great importance to the country, since they are labour intensive. In 1992 about half of all persons employed in the industrial sector were working in the agriculture-based industries, whereas the mining, petroleum and chemical industries together employed only 13.1 per cent of industrial workers (CAPMAS 1994e: 9ff).

Mechanization of the textile industry in Egypt began in 1899 in Alexandria with the support of European expatriates living there. However, a modern textile industry came into being only in 1927 with the foundation by Talaat Harb of the Misr Textile Company in El-Mahalla el-Kubra. During the following years the textile industry in Alexandria also expanded and was modernized through the establishment of factories in the town's suburbs of Kafr ed-Dawar and El-Beida. The location of Alexandria, with its hinterland in the north-western Nile delta, was particularly favourable to the textile industry, because owing to the relatively humid air from the Mediterranean, cotton fibres retained their elasticity. Moreover, the town in general has a good infrastructure and in particular a trading port, and is itself a significant market for goods of all kinds.

Until 1940 Cairo was not of great importance as a location for the textile

Table 9.4 Power generation in Egypt 1981/82 and 2000/01

Source of power	1981/82		2000/01	
	billion kWh	Relative importance (%)	billion kWh	Relative importance (%)
Hydraulic and wind	10.5	47.7	13.1	17
Thermal	11.5	52.3	63.9	83
Total	*22.0*	*100*	*77.0*	*100*

Sources: after Ministry of Information 1999: 24; 2002b

industry. While Alexandria and Kafr ed-Dawar together contributed 51 per cent and El-Mahalla el-Kubra 45 per cent to the production of the spinning mills in the country, Cairo contributed only about 1.3 per cent (Eman 1943: 66). It was not until after the Second World War that the textile industry established itself in the country's capital, particularly in its north in Shubra el-Kheima. In the late 1970s Greater Cairo supplied 28.5 per cent of the total production value of the Egyptian textile industry and employed 37.5 per cent of its labour force. During the years that followed, Alexandria and Kafr ed-Dawar, unlike El-Mahalla el-Kubra, were to some extent able to retain their former importance by assuming a leading position in the manufacture of ready-to-wear clothes. Through the policy of decentralization during the time of Nasser the textile industry spread to nearly all governorates, but retained its old centre in the north of the country. A general decline can be observed in the textile industry today, however, owing to the massive imports of cheap articles from South-East Asia.

Since the 1970s there has been a very rapid development in the food industry. Although the textile and food industries had a roughly equal share of total industrial production in 1973, the value of the food industry was nearly twice that of the textile industry twenty years later. For the food industry the availability of raw materials is still of prime importance in terms of location. Thus the sugar industry was mainly concentrated in the best areas for the cultivation of sugar cane in the south until in the 1990s, when the northern delta became the location for sugar beet cultivation. In 2000/01 sugar production in Egypt amounted to 1.4 million tons and fulfilled 56.6 per cent of the country's requirements (Ministry of Information 2002b). The production of edible oil is located primarily in the north, in the areas of Tanta, Kafr es-Saiyat and Alexandria. This is where the cultivation and processing of cotton takes place, for in Egypt most edible oil is produced from cottonseed. In 1999/2000 the production of edible and hydrogenated oil in the country was about 403,000 tons (CAPMAS 2001b: 82), which fulfilled only about 35.5 per cent of Egypt's demand (see Table 8.6).

Among the most important food industries in Egypt are the rice-polishing factories and the grain mills, as well as the factories for the processing and tinning of fruit and vegetables, which are concentrated in the areas of the Nile delta, where these products are grown.

2.2 Small-scale industries

In 1996 2.41 million persons were classified as 'craftsmen' in Egypt, while those classified as 'production workers', i.e. industrial employees, amounted to only 1.07 million (CAPMAS 2000: 29). Despite their importance for the labour market small-scale industries are officially neglected. If they appear in the official Egyptian statistics at all, they are defined as 'enterprises of the productive sector with fewer than ten employees'. Mostly they are craftsmen's establishments that form part of the informal sector. In some cases there are more than ten employees in a business; however, these do not possess legal contracts. In this part of the private economic sector the social benefits paid by the employers are less than those paid in the formal sector, but the wages are higher and working efficiency is much greater. The working conditions in most of the traditional artisans' establishments are bad. Partly the work is carried out by children. Important branches of the small-scale industries are related to the tourist industry. This is particularly the case with the weaving of tapestries (see Illustration 22), some branches of woodwork, the papyrus-painting craft, stone-cutting and glass production (see Illustration 26) as well as a wide range of other artisanship. These branches of the economy are subject to the same fluctuations as tourism in the country. During the socialist period under Nasser the small-scale industries suffered owing to restricted imports of necessary raw materials and machinery. On the other hand, like all other industrial branches, they profited from the policy of high protective tariffs on imported goods, which guaranteed that the local products found a market, even if they were of inferior quality. Through the Open Door policy under Sadat, and particularly later, through the application of the GATT regulations in Egypt, development went in the opposite direction.

2.3 New industries founded after the mid-1950s

The most important branches of these industries are the chemical industry, the engineering industry, the metalworking industry and the electronics industry. Some of these branches have historical roots in older branches, but they should be counted among the new industries today because of the high technological standards they have acquired in the meantime.

The basis of the expansion of the chemical industry in Egypt is the rapid increase in the production of petroleum since the beginning of the 1970s. Cairo, Alexandria and Suez are its main centres. The most important products of Egypt's chemical industry are dyes to be used in the textile industry, fertilizers for agricultural use and pharmaceuticals. Egypt possesses seven factories producing fertilizers: four in the country's north, one in the south and two in Greater Cairo. Five of them produce super-phosphates and two calcium nitrates. For the latter petroleum and natural gas provide the energy required. Only in the Kima agricultural fertilizer factory, located in Aswan and established in 1960 with German support, is electrical power used, which is produced with the help of the turbines installed in the High Dam. Hamdan (1984a: 764f) argues that this factory is based on false premises. According to a World Bank study, the production of 1 ton of nitrogenous fertilizer there requires electrical power the price of which is seven times higher than that of petroleum, which could be used as an energy source if production took place in the north of the country, and the overall costs are four to five times higher than the world market price. On account of the high costs of hydro-energy the Kima factory is making huge losses, which reached LE33

22. Carpet production: Carpet-making and tapestry-weaving are income-generating activities which were boosted by growing tourist demand from the 1980s and later by growing domestic demand. (Photo: F. Ibrahim)

million in 1996 (*Al Ahram Iktisadi*, 5 August 1996: 39). Moreover, the factory uses as a raw material limestone, which can be quarried nearly everywhere in Egypt – except at Aswan. So this has to be transported to the factory from Kom Ombo. In 2001/02, Egypt produced about 10.4 million tons of calcium nitrate with a 15.5 per cent nitrogen content as fertilizer. These amounts are 35 per cent above the country's requirements (*Al-Ahram Ektesady*, 20 January 2003: 32). The ecological impact of the extremely high input of fertilizers in Egyptian agriculture has already been mentioned.

Egypt is the largest producer and with its 70 million inhabitants (2003) also consumer of pharmaceuticals in the Middle East and North Africa. Production met 83 per cent of the country's demand in 2000/01, in which year it attained a value of LE3.9 billion. As in all branches of industry the private sector is rapidly gaining ground here too. Its share of production increased from 33 per cent in the 1980s to 69 per cent in 2001. This sector is more efficient and more innovative and consists of thirty-nine companies, compared to eight companies in the public sector (CAPMAS 2000/01).

Modern production in heavy industry started in Egypt in 1958–60 with the construction of the two furnaces in Helwan with an annual capacity of 265,000 tons of steel. Work there did not go smoothly, partly because the iron ore had to be transported from Aswan. The ore in the sandstone formations mined there at the time also proved to be of inferior quality, so the iron ore at El-Bahariya oasis in the New Valley, which is of higher quality, closer to Helwan and can also be mined more easily, began to be exploited. Gas-coke had to be imported from abroad and limestone was transported over a distance of 200 km from Middle Egypt to Helwan. In 1982 the Alexandria National Iron and Steel Co. was established in Ed-Dekheila/Alexandria with Japanese support. Imported iron ore can be transported there through the new port of Ed-Dekheila, in whose immediate neighbourhood the factory is situated. Instead of gas-coke local natural gas is used in the modern reduction furnace. The factory specializes in the production of reinforced steel. At the beginning of the 1990s production was 745,000 tons annually, about one-third of the country's total production of iron and steel. In 1998 production achieved a record of 1.52 million tons (*Al-Ahram*, 11 April 1999: 27), which constituted 60 per cent of Egypt's iron production. However, the company had subsequently to reduce its production to 1 million tons owing to fierce competition from cheaply imported steel, especially from the countries of the former Soviet Union (ibid. and *Al Ahali*, 15 March 2000: 1).

Because of the construction of the Sadd el-Ali, the aluminium industry at Nag' Hammadi in Upper Egypt was established, about halfway between Aswan, the source of the energy used, and Safaga, through which port the import of bauxite and the export of the aluminium takes place. It was discovered, however, that the production costs of the aluminium produced there are not competitive on international markets. As was the case with the fertilizer factory at Aswan, the state-subsidized electric power used makes the project far from profitable and less than an asset to the national economy, not to mention the environmental pollution caused in this densely populated region of the country. However, a ready supply of raw aluminium is economically favourable, with a positive effect on employment, since hundreds of small factories in Cairo and Alexandria specialize in the production of aluminium articles which still are widely used in rural as well as in poorer urban households, although in the households of the better off steel has mostly replaced aluminium.

One important factor enhanced the development of modern industries in Egypt: the leading role played by the arms industry, which expanded greatly after 1952 because of the wars with Israel and developed highly advanced technology. The fifteen factories in the country whose production was suitable for military purposes already produced, among other things, the country's first refrigerators, washing machines, radios and television sets in the 1950s.

2.4 Modern industries of the liberalization period

With the liberalization of the Egyptian economy since the late 1970s new types of industry came into existence. Their locations are the new towns in the desert, such as El-Ashir min Ramadan, Sitta October, Madinet es-Sadat and Borg el-Arab el-Gedida (see Chapter 11 and Table 9.5). Some of these industries are relatively labour intensive, but this is the exception. They work with ultra-modern imported technology, belong to a large extent to big international trusts that are trying to open up the Egyptian market for their products, or are

Table 9.5 Egyptian industries: industrial projects established in the new towns 1981–2000

New towns	Number of factories	Value of production in 2000 in million LE*	Job opportunities in the year 2000
El-Ashir min Ramadan	996	15,175	115,600
Madinet es-Sadat	244	1,120	18,300
Sitta October	638	6,254	74,100
Es-Salhiya el-Gedida	46	663	4,200
Borg el-Arab el-Gedida	361	1,182	19,300
Dumyat el-Gedida	116	103	3,600
Beni Suef el-Gedida	25	20	1,100
Badr	78	227	5,800
Madinet en-Nubariya el-Gedida	21	27	300
El-Obur	34	160	3,000
El-Minya el-Gedida	6	1	100
Total	2,565	24,932	245,400

* 1 LE = US$0.26 in 2000

Source: after Ministry of Information 2001a

23. Sultan Hassan and El-Rifai Mosques, Cairo: At the foot of Saladin's Citadel lie the mosques of the old town of Cairo. The modern city with its skyscrapers on the Nile is visible in the background. (Photo: F. Ibrahim)

established as joint ventures. In all cases the state grants considerable financial privileges. There are enterprises engaged in producing textiles or metal-ware, as well as food processing factories, mostly drying or deep-freezing local agricultural products, such as the plant at Borg el-Arab el-Gedida. In Sohag, in Upper Egypt, where the greatest concentration of onion-growing is found, the country's biggest factory for drying onions is located.

3 The problems of Egypt's industries today

3.1 Public sector inefficiency

Although the policy of deregulation and privatization had already tentatively started under Sadat, most industrial production remained in the hands of the state until the beginning of the twenty-first century. This is also the reason why a large number of people are still employed in this part of the industrial sector. Owing to mismanagement, corruption and lack of innovation, many of these enterprises work with a low degree of productivity. Most state-owned textile factories, such as those at Kafr ed-Dawar and El-Mahalla el-Kubra, had made significant losses for years. The privatization of such businesses proved difficult, since the potential investors' first condition was generally the dismissal of large numbers of workers. So for years the state was able to sell only successful enterprises. As Table 9.3 shows, in 2000/01

98 per cent of the production of the textile industry, 90 per cent of that the engineering industry, 85 per cent of the food industry, 83 per cent of the mineral extracting industry and 79 per cent of the chemical industry was located in the private sector.

3.2 The crisis in the cotton industry

The liberalization of the cotton trade in Egypt in 1994 led to a critical situation for the whole sector of the textile industry, which depended on this raw material. The state-owned as well as the private factories had been working with guaranteed supplies of local cotton, the price of which had been kept low by the state. After the latter had given up its monopoly and compulsory cultivation was stopped, the price of cotton went up and the supply was threatened. Many of the factories that had worked at a narrow profit margin had to be closed down. Moreover, following the economic liberalization Egypt was flooded with cheap textiles from China, Pakistan and other Asian countries. Owing to the reduced energy subsidies provided by the state after the World Bank's Structural Adjustment Programmes had been implemented, production costs rose to such heights that local textiles were more expensive than imported ones from South-East Asia. In spite of the fact that the quality of Egyptian products has greatly improved, the problem of marketing them still exists, for competing with Western standards is difficult, and the products are too expensive to be sold in developing countries.

3.3 The dependency of modern industries

Most enterprises established by foreign investors or through joint ventures after economic liberalization had been officially proclaimed by Sadat are completely dependent on imported know-how, technology and often manpower. Examples of these are the automobile assembly factories owned by various international firms as well as factories belonging to other large international trusts. Besides know-how, semi-finished goods are brought into Egypt in order for these factories to function. The foreign firms often bring in their own management and train local staff for other positions.

3.4 Unsustainability of industries in the new desert towns (see Table 9.5)

An artificial climate for investment was created with the help of high state subsidies and with numerous privileges to encourage the establishment of industries in the new towns. When they come to an end, these industries will be under test. Some of the investors are mainly interested in profiting from the financial advantages granted, such as cheap land, low-interest credits, licences for import and export, exemption from customs as well as from taxes, etc., without establishing functioning businesses. Another problem affecting industries in the desert towns is the lack of a local labour force.

The daily transport of workers from Cairo and Alexandria by bus to these towns entails high costs.

Despite the various success stories which are reported from some new towns, especially from Sitta October and El-Ashir min Ramadan, industries in the other new towns seem to be confronted with serious problems. According to a report by an Egyptian weekly (Internet 2001f), more than 45 per cent of the industrial plants in Borg el-Arab el-Gedida had closed down in 2001 or were on their way to doing so. Borg el-Arab el-Gedida was planned in 1979 in an economically favourable geographical location 7 km from the Mediterranean coast as a south-western extension of the city of Alexandria (population 3.5 million) and inaugurated in 1988 (see Chapter 11). The new town has five industrial sites occupying a total area of 5 km². Investors were enthusiastic during the early years, and soon the city board had approved 1,300 applications for establishing industrial plants. In 2001 only 375 of them had actually materialized, 270 of which were still not performing fully, and LE2 billion (c. US$500 million) had been invested in industries there by private entrepreneurs employing about 16,000 workers in small and medium enterprises.

In May 1997 small investors all over the country received a fatal blow, when a new law was enforced depriving entrepreneurs with capital of less than LE300,000 (c. US$80,000) of the privilege of the ten-year tax exemption granted to investors in new towns. This law coincided with the onset of a severe economic recession in Egypt which lasted for several years. One of the main reasons was the lack of liquidity and practical insolvency of the state owing to its soaring internal and external debt. According to the former Prime Minister, Khalid Mohy-ed-Din (Internet 2001g), the internal debts of the state, together with those of its parastatals, had reached LE248 billion (c. US$60 billion) in 2000, constituting 85 per cent of the annual GDP. The critical mark, which should not be surpassed, is 60 per cent.

Among the industries that failed at Borg el-Arab el-Gedida are the furniture production, the light metal and engineering and the chemical industries. The food processing industry seems to be relatively successful because of the great demand for food in the country. However, demand is not the only decisive factor for success, as was shown by the bankruptcy of the largest school furniture plant in the town. After it had supplied state schools with furniture without any payments being made by the insolvent government, Ismat, the owner, was unable to pay his bank debts, which amounted to LE140 million (c. US$35 million). When he was sentenced to imprisonment for this, he dismissed his 700 employees, closed the factory and fled abroad.

3.5 The flooding of the Egyptian market with imported goods

Protective tariffs for the benefit of local industries existed in Egypt during the socialist period, but were abolished when it came to an end. Since Egypt's industrial products cannot compete with products from South-East Asia in price at present, the Egyptian market is today full of foreign products that the country could produce itself, and even export. At the same time Egypt has lost traditional markets like the Sudan, while the European Community has practically closed its markets to countries like Egypt. So the country's economy is confronted with a serious problem at the beginning of the new millennium.

3.6 Lack of active investors

Since Sadat's era there has arisen in Egypt a growing class of capitalists who lack experience in the different branches of industry, their ways of functioning and their technologies, and who have little or no interest in the productive sector as such. So they invest rather in real estate or import businesses that promise quick and high returns, especially for those who have the necessary connections in the administration or can increase their gains considerably by way of corruption.

3.7 Haphazard investment

When the government liberated industry and granted various incentives for investors, especially in the new towns and the free trade zones, industrial plants were established there in great numbers. Entrepreneurs imitated each other without studying the market or conducting feasibility studies. By 2001 overproduction was soaring. The situation was exacerbated by the flooding of the domestic market with imported consumer goods after the reduction of customs tariffs and the termination of the state's protective policy in compliance with the GATT and WTO regulations. As most Egyptian investors lack necessary capital, they take bank loans at relatively high interest rates, thus raising their production costs and rendering their products less competitive. At the beginning of the new millennium surplus, unused industrial capacity occurred everywhere. The stores were full to bursting with unsold goods, so production had to be reduced. According to *Al-Ahram* (Internet 2001j) the surplus industrial capacity amounted to 40 per cent in the pharmaceutical industry, 50 per cent in the gas industry, 53 per cent in the shoe industry, 40 per cent in the tanneries, 17 per cent in the fertilizer industry, 15 per cent in the cement industry, 49 per cent in the grain-milling industry and 15 per cent in the edible salt industry (see Table 9.6). Considering that the state subsidizes new industries heavily, especially those in the new towns, unused industrial capacity entails great losses for the state budget. At the same time overproduction compels investors to sell their products at uncompetitive prices, hoping to gain ground in the market. As the adverse conditions persist, bankruptcy ensues. The government is confronted with a dilemma. Should it reverse its course of liberalization and intervene, to stop the deterioration in the budding industries, or not? But unless the root causes of the problem are adequately addressed, mere temporary state intervention would hinder the process of sustainable development. The real causes are on the one hand the lack of competitiveness of Egyptian products in terms of quality and price, and on the other the absence of a data bank and an advisory body to inform investors about the market situation and the risks to be expected. Coordination between producers and marketing agencies should be improved. Even within the public sector itself there is a lack of coordination which is responsible, for example, for the import of huge amounts of rice, sugar and cotton, while the heavily subsidized national production is rotting in the stores.

Table 9.6 Utilization rates of Egypt's main industries 2000

Industry/product	Number of plants inspected	Production capacity per month (tons)	Production December 2000 (tons)	Utilization rate December 2000 (%)
Cotton spinning	23	45,500	15,000	33
Cotton weaving	242	47,000	34,000	72
Sugar refining	3	133,000	25,000	19
Wheat flour	71	625,000	404,000	65
Edible oil	33	67,500	65,000	96
Detergents	17	19,000	19,000	100
Calcium nitrate fertilizers	5	775,000	775,000	100
Super-phosphate fertilizers	2	130,000	108,000	83
Cement	9	2,142,000	1,753,000	82
Motor cars	11	10,375	2,752	27
Buses	5	563	78	14
Microbuses	6	542	112	21
Refrigerators	13	129,000	72,000	56
Washing machines	50	138,000	68,000	49
TV sets	14	97,000	45,000	46
Air conditioners	8	40,000	24,000	60
Reinforced steel	16	417,000	366,000	88
Steel sheets	3	159,000	65,000	41
Other iron industries	4	42,000	31,000	74
Aluminium production	1	11,800	11,700	99
Aluminium smelting	9	5,200	4,600	88

Source: after Internet 2001j

CHAPTER 10

Tourism in Egypt

Tourism in Egypt can be classified in two main categories:

- international (foreign) tourism
- internal (domestic) tourism.

While there is substantial data about the first category involving foreigners as guests in the country, there are hardly any statistics available about tourism involving the local population, or concerning the numerous Egyptians living abroad but holding Egyptian passports and spending their holidays in Egypt like foreigners. The Ministry of Tourism keeps records only of international arrivals and departures, and the Arabic term for tourism, *siyaha*, is only applied to the foreign variety, while domestic tourism is called *rihlat* (trips), *fushat* (excursions for recreation), *ziyarat* (visits) or *tasyiif* (a stay at a seaside summer resort) depending on its nature.

1 International tourism

1.1 Development and structure of international tourism (see Figures 10.1 and 10.2 and Tables 10.1 and 10.2)

Egypt was the first country outside their own continent which Europeans visited as tourists after such travels had become fashionable among the educated and rich elite in the nineteenth century. Travelling to Egypt became popular at the time mainly on account of the newly aroused interest in the country after Napoleon's invasion in 1798–1801. His army had been accompanied by an expedition of numerous elite scholars who explored Egypt and gave detailed reports about their discoveries in their *Déscription de l'Égypte*. One of these scholars, Vivant Denon, wrote his own description of Egyptian civilization and architecture and drew hundreds of sketches of what he observed. The book was so popular that it saw forty editions in the nineteenth century alone. The deciphering of hieroglyphic script led to further archaeological activity and discoveries through which fascination for Egyptian culture was enhanced, developing into Egyptomania. Interest in Egypt gained further support through the development of photography, which in its early stages required special light conditions that were abundant in Egypt. In addition a multitude of Pharaonic monuments and fascinating motifs drew photographers to the Nile valley as well as to the desert. During the first phase the agents of foreign tourism were individuals who belonged to the upper classes in their home countries and usually spent several weeks, if not months, in Egypt. In the 1850s there were an estimated 20,000 tourists of this type in the country annually. By the time of the First World War the numbers had risen to about 50,000. The two world wars and the worldwide economic depression between them caused the number of guests to drop drastically, however. Tourism in Egypt recovered only very slowly thereafter, with an average duration of stay of only about two weeks.

After the number of tourist arrivals had increased more than twelvefold between 1950 and 1966, the steep upward trend was interrupted by the wars between Egypt and Israel that took place in 1967 and 1973. After the peace agreement of 1979 the figures for tourist arrivals in Egypt soared, so that in 1980 there were more than 1.25 million international visitors spending a total of over 8.1 million nights in Egypt (see Table 10.1). The new peace initiated an influx of Israeli tourists into Egypt, and especially to Sinai, on Jewish public holidays. In 1999 alone 415,253 Israelis visited Egypt and spent 1,638,534 nights there. Their share of the total dropped by 21.4 per cent in 2000, however, owing to the Second Palestinian intifada the year before.

Table 10.1 International tourism in Egypt: development 1974–2002*

Year	Number of visitors	Number of nights spent per visitor	Number of hotels	Number of hotel beds	Foreign currency gained (million US$)
1974	676,000	9.3	887	53,000	~200
1980	1,253,000	6.5	1,098	62,000	562
1985	1,519,000	5.9	1,168	81,000	901
1990	2,600,000	7.7	632	101,000	1,646**
1991	2,214,000	7.3	638	106,000	***
1992	3,207,000	6.8	663	110,000	***
1993	2,508,000	6.0	692	117,000	1,760
1994	2,582,000	6.0	718	121,000	2,006
1995	3,133,000	6.5	752	129,000	2,684
1997	3,961,000	6.7	829	151,000	3,727
1998	3,454,000	5.9	869	167,000	2,565
2000	5,506,000	6.0	1,010	227,000	4,300
2001	4,648,000	6.4	1,057	241,000	3,800
2002	5,192,000	6.3	***	***	3,600

* From 1990 onwards the numbers of hotels and hotel beds do not include low-cost hotels; ** 1989; *** No figures available

Sources: CAPMAS, Statistics on tourism of various years; Ministry of Tourism 2002: 54

Among other negative effects on the Egyptian economy the 1991 Gulf War caused a severe crisis in the tourism industry. But a complete recovery took place the following year, with the figure for foreign visitors exceeding 3 million for the first time (22 million tourist nights). This boom did not last long, however, since Islamist terrorists launched a series of attacks against tourists towards the end of 1992, and more severely in 1997. Tourism recovered again and broke all records in 2000, with 5.5 million international tourists spending 32.8 million nights in Egypt. Figure 10.1 and Tables 10.1 and 10.2 show that Europeans and Americans responded more sensitively to such insecurity than other visitors, who mainly came from the Arab countries. While in 1991 and 1993 the total numbers of international tourists fell by 14.8 and 21.8 per cent respectively, the numbers of visitors from Europe and America fell by 27.5 and 28.6 per cent respectively. This entailed a tremendous loss of hard currency for Egypt. For 1991 the loss was roughly estimated at US$1 billion (Statistisches Bundesamt Wiesbaden 1993: 106). It was even greater in 1998 after the terrorist attack on tourists at Luxor the year before. In 2001 the loss in tourism revenues amounted to US$0.5 billion owing to the continuation of the intifada in Palestine and the events of 11 September.

In terms of their countries of origin and cultural backgrounds foreign visitors in Egypt can be divided into two main groups: those who come from

Table 10.2 International tourism in Egypt: nights spent 1997–2002 (in thousands)

Tourists' place of origin	1997	1998	2000	2002	% change 1997–2000
Germany	3,835	1,939	5,687	5,694	+48
Italy	3,141	2,833	5,436	4,693	+49
UK	2,187	1,235	2,047	2,214	+1
France	2,009	1,133	2,710	2,070	+3
Benelux	1,056	838	1,701	1,441	+36
Russian Federation	589	707	778	2,424	+312
All Europe	*15,616*	*10,157*	*22,441*	*22,527*	*+44*
The Americas and Australia	2,008	1,504	2,292	1,436	−28
Saudi Arabia	1,775	1,756	1,727	2,002	+13
Libya	656	578	315	1,134	+82
All Arab countries	*6,234*	*5,953*	*5,577*	*7,101*	*+14*
Israel	1,257	1,573	1,222	416	−67
Asia	1,209	643	1,041	960	−21
Africa	280	321	181	209	−25
Other areas	20	16	33	15	−25
Grand total	*26,662*	*20,167*	*32,787*	*32,664*	*+23*

Sources: after Ministry of Tourism 1999: 33ff; CAPMAS 2001a; CAPMAS 2003b

Europe, America and Asia, and those who come from Arab countries – the former constituting about three-quarters, the latter about 20 per cent of the total number of visitors on average. The fluctuation in the proportions of these two main categories as shown in Figure 10.1 and Table 10.2 can be interpreted as follows:

- In the 1950s, when classical cultural tourism still prevailed in Egypt, the majority of visitors came from Western countries. In 1952, of the total number of foreign guests, 27,000 were Europeans (35.5 per cent), 18,000 Americans (23.7 per cent), and 21,000 Arabs (27.6 per cent).
- While, owing to the Israeli–Egyptian wars between 1967 and 1973, the numbers of tourists from Western countries dropped drastically, there was a considerable number of tourists from the Middle East coming to Egypt

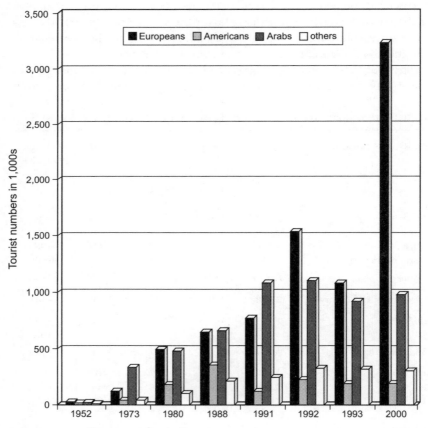

Figure 10.1 International tourism in Egypt: main tourist groups 1952–99 (Author: F. Ibrahim 2002; cartography: J. Feilner; sources of data: CAPMAS, Statistical Year Books for various years)

on business or holiday following the oil boom of the early 1970s. In 1973, of the total number of foreign guests in Egypt, 333,000 were Arabs (62.2 per cent), 119,000 Europeans (22 per cent) and 41,000 Americans (7.7 per cent).

- In 1979, immediately after the Camp David peace agreement, twice as many Western tourists visited Egypt as in 1973 – a positive development which continued throughout the 1980s. In 1988 they constituted more than half of the 2 million tourists in Egypt, so that the proportion was about the same as in the 1950s.

- In 2002 the group most strongly represented among European tourists was the Germans at 20.4 per cent, followed by the Italians at 19.6 per cent, the citizens of the USSR at 12.6 per cent, the British at 10.5 per cent and the French at 7.8 per cent. In 1992 only 1 per cent of visitors came from Eastern Europe, but their numbers increased rapidly towards the end of the millennium owing to the fall of the Iron Curtain and the accumulation of wealth in parts of society there, reaching 6 per cent in 2000. The number of Russian visitors grew from 15,900 to 451,461 between 1991 and 2002. In 2001 they occupied the third rank after Germany and Italy.

- Figure 10.1 and Table 10.1 show a marked drop of 22 per cent in the number of international tourists from 1992 to 1993, owing to the Islamist attack on British tourists in 1992. The subsequent loss of European visitors was 30 per cent. A similar situation occurred after the tragic events of 1997, when the number of European, Israeli and American tourists decreased by 35 per cent from 1997 to 1998. The loss was especially conspicuous among the Japanese and South Koreans. Their numbers had reached 118,000 in 1997, then dropped to 31,000 in 1998, reaching 126,000 again in 2000 (CAPMAS 2001a). It is interesting to note that between 1997 and 1998 the opposite development occurred among Israeli and Russian tourists. Their numbers grew by 20 and 12 per cent respectively. However, the number of Israeli visitors dropped sharply by 21.4 per cent from 1999 to 2000 owing to the troubles with Palestine (ibid.).

- Table 10.2 shows an increase of 23 per cent in the total number of tourist nights between 1997 and 2000, indicating that the crisis of 1998 had been overcome. The Europeans, who contributed more than two-thirds of the tourist nights in both years, recorded an increase of 44 per cent. Among them the Italians ranked first with an increase of 73 per cent, followed by Benelux tourists with an increase of 61 per cent. The share of tourists from the UK dropped by 6 per cent during that time, owing mainly to the changed marketing policies of the large British tourist agencies.

- Although in 1991, the year of the Gulf War, the proportion of guests from the Arab states rose considerably in relation to those from Western countries, at just over 1 million, the absolute figures for Arab guests equalled those of the two preceding years. Their countries of origin, however, were not the same as before. Whereas the number of visitors whose home countries had been supported by Egypt against Iraq increased (Kuwait by 23 per cent and Saudi Arabia by 80 per cent), the number of guests from Palestine dropped by 45 per cent and from Sudan by 49 per cent, since their governments had taken sides with Iraq during the war.

• For many years Libyans occupied first place among Arab visitors in Egypt. However, from 1992 to 2000 their share dropped from 24.8 to 15.3 per cent, while the Saudis took over the lead among Arab visitors, raising their share from 21.3 to 24.2 per cent. For political reasons there were dramatic changes in the numbers of both Sudanese visitors, dropping from 10.6 to 5.3 per cent, and Palestinians, rising from 5.6 to 15.1 per cent. The total number of Arab visitors was almost 1 million in 2000, representing a low 18 per cent of the total number of foreign tourists (CAPMAS 2001a). In 1986 the proportion of Arab visitors had been 42.3 per cent (Ministry of Tourism 1999: 41), when their absolute number was about half a million. The relative decrease in their proportion of the total number of visitors is due mainly to the enormous increase in the numbers of European tourists. While there was a boom in overseas tourism in Europe, the oil-rich Arab countries experienced an economic recession during this time.

Visitors from the Arab states differ from each other in terms of origin, the purpose of their journeys, and their attitudes. Two different groups can be recognized. One consists of rich visitors from the oil-producing countries who come either mainly to Cairo on business or as holidaymakers to spend the hot summer in Alexandria. For some of these Arabs, Egypt is a substitute for the once favoured but recently war-ridden Lebanon. They enjoy the cooler climate of the Mediterranean, and some the greater freedom regarding consumption of alcohol and other kinds of entertainment, since in their own countries these things are strictly forbidden and the *shari'a* (Islamic law) is applied in cases of contravention. Arabs of this type are to be seen in the four- and five-star hotels, where they sometimes rent whole suites. By far the greater number of Arab visitors, however, are hardly noticed by the European tourist in Egypt. They belong to a medium-income class and are more or less similar in their attitudes and consumption to Egyptians on the same level of income. For longer stays they usually rent furnished flats, for shorter stays they find accommodation in small hotels or guest houses of the *sha'bi* (people's) category, which is classified as being below the one-star category. If one compares the Americans to the Arabs as regards their choice of accommodation, one finds that in 1992, for example, only about half the Arab visitors in Egypt stayed in hotels, compared to 97.2 per cent of the American visitors, and while about one-fifth of Arab visitors chose hotels of the above-mentioned lowest category, only 5 per cent of the American visitors did so (CAPMAS 1994c).

A comparison of the duration of stay of foreign visitors of various origins shows a common trend towards shorter visits. In 1952 visits paid to Egypt lasted on average ten days, whereas five decades later, in 2000, they lasted only six days (CAPMAS 2001a). In the same period the duration of stay of Arabs was reduced from thirteen to 5.6 days, that of Europeans from twelve to about 6.5 days, and that of Americans from six to 5.6 days. The reason for the generally short periods of stay of Americans is that, although they have to endure a long flight when they come to Egypt, many of them visit the country as part of a wider-ranging tour which may include a visit to the Holy Land or Europe. In terms of their duration of stay in Egypt, the Germans and the Italians were leading among the Europeans in 2000, with an average of 7.2 nights per visitor (CAPMAS 2001a). The British and the Russians stayed a considerably shorter time at 5.4 and 4.9 nights respectively. And although Asians as a whole spent only an average of 3.8 nights, the Japanese stayed 4.7 nights. The differences among the Arabs were even greater. While the Saudis stayed for 7.2 nights, the Palestinians spent only three nights in Egypt on average, mainly because some of them cross the border to their neighbouring country for short business trips. The Libyans, who used to stay 7.2 nights on average in 1992 (ETA 1993), shortened their visits to only 2.1 nights in 2000. There are two reasons for this. The first is the deterioration in economic conditions in Libya during that period, the second the UN embargo against

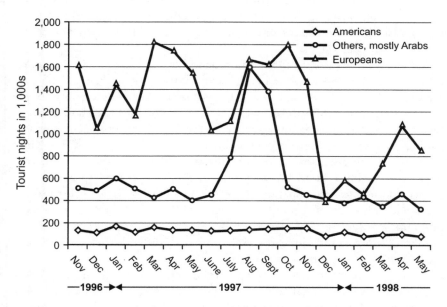

Figure 10.2 International tourism in Egypt: seasonal structure 1996–98 (Author: F. Ibrahim 2002; cartography: J. Feilner; source of data: Ministry of Tourism 1999: 22ff)

Libya in force at the time. Many Libyans travelled to Egypt by road only to fly on from there to their desired destinations abroad.

The seasonal distribution of foreign tourist arrivals in Egypt (see Figure 10.2) shows a concentration on the months of April and August on the one hand and a decrease in June and in winter on the other. To better understand this phenomenon, we have to look at the different groups of visitors separately. We see that the main season for Arab guests is summer, when they try to escape their own countries for climatic reasons during the three hottest months, which are also the time of the long school holidays. European visitors have two preferred seasons: spring and autumn. This can also be explained by climatic factors: they prefer the warm, sunny periods, but avoid summer with its extremely high temperatures. In spite of this the number of European tourists is relatively high in August, since this is the main holiday season in many parts of Europe. The visits of American tourists are much more evenly distributed over the year. For them the country is not a destination for a holiday in the sun. Many of them visit it on a tour of the Old World irrespective of the season. Figure 10.2 also shows the dramatic drop in tourist numbers, especially from Europe, after the Islamists' attack in 1997. Egypt's tourist industry suffered another severe blow in 2003, when America attacked Iraq.

1.2 Changes in foreign tourism: from old to new treasures in Egypt

Up until the 1970s tourists from the West tended to follow the classical tour of Egypt, with a main regional concentration on Cairo and Luxor with their treasures of the ancient Egyptian culture. As a rule an extension of the trip to Aswan was optional.

Since the early 1960s, with the introduction of the modern floating hotels on the Nile, the classical tour of Egypt has undergone a change. The fleet grew rapidly in number and reached 259 Nile cruise boats offering 28,270 beds in 2001. Nile cruises took place between Cairo and Luxor and between Luxor and Aswan. Most guests were still interested mainly in ancient Egyptian culture, and some groups staying at Luxor visited the Valley of the Kings on three or four successive days, studying the tombs with their guides, who were well qualified in archaeology and Egyptology besides speaking their guests' mother tongues fluently. Since the floating hotels were luxuriously equipped with swimming pools and other facilities, and varied entertainment programmes were usually offered on board, and since numerous Pharaonic monuments are found along the course of the Nile, the tourists were able to combine culture with recreation.

This new type of tourism suffered a serious blow when, in the early 1990s, Islamic terrorists started targeting the rather vulnerable Nile cruise boats. As a consequence all cruises were temporarily cancelled, and since that time practically no cruises have taken place between Cairo and Luxor since Asyut, the

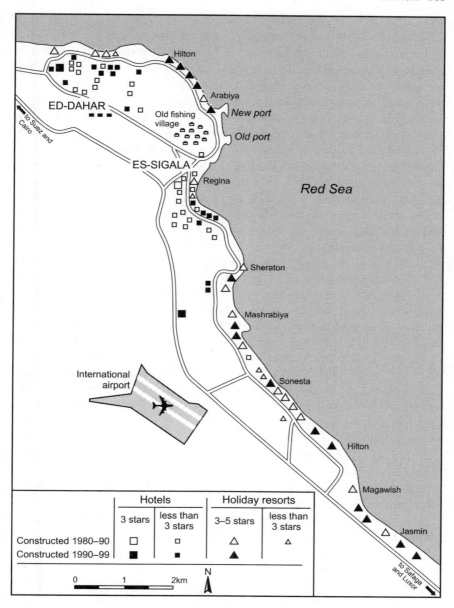

Figure 10.3 Hotel capacities at El-Ghardaqa: expansion 1980–99 (Author: F. Ibrahim 2002; cartography: J. Feilner; source: field surveys F. Ibrahim for various years)

centre of the Islamic fundamentalists, lies halfway between the two destinations. Instead, the cruises are now concentrated between Luxor and Aswan, with the result that in this part of its course the river is usually overcrowded when tourism flourishes, and in the two towns there is hardly enough space for all the boats to cast anchor. In spring 2000 they lay side by side in rows of five and more along the eastern Nile banks, spilling out great numbers of passengers daily or taking them on board after their arrival by plane. The local population is unlikely to profit from this kind of tourism, since the guests receive full-board accommodation on the floating hotels.

Roughly synchronously with the expansion of the Nile cruises in the 1980s, the purpose of the tourists' visits changed when new infrastructure for recreational and water sports tourism was developed along the Red Sea, focused on El-Ghardaqa (Hurghada; see Figure 10.3), and on Sharm esh-Sheikh on the southern tip of Sinai, after the peninsula had been returned to Egypt by Israel. Both centres of tourism are situated at a southern latitude which guarantees a warm and sunny climate all year round. While the infrastructure and the hotels at Sharm esh-Sheikh had been partly constructed by Israel after its occupation of Sinai in 1967, the extensive hotel complexes in El-Ghardaqa were often built in village style by Egyptians following the pattern of the Club Méditerranée hotel of Magawish, one of the first tourist hotels in the area, which was later taken over by the state-run Misr Travel Company. Since hotel capacities at Luxor could not keep pace with the rapid increase of tourism there, groups that had been booked in there were instead taken to El-Ghardaqa in a half-day journey. Later the combination of a classical tour of Egypt with a recreational holiday at the Red Sea gained great popularity. After the Aswan High Dam had been constructed and the Temple of Abu Simbel moved to the rim of the Sadd el-Ali reservoir, trips by plane to this monument were offered from Aswan, which takes the tourist barely more than half a day. Since a road has now been built there, the temple can also be easily reached by bus or taxi in an excursion that takes no more than one day. Tours to other temples of Nubia are also offered from Aswan, with three- to four-day cruises on the Sadd el-Ali storage lake. Usually this is combined with a cruise from Luxor to Aswan and a week at Hurghada or some other place on the Red Sea coast.

This new trend of combining culture with recreation or sports was enhanced by the following factors:

- An expansion of air traffic took place when several new airports were built, so that Luxor as well as the new holiday resorts on the Red Sea could be reached from Cairo or later in direct flights from Europe within a short time.
- Wide new tarmac roads were constructed in areas that in the 1970s had still been under the control of the military and were out of bounds to foreigners, especially in the desert areas between the Nile valley and the Red Sea, which the tourists from El-Ghardaqa or Safaga had to cross on their one- or two-day excursions to Luxor, and along the Gulf of Suez.

Today Cairo can be reached from El-Ghardaqa within five hours on the express buses which run several times daily.

- During the peak season hotel capacities at Luxor were insufficient, whereas along the Red Sea the growth in hotel capacity was extremely rapid, so that the occupancy rates of hotels in the seaside resorts allowed for more tourists. As a result travel agencies operating in both places started offering cheap package tours, including a combination of flight and hotel accommodation with half or full board, to make a stay at the coast attractive.

- During the time of terrorist attacks on tourist buses, trains and Nile cruise boats in the early 1990s, the walled and well-guarded holiday villages on the Red Sea were considered comparatively safe. Foreign travel agencies that felt responsible for the security of their customers often recommended a stay in one of the Red Sea resorts in combination with a Nile cruise between Luxor and Aswan.

- Owing to the security hazards many travel agents temporarily eliminated Egypt completely from their programmes; others, however, offered trips at very low prices. They could do so because of the enormous hotel capacities, especially in El-Ghardaqa, where hotels were mostly vacant then, with the result that accommodation was offered at prices that hardly covered the costs of the hotel companies. Through these bargain offers a completely new class of customer gained access to Egypt, sometimes paying no more than £600 sterling for a two-week all-inclusive trip; often much less for a last-minute booking. The new type of tourist was younger, much less culture oriented and of a generally lower level of formal education, so that the new trend was for a beach holiday, sometimes with children, in sunny Egypt, the oriental flair of which could be enjoyed when visiting the local bazaar.

- The recession in classical cultural tourism in Egypt as a consequence of the general demise of classical education in Europe had been foreseen by some geographers. In the 1970s it had still been possible to observe groups spending a whole week in Luxor with daily visits to the Valley of the Kings, intensively studying the various tombs. Such tourists, with a strong interest in archaeology or in Pharaonic history and art, were usually advanced in age and had often invested more than £1,500 sterling in a journey which was conducted by a highly qualified academic guide.

- After Sinai was returned by Israel, Egypt gained a reputation for offering excellent places for snorkelling and scuba-diving. Its government had to pay a high price, however, for the infrastructure erected on the peninsula by Israel during the years of occupation since 1967. When surfing became fashionable in Europe, the trend gained momentum, since for this sport, too, and also for yachting, the Red Sea and the Gulf of Aqaba, with their long white coasts and bays, offered excellent conditions practically all year round. Later some hotels started offering golfing facilities, though this type of tourism puts a heavy burden on a desert environment. Thus developed a situation quite unlike the historical beginnings of tourism in Egypt. In advertising this new kind of tourism, 'the new treasures of Egypt' were extolled. Great numbers of tourists were flown within a few hours from cold and rainy Europe to the warm coral beaches on the Red Sea, and the cheap flights often included transport of the necessary sports equipment.

Today most tourists come to Egypt with a minimum of knowledge about the country and its people, not to mention its culture or history, and during their stay they learn next to nothing about these things. Those who spend a fortnight at El-Ghardaqa or similar places usually live in a tourist ghetto and at best see a few *fellaheen* tilling their fields when they are passing through a short stretch of the Nile valley on a day trip to Luxor by bus, or a few 'Bedouin', if they join an excursion into the desert organized by the hotel they are staying at.

1.3 Regional structure of international tourism (see Figure 10.4)

Owing to its historical development tourism in Egypt shows a characteristic regional structure with decisive effects on the places concerned. However, the old regional pattern of distribution of the tourist industry has changed drastically since the 1990s with the strong expansion of tourism on the Red Sea coast and on Sinai, as described above. A comparison of the hotel capacities for 1992 and 2001 shows this change quite clearly. The share of the Red Sea and Sinai of the country's hotel bed capacity jumped from 10 to 59.8 per cent, while that of the Mediterranean coast dropped from 25 to 7.1 per cent and Greater Cairo lost its leading position, falling from 42 to 19.9 per cent. Figure 10.4 shows that this trend gained strength in the first years of the new millennium, for three-quarters of the hotel rooms under construction in Egypt in 2001 were to be found on the Red Sea coast and on the Gulf of Aqaba, while the share of the Mediterranean coast was only 2.3 per cent and that of Luxor and Aswan together 4.4 per cent. The main tourism areas are dealt with below.

Cairo and its surroundings

In 2001 Greater Cairo, with its 42,500 hotel beds, possessed 20 per cent of the total hosting capacity of Egypt (Ministry of Tourism 2002: 64). The capital is the centre of tourism in the country and of international air traffic to and from Egypt. It hosts international fairs, conferences and conventions, and moreover offers a large variety of tourist sites. The town represents a unique concentration of monuments of the seven thousand years of the Pharaonic, Greek, Roman, Byzantine, Coptic and Islamic eras (see Illustrations 19 and 23) as well as the innumerable treasures of these times. At the same time the visitor can experience a Third World metropolis of about 18 million inhabitants, which gives him impressions that are altogether different.

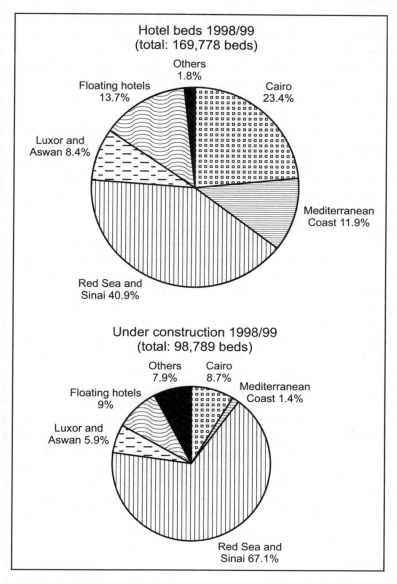

Hotel beds 1998/99
(total: 169,778 beds)

Others 1.8%

Floating hotels 13.7%

Cairo 23.4%

Luxor and Aswan 8.4%

Mediterranean Coast 11.9%

Red Sea and Sinai 40.9%

Under construction 1998/99
(total: 98,789 beds)

Others 7.9%

Cairo 8.7%

Floating hotels 9%

Mediterranean Coast 1.4%

Luxor and Aswan 5.9%

Red Sea and Sinai 67.1%

Figure 10.4 Hotel capacities in Egypt: regional distribution 1998/99 (In Cairo and Alexandria there are a considerable number of hotel beds for domestic tourism, which are not included.) Author: F. Ibrahim 2002; cartography: J. Feilner; source of data: Ministry of Tourism 1999: 54–7

Unlike the exclusively tourist-oriented places such as Luxor and Sharm esh-Sheikh, Cairo offers its visitors hotels and guest houses of all categories. Four- and five-star hotels, mostly skyscrapers, line the Nile banks or are found on the islands in exquisite districts close to the town centre. Another concentration of hotels in the higher price category, mostly one- to four-storey buildings, is situated near the Pyramids of Giza and the historical Mena House, with its breathtaking view of the Pyramids, which in the past hosted many a king or state president. Hotels in the middle category, some also dating back to the early days of tourism in Egypt, are in the colonial town centre between the quarter of Azbakiya and Tahrir Square. The government has succeeded in efforts to improve the traffic situation and the amenities here. Hotels and guest houses in the lower price categories are to be found near the main railway station and the terminals of buses and group taxis from the provinces. New hotels in the middle and higher categories have been built in the suburb of Heliopolis, conveniently located for businessmen using the international airport.

Cairo offers a large variety of restaurants, riverside casinos, restaurant boats, cafés, bars, theatres, cabarets, discos and other places for recreation, amusement or cultural events. They have a similar distribution to that of the hotels. While those serving local or lower- and medium-level demand are concentrated mainly in the town centre, those in the higher tourist categories are situated either on the Nile or along the wide arterial road that connects the town centre with Giza. The latter location sports a concentration of places for amusement and entertainment designed mainly for foreign tourists but also for rich Arabs or Egyptians. This led Islamistic terrorists to make their first bomb attacks here on Pyramid Road in 1980.

Since the mid-1950s there have been efforts to include the oasis of El-Faiyum with its Lake Qarun, situated 60 km south of Cairo, in the tourists' programmes, because it can easily be reached from the town centre. Since Pharaonic times, and especially during the reign of King Farouk, the oasis has been a popular hunting area. Today hunting takes place there illegally. The oasis is situated in the midst of a fascinating desert landscape, with hotels offering accommodation on the shores of a lake rich in fish; it has flowering fruit gardens, traditional water wheels and pigeon towers, as well as ancient monuments. Although it can offer a welcome change after a stay in noisy and dusty Cairo, so far it has remained mostly a destination for day trips only.

The Mediterranean coast

The Egyptian Mediterranean coast, with its various holiday resorts from Marsa Matruh in the extreme west to El-Arish on the Sinai Peninsula in the east, is well away from the main areas of international tourism, such as Cairo, Luxor, El-Ghardaqa and South Sinai. However, tourists with a special interest in the Greek-Roman period in Egypt usually spend one to three days on a trip to Alexandria, where new excavations are continuously taking place in the town itself and ancient treasures are being discovered offshore, and where an equivalent of the famous ancient library of Alexandria, which was burnt

24. Sitta October Bridge, Cairo: A considerable number of new bridges and flyovers were built to ease the traffic flow in Greater Cairo with its 17 million inhabitants. The picture shows Sitta October Bridge and part of the 100-km-long ring road around Egypt's capital. (Photo: F. Ibrahim)

several times and finally destroyed completely, was opened with UNESCO support at the beginning of the new millennium. The tourists usually reach Alexandria on the fast desert road from which today smaller tarmac roads lead westward over a short distance into Wadi en-Natrun in the Libyan Desert, where four of the once many Coptic monasteries can be visited. A further trip, from Alexandria westwards along the coast, can be undertaken to the British, Italian or German war memorials commemorating the deaths of thousands of mostly young soldiers in the Battle of El-Alamein on 23 October 1942, in which Rommel's troops were defeated by the British. But only a few tourists spare the time for this. The same applies to Siwa oasis, with its famous Temple of the Oracle, which Alexander the Great once consulted, and its numerous hot springs. It can be reached from Marsa Matruh within four hours by car on the tarmac road built in the 1980s. Today it is no longer a destination only for backpackers, especially since a three-star tourist hotel was opened in one of the old palm gardens and safari trips to the Great Sand Sea desert or to other oases of the Western Desert as far as Bahariya are offered. Although El-Arish on Sinai has good hotels and a fine white sandy beach, international tourism is unlikely to flourish there because of security problems at the Gaza/Israel border.

Efforts to open up the Mediterranean coast of Egypt for non-Arab international beach tourism have failed so far, partly because in summer the resorts are more than crowded by Egyptians and Arabs, and in winter the weather is not reliable and the sea rough, not unlike the European North Sea coasts in summer. Those who want to enjoy the white beaches before or after the short summer season will find most places closed or services limited. The fact that the towns along the Mediterranean coast account together for about 10 per cent of the total number of hotel beds in Egypt (see Figure 10.4) merely proves their importance for domestic and Arab tourism.

Luxor and Aswan

Every visitor to Egypt, albeit with only the slightest cultural interest, will certainly want to visit Luxor. There he can find in close proximity Thebes West with the Valley of the Kings and the Valley of the Queens, the Memnon's Colossi – one of the ancient Seven Wonders of the World – the temple of Hatshepsut and those of Karnak and of Luxor, as well as numerous other temples and sights. It was Thomas Cook who, in 1869, started tourism in Luxor and in Upper Egypt by hiring two of the Khedive's steamers and taking thirty-two Englishmen with their ladies upstream. Quantitatively further development of tourism was slow, however, so that a hundred years later there were only four tourist hotels in Luxor with a total capacity of 1,000 beds (Standl 1988/89: 213). The 1980s saw the greatest upward trend, so that by 1992 there were 9,000 hotel beds. The complete dependence of the inhabitants of the town (1996: about 300,000) on tourism had catastrophic consequences when international guests stayed away owing to the Gulf War in 1991 and terrorist attacks on tourists, which also hit Luxor in a dramatic event in 1997. There was a slight recovery of tourism in Luxor in the years in between, but the success of the mid-1980s was never achieved again, although the government made great efforts, for example by staging a spectacular performance of Verdi's opera *Aida* in front of the Hatshepsut temple on the occasion of the UN World Conference on Population in Cairo in 1994, and by investing considerably in the construction of the river promenade and a bazaar area. Included in these efforts was the building of a new Nile bridge south of the town connecting it to Thebes West, which led to negative consequences for Luxor. Instead of crossing the river on ferry boats from Luxor, today the buses take tourists to the sights on the western bank of the Nile directly, without any loss of time. So the duration of the tourists' sojourn in Luxor has been drastically reduced. Also a problem for the inhabitants of the town, who depend so much on the expenditure of foreigners, is the large number of buses transporting guests from the Red Sea coast to Luxor on day trips. They arrive at Thebes in the morning and leave Luxor in the late afternoon, so their passengers have no time to stroll through the bazaar streets and buy souvenirs or hire a sailing boat on the Nile at sunset, once popular tourist activities. Usually they are also provided with packed lunches and hot and cold drinks by the organizers of the trips. The same applies to the passengers on the floating hotels. All that tourists of this type leave behind in the once so quiet and picturesque Luxor is pollution of various kinds. In spring 2000, when tourism experienced a boom, the river was crowded with hundreds of Nile cruise boats, and one of the three daily convoys bound for the Red Sea coast consisted of about 200 buses and taxis rushing through the desert late at night to take their passengers (who had mostly spent just a few hours at Luxor) back to their holiday villages at El-Ghardaqa. Another negative effect the bridge may cause is that sooner or later new hotels and other buildings will be erected at Qurna on the west bank, close to the Valley of the Kings, further endangering the Pharaonic monuments, which are already suffering from the rising groundwater table and the great number of visitors.

Aswan still attracts numerous tourists today. Here too, however, the floating boats cause a problem for the mostly Nubian local population which depends on an income from tourism. Aswan's oldest hotel, beautifully situated overlooking the Nile cataract, opened its doors in 1899 and became a legend. Tourists coming to Aswan not only pay the ancient monuments a visit, but also go to see the High Dam, and maybe undertake a cruise on the Sadd el-Ali storage lake, to visit Abu Simbel and other Nubian temples saved from the lake floods. To interpret Luxor and Aswan's relatively small share of hotel bed capacity, as shown in Figure 10.4, we have to factor in the capacity of the floating hotels that cruise between the two towns, because passengers usually spend several nights on board the ships when these cast anchor in the two towns.

The Red Sea coast and South Sinai

Tourism along the coasts of the Red Sea, the Gulf of Suez and the Gulf of Aqaba differs greatly from tourism at the Mediterranean coast in type, in origin of guests, categories of accommodation, history of development and seasonal character. These are the most recently established tourist regions in Egypt and development is still very active, with hotels and timeshare establishments in the highest price categories being opened continuously along the white beaches (see Figure 10.3), close to what ranks among the world's most beautiful coral reefs. The large tourist villages here are often investments by rich Egyptians or are built by big international hotel companies. The tourists are fenced off from the local population and usually at a great distance from them. The only local people many foreign guests come into contact with are the hotel staff. Usually the hotels comprise several restaurants, lounges, bars and discotheques, often offering live bands, to meet the different demands of the guests, and often tennis courts, fitness studios and shopping arcades with boutiques or malls, in which guests can buy their own local newspapers as well as clothes, jewellery and souvenirs of all types. So there is no need for the guests to leave the hotel grounds and only a few of them visit the local markets or bazaars. The tourists exist in an artificial world especially created for them, usually without being aware of the fact that they are in a desert in a Third World country. Not many of the visitors at El-Ghardaqa know, for example, that practically all the water they use is brought over a distance of more than 200 km from Qena in the Nile valley, and that all the fruit and vegetables they consume have to be transported over similar distances. Since as a rule the new tourist resorts have not developed from indigenous settlements, hardly any of them had a sizeable number of inhabitants available to work in the tourist business when development started. The staff employed in the hotels usually come from Cairo or from Upper Egypt, and as a rule live together in staff residences that are provided by the hotel administration, leaving their families behind elsewhere. The impact of contact with the tourists is as a rule quite strong on the usually young male employees who live away from their families.

The average capacity per hotel or tourist village at the Red Sea and in South Sinai was 355 beds in 2001, which means that the hotels were bigger than in Cairo (301 beds/hotel) and much bigger than the average for the whole country (267 beds/hotel). According to the Governor of the Red Sea governorate, hotel capacity at the Red Sea increased from 20,000 to 34,700 rooms between 1998 and 2001. The occupancy rate in 2000 was 86 per cent, which is higher than the country's average. In 2000 the average tourist on the Red Sea coast spent US$218, which is far more than the country's average of US$131. The reason for the higher spending was the extra activities undertaken by the tourists there. Thus 32 per cent of them made a trip to Luxor for about US$90, 28 per cent went on a trip to Cairo, and 8 per cent made an excursion to Sharm esh-Sheikh. In addition, 40 per cent of them undertook diving or snorkelling tours costing on average US$25 each, and 16 per cent went on a desert safari, for which they paid US$16 on average. The Governor maintained that each hotel room generated 1.6 jobs directly and 3 additional jobs indirectly (Ali 2001).

Safaga, 50 km south of El-Ghardaqa, has become a holiday resort for windsurfers and scuba-divers and a spa for patients suffering from rheumatism. El-Quseir, 85 km south, and Marsa Alam, 138 km south, offer excellent conditions for snorkelling and for scuba-diving that surpass by far those of the northern regions, but tourism here has not yet been developed fully, although an international airport is operational. During the last two decades of the millennium El-Ghardaqa attracted so many investors that the whole area became built-up. Due to lack of proper planning the result was an amorphous settlement without all the amenities. Although this made many, including newly rich Egyptians, look for other destinations, masses of tourists continued to be flown in daily thanks to the comparatively low prices resulting from the over-capacities created. Awareness of the negative impacts of watersports tourism is gradually growing here, with the result that some hotel owners and

25. Garbage collectors (zabbaleen): The *zabbaleen* with their donkey-drawn carts collect most of the garbage in the middle-class districts of Cairo, take it to their settlements on the outskirts of the city and separate it for recycling. Gradually new systems of garbage-collecting without a recycling component are today being introduced by the government. (Photo: F. Ibrahim)

diving schools have founded Hepca, the Hurghada Environmental Protection Association, mainly for the protection of the coral reefs.

Only a few miles north of El-Ghardaqa the new tourist resort of El-Gouna was built in the early 1990s by a development company founded by a group of businessmen. Here, on an area of 17 million m² of desert land, the planners created for tourists what they called 'the brightest star on the Red Sea', a completely artificial world with a golf course, lagoons, waterways with shuttle boats, an artificial beach close to a natural coral reef, as well as a modern hospital. New concepts were embraced to try to avoid the mistakes evident at El-Ghardaqa.

The El-Ghardaqa region saw its period of most rapid development in the 1980s and 1990s. Soon after, when the government declared parts of the Gulf of Aqaba coast one of its priority zones for the development of a diversified and integrated tourism, El-Ghardaqa was overtaken in terms of tourist arrivals by the South Sinai region, beginning a trend of gradually forsaking overcrowded Sharm esh-Sheikh in favour of the coastline of the Gulf of Aqaba, the 'Egyptian Riviera' (see Illustration 20). From Sharm to Dahab, Nuweiba and Taba, what had originally been camps frequented by backpackers since the 1980s were turned into first-class hotels and expensive holiday villages. Although national parks were created in South Sinai for the protection of terrestrial and marine habitats, and to avoid linear sprawl as well as the other planning blights suffered elsewhere, at the beginning of the new millennium there was hardly a spot on the Gulf coast that was not occupied by a hotel, holiday village, gated community or a campsite later to be replaced by solid buildings. A unique desert landscape, the option of visiting St Catherine's Monastery and of climbing Jebel Musa (2,285 m), the possibility of meeting Bedouin and going on desert safaris or climbing in one of the unique canyons, white sandy beaches lined by coral reefs and colourful fish in crystal-clear water, marinas for yacht tourism and sea cruising, and a warm climate all year round attracted many tourists, including from Israel. Sharm esh-Sheikh, however, where the best diving sites in Egypt, if not in the world, can be found, with its national park of Ras Muhammad, is situated at a more southerly latitude and so enjoys higher winter temperatures. It remains the most popular destination for tourists.

Areas with predominantly individual tourism

As a consequence of the above-mentioned trends towards shorter stays and the new structure of international tourism in Egypt, above all the concentration on the southern coasts of the country, some areas well worth visiting but off the main tourist routes today receive fewer visitors. Among these places that have to fight for every single visitor these days are some sites of archaeological interest in Middle Egypt in the area of El-Minya, which are now avoided by tourists since they are close to the centres of Islamic fundamentalist terrorism, as well as other destinations such as the monasteries of the Desert Fathers near the Red Sea or the oases of the Libyan Desert in the New Valley and Siwa. In spite of all the efforts of the Egyptian government and of local administrations, famous temples or tombs such as Tuna el-Gabal, Abydos, Dandara, Idfu, Beni Hasan or Tell el-Amarna are mostly only visited by individual tourists or by groups on expensive study trips, which have become rare today. Places situated along the Nile had profited from the popularity of the cruises which started in the 1960s, but were interrupted in the early 1990s. The Coptic monasteries of St Paul (Deir Anba Pola) and St Antony (Deir Anba Antonius) in the desert mountain range at the Gulf of Suez, and the ancient monasteries in the Natrun Valley, St Makarius, St Bishoy, Syrian and Baramos, have, since the 1970s, also become destinations increasingly visited primarily by individual tourists and by study tours after access roads and facilities for accommodating guests had been constructed. A visit to the Greek Orthodox monastery of St Catherine is usually undertaken from Cairo or from Sharm esh-Sheikh by plane or by bus, and many tourists combine a visit with climbing Jebel Musa, situated close by. The whole area was turned into a national park and a new hotel opened within the walls of the monastery. The development of tourism in the oases of the Western (Libyan) Desert, in which there are also various sights of great historic and art-historic relevance to be found, started in the 1960s in tandem with construction of the New Valley Project, and is centred on El-Kharga and Ed-Dakhla. A tourist who wants to pay these a visit must allow a minimum of five days. Besides the old road from Asyut to El-Kharga there is now a good road from Giza to El-Bahariya and on via El-Farafra and Ed-Dakhla to El-Kharga, from where the tourist can reach Luxor within half a day on a public road. There is a luxurious hotel at El-Kharga and good accommodation can also be found at Ed-Dakhla as well as at El-Farafra. Capacities are limited, however. The local authorities hope to encourage adventure tourism, for example at El-Farafra, with its spectacular White Desert (see Illustration 2), and several Bedouin families already specialize in the business, offering desert safaris on four-wheel vehicles as well as camel trekking with overnight stays in tents and barbecues in the desert under the clear starry skies. Tourists on bicycles are not an uncommon sight in the oases. A large-scale development of tourism cannot be foreseen, however, although from the security point of view travelling through the New Valley is a fairly safe alternative to travelling through the Nile valley from Cairo to Luxor via Asyut.

1.4 The implications of international tourism for Egypt's economy

The Egyptian Ministry of Tourism describes tourism as 'the engine of economic development', referring to experts who see in it 'the only outlet for the economic and social problems of the developing countries' (Ministry of Tourism 1999: 3). And in fact it is of vital economic importance to Egypt. Receipts from tourism represent the most important source of foreign currency for the country, along with the remittances of Egyptians working abroad, the revenues from the Suez Canal and crude oil exports (*October*, 30 July 2000: 5). They constitute 4.4 per cent of GDP and can be estimated at 11.6 per cent of GDP if indirect tourist expenditure is taken into account as well. Unlike oil production, the highly mechanized, efficient transport activities on the Suez Canal and the modern industries in the new towns, tourism is of special significance for the national economy because of its labour intensity. The number of people earning their livelihood directly or indirectly from this branch of the economy in 2003 was estimated at 2.2 million by the Egyptian Ministry of Tourism. This figure includes not merely those employed in hotels and restaurants, but also those working in travel agencies, in the tourist transport sector, as guides and in tourist-oriented handicrafts production and trade. In addition there are numerous work opportunities created in the construction business and in the furnishing of tourist hotels. The latter saw a boom after the liberalization of the economy by Sadat in the 1970s. The huge number of hotels mushrooming along the Red Sea coast are a result of the state's Open Door policy, through which ten-year exemptions from taxes were granted for such enterprises as well as licences for duty-free import of the building materials and equipment required. Egyptian as well as foreign investors were given guarantees that their enterprises would not be nationalized. So many who possessed not only the necessary capital but also the right connections invested in the tourism industry, availing themselves of the financial advantages, exploiting them fully and quite frequently abusing them. Many of the imported goods were sold elsewhere in the country at a considerable profit. The state's policy was also to reprivatize those hotels which had been nationalized in the socialist era and which had become so run-down that they could no longer meet the demands of tourists. Egyptian as well as Arab investors saw their chance. Since they were mostly inexperienced in the hotel business many of them arranged for their hotels to be run by well-established foreign hotel companies.

It is impossible to predict the future development of tourism in Egypt. No other branch of the economy shows such an immediate response to internal as well as external instability. Although the situation within the country has improved, the danger of terrorist attacks by Islamic fundamentalists is still present. The terrorists know that if they hit tourism they hit the government, with whose policies they disagree. As two wars against Iraq, fighting between Israel and the Palestinians in the Second Intifada and the terrorist attack against the World Trade Center on 11 September 2001 showed, political events in the region or elsewhere can paralyse tourist activity overnight. It is beyond doubt that Egypt has the best resources for tourism of various types. It boasts unique monuments that are witnesses to 7,000 years of civilization and it is blessed with a favourable climate all year round and with landscapes of great scenic beauty – including mountains, deserts, beaches lined by turquoise waters with rich underwater fauna, and the green Nile valley. It has an excellent infrastructure, enough highly educated manpower to serve the tourists, for example as multi-lingual guides, and a friendly population who greet foreigners with great openness and hospitality, so on the whole the outlook should be positive. Growth rates in tourism during the years 1997–2000 were so strong (12 per cent) that it was feared that the infrastructure would collapse unless quick action was taken. The government developed urgent plans to expand the capacity of the international airport of El-Ghardaqa to 4,000 passengers/hour, that of Sharm esh-Sheikh to 1,800 passengers/hour, and that of Luxor to 2,600 passengers/hour, as well as opening a new international airport at Marsa Alam and starting construction of further international airports in various other tourist areas, such as Dahab and El-Alamein (Internet 2001h). To promote yachting tourism, eight marinas will be constructed on the Red Sea shores as well as on the Gulf of Aqaba (Saad 1999). The government hopes tourism in Egypt 'will continue in the future, to be a key contributor to GNP, foreign exchange, employment generation, regional development, and population redistribution' (Internet 2001i). However, the environmental impact should be watched carefully and the conservation of nature not be

26. Glass-blower in Old Cairo: A few glass-blowers still have their workshops in the old Fatimid part of Cairo, where they recycle the glass collected by the *zabbaleen* (garbage collectors). The products are of a high artistic quality and are nearly exclusively bought by tourists. (Photo: F. Ibrahim)

a matter of mere lip-service, since the landscapes the foreign tourists prefer are often those that are 'untouched' and ecologically particularly fragile. They will find new destinations in other parts of the world and exploit these once they find that Egyptian ones are not satisfying their demands.

2 Domestic tourism

There are more people engaged in domestic tourism in Egypt than there are in the external variety. Most probably local tourism is also of even greater importance for the national economy than foreign tourism, although there is barely any hard currency involved immediately. Domestic tourism has a tradition of several thousand years, for even during Pharaonic times Egyptians undertook regular visits on their barges to the places designated for the veneration of their gods, where the adherents of the various cults performed their religious ceremonies and celebrated with ritual feasts. These destinations were along the river, since most of the ancient cults were related to the Nile as a life-giving element. In the early Christian, i.e. Coptic, period, there was a continuation of this in the form of pilgrimages to those places along the Nile where the Holy Family is said to have rested, such as Matariya, Zaitun, Old Cairo, Baiyad (Beni Suef), Gabal et-Teir (El-Minya), as well as El-Miharraq and Durunka (Asyut), where either monasteries or churches devoted to the Virgin Mary were established. The early Christian monasteries in the deserts also became destinations for pilgrimages. The tomb of St Menas, situated in the Western Desert south-west of Alexandria, was known far beyond the borders of Egypt, and attracted so many pilgrims that a big town developed around it in the early Christian period. After excavations had been carried out there it became a place of pilgrimage again for the Copts from the middle of the last century. Today some of the desert monasteries and the old churches attract thousands of believers for prayer, fasting and retreat on certain days of the year. Pious pilgrims mingle with foreign tourists, there to study the ancient icons and the architecture of the old buildings. Local tourism of the type described here has increased considerably over recent decades for various reasons:

- A religious revival has occurred among the Copts since the 1960s.
- Thanks to the new tarmac roads, practically all desert monasteries are now accessible to normal cars.
- Many middle-class families are today more mobile since they either own cars or can afford a bus excursion organized by their parish.

The most important place for Muslim pilgrimage is Tanta, situated in the Nile delta, where the tomb of the Sufi saint Es-Saiyed el-Badawi is located. Annually in October thousands of pilgrims from all over the country gather here. Other places have similar feasts or *mulid* (birth), as such Islamic and also Christian feasts are called. Since those who attend them are mostly *fellaheen*, the infrastructure in terms of transport, accommodation, catering and entertainment has little in common with what foreign tourists demand. It is also of a much 'lower standard' than that which most Egyptians spending a summer holiday in Alexandria enjoy. Nevertheless, these popular feasts or fairs are important for the local economy, and since they attract young and old alike they are also important in keeping alive local folklore and cultural heritage.

Another, yet more important type of local tourism in Egypt is beach tourism on the Mediterranean, as well as on the Red Sea and the Gulfs of Suez and Aqaba. This type of tourism has become particularly popular among the newly rich. It is, however, not of indigenous origin. Holidaymaking of this type was first practised by the Europeans living in Egypt, especially in Alexandria, and was then adopted by the local upper class. It is significant that to this day there is no word in the Arabic language for bathing costume or swimming trunks. The French word *maillot* is used instead. Alexandria remained the classic location for Egyptians for summer holidays, although during the second half of the last century various other places gained in popularity. Today Alexandria still attracts two-thirds of the 3 million Egyptians who spend a holiday at the seaside every year. Locations between Rashid and Dumyat Nile arms, which were popular seaside resorts until the 1960s, lost their sandy beaches as a consequence of the construction of the Aswan High Dam, because of the stronger erosive power of the sea after fewer Nile sediments were deposited. Today the seaside resort that is second in popularity for local tourism is Marsa Matruh on the north coast, near the Libyan border. It developed rapidly in the 1970s, when there were close political and economic relations between Egypt and its western neighbour, at a time when Libya was able to export large amounts of crude oil and depended on Egyptian manpower. Marsa Matruh is connected to Alexandria by a railway line that formerly ended before the border but today continues to Tobruk in Libya, and by a road. As a seaside resort Marsa Matruh has certain advantages over Alexandria, which suffers badly from pollution these days. It has white sandy beaches as well as stretches of coast with bizarre rock formations (for example Cleopatra's Bath), clean sea water, unpolluted air and is much less crowded. Its greatest disadvantage is its distance (*c.* 500 km) from the places most potential visitors come from, for example Greater Cairo. This is why those who opt for a holiday here are usually wealthier people who come from Cairo or Alexandria in their own cars and who appreciate the less crowded and less polluted beaches. For others, however, Alexandria, with its great variety of entertainment, its restaurants of all categories and cafés along the corniche, is still attractive. There is, however, an enormous amount of development going on along the coastline from Alexandria to Marsa Matruh, with the result that today practically every piece of land there is subject to a planning application. The only areas not affected are at El-Alamein, where landmines of the Second World War still make development impossible, certain military areas, and an area reserved for the establishment of a nuclear reactor. The westward extension of Alexandria's holiday areas started in the mid-1950s, when the government supported the construction of large holiday villages along the coast for military personnel and the professional organizations of lawyers, doctors, etc. Likewise the big state-owned or parastatal firms and banks built or rented complete blocks of holiday flats there for their employees. Others organize day trips to Alexandria for their workforce. Through this type of social tourism the beaches close to Alexandria are crowded all summer by holidaymakers from the delta provinces, and have lost their former Mediterranean and Western-style appearance. Today the more conservative culture of the rural local population prevails along with the Islamic dress code that has characterized the urban middle class since the mid-1970s. The Westernized local bourgeoisie has shifted to the beaches farther west of Alexandria, to the Red Sea and more recently also to Sinai. West of Alexandria it is dominant in the new gated communities, which extend from Alexandria to Marsa Matruh, showing all kinds of exotic styles of architecture. Here the newly rich have their apartments, which they occupy at most from July to early September, leaving them vacant the rest of the year. Such an investment is prestigious, and may be lucrative given the high rate of inflation in the country.

Tourist locations in the Suez Canal Zone in Port Said and in Ismailiya on Lake Timsah, at the Great Bitter Lake, in Abu Sultan and in Port Fouad are more or less only of local importance and attract few visitors from Cairo and from the eastern Nile delta. Since the 1980s, however, the infrastructure for holidaymakers has been improved at Port Said in the wake of the development that followed the establishment of a duty-free trade zone near the port.

Just as the Egyptian upper class and upper middle class adopted the leisure-time behaviour of their colonial masters at the beginning of the twentieth century, today they follow the example of Western tourists, especially as regards the trend of visiting the beach resorts on the Red Sea, and more recently in South Sinai. This development began in the 1950s with day trips and weekend excursions to Ain Sukhna, a hot spring on the Gulf of Suez. Since the area lacked infrastructure, however, at first only a few foreigners living in Cairo could participate, followed by well-to-do Egyptians who owned cars. Simultaneously, at El-Ghardaqa, a Sheraton Hotel was built, and the Club Méditerranée holiday village established at Magawish. After El-Ghardaqa had become popular with foreign tourists, the proportion of Egyptian guests also increased and the state took over management of Magawish. In the summer months, with temperatures of more than 30° C, it is too hot for most Europeans. To fill the vacancies the hotel companies offer package tours at reduced prices for a week or a weekend to Egyptians. Generally Egyptians receive price reductions of 60 per cent on the room rates in the expensive tourist hotels, but complain that they are not welcome when foreign tourism flourishes. The prices they have to pay are still extremely high for the local middle class. The reduced price for a stay of one night in a four-star hotel is equivalent to a month's salary for a university graduate. Nevertheless, spending one's honeymoon in an exclusive tourist hotel has been fashionable in Egypt for some time, and many members of the middle class do so, or take a holiday there with the whole family. This may consume a good proportion of their savings, but it impresses relatives and colleagues and conveys the impression that they belong to a higher social class. When hotels and holiday villages at El-Ghardaqa were seriously under-occupied during the Gulf War and after terrorist activities in the 1990s, many big firms, banks and other organizations started holding conferences there, which were also often attended by their foreign partners or advisers. Some of the participants prolonged their stays after the function for a few days of relaxation, or brought their families, so that with this conference tourism a new type of local tourism came into being.

Although Egyptians readily adopted the foreigners' predilection for seaside tourism in the past, as well as for water sports in recent years, especially on Sinai, they are less inclined to copy the cultural tourism practised by foreigners, above all in Luxor. For them it is too expensive, too tiring and confers no prestige. Only schools, universities and various youth organizations offer cheap excursions for young people to Luxor, Aswan, Cairo or Alexandria. Of late, however, it has become a fashion for the middle class to visit the pyramids at Giza or the Egyptian Museum in Cairo on public holidays. For most people, the character of the excursions, however, is definitely more recreational than determined by an interest in ancient culture.

Egypt's Urban Centres and Rural Settlements

1 Cairo metropolis (see Figure 11.1)

1.1 Cairo – 'Mother of the World'

Cairo is the biggest and in various respects also the most important capital in Africa, the Middle and Near East and the Islamic world. For Egypt itself the town is of unequalled significance. This megalopolis is four times as big as Alexandria, which is the second-largest town in the country, and about thirty times as big as Port Said, the third-largest town (see Figure 11.1). In a term of endearment Egyptians refer to their capital as *um ed-dunya*, i.e. 'Mother of the World', and apply to it the same expression they use for their country, *masr*. This may be an adaptation of the country's name, as in the case of Tunis and Algiers, but the opposite may equally be true, since the name possibly derives from that of the first Arab settlement on the Nile, Misr al-Fustat, which was founded in AD 641. *Misr* is the old Arabic word for 'town'; however, *misrayem* is also a name for Egypt in the Old Testament. The name 'Cairo', of much later origin, is derived from the classical Arabic epithet *al-qahira*, i.e. 'the victorious one'. It is the name the Fatimids gave their capital which they founded in AD 969. It became the official name of the town as well as of the governorate belonging to it, but the expression is less frequently used by the local population today.

1.2 Genesis of the town (see Figures 11.2 and 11.3)

The place where the Nile opens out into the wide fan of the Nile delta is an ideal location for a capital. Here, in ancient times, the kingdoms of Lower Egypt and Upper Egypt bordered each other, and waterways as well as overland routes met. For centuries the place was linked to the Gulf of Suez by an artificial waterway constructed by Senostris III (1887–1849 BC). In the course of time the capital was moved westward following the shift in the course of the Nile and of the Nile fork northward. Before the founding of the comparatively young Arab towns, there existed various other settlements here:

- Heliopolis (On), situated to the north-east of the present town, was founded in 4240 BC (Muselhi 1988: 64).

- Memphis, situated on the western river bank, was the capital of the unified kingdom of Lower Egypt and Upper Egypt founded by King Menes about 2800 BC (Brunner-Traut and Hell 1966: 452ff).
- Babylon, the name of which originates in a distortion of Per-hapi-n-On, the ancient Egyptian name for the Nile island close to which it lay, which is called Roda today, was a Roman settlement with a fortress.

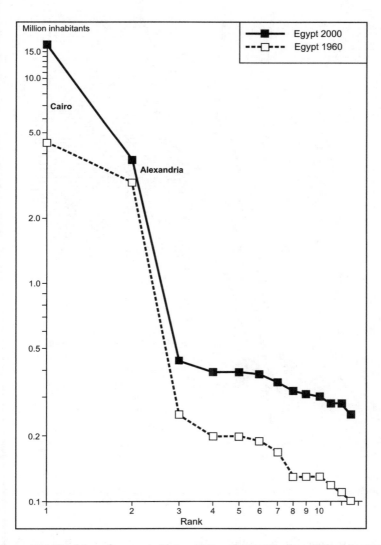

Figure 11.1 Ranking of towns in Egypt 1960 and 2000 (Author: F. Ibrahim 2002; cartography: after W. Kalis 1996; sources of data: CAPMAS, Statistical Year Books for various years)

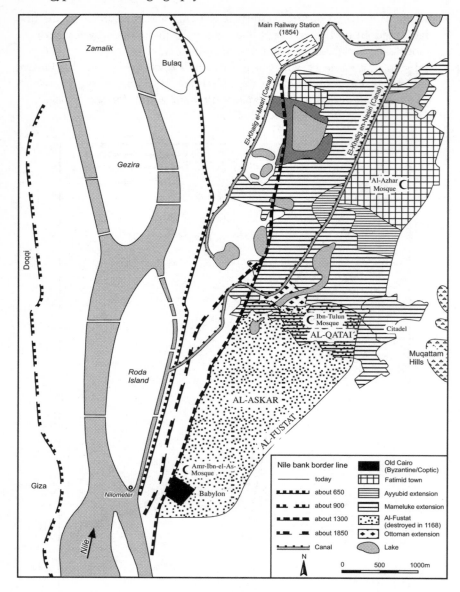

Figure 11.2 Cairo: development of the old town and changes to the Nile course in historical times (Author: F. Ibrahim 2002; cartography: J. Feilner; sources: after Said 1993: 67; Jomard 1821–29: plates 15 and 26; Muselhi 1988: 125)

Having defeated the Byzantines, who ruled over Egypt at the time, Amr Ibn el-As, the commander of the Arabs, had his own new town of Al-Fustat built north of Babylon in AD 641. In AD 750 the Abbasids founded their garrison town of Al-Askar immediately to the north of Al-Fustat. Between AD 868 and 883 Ibn Tulun, originally the Caliph of Baghdad's Abbasid governor, built his residence as well as the famous mosque of Al-Qatai' to the north-east of Al-Askar, after he had had the Christian and Jewish graves there demolished (Muselhi 1988: 82). Of these three Arab towns Fustat was the most important until it was completely burnt down in AD 1168 to forestall conquest by the Crusaders. Even when Al-Qahira was founded in the tenth century, Al-Fustat remained a major residential area and a trading centre. The town possessed the only port in the region and was connected to the Nile island of Roda and to the western bank of the river by bridges. All exchange of goods on the river, as well as by land, lay under its control. The town extended over 4.8 km in a north–south direction. Its inhabitants numbered 150,000 (ibid.: 86). After the conquest of Egypt by the Fatimids, their commander Gawhar, who was born on Sicily, founded Al-Qahira as his residence north of the existing Arab towns. The new settlement was spacious and well planned. For two centuries it remained a fortified centre of political and military power, while economic activities were concentrated on Al-Fustat, which had become the town of the common people. It was only after Saladin, who vanquished the Crusaders, and his successor had built the Citadel (1176–1207) that the rulers finally allowed the people to settle in Al-Qahira. Cairo then consisted of three parts:

- Al-Fustat, which had not completely recovered from the devastation of the fire of 1168
- the Citadel of Al-Qal'a
- Al-Qahira.

The latter consisted of different quarters (*harat*, singular *hara*), which were mostly named after the ethnic groups living in them, such as Greeks, Kurds, Berbers and Turks. Under the rule of the Baharite Mamelukes (1250–1382), Cairo became one of the biggest trading centres in the world. It had its heyday in the fourteenth century, when the number of its inhabitants was over half a million (Raymond 1975: 251). Cairo's decline began, however, in the same century, owing to political instability, the mismanagement of the Mamelukes and the plague of 1348. By the time of the Turkish conquest in 1517 the number of its inhabitants had been reduced to 385,000 (Clerget 1934: 240f). Under Turkish rule the town deteriorated further. At the end of the eighteenth century the number of its inhabitants had decreased to 263,000, of which only 34 per cent lived in Al-Qahira, while 38 per cent lived in the southern quarter, 25 per cent in the western and 3 per cent in the northern quarters of the town (Raymond 1975: 208). The population was distributed over sixty-three *harat*, each of which could be closed by doors. Twenty-three of these were in the Fatimid town of Al-Qahira.

During the time of Muhammed Ali (1805–48), the Ottoman commander who initiated a general modernization in Egypt, the town underwent great

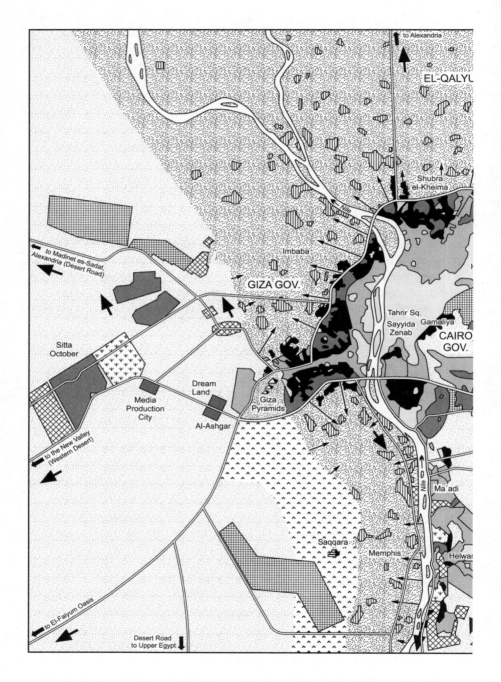

Figure 11.3 Greater Cairo: expansion of built-up areas since 1947
(Author: F. Ibrahim 2002;

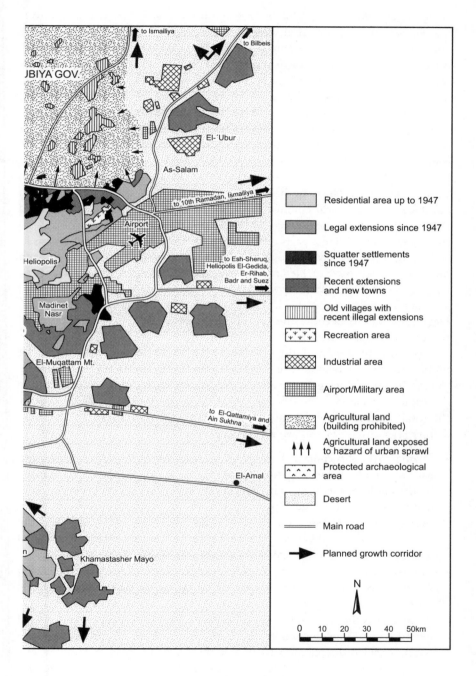

to Ismailiya

to Bilbeis

JBIYA GOV.

El-'Ubur

As-Salam

to 10th Ramadan, Ismailiya

Airport

Heliopolis

to Esh-Sheruq,
Heliopolis El-Gedida,
Er-Rihab,
Badr and Suez

Madinet
Nasr

El-Muqattam Mt.

to El-Qattamiya and
Ain Sukhna

El-Amal

Khamastasher Mayo

	Residential area up to 1947
	Legal extensions since 1947
	Squatter settlements since 1947
	Recent extensions and new towns
	Old villages with recent illegal extensions
	Recreation area
	Industrial area
	Airport/Military area
	Agricultural land (building prohibited)
↑↑↑	Agricultural land exposed to hazard of urban sprawl
	Protected archaeological area
	Desert
	Main road
	Planned growth corridor

N

0 10 20 30 40 50km

cartography: J. Feilner; sources: after General Organization of Physical Planning 1982;
Shorter 1989; field survey F. Ibrahim 2000)

changes. The doors of the *harat* were removed, police troops watched over the security of the population, new streets were built, existing ones widened, and street names, street lighting and a public scavenging service introduced. All graveyards within the town disappeared and the mountains of debris (in the older parts of town) and garbage were removed. The material was used to fill up several lakes in the surroundings. The Khedive and his Emirs had their fanciful palaces built on the outskirts of the town.

Under the Khedive Said the railway lines to Alexandria and to Suez were constructed in 1854 and 1856 with their terminals at the main station in the north-west of the town and another station close by. In 1868 the Khedive Ismail started planning the area extending from the western parts of the town towards the Nile. There he had a new European-type quarter built, which developed into a typical colonial town during British rule between 1882 and 1922. Socially, in its appearance and functions, it stood in sharp contrast to the oriental Arab-Islamic parts of the town. It was inhabited by Europeans as well as by members of the royal family. In 1906 the Belgian Baron Empain built the model town of Heliopolis on a desert plateau to the north-east of Cairo in neo-Moorish style. It was an excellently designed satellite town with all the infrastructure available at the time, linked to the capital by a tram line. Heliopolis was to become the favoured residential area for foreigners until the Egyptian upper class took over later.

From the beginning of the twentieth century Cairo developed fast. The number of its inhabitants rose from less than 1 million in 1897 to about 10 million in 1986. During that time the proportion of the population living in the capital increased from less than 10 per cent to more than 20 per cent of the total number of inhabitants of the country (Shorter 1989: 5). The main factors responsible for this were (Muselhi 1988: 215ff):

- Owing to new technical developments which allowed various weirs and canals to be built for irrigation purposes, the seasonal inundations caused by the Nile were reduced. The Nile floods thus having been brought under control, the town started expanding in a westerly and north-westerly direction along the former river bank and the Nile arms, on islands and the lakes that had been filled up. The only place where expansion efforts failed was to the east, towards the rocky plateau of Gabal el-Muqattam.
- Infrastructure was improved. In the new extensions of the town especially wide streets were built which were usually paved or had tarmac surfaces. From 1890 nine bridges were built linking the eastern and the western Nile banks across the islands. In 1896 a Belgian firm started constructing a road network. The introduction of the tram, which replaced the horse-drawn coach, enabled the planners to enlarge the town area from 6.7 km² to 13.5 km² (Muselhi 1988: 215). The newly established rail and road connections between Cairo and other parts of the country enhanced commuting as well as migration to the capital.

• There was a boom in building activity. Under the rule of the Khedive Ismail, for the first time the marketing of building plots reflected modern business practices. The Khedive gave orders in 1869 for the planning of the Ismailiya quarter. He sold the plots to people who were keen on building. In this way the high demand for modern housing which later arose through the presence of about 75,000 foreigners (Abu-Lughod 1971: 122) who lived in Egypt during the British colonial period could be met. At the beginning of the twentieth century large contractors built modern housing in suburbs such as Heliopolis, Maadi, Hadayeq el-Qubba and Doqqi.

At present Cairo is growing rapidly in a vertical as well as in a horizontal direction. Every day new skyscrapers appear with up to forty-five storeys, such as in Maadi, for example, and new storeys are constructed on top of existing buildings without the obligatory licences. The lack of vigilance and corruption within the administrative apparatus became all too obvious when in 1992 hundreds of people died and thousands were injured in an earthquake, since the houses they lived in had been constructed in a careless manner. More than 1,000 schools collapsed in Cairo alone for similar reasons.

Figure 11.3 shows the expansion of the town since the end of the Second World War. The most rapid growth has taken place so far in the north, the north-east and in the west. To the east, where we find Gabal el-Muqattam, further spread has not been possible. The blocks of flats constructed on top of the plateau suffered serious water supply and drainage problems. The extension of residential areas to the south-west took place at a relatively slow pace – the area is not attractive owing to a concentration of highly air-polluting and noise-producing industries in the narrow Nile valley, where one of the country's busiest railway lines, as well the main roads leading to the south and a main drainage canal, are found.

1.3 Recent dynamics in the mobility of Cairo's inhabitants

The exact number of inhabitants of the Cairo conurbation is not known. Egyptian statistics differentiate today between Cairo Governorate, Cairo Metropolitan Area and the Region of Greater Cairo. The Cairo Metropolitan Area includes the cities of Cairo and Giza with their immediate suburbs, as well as the city of Shubra el-Kheima. The Region of Greater Cairo was created in a consolidation uniting the Cairo Metropolitan Area with some towns in the governorates of El-Qalyubiya in the north and Giza in the south. In 1976 the number of inhabitants of Greater Cairo was estimated at about 7.5 million, ten years later at nearly 10 million, and in 2003 at about 17 million.

According to the 1986 census the distribution of the population within Greater Cairo was as follows: 62 per cent of the inhabitants lived in the Cairo Governorate, 19.2 per cent in the city of Giza, 3 per cent in smaller towns in the governorate of Giza, 7.3 per cent in the city of Shubra el-Kheima, and

8.5 per cent in smaller towns and villages in the governorate of El-Qalyubiya. The proportion of people living in Cairo Governorate decreased after that time and stood at only 57 per cent in 1996. The population of Greater Cairo grows at a rate of about 300,000 inhabitants annually at present. In addition to its inhabitants there are about 3 million people living in the immediate neighbourhood of the capital, including those in the towns of Banha in the north and El-Ayat in the south, at a distance of less than 50 km from the centre of Cairo.

Three different phases are clearly evident in the growth of Greater Cairo's population figures since the beginning of the twentieth century (see Table 11.1).

Table 11.1 Population increase: inhabitants of Egypt and of Cairo 1897–2003 (in millions)

Year	Egypt Inhabitants	Cairo Metropolitan Area	
		Inhabitants	% share of Egypt's total population
1897	9.64	0.91	9.4
1907	11.19	1.07	9.6
1917	12.72	1.25	9.9
1927	14.18	1.57	11.1
1937	15.92	1.89	11.9
1947	18.97	2.78	14.7
1960	25.98	4.53	17.5
1976	36.63	7.47	20.4
1986	48.25	9.79	20.3
1996	61.21	12.50	20.4
2003	68.20	13.58	20.0

Sources: after Shorter 1989: 5; CAPMAS 2001b: 10ff; UNDP 2002: 143

- The first phase, covering about forty years in which the number of the town's inhabitants rose from 1 million to 2 million, is characterized by steady but gradual growth at an annual rate of 1.5–2 per cent, which surpassed only slightly the growth rate of the whole country, which was 1–1.5 per cent at the time.
- During the second phase, also comprising forty years, the population increased more than fourfold. A clear indicator of this development is the rise in the number of inhabitants as a proportion of the country's total population: while it had been about 10 per cent in the first phase, it increased to more than 20 per cent in the second phase, after which it was stagnant for some time. Two main reasons account for the rapid growth of the population of the capital during this second phase:

1) Since international trade suffered serious impediments during the Second World War, which took place at the beginning of this phase, British troops based in Egypt had to be provided with local products, so the market flourished, especially in Cairo. Increasing chances of employment in the capital then acted as a pull-factor for the rural population of Egypt.

2) Following the Israeli bombardment and invasion of the Suez Canal Zone during the late 1960s and 1970s, many people fled from there, taking refuge mainly in nearby Cairo.

- A third phase, during which the growth rate of Greater Cairo's population attained a certain stability, began in about 1980 and continues to this day. For the first time in the more recent past, it fell below the growth rate of the country's total population. The following factors are responsible for this:

1) In the early 1980s, an economic recession set in in Egypt, since, owing to the Camp David Agreement of 1979, some Arab states stopped supporting the Egyptian economy. As a consequence the demand for labour decreased in Cairo.

2) The early 1980s were a time of strong labour migration from Egypt to the Arab countries, especially to the Gulf States. In Iraq alone, there were about 1 million Egyptian workers when the Gulf War broke out in 1991. Because of their generally higher level of education, greater likelihood of having contacts abroad and ability to cover travel expenses, inhabitants of the capital have better access to employment outside their own country, so that a relatively high percentage of them emigrated, thus lessening the population pressure in the area.

If we make spatial differentiation in considering the development of Greater Cairo's population, we find that the situation in the periphery of the town differs substantially from that in its centre:

- The increase was greater in outer than in central parts. Shubra el-Kheima, a northern suburb, had an annual growth rate of about 6 per cent in the decade 1976–86, whereas the governorate of Cairo, to which the inner parts of the town belong, increased only by 1.75 per cent annually.

- In terms of population density, the picture is similar. Even in the governorate of Cairo we find an immense increase in the suburbs, compared to a decrease in the town centre. In Helwan, south of Cairo, the population grew from about 20,000 inhabitants/km^2 in 1977 to nearly 90,000 in 1994, while in Bab esh-Shariya, situated in the centre of the town, the population decreased from just under 110,000 inhabitants/km^2 to slightly over 80,000 (CAPMAS 1994d: 20). In early 1994 the quarters of Esh-Sharabiya and Es-Zawya el-Hamra, close to the main station, had the highest population density, amounting to nearly 110,000 inhabitants/km^2. In 1996 the population density of the governorate of Cairo was 31,780 inhabitants/km^2.

The process described here for the Egyptian metropolis differs from the suburbanization observed in the towns of Western industrial countries in some aspects:

- The more rapid growth around the capital as compared to that in the older parts of the town, which we observed up until the end of the 1970s, was due not to a centrifugal movement of parts of the population but rather to rural–urban migration. The migrants came from all parts of Egypt, but mainly from the governorate of Giza and the governorate of El-Qalyubiya, which belong in parts to Greater Cairo. An excess of births over deaths is a prime cause of migration within the region today. During the years 1960–75 rural–urban migration was still responsible for 22 per cent of the increase in the number of inhabitants of Greater Cairo, whereas one decade later this was only the case to the extent of 10 per cent (Shorter 1989: 20).
- As a consequence of the phenomena described, the main features of suburban Cairo are not villas with gardens but fairly heteromorphous structures. We find side by side commercial blocks of flats for rent, sometimes owned by members of the middle class, dilapidated blocks of flats built by the state for low-income groups, mostly during the time of Nasser, as well as gigantic modern multi-storey buildings which are often illegally constructed. Many buildings lack plastering and look unfinished. Usually further storeys are built on top of them as soon as the necessary capital is available to the owners. Between such buildings, the poor settle in niches in their slum-like housing.

In the suburban area of Greater Cairo the government promoted the development of satellite towns and new communities with industrial and service centres by building the infrastructure and granting tax exemptions and other privileges to attract entrepreneurs. So numerous industrial plants, for example in Sitta October, and several entertainment parks were established in these peripheral settlements (see Figure 11.3).

1.4 The functional structure of Greater Cairo

The functional structure of the Greater Cairo region is also complex. For a better understanding, we give an outline of the historical development of the main functions and of their distribution today:

Trade

Retail trade The retail trade for goods in daily use, often in the form of small corner shops, is distributed all over Cairo, for obvious reasons. In many quarters, however, agglomerations of the grocery business have developed. In these we find a distinction between the shops and small stalls in which fresh vegetables and live poultry can be bought on the one hand, and the bigger food shops and, more recently, supermarkets on the other. Butchers and fishmongers can also be found in these small trading centres, meeting the daily needs of the people living in the immediate neighbourhood. While in socialist times one could find in every quarter of the town state-owned cooperatives selling subsidized foodstuffs at low prices, shops of this type have now disappeared completely. Apart from the institutions mentioned there are hawkers roaming the streets, especially in the the lower- and middle-class residential quarters, offering fruit, vegetables, milk and boiled fava beans (*ful*), the Egyptian staple food.

The location of bakeries is determined by the following factors:

- the Egyptians' high consumption of bread: it forms part of all their meals
- consumer orientation: bread is usually bought hot and consumed fresh
- the relatively low price of the product, although the World Bank has urged the government to stop subsidizing it
- the amount of space required by the bakeries.

These factors mean that ideally bakeries are located in densely populated areas, but not too close to the market zone. If they are found here, this usually indicates that they were *in situ* before the market was established.

The retail trade for goods not in daily use has the following pattern of distribution: the larger quarters of the town and the suburbs have their own shopping centres, meeting the customers' requirements by offering a wide range of clothes, jewellery and other high-value products. The centre of Cairo shows the dual structure typical of most former colonial cities. Two separate trading centres exist:

- One is in the old part of the town, serving the needs of the lower and middle classes.
- The other has developed in the modern part of town and serves the requirements of the upper middle class, and in particular of the more Westernized well-to-do. In particular the demand of the rich for fashionable Islamic women's clothes is met here too.

The shopping area in the modern part of town extends today between Opera Square and Tahrir Square, in a district that was seasonally flooded by the Nile until the nineteenth century and gradually drained thereafter. The main traditional trading centre is situated in the old Fatimid town, as well as along the streets leading from there to the main railway station. In the course of the twentieth century part of this trading centre, known as Khan el-Khalili, close to the mosque of Al-Azhar, developed into a bazaar, in which handicrafts produced all over the country, such as glass, pottery, brass or leather goods, as well as hand-woven carpets, are sold nearly exclusively to tourists. At the same time it is a place where traditional handicrafts are produced which the tourists can buy as souvenirs either there or in other parts of the country. When this part of the town started to become a tourist attraction, the local cloth traders moved out to the outer zone less frequented by tourists, whereas the goldsmiths displayed locational inertia and resorted to a new type of diversification, offering products for Egyptians as well as for the tourists who came to buy their souvenirs in the bazaar zone. As a rule, however, the goldsmiths established secondary shops in the new parts of the town. In the suburbs inhabited by the upper middle class, such as Madinet Nasr, Heliopolis, Zamalik, El-Muhandiseen and Maadi, and on Pyramid Street in Giza, shopping malls of the American type began to appear from the late 1990s. They are centres equipped with all kinds of modern shops and boutiques, as well as restaurants, cafés, halls for computer games and bowling, billiard lounges, cinemas and in some cases ice rinks.

Wholesale trade The wholesale trade in cloth, clothing and stationery is today found close to the old part of town around Al-Azhar mosque, and between there and the main station. In the area of Al-Azhar Street, in the outer zone of the old part of town, the traditional location for metal crafts, the wholesale as well as the retail trade for ironware and automobile spare parts can be found today. The craftsmen working here have great skills and produce complicated spare parts for cars as well as surgical instruments, thus recycling the scrap iron of the town. After years of heated discussions and several lawsuits between the wholesale dealers and the government, the central wholesale markets for fruit and vegetables as well as for fish were relocated in the early 1990s. The government constructed a modern central wholesale market for these goods 30 km north of Cairo in the satellite town of Al-'Ubur, situated on the desert road to Ismailiya (see Figure 11.3), and gave orders for the old markets in the town centre, where hygienic conditions had become unacceptable, to be closed down. The old locations at Rod el-Farag near the Nile and at Ghamra close to the main railway station had caused constant traffic jams. The new markets are much more spacious and provided with huge, ultra-modern cold-storage facilities. The wholesale dealers' trade unions had favoured the construction of smaller modern wholesale markets in the south, west and east of the town, with the old markets being upgraded and kept in use for the north. Their argument was that by transferring the wholesale markets to such a faraway location about six hundred women and young people employed as carriers would lose their jobs, and that the numerous retail dealers who used to collect the goods themselves with their donkey carts would also lose their livelihoods.

Transportation

Great efforts have been undertaken by the local administration during the past thirty years to improve the traffic infrastructure of the town and to keep pace with its rapid expansion, thus avoiding a total collapse of the capital's

27. *Sadat City, a new town*: The new town of Sadat City, situated in the desert west of the Nile delta halfway between Cairo and Alexandria, is still largely unoccupied, although it was built more than two decades ago. (Photo: F. Ibrahim)

transportation system. However, chaotic situations are caused during the rush hours by millions of people travelling to their places of work, universities or schools, sometimes over distances of more than 20 km, twice daily through densely populated residential areas. Trains and public buses are usually so crowded that many, especially women, prefer travelling by taxis or micro-buses in spite of the higher costs. Also, middle-class families felt obliged to buy cars in order to cope with the situation, particularly when younger women who have small children opted to go out to work. Since the early 1980s two metro lines of a total length of 22 km have been opened and are servicing an estimated 4 million passengers daily. A third line of 11 km is under construction and is scheduled to be completed by 2008. However, the new transportation system is not integrated within a policy of sustainable urban development and does not succeed in linking the old urban centres and the peripheral areas of Greater Cairo.

The reasons why a total breakdown of Cairo's traffic has been avoided can be summed up as follows:

- the main arterial roads from the centre of the town to its periphery, e.g. Ramses Street, were widened
- an eight-lane ring road was built around Cairo (see Figure 11.3), easing the traffic in the town centre

- new Nile bridges, e.g. Sitta October Bridge (see Illustration 24) and Al-Warraq Bridge, were constructed, facilitating the east–west traffic
- in many places that had formerly been bottlenecks, flyovers were built, e.g. in front of the main railway station
- a new metro was built, starting in the 1980s, which improved the traffic situation in general and in particular made transport in a north–south direction faster
- the big taxi and micro-bus terminals, especially those serving transport between the capital and the provinces, were decentralized.

The merits of the town planners who designed all this should not be under-estimated, even if mistakes occurred in certain instances, such as a disregard for the environmental problems the new roads introduced in some areas.

Administration and higher services

Until the middle of the twentieth century the country's central administrative offices were concentrated in a few places in the centre of the capital. The most important surviving sites are the following:

- the area south-east of Tahrir Square, where the parliament, most ministries and Abdin Palace, which today hosts certain parts of the government, are found
- Tahrir Square and Garden City on the eastern Nile bank, where various embassies, the Ministry of Foreign Affairs, the headquarters of the Arab League, the Egyptian Museum and the American University can be found, as well as Mugamma', a huge building containing various ministerial departments, and, close by, the main buildings of the television and radio stations
- the central railway station, close to which the main municipal power station as well as the traffic and telecommunications administrations are found.

Administrative institutions created more recently, for example the Central Agency for Public Mobilization and Statistics (CAPMAS), Misr Travel, the state-owned company for air traffic and tourism, as well as various research authorities, were established outside the town centre, where there was enough space for their premises.

With the exception of Cairo University Clinic, built in 1856, and the American University Cairo (AUC), founded in 1920, the universities are also found outside the town centre today: Cairo University, founded in 1908 in Giza, Ain Shams University, founded after 1950 in Abbasiya and Heliopolis, Al-Azhar University, founded in 1961 in Madinet Nasr, and Helwan University, founded in 1975 in the suburb of Helwan, south-east of Cairo. The head offices of banks and insurance companies as well as those of travel agencies, the catering trade and many other businesses are located in the colonial new town between Opera Square and Tahrir Square on the Nile.

During recent decades, many service enterprises have been relocated outside the town centre for lack of space for expansion. They are now mostly found in the modern multi-storey buildings in the newer parts of town, such as Madinet Nasr, the extension of Heliopolis north-east of Cairo, in Doqqi, Aguza and El-Muhandiseen in the west of the town. Various embassies are also concentrated in the latter quarters, for example the embassies of Austria and Kuwait. Others, however, have remained in their old, more central locations on the Nile, such as Garden City, where the embassies of the UK, the USA, Canada, Australia and Japan can still be found, and on the island of Zamalik, where the embassies of Germany, Argentina, the Netherlands and Sweden are located.

The most famous traditional entertainment district of Cairo is west of the Fatimid town in Mohammed-Ali Street, which is now called El-Qal'a Street. Once the traditional musicians and the belly-dancers lived there, as well as the craftsmen who produced the traditional musical instruments.

During the early twentieth century an area of modern entertainment with theatres and cinemas developed between Opera Square and the main railway station, particularly in Imad-ed-Din Street. This was the cradle of the Egyptian film industry, which gave rise to many films and film stars popular all over the world, leading to Cairo being called 'Hollywood on the Nile'. The cinemas of that time have become obsolete or are today used for other purposes. The opera house after which the square was named was completed in 1869 for the celebrations of the inauguration of the Suez Canal and destroyed by fire nearly a hundred years later. A new opera house was built by the Japanese at Zamalik on the island of Gezira as part of a gigantic modern arts centre.

In the old entertainment district of Cairo many artists appeared who became famous all over the world. More recently, owing to Westernization, the locus of entertainment has shifted to the big hotels along the Nile and near the Pyramids, following the tourists. This change of location was accomplished by a qualitative loss in the entertainment on offer. Today Western tourists and visitors from the Arab countries are offered cheap belly-dance and noisy Western music.

Egyptian men mainly pass their leisure time in the small street cafés, where they meet to drink sweet tea or Turkish coffee, to smoke the *shisha*, the oriental water pipe, and to play *taula* (backgammon). These are usually found near the markets or train and bus terminals or stops.

Housing

The lower and middle classes, that is to say the majority of the inhabitants of Cairo, are not able to pay for adequate housing. In fact there is no housing available in Cairo today which is affordable for the average citizen to rent. A young university graduate, for example, looking for a flat of two to three rooms at a price he can afford, will not find it unless he is prepared to spend his whole monthly salary of about LE200. A description of the various existing categories of housing may elucidate the situation.

Pre-1960 tenements For flats of this category, usually found in old run-down houses, rents were frozen from socialist times (1954–70), with the result that until very recently they hardly ever exceeded a few Egyptian pounds. People who occupied flats on such terms were not usually willing to move out. Rather they undertook some minor repairs to the buildings at their own expense, and their children took over the flats at the same low rent when the parents moved out or passed away. A landlord who wanted to induce his tenants to leave had to offer them a considerable sum to make them do so. He was not allowed to raise the rent after that, but he would ask the new tenants for *khiliw rigl* ('key money'), which might exceed the actual value of the flat itself, just for giving them a chance to take over the flat.

State-supported social housing programmes Since Nasser's socialist era the state has built complexes of apartment buildings called *masakin sha'biya*, i.e. 'the people's housing', but from the 1970s, since Sadat came to power, their prices have risen to such an extent that only those in the upper income groups can buy them today. Ownership is acquired by paying monthly instalments which amount to about two months' salary for a young university graduate, as well as an initial payment of about fifty times that amount.

Housing estates of the professional unions This is a programme also supported by the state. Again, mostly well-to-do and influential segments of the population profit from it, such as army officers, doctors of medicine, engineers or journalists, who are granted remarkable privileges for building their self-contained suburban colonies, as the example of El-Muhandiseen (the engineers) shows. Once planned as a housing estate exclusively for engineers, today it is a huge quarter of Cairo with inhabitants from among the higher classes of various professions.

Informal settlements About 80 per cent of the population of Greater Cairo live in houses or flats that were illegally built, and there are more than one hundred informal settlements, although the government had several demolished in the early 1990s. Such settlements are usually built on land owned by the state, as is the case at Manshiet Naser at the foot of the Muqattam Hills, where in 1993 rocks falling from the limestone escarpment destroyed several houses, killing many. Similar disasters occurred there in 1962 and 1984. The area is not at all suitable for settlement for two reasons. First it is a quarrying area where dynamite is used, and second the limestone escarpment is slowly dissolving as a result of the sewage water emanating from the blocks of flats built on the plateau above it in the 1960s.

More common is illegal construction of houses on agricultural land, or of additional storeys on top of existing houses. Here, too, casualties are recorded when one of the frequent earthquakes in the region occurs, or because of construction faults made possible by the fact that the housing authorities are bribed. Nevertheless, for housing in these informal categories, too, people pay high rents, although it is of low quality and electricity and running water are not provided.

Housing in the new towns and communities around Cairo (see Illustration 27) Housing in the new satellite towns built around Cairo during the last three decades of the twentieth century is also too expensive for the vast majority of the population, even though it was mostly built with state subsidies. The monthly instalments payable for an apartment are several hundred Egyptian pounds. The fact that many flats remain vacant for this reason has been raised in Parliament repeatedly, but no effective steps have been taken as yet to improve the situation. The same applies to the modern gated communities mushrooming in the deserts around Cairo and elsewhere in the country.

Some of the serious consequences of the housing problems in Cairo are as follows:

- A large proportion of the apartment houses built with the help of state subsidies in the so-called 'social' housing programmes, and originally conceived for low-income groups, were completed and sold, but remained unoccupied since they were acquired, usually after considerable bribes had been paid, by mostly well-to-do people who considered them a worthwhile investment. But since the state did not allow very high rents to be charged for flats, and because since the socialist era considerable legal protection for tenants has existed, owners were reluctant to let the flats they had bought and left them vacant, hoping that one day their children would move in, or they let them as 'furnished flats' with just one symbolic chair in them, at the highest prices possible, and after payment of the above-mentioned 'key money'. Thus they could get around existing laws at considerable profit.
- Families with low incomes live crowded together in a minimum of space in cellars, on the rooftops of houses and in other inadequate accommodation.
- Many young families live together in a single room in their parents' flat under unbearable conditions.
- Young people who want to get married often have to postpone the wedding for years because they are unable to find an affordable flat to move into.

The geographical distribution of the housing areas of different categories in Greater Cairo, as visible in aerial photos, forms a complex mosaic of clearly separate districts:

- The areas of high-quality housing, often consisting of very tall buildings, stretch along both sides of the Nile and occur as well in Heliopolis, Madinet Nasr and Maadi. Here live people with higher incomes, while people with lower and medium incomes live in the old part of town as well as in its older extensions to the north, such as Shubra, Zaher and Abbasiya, in the suburbs, or in the areas along the railway lines leading north and south.
- This rough pattern is interrupted by the irregularly distributed illegal settlements, but also by several concentrations of multi-storey complexes, which can be found at various locations within Greater Cairo. Figure 11.3 shows the vast areas of informal housing in which the majority of the poorer population live. However, even in areas comprising the higher categories of formal housing, illegal building is also widespread. It has been reported that some people have amassed great fortunes by illegally constructing a number of multi-storey apartment buildings in the best residential areas in town, such as Madinet Nasr (Nasr City).

In 1995 a new law came into force aimed at liberating the housing market. It allowed house owners to freely dictate the rent and the period of validity of the letting contract. The new legislation brought about changes, the most relevant of which are:

- The owners of approximately 2 million vacant flats and houses in the country, who had been unwilling to let their properties since the old legislation operated very much in favour of people who rented flats, started to look for tenants, since the new legal conditions were more favourable to owners. This eased the situation on the housing market for the upper-middle income class, but not for the lower-income classes.
- After decades in which people had been forced to buy flats because they could find none for rent, housing for rent was available, with the result that the pressure on the real estate market decreased, all the more so since at the beginning of the twenty-first century Egypt went through a time of general economic recession, especially after the extreme devaluation of the Egyptian pound in 2003.
- The beneficiaries of the new legislation were both house owners and high-income tenants. The latter could afford the higher rents. Proprietors normally now asked for an advance on the rent instead of the former 'key money'.
- One of the serious drawbacks of the new situation is that contracts can now be terminated, whereas they had been practically permanent formerly. This means great insecurity for tenants.

The following case may serve as a practical example of the change that took place. When, early in 2000, a flat built in the 1960s in a tall building became vacant, the owner raised the rent, which formerly had been frozen at LE6 monthly, to LE500. The new tenant had to pay LE25,000, i.e. fifty months'

28. *A gated community: Panorama Beach Village*: Panorama Beach Village is one of the many upper-class gated communities which occupy most of the Mediterranean coast between Alexandria and Marsa Matruh in north-west Egypt. (Photo: F. Ibrahim)

rent, in advance. The contract was limited to five years (authors' oral communication with the two tenants, 2000).

Industries

In Greater Cairo industrial sites cover 13.5 per cent of the total area and about 40 per cent of all those employed work in this sector. The industries are distributed over different parts of town. There are great concentrations, however, in the area of Helwan in the south and Shubra el-Kheima in the north, where all branches of industry are represented, especially the armaments industry. Thirteen of the country's fifteen big arms plants are found in Greater Cairo, mainly at Helwan, but also at Abu Za'bal and near the international airport in the north-east. In many instances there is an agglomeration of the munitions industry with the pharmaceutical industry, the engineering industry, the iron and steel industry, the automobile assembly industry, plants for the production of bicycles and motorbikes, railway manufacturing, wharves, the textile industry and the cement industry. Because of this concentration, and the presence of heavy industry, the regions concerned suffer from considerable pollution, as is the case at Shubra el-Kheima and at Helwan. The latter was formerly a health resort thanks to the good quality of its mineral waters. Today the people living there complain of air and groundwater pollution, of noise, and of the dumping of highly poisonous industrial waste. All efforts towards a decentralization of the industries have failed so far. Rather, the number of plants has increased. The city council would like to forbid completely the establishment of new factories in the area, exempting only businesses offering repairs, services or food supply. Noise-producing craftsmen's workshops, such as those for car repair, should be transferred to and concentrated in locations on the outskirts of town. A new centre of craftsmen's establishments of this type was built at Madinet es-Salam in the north-east of Cairo.

1.5 The problem of pollution in Cairo

The fact that 40 per cent of Egypt's industrial activities, 32 per cent of the vehicles in the country and 25 per cent of its total population are concentrated in the area of Greater Cairo has led to an extremely high degree of air pollution there. The harmful emissions are increasing dramatically year by year with the rapid increase in energy consumption, which rose by 171 per cent from 1980 to 1998 (Hassan-Gordon 2001). Additional stress is caused by the smoke produced by the burning of rice straw in the fields in the nearby Nile delta, as well as by the frequent dust storms from the Western Desert.

According to the World Health Organization (WHO), air pollution in Cairo exceeds by ten to one hundred times the level considered safe. In 2000 the US Energy Information Administration reported (ibid.): 'Levels of suspended particulate matter and lead pollution in Cairo are perhaps the highest in the world. Lead pollution is a serious threat to human health.' According to estimates quoted in the same source, air pollution in Cairo is responsible for 10,000 to 25,000 additional deaths per year. Especially noxious is the carbon monoxide contained in the exhaust fumes of the 1.2 million cars moving around Cairo daily. It causes dizziness, headaches and fatigue, as well as heart troubles, and can impede mental and physical abilities (ibid.).

The Law of the Environment of 1994 is supposed to provide the necessary framework for combating all kinds of pollution. Under this law the first steps to fight pollution have already been taken – the largest lead-smelting plant was moved from Shubra-el-Kheima to a location outside Cairo in 1999. Today strict regulations are also applied in vehicle emissions testing. Pilot projects are under way to reduce lead emissions and to use natural gas for running public buses. And, more important still, the government is gradually shifting away from its old policy of subsidizing fuel to a policy of improving the efficiency of fuel use.

2 Mediterranean metropolis: Alexandria (see Figure 11.4)

With its 3.7 million inhabitants (2002) Alexandria is the second-largest town in the country, and leaving aside the bigger towns within the Cairene agglomeration, such as Giza, Imbaba and Shubra el-Kheima, one can say that it is about seven times as big as the third-largest town in Egypt, which is

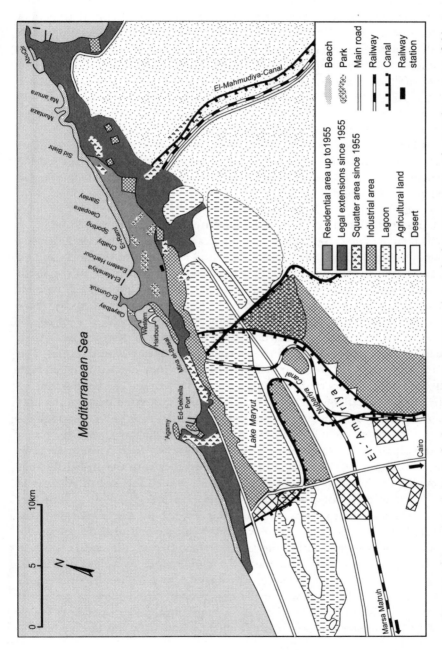

Figure 11.4 Alexandria: structure of urban growth since 1955 (Author: F. Ibrahim 2002; cartography: J. Feilner; source: field surveys F. Ibrahim 1996 and 2000)

Port Said. With a figure of 13.7 per cent for the decade 1986–96, the rate of population growth in Alexandria was clearly faster than that in the Cairo Governorate (11.9 per cent), but was slower than that of the Cairo Metropolitan Area (17.4 per cent; CAPMAS 1996). Since the late 1970s population growth in the country's two biggest towns has been less than that in the country as a whole. This new trend has arisen first because of a decrease in migration from rural areas to the overpopulated big urban centres, and second because of the success of government birth control campaigns, especially in the big towns, for which Egypt received particular recognition when it hosted the UN World Conference on Population in 1994.

Although Alexandria and Cairo have many things in common in terms of their recent development and their present problems, Alexandria has a specific character, which is determined above all by its location on the Mediterranean Sea and by its eventful history.

2.1 Historical and economic development of the town

The favourable geographical position of a bay bordered by two limestone spurs protected against invaders by the island of Pharos to the north and by Lake Maryut, which was formerly connected to the Nile river, to the south made Alexander the Great give orders in 331 BC that a port should be built here. To the immediate west, where Pompey's Pillar is found today, there had previously been an Egyptian settlement (Rhakotis), the size of which is not known for sure. The town of the Ptolemies was designed in a chessboard pattern with wide paved streets running in an east–west direction. The island of Pharos, on whose north-eastern shore they erected a 150-m-high lighthouse, was connected with the mainland by a dyke. The beacon, one of the Seven Wonders of the World of ancient times, directed boats to the port of Alexandria for sixteen centuries until it was destroyed by an earthquake in the fourteenth century. In 1480 the Mameluke Sultan Qayet Bay had a fortress built in the same place to protect the town from Turkish invasion (see Illustration 29). The island of Pharos, together with the artificially built seven-league dyke, the ancient Heptastadion, divided the Bay of Alexandria into a western harbour, which is the main port today, and an eastern harbour, which in the past was the more important one. A southern port was situated in Lake Maryut, which was much bigger and also deeper at the time than it is today. During the Greco-Roman period, Alexandria was one of the world's great centres of the arts and philosophy, as well as of science. Its famous library is said to have contained 0.5 to 1 million papyrus scrolls (GOAL 1992: 17) when it was finally destroyed by fire. Following ambitious plans to revive the spirit of the past, a huge ultra-modern building, which cost US$150 million and was partly funded by UNESCO, was opened in 2002 to house a new library of Alexandria.

In the year 30 BC, after the victory of Augustus over Cleopatra VII in a sea battle near Alexandria, Egypt became a province of the Roman Empire with Alexandria as its capital. After a subsequent extension of the town, the number of its inhabitants reached 1 million. Christianity was brought to them as early as the first century by St Mark the Evangelist, and the town developed into a centre of Christian theology. The Coptic popes of Alexandria, Athanasius, Kyrillos I and Theophilus, played important roles in the councils of Nicaea (AD 325), Constantinople and Ephesus, and the people of Alexandria suffered serious hardship during the time of the persecution of Christians by the Roman emperors, especially during the rule of Diocletian. It is believed that 144,000 Copts were martyred in AD 284. That is why the Copts date their chronology from that year, which they call 'the Year of the Martyrs'. After the split of the Roman Empire, Egypt became part of the Eastern Roman Empire, and Alexandria lost its former splendour, not only because of the general disintegration of the empire but also because of the persecution of the Copts by the rulers of Byzantium after the schism at the Council of Chalcedon in AD 451.

To the Arab conquerors who seized Alexandria in AD 642 the town nevertheless appeared a splendid metropolis. Commander Amr Ibn el-'Aas wrote at the time that he saw 4,000 palaces and as many baths, as well as 400 theatres, 1,200 vegetable vendors and 40,000 Jews (Richardson and O'Brien 1993: 462). Although Alexandria had served as a capital since the time of the Ptolemies, the Arabs established their own capital, at first at Al-Fustat and later at Cairo, while Alexandria sank into obscurity and deteriorated. Finally, the built-up area was reduced to only one-fifth of its original size. Until the end of the Turkish era the town continued shrinking, so that at last it extended only around the former dam to the island of Pharos between the western and eastern harbours. When Napoleon conquered Alexandria in 1798, it had merely 15,000 inhabitants (some authors claim only 4,000 or 5,000), while Dumyat (Damietta), more favourably situated on the eastern Nile arm, thus profiting from Nile navigation, could then claim about 20,000 inhabitants.

Thanks to Mohammed Ali, whose aim it was to make Egypt a modern trading and military power, and who for that purpose called French experts into the country to reconstruct and enlarge Alexandria's western port and build an arsenal there, the town experienced a renaissance. He also gave orders to build the Mahmudiya Canal (1819–21) to link the town to the Rosetta arm of the Nile, which flowed into the sea about 50 km to the east of the town centre. With the help of this canal the area of irrigated agricultural land could be extended. However, the canal proved of even greater importance in providing the people with drinking water. Hitherto they had depended on the limited amounts of water discharged in the wells. In the town, the canal led as far as the port of Mina al-Basal (harbour of onions), which came to be the most important quay for the transshipment of cotton. The cotton trade was expanding rapidly at the time and the cotton exchange was also close by and continued to function until the state took over the monopoly in the 1960s. During the fifty years that followed the construction of the Mahmudiya Canal, the population of Alexandria grew rapidly, increasing about tenfold. During the time of Mohammed Ali 5,500 workers were employed in the arsenal alone, while the navy employed about 20,000 sailors and workers. Many peasants from the northern Nile delta fled to Alexandria, trying to escape compulsory conscription in the army. In 1831, 10,000 men fleeing from the villages of the area were arrested in town, where they had tried to hide (Abdel-Hakim 1958: 182). The *fellaheen* were afraid of being conscripted into the army since they were usually put in the front lines and only a few of them returned to the villages alive. The Turks, Mamelukes and the well-trained soldiers who enrolled from the northern parts of the Ottoman Empire had far greater chances of survival than the Egyptian soldiers, who were poorly trained. Moreover, as native Egyptians the *fellaheen* could not identify with the military ambitions of their foreign conquerors, who ruled over Egypt to serve their own purposes. Many young men therefore mutilated their limbs or their eyes so as not to be recruited.

As the economy of Alexandria flourished throughout the nineteenth century, many foreigners settled down in the town as traders or business-men of other kinds. In 1833 they constituted more than 12 per cent of the inhabitants of the town. They mostly came from England, Malta or Tuscany; others were Jews, Greeks, Frenchmen or Austrians. Later, at the turn of the century, Greeks and Italians were in the majority. The foreigners preferred life in those parts of town with the greatest amenities, situated around the present-day central business district (CBD), and gave them a Mediterranean, or rather a cosmopolitan, character, which is reflected in the writings of various contemporary writers, for example E. M. Forster's *Alexandria: A History and a Guide*, Cavafy's *Collected Poems* and Lawrence Durrell's *The Alexandria Quartet*. This situation was ended abruptly after 1956 by a policy of nationalization. With the ensuing exodus of non-Egyptians, thousands of Jews as well as rich Westernized Egyptians who were deprived of their livelihoods left Alexandria, and the town lost its unique oriental-Mediterranean character and finally came to resemble Cairo in many ways. This trend became even more obvious with the growing influence of Islamism in the 1970s. Life on the beaches west of Alexandria, which had been used mostly by the rich, changed considerably, a fact especially visible in the women's dress code. The historical relevance of Alexandria was briefly recalled only in summer, when the government temporarily transferred its residence to the town, which remained the case till the end of the 1970s. Lately attempts have been made to restore the old splendour of the town, including efforts to upgrade the corniche, hoping to attract active investors who may initiate an economic boost in the present capitalistic era.

The modernization and general economic boom that Alexandria experienced in the first half of the twentieth century attracted thousands of Egyptians from the Nile delta and the Nile valley looking for employment, and because of the establishment of huge modern factories, especially after the Second World War, a large labour force was required. In the 1980s nearly 40 per cent of the industrial production of the country came from Alexandria, and it had a share of more than 20 per cent of the total workforce in industrial businesses with more than twenty-five employees (Governorate of Alexandria, n.d.; ~1984; no page number). Alexandria University, founded in 1942 together with several other similar institutes, today attracts more than 150,000 students from various parts of the country. Table 11.2 shows that more recently migration to Alexandria has taken place mainly from the western and central Nile delta, the greatest number of migrants coming from the neighbouring governorate of El-Beheira, with a rising trend. It has to be noted, however, that parts of this administrative district already belong to the eastern fringe of the agglomeration of Alexandria. El-Beida and Kafr ed-Dawar, with their big textile factories, have meanwhile been incorporated into the region of Greater Alexandria. The administrative district of Upper Egypt, from which the greatest number of migrants originate, is the governorate of Sohag. There, high population density and land scarcity have been strong push-factors for a long time. About three out of four of the workers

Table 11.2 Migration to Alexandria 1937–86 according to migrants' places of origin

Governorate of origin	% of the total number of migrants to Alexandria				
	1937	1947	1960	1976	1986
El-Beheira	13	17	17	19	17
El-Gharbiya	11	12	10	10	8
Kafr esh-Sheikh	*	*	7	5	4
Ed-Daqahliya	6	7	8	6	5
El-Minufiya	9	12	12	10	7
Cairo	10	6	8	6	7
Asyut	10	9	6	9	4
Sohag	15	16	16	15	13
Qena	5	6	6	5	4
Aswan	9	9	6	4	3
Other governorates	12	6	4	11	28
Total	100	100	100	100	100
Proportion of Alexandria's total inhabitants	31.5	30.6	28.4	18.4	14
Inhabitants of Alexandria	*686,000*	*919,000*	*1,516,000*	*2,318,000*	*2,876,000*

* No figures available
Sources: after Abdel-Hakim 1958: 208f; Ahmed 1989: 99; Abou Aianah 1980: 526; CAPMAS 1989c: 113ff.

in the ports of Alexandria come from Sohag, and among the costermongers the percentage is even higher. Migration from Aswan to Alexandria is less prevalent today since, thanks to the High Dam as well as to the development of tourism, new jobs have been created there. Migration from Cairo to Alexandria is negligible and easily surpassed by migration in the opposite direction. On the whole, migration to Alexandria has been constantly abating. We have a similar trend as described for Cairo above. From 1986 to 1996 both cities had a negative migration balance. The main reasons for this phenomenon are:

• Labour migration to the Arab countries partly replaced the former rural–urban migration.
• The costs of living are extremely high in Alexandria and Cairo.
• Shortage of housing in the town made many new migrants settle outside the administrative borders of these towns. Statistically they do not count, although factually they are part of the population of the town.

The strong migration of past decades, as well as the natural growth of Alexandria's population, have led to bottlenecks in the areas of services, infrastructure and especially housing. Owing to the poor infrastructure in the newly established housing areas, many people were forced to stay in the old, more central parts of town close to their places of work. One of those old parts, El-Gumruk, situated between the western and eastern harbours, had an extremely high population density of nearly 130,000 inhabitants/km^2, according to the 1986 census, which was not only the highest in town but the highest in all Egypt. Second to this came Muharram Bey, situated near the main railway station, with a population density of over 100,000 inhabitants/km^2, followed by the quarter of El-Manshiya, likewise situated in the town centre, and Er-Raml, situated on the coast north-east of the eastern port, with population densities of between 70,000 and 80,000 inhabitants/km^2. Areas like El-Muntaza in the north-east and Ed-Dekheila in the south-west had population densities of less than one-tenth of this, owing mainly to the fact that these areas have other than residential uses. In El-Muntaza, where the former royal palace is situated, there are parks and areas reserved for cultural and tourist use; in Ed-Dekheila, on the other hand, there are huge industrial sites and harbour facilities. The most thinly populated area was El-'Amriya, a stretch of desert on the south-western periphery of the town with just over 60 inhabitants/km^2.

In Alexandria, as in Cairo, the shortage of housing led to the establishment of squatter settlements. In 1994 over 1.5 million people lived in more than sixty of these in Alexandria (*Al-Ahram*, 28 March 1994: 18). This means that half the population of the town lived in undemarcated settlements. It must be noted, however, that these are not always slums, their main characteristic being merely that they are illegally built and were not planned by the responsible authorities. They can be divided into two main categories according to their appearance and social structure:

- The first category consists of illegal settlements, some of them good-quality structures but lacking the infrastructure usually available in the settlements planned by the state, such as running drinking water, drainage, tarmac roads, electricity and telephone cables, as well as schools and hospitals. If their illegal status causes no serious problems, the state usually tolerates such settlements, and may even recognize them eventually. An example of such a legally upgraded, originally undemarcated settlement is the suburb of El-Agamy, situated on the coast south-west of Alexandria, with its weekend villas built after the 1960s by the rich.
- To the second category belong the squatter settlements consisting of huts built of waste material, often interspersed with some stone buildings. Such settlements are found mostly to the south of the railway line between Alexandria and the Mahmudiya Canal in the south of the town and by Lake Maryut. Here the quality of the housing is usually very low, and the people live under constant threat of being evicted (Ahmed 1989: 121f).

One of the measures taken by the central government to solve the housing problem of Alexandria was the construction of the new satellite town of Borg el-Arab el-Gedida, situated 60 km to the south-west, but not immediately on the Mediterranean coast. This town was first conceived in 1979 for a population of half a million in its final stages. When, fifteen years later, only about one-fifth of the 9,000 flats that had then been completed had been sold, the director in charge of the construction of the new town stopped all further building (*October*, 26 December 1993: 8). However, in the first year of the new millennium another new town, Mubarak Science City, was opened nearby. The decisive reason why the flats could not be sold in spite of comparatively favourable conditions for their financing, and in spite of the general shortage of housing, was the relatively high prices. Those for whom the problem of housing is most urgent are usually penniless and cannot profit from the housing programmes that the state has offered since the 1970s. Here, cheap housing for industrial workers would have been needed, since Borg el-Arab el-Gedida was planned as an industrial town. By 2000 about £120 million had been invested to develop the industries there, and over 360 factories built employing more than 19,000 workers in the production of building materials, textiles and food supplies, as well as chemicals, metal-ware and wood products (Ministry of Information 2001a; see Chapter 9).

2.2 The regional structure of the town (see Figure 11.4)

The regional structure of Alexandria is primarily determined by the town's physical-geographical position on a narrow strip of land 2–3 km wide, between the Mediterranean Sea and Lake Maryut. This is why Alexandria grew north-eastward over about 20 km from its old centre to Abu Qir and south-westward over about 26 km. As a matter of course, the distribution of the various urban functions followed this strip-like expansion over a distance of nearly 50 km.

The dual structure of the inner city and its development

Up to the middle of the twentieth century Alexandria's CBD clearly revealed the typical dual pattern of the colonial Mediterranean towns, similar to Tunis and Algiers. On the one hand there is an old Arab town built on the site of the ancient Heptastadion. Here the town's poorer inhabitants and the rural people from El-Beheira Governorate still do their shopping in the narrow *suq* (market) lanes, which are partly roofed and where some traditional handicrafts are still practised in the back yards of the shops. Adjacent to it there is a 'modern town', which displays the features characteristic of the commercial activities of its former foreign inhabitants and the Egyptian upper class. In this more modern colonial city with its wide streets and spacious buildings there is a concentration of central services, with banks, insurance companies, travel agencies, public administration offices, hotels, restaurants, cafés, theatres, cinemas, department stores, supermarkets, pharmacies, medical surgeries and lawyers' offices. However, both the modern CBD and the traditional trading centre have become too small to cater for almost 4 million inhabitants with an additional 3 million holidaymakers in summer and another 1 million visitors from the surrounding areas. Development has taken various forms:

- The CBD of the colonial era, situated between the main railway station and the seafront, slowly expanded north-eastward along the corniche and the streets running parallel to it, extending into the former upper-class sea resorts of Chatby, Sporting, Cleopatra and Stanley. A south-westward expansion was not appropriate, since harbour traffic and industry cause pollution of various kinds.
- The trading centre serving the poorer classes expanded eastwards and southwards in spite of the pollution of the harbour area and of the Maryut lake, into which the sewage of the mega-city is discharged.
- The immense growth of some suburban areas situated at great distances from the town centre, such as 'Agamy in the south-west and Abu Qir in the north-east, has encouraged the development of smaller additional CBDs, where central goods and services are available. The result is a diffusion of the functions of Alexandria's downtown CBD, leading to a weakening of its relative importance, so that it already shows signs of stagnation. Cairo's colonial CBD, on the other hand, still retains its old vigour and is keeping pace with the demands of the steadily increasing purchasing power of certain sectors of Egyptian society.

The ports

Apart from the western port of Alexandria there is today a new port, which was built in the 1980s near the newly industrialized area of Ed-Dekheila, and three smaller ports, one of them near Abu Qir to the north-east, another at Sidi Krer to the south-west, and the old eastern port, which is no longer used for shipping freight. In the early 1990s, more than 60 per cent of Egyptian sea trade passed through the ports of Alexandria. Since this far exceeded the capacity of the main port, the new port at Ed-Dekheila was built with facilities for containers and special infrastructure for unloading imported iron ore serving the requirements of the nearby steel factory.

In 1999/2000, the transshipment of goods at Alexandria amounted to 21.7 million tons, constituting about half of the freight of all Egyptian seaports (CAPMAS 2002: 112). The fact that Alexandria's ports are still very important today, although more recently built ports exist around the Suez Canal, is determined by the favourable position of the town:

- It lies closer to the areas of origin of the goods to be exported, mainly cotton and rice from the Nile delta, and to Europe, where the imported goods originate.
- The town itself is an important market. It is also a large centre for the processing industries for which the ports play a decisive role, such as the cotton dressing, pressing and packing industries, as well as ship and car repair. Moreover, it is the location of the warehouses used for storing goods imported or exported, such as wood, cotton and agricultural fertilizers, and of fuel storage tanks and the offices of the big shipping and transport agencies, as well as the customs authorities.

In 2002 plans were under way to develop the ports of Alexandria. However, owing to limited expansion potential, the Mediterranean harbour of Dumyat was upgraded to ease the pressure on the ports of Alexandria/Ed-Dekheila and to act as a transit port, especially for container ships.

Old and new industries

During the twentieth century various factors led to a concentration of the productive sector in Alexandria in the following locations.

The east Here we find an agglomeration of the textile industry, for which the comparatively low price of formerly cultivated land is responsible, together with the availability of labour migrants from the Nile delta, and readily available transport on the Mahmoudia Canal as well as on the direct road to the Nile delta.

The south Not far from the railway line to Cairo numerous textile, food and paper factories can be found, as well as cigarette factories. There are considerable transport advantages in this location. The nearby crowded town quarters of Muharram Bey, Karmus and El-Hadra provide not only the necessary labour force but also ready consumer markets.

Near the main port Here we find the cotton presses as well as the former location of the tanneries and other leather-processing industries, determined by the nearby slaughterhouse. The latter was shifted to El-'Amriya, in the south-west of the town, and the tanneries as well as the leather industries were relocated to Borg el-Arab el-Gedida.

The south-west This is the location of the large modern state-owned industries. After the government had passed a law forbidding the construction of buildings on agrarian land, the rocky desert areas and the dried-out parts of Lake Maryut, south-west of Alexandria, were designated for the new industries. This is why a Portland cement factory as well as soda and salt factories were built at El-Maks, and various branches of the petrochemical industry were established near the oil refineries. In addition, the Alexandria National Iron and Steel Company was built with Japanese support in the early 1980s at Ed-Dekheila, producing reinforced steel mainly for construction purposes. In 2001 it employed 3,180 workers. It is provided with direct access to the nearby port, from which the imported iron-ore pellets and scrap iron are transported directly to the steel works on conveyor belts. The direct reduction process is applied here in electric arc furnaces, with domestic natural gas as the reducing agent. The steel produced is partly for export.

Tourism in and around Alexandria (see also Chapter 10)

Annually between mid-June and mid-September, Alexandria has to cope with an influx of about 3 million people from all over Egypt, but mainly from the agglomeration of Cairo, who want to enjoy the fresh cool air and relax on the white beaches. During the rest of the year people come to this metropolis on the shores of the Mediterranean Sea to spend a weekend or a public holiday there. It takes no more than three hours by train or by car on the desert road to get from Cairo to Alexandria. The visitors who come in summer, mostly families, often stay for one to four weeks. Many of the inhabitants of Alexandria, especially those living close to the sea, let parts of their flats to them. Practically all accommodate members of their extended families, who take the opportunity of visiting them. Since more Egyptian families own cars today, the proximity of the beaches plays a lesser role now, though it is decisive in terms of room rates, of course. Well-to-do people who have invested their money in villas or flats close to the seaside let them at the highest prices possible for two to three months, while they usually remain unoccupied for the rest of the year. This makes the housing problem in Alexandria especially acute for the majority of the town's inhabitants, who cannot afford the high rents.

The local tourism described was until the 1950s concentrated on the coastal

29. Alexandria: Eastern Port and the fortress of Qayet Bay: The Eastern Port of
Alexandria is the site around which Alexander the Great founded his capital. Later the
Mamalukes built a fortress there. On public holidays the area is now visited by many
people from Alexandria and its rural surroundings. In recent years archaeologists have
lifted important artefacts from the bottom of the sea, and their work is still going on
here. (Photo: F. Ibrahim)

strip from east of the eastern harbour to the area of El-Muntaza Palace. The
public had no access to the latter until the revolution of 1952. North-east of
this there was a stretch of about 4 km of undeveloped coast up to the small
harbour of Abu Qir, where we find the terminal of a railway line connecting
it to Alexandria. Abu Qir was once known as a quiet, cheap, Westernized
holiday resort for the middle classes. Today the area is densely populated
and very polluted owing to the agrarian fertilizer industry established there.
Since the second half of the 1950s, the beaches of El-Muntaza and the village of El-Ma'amura, adjacent to it to the south-east, have been developed
for the well-to-do. At the same time, the trend of opening up new beaches
in the south-west gathered pace. There is a built-up area stretching about 15
km along the coast south-west of the main port and the military area of Ed-
Dekheila, as well as the industrial areas of El-Maks and Ed-Dekheila, with
their highly polluting industries. It is unsuitable as a residential area. However,
to the immediate south-west of these, on the excellent beaches of El-'Agamy,
many people acquired land and built villas, which they used in summer or
at weekends when they brought their families by car. The whole settlement
was illegal; nevertheless a casino was opened there as well as the splendid

hotel of Hannoville. In the 1970s and the 1980s, the fine white sandy beaches of El-'Agamy up to Sidi Abdel Rahman, 127 km west of Alexandria, were systematically occupied by the rich and influential, and by the professional organizations of army officers, police officers, medical doctors and university professors, as well as by private investors who had acquired the necessary capital after the Open Door policy had brought about great changes in the economy of the country. Holiday villages, some gigantic, were built for the Egyptian upper class (see Illustration 28), as well as a few beach resorts for foreign tourists. However, it has not been possible to establish international tourism here so far in spite of the proximity of the small international airport south-west of Alexandria. The main reasons are:

- Until the end of the 1980s there was a lack of attractive hotels. Since the early 1990s, international tourism has suffered repeatedly owing to political events such as the Gulf War of 1991, the war of 2003 against Iraq and various terrorist attacks on foreign tourists.
- Alexandria is away from the main tourist destinations from Cairo to Luxor and Aswan, at the Red Sea and on Sinai.
- The majority of non-Arab foreign tourists visit Egypt between October and April. During this time the weather is rather cool and unreliable at the Mediterranean coast.
- In terms of climate and potential for water sports such as scuba-diving, snorkelling, surfing and sailing, El-Ghardaqa and South Sinai, situated much farther south, offer excellent conditions all year round, and Alexandria cannot compete with them.
- Foreign tourists interested in the Greco-Roman past of Alexandria will usually spend a few days in a hotel in the town centre. If they visit the beaches in the south-west, they soon discover that adequate service is offered only in one or two exclusive hotels.

However, in the summer months Alexandria attracts many rich Arabs. For them the town offers not only a climate much cooler than that of their own countries, but also much more liberal kinds of entertainment without strict control of alcohol consumption or segregation of the sexes.

Pollution of the sea water has become a major problem, not only for tourism in Alexandria but for the town as a whole. Since the sea-water currents flow in a west–east direction, the problem arises from El-'Agamy to Abu Qir. Until 1991 all municipal sewage (in summer that of over 6 million people) and all industrial waste water passed into the sea without prior purification. By 1994 the government had implemented 70 per cent of a project for waste water disposal. The water is now purified and then diverted into Lake Maryut. Seemingly, however, the treatment was inadequate, since Lake Maryut has become seriously polluted and local fishermen have sued the state. In the area of Ed-Dekheila and to the south-west of it no water treatment plans have been drawn up.

3 The regional capitals

In the hierarchy of Egyptian towns, ranked according to their number of inhabitants, there is a big gap between Cairo and Alexandria on the one hand and all other towns on the other. The sizes of other capitals of their respective governorates range between 100,000 and 500,000 inhabitants (see Figure 11.1) and they differ greatly from one another. A comparison of their characteristics shows the following main features:

- These towns have different degrees of dependency on Cairo. Dependency is greatest in those towns situated closer to the capital, of course, but also in those which have a limited labour market owing to a lack of industry.
- They also differ in their urban character, independent of the number of their inhabitants. The towns of Damanhur, Shebin el-Kom, Beni Suef and Qena are of a considerable size, but they have at the same time a predominantly rural character owing to their large agrarian hinterlands, very different from towns like Port Said, Suez, Aswan and El-Ghardaqa.
- Since the era of Nasser the administrations of all governorate capitals have pursued in more or less the same ambitious manner a policy of establishing their own universities. Except in the capitals of the desert governorates, with their small populations, these have materialized, although securing the necessary capital, technical infrastructure and staff required a major investment of energy. Today many of these universities depend on the services of professors from Cairo or Alexandria who spend only a few days each week at their places of work.
- Similarly, since the era of Sadat most of the governorate capitals have tried to establish their own satellite towns, usually in adjacent desert areas, since the government forbade the construction of settlements on agricultural land. These twin towns normally bear the name of the original town with the addition of *el-Gedida* (the new one). Most of these hugely prestigious projects have been realized in part at least, consuming tremendous sums of money even though the necessary infrastructure was completed only in some cases, while in others it is not yet sufficient to enable the new towns to function, and in still others it is more or less only in the planning stage. The fact that apartment blocks were often finished but remained vacant led people to call these settlements *madinet el-ashbah* (ghost town). It should be acknowledged however, that on the plus side these towns represent a serious effort to halt the expansion of built-up areas at the expense of the country's scarce agricultural land.

3.1 The example of Beni Suef

To give an example of a regional capital situated in the rural parts of the Nile valley or the Nile delta, the town of Beni Suef is described here. This example is typical in many ways, although it should be mentioned that towns such as Tanta or Asyut, which have twice as many inhabitants, are of a more complex structure.

The social and economic characteristics of Beni Suef (see Figure 11.5)

Beni Suef is located 123 km south of Cairo, under the strong influence of which it comes. Thus it may be considered as part of Middle Egypt, though officially it belongs to Upper Egypt. In terms of dialect and other cultural characteristics, its inhabitants are very similar to the people living in the southern parts of the Nile valley, but they do not consider themselves as *sa'idi*, i.e. Upper Egyptian. The region of Beni Suef boasts a long and rich history. Here we find the pyramid of Medum, which is older than the pyramids of Giza. Close by is the town of Ihnasya, which was the capital of Egypt during the Ninth and Tenth Dynasties (2242–2133 BC), and at Deir el-Maymun, 25 km to the north of Beni Suef on the eastern bank of the Nile, lies the cradle of Christian monasticism, for here, St Antony the Great began his ascetic life until he retired into the Eastern Desert.

In 2002, Beni Suef had more than 200,000 inhabitants. The growth in population for the decade 1980–90 was 2.6 per cent (Mikhael 1986), similar to the average for the whole country as well as to that of the whole governorate of Beni Suef. The town's growth is mainly a natural increase. Migration to Beni Suef from its rural surroundings is mostly balanced by emigration to Cairo. The governorate of Beni Suef is situated so close to Cairo that migrants from its rural areas prefer to move to Cairo directly, without previous migration to Beni Suef. The mobility of the population within the town is centrifugal, in nearly all directions. The old parts of the town are extremely degraded and cannot absorb any further population (ibid.). This is particularly evident in the town centre, which does not reflect at all the actual size of the town. The land cultivated by the *fellaheen* extends to the borders of the town; many of them live within Beni Suef, thus contributing to its rural character. The structure of employment in the formal sector of the town shows that about two-thirds are state-employed (Mikhael, oral communication, March 1994). Second in number are those occupied in trade and other services. Industrial employment is of subordinate relevance, which is not necessarily so in other governorate capitals.

However, a process of restructuring began in the industrial sector in Beni Suef after the implementation of the policy of reprivatization. Thus the largest factory in the town, with about 2,000 employees, a state-owned textile plant, was offered for sale in 1993 after it had been making losses for years. When by 2001 no buyer had been found, the government closed down

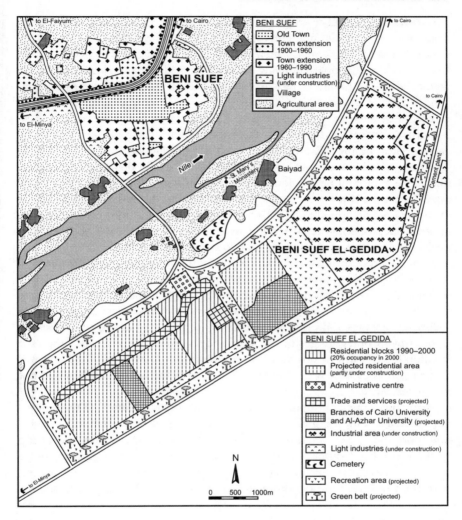

Figure 11.5: Beni Suef and its satellite town of Beni Suef el-Gedida (Author: F. Ibrahim 2002; cartography: J. Feilner; sources: after Mikhael 1986; Ministry of Housing 1998; field survey F. Ibrahim 2000)

the plant. The dismissed workers received lump sums ranging from US$5,000 to US$9,000. The cotton ginnery, which used to employ some five hundred workers seasonally, was also closed down. This marked the end of the traditional cotton industry in Beni Suef. Similar closures of textile plants in the public sector took place all over Egypt after the liberalization of the economy and the opening up of the market. The public sector businesses could not compete any more, owing not only to their poor technical standards but also to widespread mismanagement and corruption. In the early 1990s a soft-drinks factory at Beni Suef, employing five hundred workers, was bought by a businessman from Yemen, who also held shares in the reprivatized Egyptian Coca-Cola International company. In 2001 he had already closed down the factory after the period of tax exemption had elapsed, and opened another similar plant at El-Minya to avail himself of another ten-year term of financial privileges granted to new enterprises. The youngest and economically most promising enterprise is a cement factory built with Japanese support on the eastern bank of the Nile, which commenced production in the early 1990s. The raw material used is the marl of the local Tertiary deposits. In its initial phase one thousand people found employment here. In 2001 the French had taken over the plant and were also constructing another similar factory in the same area, while a private Egyptian company opened a third cement factory at Beni Suef offering 1,300 work opportunities (Governorate of Beni Suef 1994; Governorate of Beni Suef, oral communication, 2001).

Other sources of income in Beni Suef are found in the smaller businesses, such as brick yards, quarries or plants for the production of other building materials, of foodstuffs and clothing. In the 1990s plans were made to free the old part of the town from the noise and dirt produced by small-scale industries, garages and other workshops by removing them to two locations in the town's outer fringes to the west and the south-west. In 2001 the new location for 144 workshops in the west had already been established and was 50 per cent occupied, while the second new area for light industries had not yet materialized.

Beni Suef gained in importance when in the 1980s a branch of the University of Cairo comprising six faculties was established here. Ten years later it had more than seven thousand students, mostly from the region, but owing to the centralized system of university admission in Egypt, also from other parts of the country. Further faculties were established in nearby El-Faiyum, with the result that the two branches are now complementing each other.

Housing problems at Beni Suef

According to El-Nahhas (1997: Appendix), there are eight squatter settlements in the town of Beni Suef, which are part of the fifty-two illegal settlements in the whole governorate. Table 11.3 gives a comparison between the urban housing situation in Beni Suef and that of Cairo/Giza, Alexandria and the Egyptian average. It reveals the particularly bad housing situation in Beni Suef:

• Only 63.6 per cent of the urban population of Beni Suef Governorate live in appropriate types of housing (flats and houses), as compared to the country's average of 83.7 per cent, not to mention the higher percentages in the mega-cities of Greater Cairo and Alexandria. Though living in a flat does not guarantee that the dwelling is appropriate, it is at least considered better than having no self-contained dwelling, as, for example, one of the other housing types mentioned below.

- 27 per cent of the urban inhabitants of Beni Suef live in *fellaheen*-type houses, which are built of Nile silt, cow dung and straw. Although this type of house could be quite appropriate in rural areas, it is usually narrow and poorly built in towns. It lacks running water and sanitary facilities. Often it is illegally built on the margins of public roads, along railway lines, canals and on whatever public spaces are available.
- 9.3 per cent of the urban dwellings of Beni Suef are of an even poorer quality. They usually consist of single rooms, either separate or part of a shared dwelling. In most cases they have no toilet facilities and no access to running water.

According to the same source 38 per cent of the urban population of Beni Suef Governorate live in unacceptable housing conditions. It must be noted that the town of Beni Suef accommodates nearly half the urban population of the governorate and that the housing situation there can be considered representative of the other urban centres in the governorate.

Beni Suef's new twin town, Beni Suef el-Gedida (see Figure 11.5)

When in the early 1980s the eastern and the western Nile banks near Beni Suef were linked by a bridge, eastward expansion of the town was made possible. In 1986 the Egyptian parliament decided that the town of Beni Suef el-Gedida was to be built on a desert plateau on the eastern bank of the Nile opposite Beni Suef. The aim was on the one hand to solve the housing problems and on the other to protect the fertile agricultural land from further building encroachment. At the same time, a fast new desert road was built between Cairo and Asyut, close to which the new town is situated, so that its location is particularly favourable for commuters who work in Cairo. However, the new cement factories cause a problem, since they lie to the

Table 11.3 Housing in Egypt's towns: proportion of different types of urban dwellings in selected Egyptian governorates 1996 (%)

Type of housing	Cairo/Giza	Alexandria	Beni Suef	Egypt
Flat	86.4	84.1	51.8	79.3
House	2.2	3.0	11.8	4.4
Mud house	1.3	1.7	27.1	7.0
Shared one-room dwelling	5.4	6.6	4.8	5.4
Separate one-room dwelling	3.4	4.4	4.4	3.7
Tent, hut, etc.	1.3	0.2	0.1	0.2

Source: after CAPMAS 1999b: 1–3

north-east of Beni Suef el-Gedida, and thus the north-easterly trade winds prevailing in this part of Egypt seasonally carry the pollution to the settlement and cause the same problem there as the other big cement factory does at Turra/Helwan. The projected green belt around the town will hardly be able to solve the problem.

Based on a publication from the Ministry of Housing (1998) and the authors' survey of 2000, the Beni Suef el-Gedida project can be summarized in the following points:

- The project is scheduled to be completed in 2007.
- The target population is 420,000.
- Employment should be provided for 30,000 people.
- The total area is 163 km², of which 140 km² are reserved for green belts.
- The total area to be built up is 23 km², divided as follows:

Residential areas (six districts)	19 per cent
Trade and services	23 per cent
Industry	30 per cent
Roads and open space	28 per cent

- District 1 of the residential area has 1,265 plots, which are available to private enterprises (5–7 per cent of the plots had been built up in 2000).
- District 2 of the residential area consists of 9,120 flats in the low-cost housing category, with floor spaces of 62–93 km² each. (In 2000 all apartment blocks had been completed but the occupancy rate did not exceed 25 per cent. One of the reasons was the shortage of drinking water.)
- District 3, with 1,230 plots, was meant to be handed over to contractors and professional associations to develop. (In 2000 only about 2 per cent had actually been built up.)
- Districts 4, 5 and 6 are projected residential areas.
- The town centre consists of 691 plots for functions such as administration, trade and services. (In 2000 there were already a medical centre, a hospital for teachers, two mosques, a centre for social services, an Islamic college for girls, five technical schools, a primary school and four nurseries; the post office, the central telephone office and the town hall were under construction.)
- Three areas were reserved for industrial activities:
1) For light industries: a small strip of land near the residential areas. (In 2000 some plants had started production. They were smelting iron bars, producing detergents, drying onions for export, and producing fodder.)
2) For moderately heavy industries: a large area of 800 acres.
3) For agro-industries ('food security'): an area of about 700 acres.

It cannot be overlooked, however, that, in spite of all the efforts made, the new town does not meet the demands of the people. In particular the needs of the poor, about 13,000 families, were neglected. Therefore, about 75 per cent of all the completed flats in the lowest price category were vacant in 2000. The system of allocation for these was as follows: The government offered them for sale at a price of LE30,000 (*c.* £5,000). The buyers had to pay LE3,000 of this in advance and could pay the rest in monthly instalments of LE65 over thirty years. Of all the housing programmes offered by the government the 'Suzanne Mubarak Housing Programme' for newly married couples is the most attractive, offering small, nicely built flats at a relatively low price. In Beni Suef el-Gedida 4,000 flats of this type were constructed. They were immediately sold and in 2001 about 90 per cent of them were already occupied, a much higher occupancy rate than in other housing programmes, which only the higher income groups can afford. In Beni Suef – just as in Cairo, Alexandria and other towns – those who have the money can profit from these governmental programmes, which are publicly claimed to be for the poor. For decades those who had the money invested in the newly built residential areas and did not care if the infrastructure remained uncompleted for years, since they had bought the properties for their (sometimes still young) children while they themselves preferred to remain living in the usually more spacious and cheaper flats in the older parts of the towns. Since in recent years the legal situation regarding the letting of flats has been changed, granting greater rights to landlords, flats were sometimes let for high rents to other well-off citizens. The problems experienced in Beni Suef el-Gedida arose also in El-Minya el-Gedida and elsewhere, but housing continues to be planned and built in the same way. As long as the state does not change its policy and offer cheap housing on a large scale, as during the time of Nasser, the problem will not be solved. In early 2000 several of the new still-uninhabited buildings in Beni Suef el-Gedida had already been partly demolished by an earthquake. Instead of instituting grandiose plans, it might have been far more sensible first to upgrade parts of the old town of Beni Suef, where the houses are utterly run down. Then new housing could have been created. The point is being discussed in the town, but no steps have been taken so far.

4 Towns in the desert – a rediscovered urbanization strategy for Egypt (see Table 11.4)

In connection with the construction of the Suez Canal in the nineteenth century, the Khedives had already had modern towns built in the desert by European architects. This is the origin of towns such as Ismailiya and Port Tawfiq, with their green parks, alleys and characteristic architecture in colonial style with verandas, balustrades and gardens. These towns are completely un-Egyptian and lack a rural hinterland. Also, when modern Cairo emerged, its rulers craved a life of luxury and, in spite of their high debts, spent enormous sums on building their palaces and elegant cities. Already in

Table 11.4 New towns in Egypt – from planning stage to realization

Name of town	Year of foundation	Population 1986	Population 1996	Target popul. 2000–10	Housing units built 1982–2001
Badr	1982	–	248	280,000	11,500
El-Ubur	1982	1,037	991	477,000	19,500
Khamastasher Mayo (15 May)	1978	24,106	65,865	250,000	17,100
El-Amal, El-Qahira el-Gedida, El-Qattamiya, El-Tagammuat	1986	–	34,819	250,000	32,000
Esh-Sheruq	,,	–	–	–	24,800
Esh-Sheikh Zayed	under construction	–	*	*	8,400
Sitta October	1979	528	35,477	500,000	42,100
Total of new towns in Greater Cairo	Since 1977	25,671	137,400	2,257,000	155,400
El-Ashir min Ramadan	1977	8,509	47,839	500,000	26,700
Madinet es-Sadat	1978	669	16,312	500,000	8,000
Borg el-Arab el-Gedida	1979	*	7,055	510,000	8,200
Gharb en-Nubariya	1986	25,754	25,924	50,000	2,500
Es-Salhiya el-Gedida	1982	464	8,133	100,000	6,000
Dumyat el-Gedida	1984	70	6,517	270,000	11,000
Beni Suef el-Gedida	1988	–	203	420,000	4,900
El-Minya el-Gedida	1986	–	68	120,000	3,000
Asyut el-Gedida	under construction	–	–	131,000	3,000
Akhmim/Sohag el-Gedida	,,	–	–	120,000	*
Tiba el-Gedida (Luxor)	,,	–	*	–	1,500
Aswan el-Gedida	,,	–	–	120,000	*
Grand total	Since 1977	61,237	249,451	4,598,000	230,200

* No figures available

Sources: after CAPMAS 1996; El-Hady 1993: 113ff; Soliman 1996: 200; Ministry of Information 2001a and 2002a

1877, one of these new settlements, the health resort of Helwan, was linked to Cairo by a modern railway line (today the metro). At the beginning of the twentieth century, further new towns in a grand style were founded in the desert areas around Cairo, such as the satellite towns of Heliopolis and Hadayeq el-Qubba to the north-east, and El-Maadi el-Gedida in the south, likewise linked to the town centre by a railway or metro line, which was a revolutionary innovation at the time.

Less spectacular, but also very important, was the later construction of new settlements of urban character in desert areas in accordance with the development of new agrarian land, such as Gianaklis to the south-west of Alexandria, as well as settlements in Tahrir Province, in the area of Lake Maryut, in El-Wadi el-Gedid and, presently, in various parts of Sinai. Here, uniform blocks of flats were dominant for a long time, but the rents were often affordable for the masses for whom the houses had been built. Also, as part of the socialist housing programmes of the 1950s, in many places huge urban colonies were constructed, such as Madinet Nasr (= town of victory, named after the secret password of the revolution of 1952), built in the desert beween Cairo and Heliopolis but now an integral part of the Cairene agglomeration. In 1994 it had more than 180,000 inhabitants.

In the course of time, the state formulated more radical concepts of area planning, with the result that in the 1960s and 1970s an urbanization strategy was proclaimed, which can be summarized as follows (see Knaupe and Wurzel 1995: 53): The main aim was to create a regional structure all over the country, allowing a more homogeneous distribution of the population, greater economic balance and the protection of fertile arable land, as well as the necessary infrastructure. To fulfil these aims, zones of development were designed to divert the settlement of the fast-growing population to areas outside the traditionally inhabited but now overcrowded regions. As part of these, new towns were to be built, to function as nuclei of further development. The planners conceived four different categories of new towns in their regional programmes:

- independent new towns
- dependent new settlements
- dependent new urban communities
- dependent new twin towns.

So far, seven new towns in the first category have been built. The following four are closely oriented towards Cairo: Madinet el-Ashir min Ramadan (10th of Ramadan), Madinet Badr, Ash-Shuruq and Madinet es-Sadat. Two of the new towns are situated near Alexandria: Borg el-Arab el-Gedida and En-Nubariya el-Gedida. Another new town, Es-Salhiya el-Gedida, lies between Cairo and Ismailiya in the land reclamation area it is named after.

The dependent new settlements were meant in the first place to reduce the high population pressure on Greater Cairo. So far, three towns have been built to serve this purpose: Madinet Sitta October (6 October) in the south-west, Madinet Khamastasher Mayo (15 May) in the south-east, and Al-Ubur in the north-east. Although Madinet Sitta October was not able to fulfil its original aim, like most of the other new towns it became an important location for various new industries, owing mainly, of course, to state subsidies. Among the foreign investors are US firms such as General Motors and Xerox, each employing more than 500 people. According to the semi-official daily *Al-Ahram*, Madinet Sitta October has 1,200 industrial plants contributing 15 per cent of the value of the country's export of industrial commodities (Internet 2002). Industries in the other two towns were less successful. In the case of Al-Ubur, this was because of conflicts between the Ministry of Agriculture and the ministry responsible for the new town. Madinet Khamastasher Mayo had been planned from the start to house the great number of workers in the Helwan industries, and not as an industrial town itself.

To reduce migration from the provinces to the country's capital, new towns were established as twin towns for the capitals of some governorates. In 2002 six of these were under construction: Esh-Sheikh Zayed, El-Minya el-Gedida, Asyut el-Gedida, Akhmim/Sohag el-Gedida, Tiba el-Gedida (Luxor) and Aswan el-Gedida, as well as Beni Suef el-Gedida, which is described above. All these were established in the desert areas bordering the Nile valley, usually on the Nile bank opposite the original town. In tandem, new Nile bridges were built at Beni Suef, El-Minya, Luxor and Aswan.

While the new towns were in the planning stage, the government passed a law that forbade all further establishment of settlements on agricultural land.

Though those responsible in government had a vision for the regional planning of Egypt that is certainly clear-headed in many respects, the likely success of the new programmes is doubtful. In 1992 a mere 160,000 people were living in the 200,000 flats that had been built in twenty-one new towns. The state had contributed US$5,000 to every single one of them, which in relation to other prices in Egypt is an extremely high sum, while the number of beneficiaries is relatively small and, moreover, they do not belong to the low-income groups the state should support in the first place. In 1995 the advance payment for a flat in Khamastasher Mayo, which is not in a favourable location because of the pollution caused by the industries of nearby Helwan, was about US$1,170, and the monthly instalments were US$17. At the time the average state employee or worker received about US$28 as his monthly income, and as a result he was not in a position to acquire such property.

The new towns have, however, proved beneficial in terms of the modern factories established in them. In 2000 these employed 245,400 people (see Table 9.5). The drawback was, however, that most of the workers lived in their old towns and had to be taken to their places of work daily in buses. Unfortunately the establishment of effective suburban public transport systems had been neglected by the planners. There are no tram or metro lines, in contrast to the first desert towns built near Cairo. Moreover, it is doubtful that the newly founded industries will survive when the many privileges, such as tax exemption and high subsidies, are terminated.

In addition to the above-mentioned types of new towns and new communities that are planned and strongly subsidized by the state, there are a growing number of gated communities. They made their first appearance as 'holiday villages' on the Mediterranean coast (see Illustration 28) and spread fast to cover the whole 300 km strip between Alexandria and Marsa Matruh, parts of the Red Sea coast, of the Gulfs of Suez and Aqaba as well as the outskirts of Cairo and Giza. The new gated communities are often copies of settlements in the USA, especially in California. They are provided with security services, schools, hospitals, mosques, recreation areas, sports clubs, shopping malls and other services. These communities are built by private companies for the affluent classes. Nevertheless, huge sums of money are contributed by the state for building the costly infrastructure, which is all that makes the creation of such settlements in desert areas possible. In this way the problem of social segregation and social disparities is exacerbated in the country.

5 Egypt's rural settlements

Although a comparison of the data from the Egyptian population censuses of 1986 and 1996 shows a slight rise in the proportion of rural inhabitants, urbanization is still proceeding rapidly, for many settlements that are statistically classified as rural have a clearly urban character. Many 'villages' have more than 30,000 inhabitants, who are mostly engaged in urban professions (Müller-Mahn 2001a). According to the 1996 census there were 4,132 rural settlements in Egypt with an average number of 8,150 inhabitants. This shows that Egypt's rural settlements are relatively big. They differ considerably among themselves in character, depending on their closeness to a town, their size and their central functions. Many *fellaheen* from villages situated close to a town take the opportunity of earning their livelihood in the informal as well as in the formal urban sectors. Big villages fulfil central functions for many of the smaller villages, which belong to them administration-wise, providing their schools, hospitals, mosques, churches, banks, branches of agricultural cooperatives, administration and other services. For the bigger villages, the classical Arabic term *qarya* is used, for the smaller ones the term *'izbet* (possessive of *'izba*). In Upper Egypt, some smaller villages are called *nag'*, as for example in the name of the town of Nag' Hammadi (i.e. Hammadi's village). Officially, every independent village or part of a larger settlement is called *shiyakha* (plural *shiyakhat*).

The usual building material of the *fellaheen* was formerly bricks made of a mixture of mud, cow dung and straw, which were dried in the sun. Farmers normally used the topsoil of their fields for this purpose (see Illustration 16), which consisted of Nile silt. Eventually the government forbade this, but illegal making of bricks using the precious Nile deposits goes on in many parts of Upper Egypt, and a farmer who is in dire need of money may sell some of his best soil for this purpose. The walls of the typical *fellaheen* house are plastered over with the same material as is used in brick-making; the flat roof consists of wood, mostly the trunks of date palm trees. Inside the house a part is usually reserved for animals, another contains the oven, which equally is built of mud (see Illustration 13), and in which the flat round bread is baked by the *fellaha*. Traditionally in the bigger houses, such as that of the *sheikh el-balad* or *omda* (mayor), there is a terrace or hall with a *mastaba*, i.e. a mud bench, usually covered with a mat of plaited reeds. The roofs of the houses are still used today for storing fuel, which mainly consists of dried maize and cotton stalks, as well as of animal dung mixed with straw and formed into a disc-like shape. The inner parts of the maize cobs serve for lighting the fire, and are usually stored beside the oven. In small tower-like structures on the roofs the grain that is not needed for immediate consumption after the harvest is stored. Many *fellaheen* have pigeon towers on the roofs of their houses (see Illustration 15). Small openings in the house walls at a height of about 2 m from the ground serve for ventilation.

During the second half of the twentieth century a conspicuous change was to be observed in the appearance of Egyptian villages, since remigrants who had worked in the oil-rich Arab states invested their savings mostly in the construction of houses of a more urban type in their home villages. More and more villages thus lost their traditional character. Because of the land shortage prevailing, the extension often had to be vertical rather than horizontal.

A certain area of agricultural land, called *hiyasa*, belongs to each village. It consists of the land owned by the villagers, and additionally of the land they have rented from people who usually live in town. In spite of the socialist land reforms, absenteeism has not quite been eradicated in Egypt.

The infrastructure of the small villages is lacking in many respects, although most of them have electricity these days, as well as a central distribution of clean water, which is gradually being replaced by water pipes leading to individual houses, since people have to pay for the water now. Usually there is a weekly market (*suq*) and a number of small shops. In the weekly markets the women of the village can sell their surplus agricultural produce, such as vegetables, poultry, eggs and milk or milk products. Since the Nile valley is very narrow, the villages lie close together, and it is usually not difficult to reach a nearby town. However, since most *fellaheen* are poor, they do not go to town very often.

CHAPTER 12

The Prospects for Egypt's Economy at the Beginning of the Twenty-first Century

Its fast-growing population of almost 70 million and its limited natural resources are hard challenges for Egypt. With more than half this population existing below the poverty line and an inevitable confrontation with economic globalization looming, Egypt does not have many options. The implementation of some macroeconomic objectives within the first two decades of the twenty-first century appears to be of vital importance to improve the country's economic prospects. The most urgent of these are:

- the privatization of the state economic sector – it must be considered the key to all economic reform
- the improvement of the general investment environment
- the advancement of research and technology – without these Egypt will not be able to participate efficiently in the globalization process
- the successful implementation of agricultural projects in various parts of the country
- taking greater care of the social and economic sustainability of development.

These various areas are dealt with below.

1 The struggle for economic transformation

The privatization of the public sector, an essential part of the World Bank's Structural Adjustment Programme, was made one of the preconditions for writing off about US$25 billion of external debt, which constituted about one-half of Egypt's total external debt in 1990/91. The Egyptian government was able to convince the international donors of the seriousness of its intention to sell most of the holding companies in the public sector (Wurzel 2001: 13). By 2001, 155 of the 314 state-owned companies coming under the privatization programme of 1991 had been sold or transferred to the private sector (Essam El-Din 2000; Fekry 2001a). The transactions took various forms:

- For 37 companies majority shares were floated on the stock market.
- 24 companies were sold to investors.

- In 30 companies majority stakes were sold to the shareholders' associations of the companies' employees.
- Another 36 concerns had majority stakes sold as assets.
- In 16 companies minority shares were sold.
- The remaining 12 companies were leased.

Up to 2001 privatization had yielded LE16 billion, only LE5.8 billion of which were sent to the state treasury, while most was spent on repaying the debts of the companies sold, on compensating dismissed workers and on restructuring and rehabilitating businesses to prepare them for sale.

Some negative consequences of the privatization policy soon emerged, the most serious being the loss of employment of thousands of workers within the process. Moreover, monopolies began to appear in certain strategic industries, such as those producing cement, steel, fertilizers and beverages. Also, for the remaining unsold companies, most of which were loss-making ones, there were no effective reform programmes. In his overall assessment of the application of the privatization programme in Egypt the German economist Wurzel (2000; 2001), who has considerable insight into the Egyptian economy, comes to an extremely negative judgement. He maintains that from the very beginning the government was not in favour of privatization of the economy, which is incompatible with the interests of the political elite in a rentier state. It deprives those in power of the economic rents they otherwise receive, both external and internal ones – and, as described in Chapter 7, more than 60 per cent of Egypt's state budget in 1996/97 came from rents acquired through state monopolies. Moreover, there was apprehension that the liberalization of the economy could give rise to a new class with independent political views which might jeopardize the political regime. Wurzel (ibid.) argues that the Egyptian government finds itself in a dilemma. On the one hand it wants to satisfy donors by carrying out the privatization programme and thus achieve a write-off of its external debt and an increase in its international rents. On the other hand, it wants to keep control over the country's economy so as not to lose the economic rents it can draw from it. According to Wurzel (2001: 14ff), the government made a show of privatization and was more or less successful in convincing international donors that it was taking steps in this direction. This show was regularly staged before the evaluations of the World Bank, the IMF and the donor countries were due. Such pseudo-privatization plays could be quite dramatic, involving a change of prime minister and cabinet members. The new ministers would then vow to promote privatization strongly. In fact, Privatization Law No. 203 of 1991 stipulated the privatization of 314 state companies with an estimated value of US$26 billion, which constituted only 15 per cent of the total value of the public economic sector at that time. However, other enterprises, amounting to a total value of 85 per cent, which were exempted from the Privatization Law, included

30. Convoy of ships passing through the Suez Canal: The Suez Canal, constructed 1859–69, shortened the sea journey between Europe and Asia considerably. Fully loaded tankers of 170,000 tons and unloaded ones of 400,000 tons can pass through it today. The revenues Egypt gains from the canal are of great importance for the country's economy. (Photo: F. Ibrahim)

the most important economic sectors, such as the petroleum industry, the Suez Canal Authority and the military industry. Repeatedly the government announced privatization negotiations which did not take place or conducted various forms of pseudo-privatization, for example offering enterprises for sale and ultimately selling them to other companies in the public sector, or 'selling' a proportion of the companies' shares to their employees without actually transferring ownership to them. Some companies were offered for sale for years, while the government simultaneously undertook efforts to make them unattractive to buyers, for example by demanding unrealistically high prices or by leaving the enterprises in a poor condition. The result of these manoeuvres was that by 1998, the year in which the privatization pro-gramme should have been completed, only 17.5 per cent of state enterprises stipulated under the privatization programme had actually been transferred to the private sector (Wurzel 2001: 16). Wurzel concludes that the Egyptian make-believe privatization achieved its objective, for international donors rewarded Egypt's efforts by writing off the last tranche of its external debt. Having achieved this, the government turned down a USAID offer to fund a privatization support programme.

2 Egypt's capital investment environment

Egypt has been trying to attract foreign investors since 1974, and encouraging domestic ones since 1977. The government hopes that foreign investment may enhance technological development, leading to cost-effective production, rendering the country able to compete with other producers worldwide. This would in turn support the development of industrial sectors in which Egypt has comparative advantages, such as the production of textiles, in particular ready-made garments, chemicals and agro-industrial goods. Globalization should allow for greater cross-border mobility of goods and services, stimulating the development of new industries in Egypt. However, the government's success in attracting foreign investors has been limited so far. The reason is that the investment environment is still less favourable than in other countries of the region. To make it more attractive, some measures must be taken, such as (see Giugale and Mobarak 1996: 137ff):

- The regulatory and bureaucratic environment must be improved. Bureaucratic regulations are a great impediment to international trade in Egypt. They cause a loss of time, increase production costs, lower productivity and weaken competitiveness.
- The infrastructure still needs upgrading. The port of Alexandria, for example, is disastrously inefficient.
- Free flow of capital and goods across the borders should be guaranteed. Presently trade barriers are still a serious obstacle.
- State intervention must be removed.
- State monopoly must come to an end.
- Although prices were liberated, the markets are still controlled by the state. They, too, require liberalization.
- Control of the economy as a whole should be relaxed.
- Private sector monopolies, especially those resulting from the privatization process in the public sector, should be removed. Consumer rights should be respected, and fair competition guaranteed.
- There are still legal and judicial deficiencies: law and order must be preserved, corruption combated, contracts enforced and property rights protected.

In the establishment of special industrial zones and customs-free zones, the government has started moving in the right direction. However, too many concessions to new investors affect the old industrial centres negatively, since an imbalance is created which hampers competition.

With little success, the government has in recent years been applying the GATT agreement. Egypt had hoped for easier access to the larger global market and for a greater demand for the country's industrial capacities. In fact GATT impeded the industrialization process in the country, just as the liberation of commerce had already led to the flooding of the Egyptian market with foreign goods, which made local industry even less competitive (ibid.).

3 Boosting research and technological development

Recognizing that science and technology are vital for Egypt's ability to participate in the process of globalization, in 1995 the government proclaimed the start of a huge undertaking called the 'Valley of Technology Project', to be established on Sinai on the east bank of the Suez Canal. The total investment to be made was estimated at about US$12 billion. In 2002 the Egyptian 'Silicon Valley' was still on the official agenda of mega-projects (Ministry of Information 2002b), but the Minister of Communication and Information, Nazif, had already signalled a change of strategy regarding this project. He maintained (Howeidy 2000): 'We haven't dropped that idea. But we must be more selective in identifying areas, that they should be closer to existing communities rather than being built from scratch. The second thing is to start with small areas that can grow later on.' From this statement it becomes clear that the government had in fact dropped the idea of the technology mega-project on Sinai. The reasons given by the minister are indeed quite valid, since it is always wise to start small and grow gradually, and to choose locations where agglomerations of consumers are found nearby. In this respect, the choice of Alexandria or Cairo as locations for the two smaller science centres discussed below is a much better one than that of the Valley of Technology Project in the Sinai desert.

In 2000 President Mubarak inaugurated a new scientific research centre, the Mubarak Science City (MSC), in Borg el-Arab el-Gedida near Alexandria, built on 100 acres of land at a cost of LE100 million in the first phase. The ambitious city, which the Minister of Higher Education compared to the US Silicon Valley, has three spectacular pyramid-shaped buildings in imitation of the Pharaonic monuments at Giza. The MSC started up with the following institutions: the Genetic Engineering and Biotechnology Institute, the Information Technology Institute, the New Materials and Advanced Technology Institute, the Scientific and Technological Abilities Development Centre and the Small-Scale Industries Development Centre. The government hopes that the MSC will act as a motor for modernizing the industry in the Alexandria region, where 40 per cent of Egyptian industries are concentrated (*Egypt* magazine 2001), and at the same time enhance the modernization of agriculture. In the latter respect an agreement was signed in 2001 granting to the institution oversight of the first major organic farm in Siwa oasis, with an organic fertilizers factory, a sophisticated irrigation system and various solar power stations (Fekry 2001b).

Another similar science city was planned for Sitta October near Giza on an area of 130,000 m² with an initial budget of LE250 million. The private sector is being called upon to supply a major share of the necessary funds. The Minister of Higher Education compared this new science city to the Franklin Science Institute, the Virginia Science Institute and the New York Sciences Centre in America. According to him, the aims of such a project are (El-Saqqar 2001):

- to create a favourable environment for research in new scientific areas
- to produce hardware and software in the area of information technology.

But Egypt has still a long way to go in IT, for in 2000 Internet users were merely 0.73/10,000, as compared to 1.27/10,000 in Jordan and 1,218.42/10,000 in Finland (World Bank 2001: 310).

4 Agricultural mega-projects for the third millennium

In 1997 the government announced the launch of several agricultural mega-projects to run until the year 2017. They are grouped under two programmes:

- the Southern Valley Project, comprising sub-projects in the southern governorates, with the main sub-project in Toshka
- the National Project for the Development of Northern Sinai and the Northwestern Coast, in which As-Salam Canal in the east and An-Nasr/ Al-Hammam Canals in the west form the projected development axes.

It is obvious that the government chose desert areas for the purpose of population redistribution, trying to pull people out of the congested Nile valley. One of the political intentions was also to boost development in areas that had so far been neglected by the central administration in Cairo.

While As-Salam-Canal Project and An-Nasr/Al-Hammam-Canals Project have been dealt with in Chapter 8, the projects at Toshka and East Uweinat will be briefly reviewed here. The backbone of the Toshka Project, which is in the first place a desert cultivation project, is the Sheikh Zayed Canal. It was constructed in the south-east of the Libyan Desert, branching off from the western flank of the Sadd el-Ali reservoir and running north-westward following the Darb el-Arbain to the New Valley over a distance of 850 km (Al-Kharbutli and Abdel-Ati 1998: 49). A giant pumping station will lift the water to a level 50 m above that of Lake Nasser to make it flow into the desert. The LE300 billion project is intended to underpin the livelihood of the 6 million inhabitants expected to live in the area one day (Ministry of Information 2000: 135). The project, the construction of which started in 1996, aroused considerable controversy among scientists and politicians. One of the critics of the project is the Egyptian pedologist Kishk (Kishk 1999b). The main points of criticism raised by him, as well as by other scientists, are:

- Egypt is already suffering from a water shortage. If one day 5 billion m³ of water are extracted from Lake Nasser for this project alone, certain disaster will befall irrigated agriculture in the whole of Egypt, especially given that at the same time that As-Salam Canal on northern Sinai is being constructed, which is to draw another 4.45 billion m³ of water annually from the Nile, as well as the An-Nasr/Al-Hammam Canals and their western extension, which are to irrigate 530,000 *feddans* of desert land west of Alexandria which will require about 4.5 billion m³ of water, too. For three decades the planners have been talking of saving water through more rational use, by reducing the area of rice cultivation and recycling drainage water. But little has been achieved so far in this respect. Besides, ecologists and agronomists warn against the reduction in the areas of rice cultivation in the northern delta for different reasons.
- The soils of the Toshka Depression are by no means better than the soils of alternative desert areas on the flanks of the Nile delta, where sufficient landless labourers are available. Transferring *fellaheen* into a desert against their will is neither socially nor economically sustainable.
- The Toshka region is one of the hottest and driest areas in the world. The water consumption of crop plants there will be twice that in northern Egypt.
- Despite the huge size of the project no serious study has been carried out so far on its possible ecological impact. Pumping 5 billion m³ of water annually into the Toshka Depression, where no drainage is possible, will turn it into a salt lake, as previous experience in Ed-Dakhla, Siwa and Wadi en-Natrun showed. There salt lakes (constantly growing in size) have appeared in recent years as a result of excessive irrigation.
- So far, in the first phase of the project, 540,000 *feddans* of land have been reclaimed and given to four investors from Saudi Arabia, the UAE and Egypt. As these capitalists will apply modern methods of agriculture, similar to those applied in the USA and in Australia, the number of the jobs created will be very limited, leaving aside the ecological consequences. Owing to the tax exemption and other concessions granted to the investors, the revenues for the state budget will be negligible. The state is giving away billions of LE in the form of infrastructure and water to four private investors, without gaining anything for the country's poor, whose resources are being spent.

The mega-project at East Uweinat for the reclamation and cultivation of 200,000 *feddans* using groundwater is also controversial. It is doomed to failure for the very reasons that caused the failure of the New Valley Project (see Chapter 8). Cultivating staple crops by water lifted from a depth of 200 m is uneconomic, for the high water costs will inflate the production costs. Most crop production costs in the Nile valley, where good soils and cheap water are available, are already above the world average. Domestically produced wheat, rice, cotton and sugar are an example of this.

In 2001 the number of wells dug in East Uwainat reached 354 and the area cultivated was 28,000 *feddans* (Ministry of Information 2002b).

Egypt's government is optimistic about the new projects – scientists and other experts, on the other hand, warn that the mega-projects will lead to a mega-catastrophe. The future will show us who is right.

5 Sustainability of development in Egypt

The private sector has been responsible for the growth of industrial production over the past decade. However, in the case of the multinationals, revenues are to a great extent often transferred out of the country. Some of them are also restricted to operating exclusively within the Egyptian market so as to avoid competition with the mother company. So they are not helpful in terms of opening up export opportunities for Egypt's economy.

As has been shown here, some of the preconditions of sustainable economic development are still lacking in Egypt. Among them is the favourable and sustainable investment environment just mentioned, but also social sustainability, which should be based on an active civil society (see Chapter 3). Respect for workers' rights is being neglected, in particular through liberalization of the economy. Labour laws seem to exist only on paper, and in the new industrial and customs-free zones they are either hardly observed at all or they do not exist. Egyptian labour unions and militant labour activists have been utterly silenced since the bread revolts of the 1970s. This neglect of rightful claims may enhance economic investment in the short term but will be detrimental to it in the long run.

Equally serious is the ecological situation in Egypt, with environmental destruction caused by excessive irrigation in agriculture, the dumping of garbage in and outside towns, the construction of whole towns in desert areas, and the establishment of industries or tourist infrastructure such as golf courses there or in other virgin environments. The once unique terrestrial and aquatic ecosystems in the areas of El-Ghardaqa and Sharm esh-Sheikh are glaring examples of the latter. Hundreds of square kilometres have already been buried under the newly constructed holiday resorts and the sands of the artificial beaches. In addition to this, hundreds of motor boats cast anchor on the coral reefs there daily, ferrying tourists for diving or snorkelling. Egypt really is killing the goose that is laying the golden eggs.

The country is in dire need of reforms to bring about numerous structural changes, and should at the same time revise its policy of development, or else sustainable economic development will not be achieved.

References

Abdel-Fadil, M. (1975) *Development, Income Distribution and Social Change in Rural Egypt (1952–1973)* (Cambridge).

Abdel Fattah, M. M. (1992) 'Resources and Food in Rural Egypt', in Arab Research Centre, Cairo (ed.), *The Agricultural Question in Egypt* (in Arabic) (Cairo), pp. 98–132.

Abdelghani, M .I. M. (2002) *Handslungsstrategien verwundbarer Bevölkerungsgruppen zur Sicherung ihrer Existenz in den Hüttensiedlungen der Stadt El-Minya, Ägypten.* Doctoral thesis, University of Bayreuth.

Abdel-Hakim, M. S. (1958) *The City of Alexandria* (in Arabic) (Cairo).

— (1967) 'The Population of Egypt: a Demographic Study', *Bulletin of the Faculty of Arts*, vol. 29, nos 1/2 (Cairo), pp. 17–44.

Abdel-Latif, A. (1974) *Fisheries of Lake Nasser*, Aswan Regional Planning, Lake Nasser Development Centre (Aswan).

Abdel-Malek, A. (1971) *Ägypten – Militärgesellschaft. Das Armeeregime, die Linke und der soziale Wandel unter Nasser* (trans. from French and English by R. Kruse) (Frankfurt).

Abdel-Moiti, A., and H. Kishk (1992) 'The Most Important Changes in the Egyptian Village' (in Arabic), in Centre of Arab Research, *The Agricultural Question in Egypt* (Cairo), pp. 201–29.

Abdel Motaal, D., and E. Volpi (1997) 'The Zabbalin Community of Mokkatam', *Cairo Papers in Social Science*, vol. 11, no. 4 (Cairo).

Abou Aianah, F. M. (1980) *A Population Geography of Alexandria* (in Arabic) (Alexandria).

Abou El-Magd, N. (1999) 'Feminists Seek Unity', *Al-Ahram Weekly*, no. 435, 24–30 June (Cairo). <http://www.ahram.org.eg/weekly/1999/435/eg19.htm>

Abu Al-Izz, M. S. (1971) *Landforms of Egypt* (Cairo).

Abu-Lughod, J. L. (1961) 'Migrant Adjustment to City Life: the Egyptian Villager in Cairo', *Ekistics*, vol. 12, no. 71 (Athens), pp. 192–202.

— (1969) 'Varieties of Urban Experience: Contrast, Coexistence and Coalescence in Cairo', in I. M. Lapidus (ed.), *Middle Eastern Cities* (Berkeley, CA), pp. 159–87.

— (1971) 'Cairo. 1001 Years of the City Victorious', in L. C. Brown (ed.), *From Madina to Metropolis. Heritage and Change in the Near East City* (Princeton, NJ).

— (1973) 'Cairo. Perspective and Prospectus', in L. C. Brown (ed.), *From Madina to Metropolis. Heritage and Change in the Near East City* (Princeton, NJ), pp. 95–113.

— (1975) 'A Comparative Analysis: Cairo, Tunis, and Rabat-Salé', *Ekistics*, vol. 39, no. 233 (Athens), pp. 236–45.

— (1998) 'Television and the Virtues of Education: Upper Egyptian Encounters with State Culture', in N. S. Hopkins and K. Westergaard (eds), *Directions of Change in Rural Egypt* (Cairo), pp. 147–65.

Abu-Zeid, M. (1987) 'Environmental Impact Assessment for the Aswan High Dam', in A.K. Biswas and Q. Geping (eds), *Environmental Impact Assessment for Developing Countries*, Natural Resources and Environment Series, vol. 19, pp. 168–90.

Adams, R. H., Jr (1991) *The Effects of International Remittances on Poverty, Inequality, and Development in Rural Egypt*, International Food Policy Research Institute, Research Report 86 (Washington, DC).

Ahmed, A. A. (1959/60) 'An Analytic Study of the Storage Losses in the Nile Basin, with Special Reference to Aswan Dam Reservoir (Sadd-Al-Ali)', *Institution of Civil Engineers Proceedings*, vol. 17, session 1959/60, pp. 181–200. Discussion of the paper in vol. 19, session 1960/61, pp. 337–415.

Ahmed, J. M. (1960) *The Intellectual Origins of Egyptian Nationalism* (London).

Ahmed, S. A. H. (1989) *Modern Town Planning for Alexandria* (in Arabic), MA thesis, University of Alexandria (Alexandria).

Al-Ahram (1984) *Drying the Northern Lakes* (in Arabic) (Cairo), p. 3.

Al-Ali, N. (2000) *Secularism, Gender and the State in the Middle East: the Egyptian Women's Movement* (Cambridge).

Al-Attar, A. (2001) *Haphazard Investment (1)*. <http://www.ahram.org.eg/arab/ahram/2001/3/7/ECON1.htm>

Al-Basil, A. (2001) *Export is the Battle of Challenge*. <http://www.ahram.org.eg/arab/ahram/2001/2/23/INVE3.htm>

Aldridge, J. (1969) *Cairo* (Boston).

Alexandria National Iron & Steel Co. (1992) *1982–1992* (no location).

Al-Hady, H. A. (1993) *The New Settlements between Universality and Locality. A Study of the Egyptian Situation* (in Arabic) (Cairo).

Ali, S. (2001) *Tourism on the Red Sea Coast*. <http://www.ahram.org.eg/arab/ahram/2001/3/6/INVE2.htm>

Al-Mahdi, A. (2000) *The Nile Waters. The Promise and the Threat* (in Arabic) (Cairo).

Al Sayyid, M. K. (1990) 'Privatization: The Egyptian Debate', *Cairo Papers in Social Science*, vol. 13, monograph 4 (Cairo).

Altorki, S., and C. Fawzi El-Solh (1989) *Arab Women in the Field: Studying Your Own Society* (Cairo).

American University Cairo Press (1993) 'The Economics and Politics of Structural Adjustment in Egypt. Third Annual Symposium', *Cairo Papers in Social Science*, vol. 16, monograph 3 (Cairo).

— (1994) 'Human Rights: Egypt and the Arab World. Fourth Annual Symposium', *Cairo Papers in Social Science*, vol. 17, monograph 3 (Cairo).

Amin, Q. (1899/1900; 2000) *The Liberation of Women: The New Woman* (English trans.) (Cairo).

Ammoun, D. (1991) *Crafts of Egypt* (Cairo).

Anhoury, J. (1941) 'L' Economie Agricole de l'Egypte', *Eg. Contemp.* 32, pp. 497–647.

Ansari, H. (1986) *Egypt. The Stalled Society* (Cairo).

Arafa, B. (1954) *The Social Activities of the Egyptian Feminist Union* (Cairo).

Arafa, M. (1965) *Es-Sadd el-Ali* (in Arabic) (Cairo).

Assaad, M., and N. Garas (1994) 'Experiments in Community Development in a Zabbaleen Settlement', *Cairo Papers in Social Science*, vol. 16, monograph 4 (Cairo).

Assmann, J. (1999) *Ägypten – Eine Sinngeschichte* (Frankfurt).

Awad, L. (1968) 'Cultural and Intellectual Developments in Egypt since 1952', in P. J. Vatikiotis (ed.), *Egypt since the Revolution* (London), pp. 143–61.

Ayrout, H. H. (1963) *The Egyptian Peasant* (Boston).

Baden, S. (1992) *The Position of Women in Islamic Countries: Possibilities, Constraints and Strategies for Change*, BRIDGE Report no. 4, Institute for Development Studies (Brighton).

Badran, M. (1999/2000) 'Feminism in a Nationalist Century', *Al-Ahram Weekly*, no. 462, 30 December 1999–5 January (Cairo). <http://www.ahram.org.eg/weekly/1999/462/women.htm>

Baer, G. (1957) 'The Settlement of the Beduins', in G. Baer, *Studies in the Social History of Modern Egypt. Die Welt des Islams*, vol. 5, nos 1–2 (Chicago, London), pp. 84–98.

— (1962) *A History of Landownership in Modern Egypt, 1800–1950* (London, New York).

— (1969) *Studies in the Social History of Modern Egypt* (Chicago).

Ball, J. (1933) 'The Qattara Depression of the Libyan Desert and the Possibility of Its Utilization for Power-production', *Geographical Journal*, vol. 82, no. 4, pp. 289–314.

Barbour, K. M. (1972) 'The Growth, Location and Structure of Industry in Egypt', *Praeger Special Studies in International Economics and Development* (New York, Washington, London).

Barth, H. K., and A. A. Shata (1987) 'Natural Resources and Problems of Land Reclamation in Egypt, *Beihefte zum Tübinger Atlas des Vorderen Orients, Reihe A*, no. 23 (Wiesbaden).

Beddis, R. A. (1963) 'The Aswan High Dam and the Resettlement of the Nubian People', *Geography*, vol. 48/1, no. 218 (Sheffield), pp. 77–80.

Behrens-Abouseif, D. (1972) *Die Kopten in der ägyptischen Gesellschaft von der Mitte des 19. Jahrhunderts bis 1923* (Hamburg).

Benin, J., and Z. Lockman (1987) *Workers on the Nile: Nationalism, Communism, Islam and the Egyptian Working Class, 1882–1954* (Princeton, NJ).

Berger, M. (1970) *Islam in Egypt Today. Social and Political Aspects of Popular Religion* (Cambridge).

Berliner Geowissenschaftliche Abhandlungen (1988) *Egypt Atlas for Ground Water* (Berlin).

Billerbeck, K. (1956) *Struktur und Entwicklung der ägyptischen Wirtschaft* (Hamburg).

Biswas, A. K., et al. (1978) *Water Management for Arid Lands in Developing Countries* (Oxford).

Blackman, W. S. (1968) *The Fellahin of Upper Egypt. Their Religious, Social and Industrial Life with Special Reference to Survivals from Ancient Times* (London).

Blankenhorn, M. (1921) 'Ägypten', *Handbuch der Regionalen Geologie* (Heidelberg).

Bliss, F. (1984) 'Wüstenkultivierung und Bewässerung im "Neuen Tal" Ägyptens', *Geographische Rundschau*, vol. 36, no. 5, pp. 256–62.

— (1989) 'Wirtschaftlicher und sozialer Wandel im "Neuen Tal" Ägyptens, *Beiträge zur Kulturkunde*, no. 12 (Bonn).

— (1998) 'Siwa, die Oase des Sonnengottes', *Beiträge zur Kulturkunde*, no. 18 (Bonn).

Boulos, L., and M. N. El-Hadidi (1984) *The Weed Flora of Egypt* (Cairo).

Bourguet, P. du (1967) *Die Kopten* (Baden-Baden).

Brendl, O., Jr (1957) 'Die Obstgartenwirtschaft Ägyptens', *Die Bodenkultur* (Vienna), pp. 469–87.

Brown, N. J. (1990) *Peasant Politics in Modern Egypt. The Struggle against the State* (New Haven, CT, London).

Brunner-Traut, E., and V. Hell (1966) *Ägypten. Studienreiseführer mit Landeskunde* (Stuttgart).

Budde, A. (1988) *'Ägyptens Landwirtschaft im Entwicklungsprozess', Sozialökonomische Schriften zur ruralen Entwicklung* (Göttingen).

Bush, R. (1998) 'Facing Structural Adjustment: Strategies of Peasants, the State, and the International Institutions', in N. S. Hopkins and K. Westergaard (eds), *Directions of Change in Rural Egypt* (Cairo), pp. 88–109.

Cancel, C. M. (2002) *Women's Movements in Egypt.* <http://www.globalwomensrights.net/library/weekly/aa032300.htm>

CAPMAS (Central Agency for Public Mobilisation and Statistics) (1980) *Egypt: Statistical Indicators 1952–1979* (Cairo).

— (1986) *Arab Republic of Egypt: Census of Population, Housing and Establishments*, vol. 1, part 1 (Cairo).

— (1987) *Water Resources* (in Arabic) (Cairo).

— (1988a) *Statistical Year Book: Arab Republic of Egypt 1952–1987* (Cairo).

— (1988b) *Egypt – Demographic Responses to Modernization* (Cairo).

— (annually 1988–95) *Consumer Price Index Report* (in Arabic) (Cairo).

— (1989a) *Statistical Year Book: Arab Republic of Egypt 1952–1988* (Cairo).

— (1989b) *Communiqué on the Press Conference on the Occasion of Egypt's Population Reaching 55 million on 17/12/1989* (in Arabic) (Cairo).

— (1989c) *Alexandria Governorate 611/89/AMT* (in Arabic) (Cairo).

— (1992) *Statistical Year Book 1952–1991* (Cairo).

— (1993) *Statistical Year Book 1952–1992* (Cairo).

— (1994a) *Statistical Year Book 1952–1993* (Cairo).

— (1994b) *Annual Report on Newly Cultivated Land in the Arab Rep. of Egypt* (in Arabic) (Cairo).

— (1994c) *Statistics of the Activities of Hotels, Inns and Tourist Villages for the Third Quarter of 1992* (in Arabic) (Cairo).

— (1994d) *Estimation of the Population Number of the Arab Rep. of Egypt on 1/1/1994* (in Arabic) (Cairo).

— (1994e) *Economic Statistics 1991/92*, vol. 2. (in Arabic) (Cairo).

— (1995) *Statistical Year Book 1992–1994* (Cairo).

— (1996) *Preliminary Results of the 1996 Census of Population, Housing and Establishments* (in Arabic) (Cairo).

— (1998) *Statistical Year Book 1992–1997* (Cairo).

— (1999a) *Ref. No. 71-12422/97* (in Arabic) (Cairo).

— (1999b) *Ref. No. 1103/1998/AMT* (in Arabic) (Cairo).

— (1999c) *Statistical Year Book 1993–1998* (Cairo).

— (2000) *Statistical Year Book 1993–1999* (Cairo).

— (2000/01) *Pharmaceutical Industry* (in Arabic) (Cairo).

— (2001a) *Tourist Movement, December 2000* (Cairo).

— (2001b) *Statistical Year Book 1993–2000* (Cairo).

— (2002) *Statistical Year Book 1994–2001* (Cairo).

— (2003a) *Ref. No. 71-12422/2001* (in Arabic) (Cairo).

— (2003b) 'Number of Nights Jan. 2002/Dec. 2002' (unpublished sheet) (Cairo).

CAPMAS/UNICEF (Allen, L. F.) (1989) *The Situation of Children in Upper Egypt* (Cairo).

Carapico, S. (2000) 'NGOs, INGOs, GO-NGOs and DO-NGOs. Making Sense of Non-Governmental Organizations', *Middle East Report*, spring 2000, pp. 12–15.

Carter, B. L. (1986) *The Copts in Egyptian Politics* (London, Sydney, Dover, NH).

Chitham, E. J. (1986) *The Coptic Community in Egypt. Spatial and Social Change*, Centre for Middle Eastern and Islamic Studies, Occasional Papers Series, no. 32 (Durham).

Clerget, M. (1934) *Le Caire. Etude de géographie urbaine et d'histoire économique*, 2 vols (Cairo).

Cole, D. P., and S. Altorki (1998) *Bedouin, Settlers, and Holiday-Makers – Egypt's Changing Northwest Coast* (Cairo).

Commander, S. (1987) *The State and Agricultural Development in Egypt since 1973* (London).

— (1989) 'Egypt: Some Issues in Agricultural Sector Policy', in C. Tripp and R. Owen (eds), *Egypt under Mubarak* (London, et al.), pp. 137–57.

Commander, S., and A. A. Hadhoud (1986) 'From Labour Surplus to Labour Scarcity? The Agricultural Labour Market in Egypt', *Development Policy Review*, vol. 4, no. 2, pp. 161–80.

Cramer, M. (1959) *Das Christlich-Koptische-Ägypten – Einst und Heute. Eine Orientierung* (Wiesbaden).

Cromer, Earl of (1908) *Modern Egypt* (London).

Degens, E. T. (1962) 'Geochemische Untersuchungen von Wässern aus der ägyptischen Sahara', *Geologische Rundschau* 52, pp. 625–39.

Dittmann, A. (1989) 'Cities and Markets in Egypt. Marketing Systems in Fayoum as a Case Study', *BRISMES – Proceedings of the 1989 International Conference on Europe and the Middle East* (Durham), pp. 526–41.

— (1990) 'Periodische Märkte in Ägypten. Wochenmärkte und ambulanter Einzelhandel in der Oase Faiyum', *Geographische Rundschau* 42, pp. 143–50.

Dittmann, A., E. Ehlers and R. Grafe (1990) 'Traditionelle und moderne Stadt-Umland-Beziehungen im islamischen Orient: Das Beispiel Faiyum (Ägypten)', *Die Erde*, vol. 121, no. 2, pp. 119–34.

— (1991) 'Traditional and Modern City–Hinterland Relationships in the Islamic Middle East: The Example of Faiyum (Egypt)', *Applied Geography and Development* 38 (Tübingen).

Early, E. A. (1993) *Baladi Women of Cairo. Playing with an Egg and a Stone* (Cairo).

Egypt Magazine (2001) *Mubarak Science City – New Pyramids of Egypt.* <http://www.sis.gov.eg/public/magazine/iss022e/html/mag08.htm>

Ehlers, E. (1984) 'Ägypten. Zur Urbanisierung einer agraren Gesellschaft', *Geographische Rundschau* 36, pp. 220–8.

El-Batriq, et al. (2001) *The Problem of Sugar.* <http://www.ahram.org.eg/arab/ahram/2001/1/5/INVE1.htm>

El-Gawhary, K. M. (2000) 'Egyptian Advocacy NGOs. Catalysts for Social and Political Change?', *Middle East Report*, spring 2000, pp. 38–41.

El Gowhary, Y. (1966a) 'Geography and Town Planning: the Example of Mansura', *Bulletin de la Soc. de Géogr. d'Egypte* 39, pp. 115–36.

— (1966b) 'Rise of Urbanism in Lower Egypt', *Geographicky Casopis* 18 (Bratislava), pp. 201–17.

El-Hady, H. A. (1993) *New Communities between Globalization and Locality, a Case Study of Egypt* (in Arabic) (Cairo).

El-Kammash, M. M. (1968) *Economic Development and Planning in Egypt* (New York).

El-Karanshawy, S. (1998) 'Class, Family and Power in an Egyptian Village', *Cairo Papers in Social Science*, vol. 20, no. 1 (Cairo).

El-Katsha, S., and S. Watts (1993) 'The Empowerment of Women: Water and Sanitation Initiatives in Rural Egypt', *Cairo Papers in Social Science*, vol. 16, monograph 2 (Cairo).

El-Katsha, S., et al. (1989) 'Women, Water and Sanitation: Household Water Use in Two Egyptian Villages', *Cairo Papers in Social Science*, vol. 12, monograph 2 (Cairo).

El-Kharbutli, O. A. and A. S. Abdel-Ati (1998) *Toshka* (Tanta).

El-Khayar, A. (1982) *Politics of Income Distribution in Egypt* (in Arabic) (Cairo).

Ellis, W. S. (1972) 'Troubled Capital of the Arab World: Cairo', *National Geographic Magazine*, vol. 141, no. 5 (Washington, DC), pp. 639–67.

El-Menshaui, M. (1974) *Analyse und Entwicklungsmöglichkeiten von Bewässerungsbetrieben auf Neuland – untersucht am Beispiel des ABIS-Projektes/Ägypten* (Stuttgart-Hohenheim).

El-Messiri, S. (1983) 'Tarahil Labourers in Egypt', in A. Richards and P. Martin (eds), *Migration, Mechanization, and Agricultural Labour Markets in Egypt* (Boulder, CO), pp. 79–100.

El-Naggar, A. E. (1999) *From El-Sadd to Toshka* (in Arabic) (Cairo).

El-Nahhas, A. M. I. (1997) *Squatter Settlements and the Increase in Crime Rates*, diploma thesis, National Planning Institute (in Arabic) (Cairo).

El Saiyad, M. M., and M. A. Saudi (1966) *The Sudan* (in Arabic) (Cairo).

El-Saqqar, W. (2001) *Science City for Modernizing Egypt*. <http://www.ahram.org.eg/arab/ahram/2001/2/18/INVE1.htm>

El-Shagi, E. (1970) '*Die Wahl der Betriebsform für die neu kultivierte Fläche in Ägypten*', *Internationales Afrika-Forum*, vol. 6, no. 2 (Munich).

El-Sokkari, M. A. (1984) 'Basic Needs, Inflation and the Poor of Egypt, 1970–1980', *Cairo Papers in Social Science*, vol. 7, monograph 2 (Cairo).

El-Wakil, Y. A. (1967) *Bilharziose in Ägypten. Unter besonderer Berücksichtigung des Standes in der Provinz El-Baheira* (Göttingen).

El-Wali, M. (1993) *The Inhabitants of Shanty Towns and Squatter Settlements* (in Arabic) (Cairo).

Eman, A. (1943) *L'industrie du coton en Egypte* (Cairo).

Ende, W. (1975) *Arabische Nation und islamische Geschichte. Die Umayyaden im Urteil arabischer Autoren des 20. Jahrhunderts* (Wiesbaden).

Esbeck-Platen, H.-H. v. (1962) '*Ingenieurgeologische Vorarbeiten für das Projekt des Nilstaudammes Sadd el-Ali (Ägypten)*', *Geologische Mitteilungen*, vol. 3, no. 1 (Aachen), pp. 43–66.

Essam El-Din, G. (2000) *A New Boost for Privatization*. <http://www.ahram.org.eg/weekly/2000/511/ec5.htm>

ETA (Egyptian Tourist Authority) (1993) *Total Number of Tourists, December 1992* (Cairo).

— (1998) *Tourist Movement, December 1998* (Cairo).

Ezzat, D. (2000) 'Arabs Need Globalisation and Democracy', *Al-Ahram Weekly*, no. 469, 17–23 February (Cairo).

Fahim, H. M. (1981) *Dams, People and Development. The Aswan High Dam Case* (New York, Oxford, Toronto, Sydney, Paris, Frankfurt).

— (1983) *Egyptian Nubians. Resettlement and Years of Coping* (Salt Lake City, UT).

Fakhry, A. (1982) *Siwa Oasis* (Cairo).

— (1983) 'Bahriyah and Farafra Oases', in *The Oases of Egypt*, vol. 2 (Cairo).

Farag, F. (2000) *Labour on the Fence.* <http://www.ahram.org.eg/weekly/2000/481/ec7.htm>

Farag, M. (1980) 'Aluminium Industry in Egypt', *Proceedings of the Symposium*, 18–19 February (Cairo).

Fathi, A. (1981) 'Egypt – the Sadd el-Ali', *Al-Ahram Iktisadi*, 22 June (in Arabic).

Fekry, A. (2001a) *Privatization Drive Set to Speed Up after Downward Trend.* <http://metimes.com/2K1/issue2001-2/bus/privatization–drive–set.htm>

— (2001b) *Siwa Oasis to Have First Major Organic Farm.* <http://metimes.com/2K1/issue2001-22/bus/siwa–oasis–to.htm>

Fentzloff, H. E. (1961) 'Die Naturgegebenheiten des Sadd-el-Ali-Projekts – Hochstaudamm von Assuan, Ägypten', *Die Erde* 92 (Berlin), pp. 6–17.

Fernea, E. W. (ed.) (1994) *Women and the Family in the Middle East. New Voices of Change* (Austin, TX).

Fernea, R. A. (1973) *Nubians in Egypt: Peaceful People* (Austin, TX).

Fouad, N. A. (1973) *Rewrite History* (in Arabic) (Cairo).

Gadalla, S. M. (1962) *Land Reform in Relation to Social Development, Egypt* (Columbia).

Gamal-el-Din, S. (2001) 'The Most Recent Survey on Family Income and Expenditure in Egypt', *Al-Ahram*, 19 July (in Arabic).

General Organization of Physical Planning (1982) *Master Plan for Greater Cairo* (in Arabic) (Cairo).

Ghanem, M. (1999) *The Tragedy of Administrative Detention.* <http://metimes.com/issue99-24/opin/detention.htm>

Ghonaim, O. A. (1980) *Die Wirtschaftsgeographische Situation der Oase Siwa (Ägypten)* (Stuttgart).

Ghonaim, O. A., and B. Gabriel (1980) 'Desertification in Siwa Oasis (Egypt) – Symptoms and Causes', in W. Meckelein (ed.), *Desertification in Extremely Arid Environments*, Stuttgarter Geographische Studien, vol. 95 (Stuttgart), pp. 157–73.

Ghonem, M. M. (1993) *Weizenversorgung und Ernährungssicherung in Ägypten* (Aachen).

Gillespie, K. (1984) *The Tripartite Relationship: Government, Foreign Investors, and Local Investors During Egypt's Economic Opening* (New York).

Girgis, M. (1973a) 'Determinanten der industriellen Entwicklung in Ägypten', *Die Weltwirtschaft* 1 (Kiel), pp. 113–40.

— (1973b) 'Labour Absorptive Capacity of Export Expansion and Import Substitution in Egypt 1954–1970', *Kieler Arbeitspapiere*, no. 1, Institut für Weltwirtschaft (Kiel).

— (1977) *Industrialisation and Trade Patterns in Egypt* (Kiel).

Giugale, M. M., and H. Mobarak (eds) (1996) *Private Development in Egypt* (Cairo).

GOAL (The General Organization of the Alexandria Library) (1992) *The Revival of Alexandria* (Alexandria).

Gomaa, S. S. (1995) 'Environmental Threats in Egypt: Perceptions and Actions', *Cairo Papers in Social Science*, vol. 17, monograph 4 (Cairo).

— (1997) *Environmental Policy Making in Egypt* (Cairo).

Governorate of Alexandria (nd, ~1984) *Comprehensive Plan – Alexandria 2005* (in Arabic) (Cairo).

Governorate of Beni Suef (1994) *Regional Exposition* (in Arabic) (Beni Suef).

Grafe, R. (1994) *Ländliche Entwicklung in Ägypten: Strukturen, Probleme und Perspektiven einer agraren Gesellschaft, dargestellt am Beispiel von drei Dörfern im Fayyum* (Bonn).

Graves, W. (1975) 'New Life for the Troubled Suez Canal', *National Geographic Magazine*, vol. 147, no. 6, pp. 792–817.

Griffiths, J. F. (ed.) (1972) 'Climates of Africa', *World Survey of Climatology*, vol. 10 (Amsterdam, London, New York), pp. 79–92.

Grzeskowiak, M., D. Norouzi and M. Robbe (1976) *Aufbruch am Nil. Politik und Ideologie in der ägyptischen Befreiungsbewegung unter Gamal Abdel Nasser* (Berlin).

Habib-Hassan, F. M. (1967) *Böden des ägyptischen Niltals und ihre Charakterisierung durch das Rissbild* (Giessen).

Hagel, J. (1972) 'Geographische Aspekte der Umweltgestaltung (u.a. am Beispiel des Sadd-el-Ali)', *Geographische Rundschau*, vol. 24, no. 1 (Brunswick), pp. 20–9.

Hamdan, G. (1959) *Studies in Egyptian Urbanism* (Cairo).

— (1961) 'Evolution of Irrigation Agriculture in Egypt', in D. Stamp (ed.), *Arid Land Research XVII. A History of Land Use in Arid Regions* (Paris).

— (1980–84) *Egypt's Character* (vol. 1: 1980; vol. 2: 1981; vol. 3: 1984a; vol. 4: 1984b) (in Arabic) (Cairo).

Hamdy, M. (1963) *Long Term Manpower Planning Research. A Proposed Occupation Structure for the Manpower for UAR in 1985* (Cairo).

Hamida, I. H. (1992) *Overview of the Development and Utilization of Nubian Artesian Basin, Northeast Africa*, paper presented to the SSO-DRC Workshop on the Aquifers of Major Basins, November (Cairo).

Hamra, A. (1984) 'Verkehrsplanung in Ägypten', *Arbeitshefte des Instituts für Stadt- und Regionalplanung der TU Berlin* (Berlin).

Handoussa, H., and G. Potter (eds) (1991) *Employment and Structural Adjustment. Egypt in the 1990s* (Cairo).

Hanna, F. S., and H. Beckmann (1975) 'Clay Minerals of Some Soils of the Nile Valley in Egypt', *Geoderma*, vol. 14, no. 2 (Amsterdam), pp. 159–70.

Hanna, M. (1989) *The Seven Pillars of Egyptian Identity* (in Arabic) (Cairo).

— (1996) *Housing and Politics* (in Arabic) (Cairo).

Hanna, N. S. (1982) 'Ghagar of Sett Guiranha. A Study of a Gypsy Community in Egypt', *Cairo Papers in Social Science*, vol. 5, monograph 1 (Cairo).

Hansen, B., and G. A. Marzoug (1966) *Development and Economic Policy in the UAR (Egypt)* (Amsterdam).

Harbison, F., and A. I. Ibrahim (1958) *Human Resources for Egyptian Enterprise* (New York, Toronto, London).

Harik, I. (1979) *Distribution of Land, Employment and Income in Rural Egypt*, Cornell University Rural Development Committee, Center for International Studies, Special Series on Landlessness and Near-Landlessness, no. 5 (Ithaka).

— (1996) *Economic Policy Reform in Egypt* (Gainesville, FL).

Hartung, F. (1957) 'Das Wasser im alten und neuen Ägypten', *Naturwissenschaftliche Rundschau* 10 (Stuttgart), pp. 342–8.

— (1979) *75 Jahre Nilstau bei Assuan. Entwicklung und Fehlentwicklung* (Munich).

— (1991) 'Der Hochstaudamm von Assuan', Praxis Geographie, July/August, pp. 80–1.

Hassan, F. (2001) 'Speaking for the Other Half', Al-Ahram Weekly On-line, no. 523, 1–7 March (Cairo). <http://www.ahram.org.eg/weekly/2001/523/sc3.htm>

Hassan-Gardon, T. (2001) Cairo's Air Pollution Catches International Eye. <http://metimes.com/2K1/issue2001–16/eg/cairos_air_pollution.htm>

Haude, W. (1959a) 'Die Verteilung der potentiellen Verdunstung in Ägypten', Erdkunde, vol. 13, no. 3 (Bonn), pp. 214–24.

— (1959b) 'Verdunstung und Wasserbilanz im Flußgebiet des Nils', Geografiska Annaler, vol. 41, no. 1 (Stockholm), pp. 49–66.

— (1961) 'Die naturgegebene Wasserspende an Ägypten und den Nil', Die Erde 92 (Berlin), pp. 18–42.

Hecht, G., and J. Kniesel (1968) 'Die Oase Siwa (VAR) – Bemerkungen zur Geographie', Geographische Berichte 47 (Leipzig), pp. 93–104.

Hefny, W. (1963) 'Zur Bestimmung der Verdunstung und des Wasserhaushaltes in Trockengebieten des Vorderen Orients zwischen Nil und Euphrat', Die Wasserwirtschaft, vol. 53, no. 12 (Stuttgart), pp. 427–38.

Heikal, M. H. (1992) The Gulf War – Illusions of Power and Victory (in Arabic) (Cairo).

— (1995) 1995 – Egypt's Gate into the Twenty-First Century (in Arabic) (Cairo).

Heinl, M., and U. Thorweihe (1993) 'Groundwater Resources and Management in SW Egypt', Catena Supplement 26, pp. 99–121.

Helck, W. (1974) 'Die altägyptischen Gaue', Beihefte zum Tübinger Atlas des Vorderen Orients, Reihe B, Geisteswissenschaften, no. 5 (Wiesbaden).

— (1977) Das vorislamische Ägypten, in: H. Schamp, Ägypten (Tübingen, Basel), pp. 100–21.

Herrera, L. (1992) 'Scenes of Schooling: Inside a Girls' School in Cairo', Cairo Papers in Social Science, vol. 15, monograph 1 (Cairo).

— (2000) 'Downveiling: Shifting Socio-Religious Practices in Egypt', ISIM Newsletter, no. 6, October (Leiden), pp. 1 and 32.

Herzog, R. (1957) 'Die Nubier. Untersuchungen und Beobachtungen zur Gruppengliederung, Gesellschaftsform und Wirtschaftsweise', Völkerkundliche Forschungen 2 (Berlin).

Hetzel, W. (1959) 'Die Gewinnung landwirtschaftlicher Nutzflächen in Ägypten', Erdkunde, vol. 13, no. 4 (Bonn), pp. 436–55.

Hobbs, J. (1990) Bedouin Life in the Egyptian Wilderness (Cairo).

Höber-Kamel, G. (1995) 'Ägypten heute: Der nationale Tag der ägyptischen Frau', Kemet, Zeitschrift für Ägyptenfreunde, vol. 4, no. 3 (Berlin), p. 57.

Hochholzer, H. (1967) 'Kairo. Geschichtliches Raumgefüge und Gegenwartsdynamik einer Weltstadt', Forschungen und Fortschritte, vol. 41, no. 5 (Berlin), pp. 137–40.

— (1968) 'Grundzüge der Demographie und Sozialanthropologie der ägyptischen Bevölkerungen', Afrika heute 22 (Bonn), pp. 334–8.

Holmèn, H. (1991) Building Organizations for Rural Development. State and Cooperatives in Egypt (Lund).

Hoodfar, H. (1999) Between Marriage and the Market: Intimate Politics and Survival in Cairo (Cairo).

Hopkins, N. S. (ed.) (1991) 'Informal Sector in Egypt', Cairo Papers in Social Science, vol. 14, monograph 4 (Cairo).

Hopkins, N. S., and S. E. Ibrahim (eds) (1985) 'Arab Society', *Social Science Perspectives* (Cairo).

Hopkins, N. S., and K. Westergaard (eds) (1998) *Directions of Change in Rural Egypt* (Cairo).

Hopwood, D. (1989) *Egypt – Politics and Society 1945–1984*, 2nd edn (London).

Hornung, E. (1965) '*Grundzüge der ägyptischen Geschichte*', *Grundzüge* 3 (Darmstadt).

Hourani, A. (1962) *Arabic Thought in the Liberal Age, 1898–1939* (London).

Howeidy, A. (2000) *Gateways to IT.* <http://www.ahram.org.eg/weekly/200/467/ec4. htm>

Hurst, H. E. (1957) *The Nile, a General Account of the River and the Utilization of Its Water*, revised edn (London).

Hvidt, M. (1998) *Water, Technology and Development. Upgrading Egypt's Irrigation System* (London, New York).

Ibrahim, A. (2001) *A Debate on Energy and Development.* <http://www.ahram.org.eg/ arab/ahram/2001/6/10/Econ6.html>

Ibrahim, B. and F. N. (1995) '*Islam – Weltreligion und politische Waffe*', *Geographie heute* 127, pp. 40–5.

— (1997) '*Die Nilländer*', *Die Große Bertelsmann Lexikothek. Länder, Völker, Kontinente*, vol. III (Gütersloh), pp. 42–54.

— (1998) '*Weltbilder ägyptischer Kinder und Jugendlicher*', *Regensburger Beiträge zur Didaktik der Geographie* 4 (Regensburg), pp. 135–45.

— (2000) 'The Contribution of Immigration towards Processes of Globalization in Germany – the Example of the Egyptian Copts', in M. Koller (ed.), *Migration aus Nordafrika* 94 (Neuried), pp. 86–117.

Ibrahim, B. and F. Ibrahim (2002) '*Tourismus in Ägypten – ein starker Wirtschaftsfaktor?*', in K. Schliephake (ed.), *Die Beziehungen zwischen der BR Deutschland und der AR Ägypten*, Würzburger Geographische Manuskripte, vol. 60 (Würzburg), pp. 85–90.

Ibrahim, B. and I. (1992) '*Die arabische Frau zwischen orientalisch-islamischer Tradition und Moderne*', *Geographie heute* 103, pp. 23–30.

Ibrahim, Ferhad (ed.) (1995) '*Staat und Zivilgesellschaft in Ägypten*', *Demokratie und Entwicklung* 19 (Münster).

Ibrahim, F. N. (1980) *Der Hochstaudamm von Assuan – Ziele und Folgen* (slide series with explanatory text) (Stuttgart).

— (1982a) 'Ecological and Economic Problems of the Qattara-Depression Project, Egypt', *GeoJournal*, vol. 6, no. 1 (Wiesbaden), pp. 88–9.

— (1982b) '*Kairo. Städtische Siedlungsräume im Vergleich*', in Diercke Weltraumbildatlas, *Textband* (Braunschweig), p. 270.

— (1982c) '*Nil und Assuan-Hochstaudamm, Eingriff in ein Flußsystem*' (set of transparencies) (Düsseldorf).

— (1982d) *Teacher's Manual for the Set of Transparencies: Nil und Assuan-Hochstaudamm* (Düsseldorf).

— (1982e) 'Nile Valley (El Minia Province)', in H. Mensching (ed.), *Problems of the Management of Irrigated Land* (Hamburg), pp. 165–7.

— (1982f) *Geographical Information for the Set of Transparencies: Nil und Assuan-Hochstaudamm* (Düsseldorf).

— (1982g) 'Social and Economic Geographical Analysis of the Egyptian Copts', *GeoJournal*, vol. 6, no. 1, pp. 63–9.

— (1982h) 'The Aswan High Dam: Serious Human Interference with the Ecosystem', *Development and Cooperation*, no. 6 (Bonn), pp. 12–15.

— (1982i) 'The Ecological Problems of Irrigated Cultivation in Egypt', in H. Mensching (ed.), *Problems of the Management of Irrigated Land* (Hamburg), pp. 61–70.

— (1983a) '*Der Assuan-Staudamm – vom Scheitern eines Großprojekts*', *Bild der Wissenschaft* 4 (Stuttgart), pp. 76–83.

— (1983b) '*Die Kopten und ihre gegenwärtige Situation*', in S. Labib et al. (eds), *Die Kopten* (Hamburg), pp. 113–21.

— (1984a) *The Environmental Problems of the Aswan High Dam*, Proceedings of the Shiga Conference on the Conservation and Management of the World Lake Environment (Shiga, Japan), pp. 119–21.

— (1984b) '*Der Hochstaudamm von Assuan – eine ökologische Katastrophe?*', *Geographische Rundschau*, vol. 36, no. 5 (Brunswick), pp. 236–42.

— (1984c) '*Der Wasserhaushalt des Nils nach dem Bau des Hochstaudamms von Assuan*', *Die Erde* 115, pp. 145–61.

— (1985a) '*Flußoase Nil. Gezira-Bewässerungsgebiet*' (2 maps), in *Westermann Atlas Heimat und Welt* (Brunswick), p. 76.

— (1985b) '*Erfolge und Fehleinschätzungen bei den Landgewinnungsmaßnahmen auf der Sinaihalbinsel und an der östlichen Mittelmeerküste Ägyptens*', *Erlanger Geographische Arbeiten* 17, pp. 163–77.

— (1986a) '*Der Assuan-Staudamm und seine Folgen*', in Kreditanstalt für Wiederaufbau (ed.), *Analysen, Meinungen, Perspektiven* (Frankfurt), pp. 55–9.

— (1986b) '*Nubien – Ende einer Kultur im Stausee. Die Auswirkungen des Hochstaudammes von Assuan in ökologischer und ethnischer Sicht*', in P. E. Stüben (ed.), *Ökozid 2: Nach uns die Sintflut* (Giessen), pp. 99–118.

— (1986c) '*Ressourcenknappheit und Bevölkerungsexplosion in Ägypten*', in H. Jäger (ed.), *Beiträge zur Didaktik der Geographie* 9 (Frankfurt), pp. 249–69.

— (1987) 'Recent Impact of Irrigated Cultivation on the Nile Delta', in J. Béthemont and C. Villain-Gandoss (eds), *Les Deltas Mediterranéens* (Vienna), pp. 347–63.

— (1989) '*Die wachsende Islamisierung in Ägypten und die Situation der Kopten*', St Markus, October–December (Kopt.-Orth. Zentrum, Waldsolms/Kröffelbach/Ts.), pp. 8–15.

— (1990a) '*35 Jahre Kontroverse: Sadd el-Ali – der Hochstaudamm von Assuan*', Part I, *Praxis Geographie*, September, pp. 48–50; Part II, *Praxis Geographie*, October, pp. 54–6.

— (1990b) '*Das wunderbare Wirken des koptischen Papstes Kyrillos VI*' (Fürth).

— (1992a) '*Die arabische Welt in einer Identitätskrise*', *Geographie heute* 103, pp. 4–10.

— (1992b) '*Hunger am Nil – Die Überlebensstrategien der Fellachen von Beni Khalil*', *Geographische Rundschau*, vol. 44, no. 2, pp. 94–7.

— (1992–93) 'Vulnerable Groups among the Fellahin – a Case Study of a Village in Middle Egypt', *Bulletin of the International Committee of Urgent Anthropological and Ethnological Research of the IUAES*, nos 34–5 (Vienna), pp. 117–32.

— (1993a) *The Ecological Impact of Groundwater Use in the Arid Regions* (Bonn).

— (1993b) '*Ägypten. Naturräumliche Voraussetzungen – Bevölkerungs- und Sozialstruktur – Wirtschaft*', *Staatslexikon* 7 (Fribourg, Basle, Vienna), pp. 513–19.

— (1996) *Ägypten – Eine geographische Landeskunde* (Darmstadt).

— (2001a) 'Egypt's Disposition towards Self-Determination for Southern Sudan', *Sudan Rundbrief*, July. Amnesty International (Bielefeld), pp. 50–9.

— (2001b) '*Ägyptens Weg in die Moderne*', in *Afrika II. Informationen zur Politischen Bildung* 272 (Bonn), pp. 42–3.

— (2001c) Contributions on Egypt, Horn of Africa, Maghreb, North Africa, East Africa, South Africa and West Africa, in J. E. Mabe (ed.), *Lexikon der afrikanischen Kulturen* (Stuttgart and Weimar).

Ibrahim, F. and B. Ibrahim (2002) '*Ägypten – eine landeskundliche Einführung*', in K. Schliephake (ed.), *Die Beziehungen zwischen der BR Deutschland und der AR Ägypten*, Würzburger Geographische Manuskripte, vol. 60 (Würzburg), pp. 3–10.

Ibrahim, F. N., M. A. Kishk and M. S. El-Zanaty (1993a) 'Rural and Urban Poverty – Comparative Case Studies in Egypt', in H.-G. Bohle, T. E. Downing, J. O. Field and F. N. Ibrahim (eds), *Coping with Vulnerability and Criticality*, Freibourg Studies in Development Geography (Saarbrücken), pp. 97–112.

Ibrahim, F. N., S. Labib, K. Khella and Y. Farag (eds) (1980) *Die Kopten* 1 (Hamburg).

— (1981) *Die Kopten* 2 (Hamburg).

— (1983) *Die Kopten* 3 (Hamburg).

Ibrahim, F. N., N. K. Marcos and M. Al Sanady, M. (1993) *The Poor and the Extremely Poor – A Case Study of the Egyptian Fellahin*, Freiburg Studies in Development Geography (Saarbrücken), pp. 71–86.

Ibrahim, F. N., and H. Mensching (1976) *Desertification im zentraltunesischen Steppengebiet*, Nachrichten der Akademie der Wissenschaften, II. Math.-Phys. Klasse 8 (Göttingen), pp. 99–118.

Ibrahim, S. E. (1995) 'Civil Society and Prospects of Democratization in the Arab World, in A. R. Norton (ed.), *Civil Society in the Middle East*, vol. 1 (Leiden, New York, Cologne), pp. 27–54.

Ibrahim, S. E., C. Keyder and A. Öncü (eds) (1994) *Developmentalism and Beyond. Society and Politics in Egypt and Turkey* (Cairo).

Ikram, K. (1980) *Egypt. Economic Management in a Period of Transition* (Baltimore, London).

ILO (2001) *Egypt. Unemployment, General Level, 3A.* <http://laborsta.ilo.org/cgi-bin/broker.exe>

International Migration Project (1978) *Country Case Study: Arab Republic of Egypt* (co-directors and principal researchers: J. S. Birks and C. A. Sinclair) (Durham).

Internet (1999a) *Urgent Investigations* (in Arabic). <http://www.ahram.org.eg/arab/ahram/1999/12/20/INVE1.html>

Internet (1999b) *Transparency International (TI). 1998 Corruption Perceptions Index – Index Data.* <http://www.gwdg.de/~uwvw/CPI1998.html>

Internet (2000a) *Report on Egypt's Economy by US Embassy, Cairo.* <http://www.sis.gov.eg/online/html2/o050820d.htm>

Internet (2000b) *Year Book 1999.* <http://www.sis.gov.eg/public/yearbook99/html/enrg07.htm>

Internet (2000c) *The Western Delta Project* (in Arabic). <http://www.ahram.org.eg/arab/ahram/2000/12/24/FRON4.htm>

Internet (2000d) *Remittances of Egyptians Abroad in 1999* (in Arabic). <http://www.ahram.org.eg/arab/ahram/2000/12/26EGYP5.htm>

Internet (2001a) *PM Cairo Outlines Egypt's Economic Fundamentals.* <http://metimes.com/2K1/issue 2001-4/bus/pm–outlines–egypts.htm>

Internet (2001b) *Economic and Administration Experts Outline the Programme of Modernizing Economic and Administrative Institutions* (in Arabic). <http://www.ahram.org.eg/arab/ahram/2001/1/9/ECOM.html>

Internet (2001c) *Government Destroyed the Milk Industry* (in Arabic). <http://www.alahali.com/3-1-2001/sub2-1.html>

Internet (2001d) *The El-Faiyum Sugar Beet Project* (in Arabic). <http://www.ahram.org.eg/arab/ahram/2001/3/15/EGYP10.htm>

Internet (2001e) *Minister of Housing Reviews New AUC Plan* (in Arabic). <http://www.ahram.org.eg/arab/ahram/2001/2/2/EGYP7.htm>

Internet (2001f) *Half of the Projects of Borg el-Arab el-Gedida are in Trouble* (in Arabic). <http://www.alahali.com/21-3-2001/sub2-2.html>

Internet (2001g) *Khalid Mohy-ed-Din Demands the Disclosure of the Actual Distribution of Income* (in Arabic). <http://www.alahali.com/14-3-2001/sub1-1.html>

Internet (2001h) *An Urgent Plan to Develop the Airports* (in Arabic). <http://www.ahram.org.eg/arab/ahram/2001/3/14/EGYP2.htm>

Internet (2001i) *The Egyptian Riviera.* <http://www.tourinvest.com.eg/proj–1.htm>

Internet (2001j) *A Study by the Authority for Industrialization* (in Arabic). <http://www.ahram.org.eg/arab/ahram/2001/3/13/ECOM1.htm>

Internet (2001k) *Egypt and Jordan Sign Gas Pipeline Deal.* <http://metimes.com/2K1/issue2001-23/bus/egypt–and–jordan.htm>

Internet (2001l) *Sector Survey Pharmaceuticals.* <http://www.businesstoday-eg.com/surv1.htm>

Internet (2002a) *The Minister of External Trade Visits the Export-oriented Projects in Madinet Sitta October* (in Arabic). <http://www.ahram.org.eg/arab/ahram/2002/7/25/ECON2.htm>

Internet (2002b) *Cairo Resists Pressure from Washington for Releasing Saad Eddin Ibrahim* (in Arabic). <http://www.asharqalawsat.com/pcdaily/16-08-2002/front/front.html>

Ireton, F. (1998) 'The Evolution of Agrarian Structures in Egypt: Regional Patterns of Change in Farm Size', in N. S. Hopkins and K. Westergaard (eds), *Directions of Change in Rural Egypt* (Cairo), pp. 41–65.

Ismael, J. and T. Y. (1995) 'Social Policy in the Arab World', *Cairo Papers in Social Science*, vol. 18, monograph 1 (Cairo).

Ismail, M. M. (1988) *The Economic Problem of Egypt* (in Arabic) (Alexandria).

Issa, H. M. (1970) *Capitalisme et sociétés anonymes en Egypte* (Paris).

Jany, E., and H. Kanter (1972) '*Einige Bemerkungen über Krankheiten (in der Sahara)*', in H. Schiffers (ed.), *Die Sahara und ihre Randgebiete*, vol. II: *Humangeographie* (Munich), pp. 457–62.

Jobbins, J. (1993) *The Red Sea Coasts of Egypt. Sinai and the Mainland* (Cairo).

Jobbins, J., and M. Megalli (1993) *The Egyptian Mediterranean* (Cairo).

Jomard, E. F. (1821–29; 1988) 'Le Caire', in *La Description de l'Égypte* 18 (Paris), Arabic trans. by A. F. Sayid (Cairo), pp. 113–535.

Kamel, A. (ed.) *Kemet – das Schwarze Land: Ägypten* Zeitschrift für Ägyptenfreunde, quarterly journal (Berlin).

Kamel, I. A. (1970) *The Impact of Nasser's Regime on Labour Relations in Egypt* (Michigan).

Karam, A. M. (1998) *Women, Islamists and the State: Contemporary Feminisms in Egypt* (London).

Kassas, M. (1971) 'Pflanzenleben in der Östlichen Sahara', in H. Schiffers (ed.), Die Sahara und ihre Randgebiete (Munich), pp. 477–97.

— (1980) 'Environmental Aspects of Water Resources Development', in A. K. Biswas et al., Water Management for Arid Lands in Developing Countries (Oxford), pp. 67–77.

Kassas, M., and M. A. Zahran (1965) 'Studies on the Ecology of the Red Sea Coastal Land, II. The District from El-Galala El-Qibilya to Hurghada', in Bull. de la Soc. de Géogr. d'Égypte 38 (Cairo), pp. 155–94.

Kassem, N. (1987) Development of Egyptian Industry from the Time of Mohammed Ali to the Time of Abdel-Nasser (in Arabic) (Cairo).

Kelley, A. C., A. M. Khalifa and M. N. Khorazaty (1982) Population and Development in Rural Egypt, Duke Press Policy Series, Studies in Social and Economic Development, no. 5 (Durham).

Kerr, M. H., and El S. Yassin (eds) (1982) Rich and Poor States in the Middle East. Egypt and the New Arab Order (Cairo, Boulder, CO).

Khafagi, F. (1984) Women and Labour Migration: One Village in Egypt, MERIP Reports, no. 124, pp. 17–21.

Khalifa, A. M. (1973) The Population of the Arab Republic of Egypt, Inst. of Statistical Studies and Research (Cairo).

Kirsch, O., and J. Wörz (1984) Genossenschaftliche Produktionsförderung in Ägypten, Forschungsstelle für internationale Agrarentwicklung (Heidelberg).

Kishar, H. A. (1975) Die Auswirkungen des Assuan-Hochstaudammes auf die ägyptische Landwirtschaft (Innsbruck).

Kishk, M. A. (1985) 'Desert Encroachment in Egypt's Nile Valley', in S. A. El-Suwaify et al. (eds), Soil Erosion and Conservation, pp. 15–23.

— (1986) 'Land Degradation in the Nile Valley', Ambio, vol. 15, no. 4, pp. 226–30.

— (1993) 'Combating Desertification, is It Always Possible? The Case of Small Egyptian Farmers', GeoJournal, vol. 31, no. 1, pp. 77–84.

— (1999a) Land and Water in Egypt (in Arabic) (Cairo).

— (1999b) Toshka – Illusions and Facts (in Arabic) (Cairo).

Knaupe, H., and U. G. Wurzel (1995) 'Aufbruch in der Wüste. Die Neuen Städte Ägyptens', Leipziger Beiträge zur Orientforschung 5 (Frankfurt, Berlin, Bern, New York, Paris, Vienna).

Knetsch, G. (1957) 'Eine Struktur-Skizze Ägyptens und einiger seiner Nachbargebiete', Geologisches Jahrbuch 74 (Hanover), pp. 75–86.

Knetsch, G., and M. Yallouze (1955) 'Remarks on the Origin of the Egyptian Oasis-depression', Bull. de la Soc. de Géogr. d'Égypte 28 (Cairo), pp. 21–33.

Knetsch, G., A. Shata, E. Degens, K. O. Münnich, J. C. Vogel and M. M. Shazly (1962) 'Untersuchungen an Grundwässern der Ost-Sahara', Geologische Rundschau 52, pp. 587–610.

Knörnschild, L. (1993) 'Zur Geschichte der Nilwassernutzung in der ägyptischen Landwirtschaft von den Anfängen bis zur Gegenwart', Leipziger Beiträge zur Orientforschung 1 (Frankfurt, Berlin, Bern, New York, Paris, Vienna).

Kolbe, H. (1957) 'Zur Geologie der Eisenerzvorkommen Ägyptens', Geologisches Jahrbuch 74, pp. 611–28.

Koller, M. (2000) Sadats Wende (Neuried).

Korayem, K. (1996) 'Structural Adjustment, Stabilization Policies, and the Poor in Egypt', Cairo Papers in Social Science, vol. 18, monograph 4 (Cairo).

Kovda, V. A. (1958) 'Salinity Problems of Irrigated Soils in Egypt', in *Studies on the Soils of Egypt, Publications de l'Inst. du Désert d'Égypte*, no. 11, pp. 3–60.

Kramer, T. W. (1977) 'Neuere Geschichte Ägyptens', in H. Schamp (ed.), *Ägypten* (Tübingen), pp. 170–222.

Krause, R. F. (1985) 'Untersuchungen zur Bazarstruktur von Kairo', *Marburger Geogr. Schriften* 99 (Marburg).

Kreditanstalt für Wiederaufbau (KfW) (1986) 'Der Assuan-Staudamm und seine Folgen', *Analysen, Meinungen, Perspektiven* (Frankfurt).

Labib, S. (2001) *Giving Tourism a Better Deal*. <http://www.org.eg/weekly/2001/523/ec.3.htm>

Labib, S. Y. (1965) 'Handelsgeschichte Ägyptens im Spätmittelalter (1171–1517)', *Beihefte der Vierteljahrschrift für Sozial- und Wirtschaftsgeschichte* 46 (Wiesbaden).

Lane, E. W. (1908) *Manners and Customs of the Modern Egyptians. Written in Egypt during the Years 1833–1835*, 3rd edn (London, 1989).

Lapidus, I. M. (1967) *Muslim Cities in the Later Middle Ages* (Cambridge, MA).

— (1972) 'The Conversion of Egypt to Islam', *Israel Oriental Studies*, vol. 2 (Jerusalem), pp. 248–62.

Lebon, J. H. G. (1970) 'The Islamic City in the Near East. A Comparative Study of Cairo, Alexandria and Istanbul', *Town Planning Review*, vol. 41, no. 2 (Liverpool), pp. 179–94.

Lichtenstadter, I. (1948) 'The New Woman in Modern Egypt: Observations and Impressions', *Muslim World*, vol. 38 (Hartford, CT), pp. 36–71.

Lippman, T. W. (1989) *Egypt after Nasser. Sadat, Peace and the Mirage of Prosperity* (New York).

Lloyd, J. W. (1992) 'Deep Aquifers and the Impact of their Exploitation', in Friedrich Ebert Stiftung (ed.), *Jordan's Water Resources and Their Future Potential* (Amman).

Lobban, R. A. (ed.) (1983) 'Urban Research Strategies for Egypt', *Cairo Papers in Social Science*, vol. 6, monograph 2 (Cairo).

Loersch, H. v. (1966) *Ernährung und Bevölkerung in der Entwicklung der ägyptischen Wirtschaft. Eine Untersuchung gegenwärtiger Bedingungen des wirtschaftlichen Wachstums Ägyptens* (Munich).

Luger, P., F. Hendriks, H. Kallenbach, E. Klitzsch and P. Wycisk (1990) 'Im Geländewagen durch 600 Millionen Jahre Erdgeschichte', *Die Geowissenschaften*, vol. 5, no. 8, pp. 121–9.

Lynch, P. D., and H. Fahmy (1984) *Craftswomen in Kerdassa, Egypt. Household Production and Reproduction* (Geneva).

Mabro, R. (1974) *The Egyptian Economy 1952–1972* (Oxford).

Mabro, R., and S. Radwan (1976) *The Industrialization of Egypt 1939–1973. Policy and Performance* (Oxford).

Macleod, A. E. (1991) *Accommodating Protest: Working Women, the New Veiling, and Change in Cairo* (Cairo).

Marei, S. (1960) *UAR Agriculture Enters a New Age. An Interpretative Survey* (Cairo).

— (1970) *Egyptian Agriculture* (in Arabic) (Cairo).

Marthelot, P. (1969a) 'Dimensions nouvelles d'une métropole: Le Caire', *Revue Géographique de l'Est*, vol. 9, nos 3–4 (Nancy), pp. 379–90.

— (1969b) 'Le Caire, nouvelle métropole', *Annales d'Islamologie*, vol. 8 (Paris), pp. 189–221.

— (1970) 'Le Caire, nouvelle métropole', Acta Geographica, vol. 3, no. 1 (Paris).

— (1974) 'Recherche d'identité et mutation urbaine: L'example du Caire', Revue de l'Occident Musulman et de la Méditerranée, vol. 18, no. 2 (Aix-en-Provence), pp. 111–18.

Martonne, E. de (1948) 'Reconnaissance géographique au Sinai', Bull. de la Soc. Royale de Géogr. d'Égypte, vol. 22, nos 3–4 (Cairo), pp. 105–36.

Mayfield, J. B. (1971) Rural Politics in Nasser's Egypt. A Quest for Legitimacy (foreword by George Lenczowski) (Austin, TX, London).

Mehanna, S., R. Huntington and R. Antonious (1984) 'Irrigation and Society in Rural Egypt', Cairo Papers in Social Science, vol. 7, monograph 4 (Cairo).

Meinardus, O. (1961) 'The Monastery of St Paul in the Eastern Desert', Bull. de la Soc. de Géogr. d'Égypte, vol. 34 (Cairo), pp. 81–110.

— (1962) 'The Coptic Monuments in the Nile Valley between Sôhag and Aswân', Bull. de la Soc. de Géogr. d'Égypte, vol. 35 (Cairo), pp. 177–216.

Meinardus, O. F. A. (1969) 'The Coptic Church in Egypt', in A. J. Arberry (ed.), Religion in the Middle East, vol. I (Cambridge).

— (1970) Christian Egypt: Faith and Life (Cairo).

— (1977) Christian Egypt Ancient and Modern (Cairo).

Messiha, S. A. (1983) 'Export of Egyptian School Teachers', 2nd edn, Cairo Papers in Social Science, vol. 3, monograph 4 (Cairo).

Meyer, G. (1978) 'Erschließung und Entwicklung der ägyptischen Neulandgebiete', Erdkunde, vol. 32, no. 3, pp. 212–27.

— (1979) 'Auswirkungen des Projektes "Neues Tal" auf die Entwicklung der ägyptischen Oasen', Geographische Zeitschrift 67, pp. 240–62.

— (1980) 'Die Zuwanderung aus den ägyptischen Oasen nach Kairo', Der Islam 57, pp. 36–50.

— (1984) 'Ländliche Lebens- und Wirtschaftsformen Syriens im Wandel. Sozialgeographische Studien zur Entwicklung im bäuerlichen und nomadischen Lebensraum', Erlanger Geographische Arbeiten 16 (Erlangen).

— (1987a) 'Abfall-Recycling als wirtschaftliche Existenzmöglichkeit im informellen Sektor – das Beispiel der Müllsammler in Kairo', Die Erde 118, pp. 65–76.

— (1987b) 'Manufacturing in Old Quarters of Central Cairo', in Material on City Centers in the Arab World (Tours), pp. 75–90.

— (1988a) 'Sozioökonomische Strukturen und Verflechtungen der Kleinindustrie in Kairo', Würzburger Geographische Arbeiten 70 (Würzburg), pp. 213–25.

— (1988b) 'Wirtschaftsgeographische Probleme der Industrieansiedlung in den neuen Entwicklungsstädten der ägyptischen Metropole', Die Erde 42, pp. 284–94.

— (1989) 'Kairo. Entwicklungsprobleme einer Metropole der Dritten Welt', Problemräume der Welt 11 (Cologne).

— (1998) 'Economic Changes in the Newly Reclaimed Lands: From State Farms to Small Holdings and Private Agricultural Enterprises', in N. S. Hopkins and K. Westergaard (eds), Directions of Change in Rural Egypt (Cairo), pp. 334–53.

— (2001) 'Wirtschaftliches Überleben im Zeichen der Strukturanpassungspolitik', inamo 26, pp. 21–3.

Middle East Times (2001) Egypt Business Notes. <http://metimes.com/2K1/issue2001-5/bus/egypt–business–notes.htm>

Migahid, A. M. (1966) 'Ecology of Egyptian Desert Plants', in Das Wasser in den ariden Gebieten der alten Welt, Nova Acta Leopoldina, vol. 31, no. 176 (Leipzig), pp. 179–87.

Mikhael, M. H. (1986) *The Urban Settlements in Beni Suef Governorate*, unpublished dissertation, Cairo University (in Arabic) (Cairo).

Ministry of Agriculture and Land Reclamation (1989) *Agricultural Economy* (in Arabic) (Cairo).

— (1991) *Agricultural Economy* (in Arabic) (Cairo).

— (1992) *Development Strategy for Agriculture in Egypt in the Nineties* (in Arabic) (Cairo).

Ministry of Housing (1998) *Madinet Beni Suef El-Gedida* (in Arabic) (Cairo).

Ministry of Information (1998) *Irrigation*. <http://www.sis.gov.eg/public/yearbook97/html/agri603.htm>

— (1999) *18 Years of Achievements* (Cairo).

— (2000) *Egypt Year Book 1999* (Cairo).

— (2001a) *19 Years Achievements*. <http://www.sis.gov.eg/19years/html/ach01.htm>

— (2001b) *Egypt Year Book 2000*. <http://www.sis.gov.eg/Yearbook2000/html/tour00.htm>

— (2002a) *20 Years of Achievements*. <http://www.sis.gov.eg/public/achiev21/html/ach3.htm>

— (2002b) *Egypt Year Book 2001*. <http://www.sis.gov.eg/yb2001f>

Ministry of Tourism (1999) *Egypt – Tourism in Figures – 1998* (Cairo).

— (2002) *Egypt 2001 – Tourism in Figures* (Cairo).

Mitchel, R. P. (1969) *The Society of the Muslim Brothers* (New York).

Mitchell, T. (1989) *Colonising Egypt* (Cairo).

— (1998) 'The Market's Place', in N. S. Hopkins and K. Westergaard (eds), *Directions of Change in Rural Egypt* (Cairo), pp. 19–40.

Mohamed, E. A.-A. (1989) *Entwurf einer Entwicklungsstrategie für das Niltal Ägyptens, dargestellt am Beispiel der Provinz Assiut* (Berlin).

Mohie el-Din, A. (1982) 'Income Distribution and Basic Needs in Urban Egypt', *Cairo Papers in Social Science*, vol. 4, monograph 3 (Cairo).

Müller, C. D. G. (1969) '*Grundzüge des christlich-islamischen Ägypten von der Ptolemäerzeit bis zur Gegenwart*', *Grundzüge* 11 (Darmstadt).

Müller-Mahn, H.-D. (1989) '*Die Aulad 'Ali zwischen Stamm und Staat. Entwicklung und sozialer Wandel bei den Beduinen im nordwestlichen Ägypten*', *Abhandlungen – Anthropogeographie, Institut für Geographische Wissenschaften* 46 (Berlin).

Müller-Mahn, D. (1991) 'Entwicklungsprojekte mit Nomaden in Nordafrika', in F. Scholz (ed.), *Nomaden – Mobile Tierhaltung* (Berlin), pp. 371–98.

— (1995) '*Nomaden im Niemandsland*' – *Die Demarkation der ägyptisch-libyschen Staatsgrenze und ihre Auswirkungen auf die Stämme der Aulad 'Ali*', in S. Frank and M. Kamp (eds), *Libyen in Geschichte und Gegenwart* (Hamburg).

— (1998a) 'Spaces of Poverty: The Geography of Social Change in Rural Egypt', in N. S. Hopkins and K. Westergaard (eds), *Directions of Change in Rural Egypt* (Cairo), pp. 256–76.

— (1998b) '*Du "Zoning familial" au "Zoning économique". La transformation des structures sociospatiales dans deux villages égyptiens*', *Révue de Géographie de Lyon* 73, pp. 227–34.

— (1999) '*Migrationskorridore und transnationale soziale Räume. Eine empirische Skizze zur Süd-Nord-Migration am Beispiel ägyptischer "Sans-papiers" in Paris*', in J. Janzen (ed.), *Räumliche Mobilität und Existenzsicherung* (Berlin), pp. 167–200.

— (2001a) 'Ägyptens ländlicher Raum im Umbruch', Geographische Rundschau 6, pp. 4–10.

— (2001b) 'Fellachendörfer. Sozialgeographischer Wandel im ländlichen Ägypten', Erdkundliches Wissen 127 (Stuttgart).

— (2001c) 'Vertreibung der Pächter – Rückkehr der Paschas?', inamo 26, pp. 18f.

Muselhi, F. M. (1988) The Development of the Egyptian Capital and Greater Cairo (in Arabic) (Cairo).

— (1993) Geographical Studies on Egypt (in Arabic) (Cairo).

Nada, A. H. (1991) 'Impact of Temporary International Migration on Rural Egypt', Cairo Papers in Social Science, vol. 14, monograph 3 (Cairo).

Nagi, M. H. (1971) 'Labor Force and Employment in Egypt: a Demographic and Socio-economic Analysis', in Praeger Special Studies in International Economics and Development (New York, Washington, London).

National Council for Production and Economic Affairs (1976) The High Dam and Its Effects (in English and Arabic) (Cairo).

Nelson, C. (1996) Doria Shafik – Egyptian Feminist, a Woman Apart (Cairo).

Nielsen, E. (1973) 'Coastal Erosion in the Nile Delta', UNESCO: Nature and Resources, vol. 9, no. 1 (Paris), pp. 14–18.

Niemeyer, W. (1936) Ägypten zur Zeit der Mamluken. Eine kultur-landeskundliche Skizze (Berlin).

Niemz, G. (1986) '25 Jahre Projekt "Neues Tal", Erfolge und Mißerfolge bei dem wichtigsten Erschließungsprojekt in der ägyptischen Wüste', in H. Jäger (ed.), Afrika im Spiegel neuer Forschung (Frankfurt), pp. 223–48.

Niethammer, G. (1971) 'Die Fauna der Sahara', in H. Schiffers (ed.), Afrika-Studien Nr. 60: Die Sahara und ihre Randgebiete I (Munich), pp. 499–587.

Norton, A. R. (ed.) (1995) Civil Society in the Middle East, vol. 1 (Leiden, New York, Cologne).

Office of the Egyptian Prime Minister (1993) Description of Egypt in Figures (in Arabic) (Cairo).

Oldham, L., H. El Hadidi and H. Tamaa (1987) 'Informal Communities in Cairo: the Basis of a Typology', Cairo Papers in Social Science, vol. 10, monograph 4 (Cairo).

Omran, A. R. (ed.) (1973) Egypt: Population Problems and Prospects (Chapel Hill, NC).

Otto, E. (1966) 'Ägypten. Der Weg des Pharaonenreiches', Urban-Bücher 4 (Stuttgart).

Oweiss, I. M. (ed.) (1990) The Political Economy of Contemporary Egypt (Washington, DC).

Parker, J., and J. Coyle (1981) Urbanisation and Agricultural Policy in Egypt (Washington, DC).

Passarge, S. (1940) 'Die Urlandschaft Ägyptens und die Lokalisierung der Wiege der altägyptischen Kultur', in Dt. Akademie der Naturforscher (ed.), Nova Acta Leopoldina vol. 9, no. 58 (Halle/Saale).

Pfannenstiel, M. (1953) Das Quartär der Levante. Teil II. Die Entstehung der ägyptischen Oasendepression (Wiesbaden).

Platt, K. B. (1970) 'Land Reform in the United Arab Republic', in Agency for International Development, Spring Review of Land Reform, vol. 8, pp. 1–68.

Poncet, E. (1970) 'Notes sur l'évolution récente de l'agglomération du Caire', Annales de Géographie, vol. 79, no. 431/1 (Paris), pp. 78–111.

Prehn, M. (1990) 'Die Relativierung des Fortschritts – dargestellt am Fallbeispiel der

Oase Fayum, Ägypten', Mitteilungen der Geographischen Gesellschaft in München 75, pp. 61–95.

Pudney, J. (1955) *Alles inbegriffen. Die Geschichte des Hauses Cook* (Stuttgart).

Radwan, S. (1977) *Agrarian Reform and Rural Poverty: Egypt 1952–1975* (Geneva).

Radwan, S., and E. Lee (1986) *Agrarian Change in Egypt – An Anatomy of Rural Poverty* (London).

Rady, H. M. (1968) *Rentabilität von Bewässerungsvorhaben* (Stuttgart-Hohenheim).

Ravaisse, P. (1886/90) *'Essai sur l'histoire et sur la topographie du Caire d'après Maqrizi'*, in *Mémoires de la Mission Archéol. Française au Caire*; vol. I: 1886, pp. 409–81; vol. III: 4/1890, pp. 33–115.

Raymond, A. (1973/1974) *Artisans et commerçants au Caire au XVIII siècle*, 2 vols (Damascus).

— (1975) *'La population du Caire de Maqrizi à la Description de l'Égypte'*, BEO 28.

Reh, H. (1965) *'Geologie, Lagerstätten und Bergwirtschaft der Vereinigten Arabischen Republik'*, Zeitschrift für angewandte Geologie 11, pp. 608–13.

Rejwan, N. (1974) *Nasserist Ideology. Its Exponents and Critics* (New York, Toronto, Jerusalem).

Richards, A. (1982) *Egypt's Agricultural Development, 1800–1980: Technical and Social Change* (Boulder, CO).

Richards, A., and P. L. Martin (eds) (1983) *Migration, Mechanization and Agricultural Labor Markets in Egypt* (Boulder, CO, Cairo).

— (1985) *'Rural Wages and Agricultural Policy – The Case of Egypt'*, Third World Planning Review 7, pp. 45–59.

Richards, A., and J. Waterbury (1991) *A Political Economy of the Middle East: State, Class, and Economic Development* (Cairo).

Richardson, D., and K. O'Brien (1993) *Egypt* (London).

Rida, I. T. (1961) *Untersuchungen über den Stadtkern von Kairo* (Zurich).

Ritter, W. (1974) *'Recreation and Tourism in the Islamic Countries'*, Recreatievoorzieningen 6 (Breda), pp. 241–5.

— (1977) *'Der Fremdenverkehr'*, in H. Schamp, Ägypten (Tübingen, Basle), pp. 646–53.

Rivlin, H. A. B. (1961) *'The Agricultural Policy of Muhammad Ali in Egypt'*, Harvard Middle Eastern Studies 4 (Cambridge, MA).

Riyad, H. et al. (1987) *Alexandria* (Alexandria).

Rubin, G. (1990) *Islamic Fundamentalism in Egypt's Politics* (London).

Rugh, A. (1984) *Family in Contemporary Egypt* (Syracuse).

Russel, D. (1962) *Medieval Cairo and the Monasteries of the Wadi Natrun – a Historical Guide* (London).

Rzôska. J. (ed.) (1976) *'The Nile, Biology of an Ancient River'*, Monographiae biologicae, vol. 29 (The Hague).

Saab, G. S. (1967) *'The Egyptian Agrarian Reform 1952–1962'*, Middle Eastern Monographs 8 (London, New York, Toronto).

Saad, R. (1988) *'Social History of an Agrarian Reform Community in Egypt'*, Cairo Papers in Social Science, vol. 11, monograph 4 (Cairo).

— (1998) *'State, Landlord, Parliament and Peasant: the Story of the 1992 Tenancy Law in Egypt'*, in A. Bowman and E. Rogan (eds), *Agriculture in Egypt from Pharaonic to Modern Times*, Proceedings of the British Academy 96, Oxford University Press, pp. 387–404.

— (1999) *Planning for Yachting Tourism.* <http://www.ahram.org.eg/weekly/1999/434/tr1.htm>

Sadowski, Y. M. (1991) *Political Vegetables? Businessman and Bureaucrat in the Development of Egyptian Agriculture* (Washington, DC).

Safran, N. (1961) *Egypt in Search of Political Community. Analysis of the Political Evolution of Egypt, 1804–1952* (Cambridge, MA).

Said, G. (1959) 'Some Problems of Industrialization in Egypt', *L'Égypte Contemporaine*, vol. 50 (Cairo), pp. 29–104.

Said, R. (1981) *The Geological Evolution of the River Nile* (New York).

— (ed.) (1990) *The Geology of Egypt* (Rotterdam, Brookfield, MO).

— (1993) *The River Nile* (Oxford, New York, Seoul, Tokyo).

Saleh, S. A. W. (1983) 'The Brain Drain in Egypt', 2nd edn, *Cairo Papers in Social Science*, vol. 2, monograph 5 (Cairo).

Salem-Murdock, M. (1984) *Nubian Farmers and Arab Herders in Irrigated Agriculture in the Sudan: From Domestic to Commodity Production* (Ann Arbor, MI).

Samaha, M. A. H. (1980) 'The Egyptian Master Water Plan', in A. K. Biswas et al. (eds), *Water Management for Arid Lands in Developing Countries. Water Development, Supply and Management*, vol. 13 (Oxford, Frankfurt), pp. 29–45.

Saunders, L. W., and S. Mehanna (1986) 'Village Entrepreneurs: An Egyptian Case', *Ethnology*, vol. 25, no. 1, pp. 75–88.

Schamah, M. (1968) *Die Stellung der Frau im sunnitischen Islam unter besonderer Berücksichtigung Ägyptens* (Berlin).

Schamp, H. (1965) 'Die Umsiedlung der Nubier in Oberägypten. Eine sozialgeographische Studie', *Tagungsbericht und Wissenschaftl. Abhandlungen des 35. Dt. Geographen tages Bochum* (Wiesbaden), pp. 283–92.

— (1966) 'Der Hohe Damm von Assuan und das Gabgaba-Projekt', *Geographische Rundschau*, vol. 18, no. 12 (Braunschweig), pp. 468–74.

— (1967) 'Kharga. Von der Oasis magna zum Neuen Tal', *Die Erde*, vol. 98, no. 3 (Berlin), pp. 173–202.

— (1977) *Ägypten* (Tübingen, Basle).

— (1983) 'Sadd El-Ali, der Hochstaudamm von Assuan', *Geowissenschaften in unserer Zeit*, vol. 1, no. 2 (Weinheim), pp. 51–85.

Scheffler, R. (1990) 'Entwicklungsprobleme der Region Groß-Kairo', *Geographische Berichte* 4, pp. 252–65.

Schendel, U. (1967) *Vegetationswasserverbrauch und –wasserbedarf* (Kiel).

Schmidt, C. (1991) *Das Konzept des Rentier-Staates. Ein sozialwissenschaftliches Paradigma zur Analyse von Entwicklungsgesellschaften und seine Bedeutung für den Vorderen Orient* (Münster, Hamburg).

Schmitthenner, H. (1931) 'Die Stufenlandschaft am Nil und in der Libyschen Wüste', *Geographische Zeitschrift* 37 (Leipzig, Berlin), pp. 526–40.

Scholz, F. (ed.) (1991) *Nomaden – Mobile Tierhaltung* (Berlin).

Schoske, S., B. Kreissel and R. Germer (1992) 'Anch' *Blumen für das Leben – Pflanzen im alten Ägypten* (Munich).

Schulze, R. (1981) *Die Rebellion der ägyptischen Fallahin 1919: Zum Konflikt zwischen der agrarisch-orientalischen Gesellschaft und dem kolonialen Staat in Ägypten 1820–1919* (Berlin).

Schwarz, R. (1992) *Ägypten* (Reinbek).

Sell, R. R. (1987) 'Gone for Good? Egyptian Migration Processes in the Arab World', *Cairo Papers in Social Science*, vol. 10, monograph 2 (Cairo).

Serag, M. A. (1980) *Erschließung der Nordwestküste Ägyptens für den internationalen Badetourismus* (Stuttgart).

Shafia, H. (1968) *Gegenwartsprobleme der Bilharziose in Ägypten. Möglichkeiten einer Sanierung* (Hamburg).

Shalash, S. (1977) 'Hydrology of Lake Nasser in Twelve Water Years 1964/76', in Research Inst. of the Side Effects of the Sadd el Ali, Report no. 21 (Cairo).

Shata, A. (1956) 'Structural Development of the Sinai Peninsula – Egypt', *Bull. de l'Inst. du Desert d'Égypte*, vol. 6 (Heliopolis), pp. 117–57.

— (1961) 'Remarks on the Regional Geologic Structure of the Ground Water Reservoirs at El Kharga and El Dakhla Oases (Western Desert, Egypt, UAR)', *Bull. de la Soc. de Géogr. d'Égypte*, vol. 34 (Cairo), pp. 151–66.

Shata, A., and I. F. El-Fayoumi (1967) 'Geomorphological and Morpho-pedological Aspects of the Region West of the Nile Delta with Special Reference to Wadi El-Natrun Area', *Bull. de l'Inst. du Desert d'Égypte*, vol. 17, no. 1 (Cairo).

Shata, A., M. Pavlov and K. Saad (1962) *Preliminary Report on the Geology, Hydrogeology and Ground Water Hydrology of Wadi El-Natrun and Adjacent Area* (Cairo).

Sherbiny, N. A., D. P. Cole and N. M. Girgis (1992) 'Investors and Workers in the Western Desert of Egypt: An Exploratory Survey', *Cairo Papers in Social Science*, vol. 15, monograph 3 (Cairo).

Shibl, Y. (1971) *The Aswan High Dam* (Beirut).

Shorter, F. (1989) 'Cairo's Leap Forward. People, Households, and Dwelling Space', *Cairo Papers in Social Science*, vol. 12, monograph 1 (Cairo).

Simaika, Y. M. (1962) *Alternative Uses of Limited Water Supplies in the Egyptian Region of the UAR*, UNESCO Arid Zone Research Series, no. 18 (Paris).

Simons, P. (1968) '*Die Entwicklung des Anbaus und die Verbreitung der Nutzpflanzen in der ägyptischen Nilstromoase von 1800 bis zur Gegenwart*', Kölner Geographische Arbeiten 20 (Wiesbaden).

— (1973) '*Die Nilwüste*', in H. Schiffers (ed.), *Regionalgeographie (Die Landschaften)*, vol. 3: *Die Sahara und ihre Randgebiete. Darstellung eines Naturgroßraumes* (Munich).

— (1977) '*Die Landwirtschaft*', in H. Schamp (ed.), *Ägypten* (Tübingen), pp. 569–98.

Singerman, D. (1997) *Avenues of Participation: Family, Politics, and Networks in Urban Quarters of Cairo* (Cairo).

Smith, S. C. (1986) 'General Impact of High Aswan Dam', ASCE, *Journal of Water Resources Planning and Management*, vol. 112, no. 4.

Soliman, A. M. (1996) *Housing and Sustainable Development in Developing Countries* (in Arabic) (Cairo).

Soliman, K. H. (1972) 'The Climate of the United Arab Republic', in J. F. Griffiths (ed.), *Climates of Africa*, World Survey of Climatology, vol. 10 (Amsterdam, London, New York), pp. 79–92.

Soliman, S. (1999) 'State and Industrial Capitalism in Egypt', *Cairo Papers in Social Science*, vol. 21, no. 2 (Cairo).

Springborg, R. (1982a) 'Patrimonialism and Policy Making in Egypt: Nasser and Sadat and the Tenure Policy for Reclaimed Lands', *Middle Eastern Studies* 15, pp. 49–69.

— (1982b) *Family, Power and Politics in Egypt* (Philadelphia).

— (1989) *The Political Economy of Mubarak's Egypt* (Boulder, CO).

— (1990) 'Agrarian Bourgeoisie, Semiproletarians, and the Egyptian State. Lessons for Liberalization', *International Journal of Middle East Studies*, vol. 22, no. 4, pp. 447–72.

Standl, H. (1988/1989) 'Wirtschafts- und sozialgeographische Untersuchungen zur Entwicklung und Struktur der touristischen Dienstleistungsunternehmen in Luxor/Ägypten', *Mitteilungen der Fränkischen Geographischen Gesellschaft* 35/36, pp. 203–71.

Stanford, J. S. (1962) *The Financial and Administrative Organization and Development of Ottoman Egypt 1517–1798* (Princeton, NJ).

Statistisches Bundesamt Wiesbaden (1988) *Statistik des Auslandes. Länderbericht Ägypten 1988* (Stuttgart, Mainz).

— (1993) *Statistik des Auslandes. Länderbericht Ägypten 1993* (Stuttgart, Mainz).

Stauth, G. (1983) *Die Fellachen im Nildelta: Zur Struktur des Konflikts zwischen Subsistenz- und Warenproduktion im ländlichen Ägypten* (Wiesbaden).

Sterling, C. (1971) 'The Aswan Disaster', *National Parks and Conservation Magazine* 41, pp. 10–13.

Stewart, D. (1968; 1981) *Great Cairo. Mother of the World* (Cairo).

Strelocke, H. (1976) *Ägypten. Geschichte, Kunst und Kultur im Niltal: Vom Reich der Pharaonen bis zur Gegenwart* (Cologne).

Sullivan, D. J., and S. Abed-Kotob (eds) (1999) *Islam in Contemporary Egypt* (Boulder, CO, London).

Sullivan, E. L. (ed.) (1984) 'Impact of Development Assistance on Egypt', *Cairo Papers in Social Science*, vol. 7, monograph 3 (Cairo).

Sullivan, E. L., el S. Yassin, A. Leila and M. Palmer (1990) 'Social Background and Bureaucratic Behavior in Egypt', *Cairo Papers in Social Science*, vol. 13, monograph 3 (Cairo).

Tadros, H. F. (2001) *The Development of School Education.* <http://www.ahram.org.eg/arab/ahram/2001/3/14/OPIN7.htm>

Tadros, H. R. (1984) 'Social Security and the Family in Egypt', *Cairo Papers in Social Science*, vol. 7, monograph 1 (Cairo).

Tadros, H. R., M. Feteeha and A. Hibbard (1990) 'Squatter Markets in Cairo', *Cairo Papers in Social Science*, vol. 13, monograph 1 (Cairo).

Tadros, T. M. (1956) 'An Ecological Survey of the Demi-arid Coastal Strip of the Western Desert of Egypt', *Bull. de l'Inst. du Désert*, vol. 4, no. 2 (Heliopolis).

Tafesse, T. (2001) *The Nile Question: Hydropolitics, Legal Wrangling, Modus Vivendi and Perspectives* (Münster, Hamburg, London).

Technau, G. (1974a) 'Bilharziose – ein lösbares Problem', *Die Naturwissenschaften*, vol. 61, no. 3 (Berlin, Heidelberg, New York), pp. 111–16.

— (1974b) 'Bilharziosebekämpfung in Fayyum', in H. v. F. Kochwasser and H. R. Roemer (eds), *Araber und Deutsche. Begegnungen in einem Jahrtausend* (Tübingen), pp. 391–4.

Thompson, H. M. (ed.) (1983) 'Studies in Egyptian Political Economy', 2nd edn, *Cairo Papers in Social Science*, vol. 2, monograph 3 (Cairo).

Thorweihe, U. (1990) 'Nubian Aquifer System', in R. Said (ed.), *The Geology of Egypt* (Rotterdam, Brookfield, MO), pp. 601–11.

Thorweihe, U., and M. Heinl (1998) *Groundwater Resources of the Nubian Aquifer System* (Paris, Berlin).

Thorweihe, U., and H. Schandelmeier (eds) (1993) *Geoscientific Research in Northeast Africa* (Rotterdam, Brookfield, MO).

Tignor, R. L. (1977) 'Bank Misr and Foreign Capitalism', *International Journal of Middle East Studies*, vol. 8, no. 2 (London).

Tondok, W. and S. (1999) *Ägypten individuell* (Munich).

Toth, J. F. (1980) 'Class Development in Rural Egypt', in T. K. Hopkins and I. Wallerstein (eds), *Processes of the World-System* (Beverly Hills, CA, London).

United Nations Development Programme (UNDP) (2000) *Human Development Report* (New York).

— (2002) *Arab Human Development Report* (New York).

Valaoras, V. G., N. Maghoub and M. Farag (1972) *Population Analysis of Egypt, 1935–1970* (Cairo).

van Nieuwenhuijze, C. A. O., et al. (1985) *The Poor Man's Model of Development. Development Potential at Low Levels of Living in Egypt* (Leiden).

Vatikiotis, P. J. (1991) *The History of Modern Egypt from Muhammad Ali to Mubarak* (London).

Vielhaber, A. (1979) *Tourismus in Ägypten* (Starnberg).

Villa Hügel eV (1963) '*Koptische Kunst. Christentum am Nil*', *Katalog einer Ausstellung*, 3 May–15 August (Essen).

Vivian, C. (1990) *Islands of the Blest. A Guide to the Oases and Western Desert of Egypt* (Cairo).

Volkoff, O. V. (1984) *1000 Jahre Kairo – Die Geschehnisse einer verzauberten Stadt* (Mainz).

Wakin, E. (1963) *A Lonely Minority: The Modern Story of Egypt's Copts* (New York).

Wali, Y. (1985) 'Land Reclamation in Egypt', *Al-Mussawar*, 6 September, p. 37.

Walters, C. C. (1974) *Monastic Archaeology in Egypt* (Warminster).

Waterbury, J. (1973a) 'Egyptian Elite Perceptions of the Population Problem', AUFS, Field Staff Reports, Northeast Africa Series, *Africa*, vol. 18, no. 3 (Hanover, NH, New York).

— (1973b) 'Cairo, Third World Metropolis, Pt II: Transportation', AUFS, Field Staff Reports, Northeast Africa series, *Africa*, vol. 18, no. 7 (Hanover, NH, New York).

— (1973c) 'Cairo, Third World Metropolis, Pt III: Housing and Shelter', AUFS, Field Staff Reports, Northeast Africa Series, *Africa*, vol. 18, no. 8 (Hanover, NH, New York).

— (1973d) 'The Balance of People, Land and Water in Modern Egypt', AUFS, Field Staff Reports, Northeast Africa Series, *Africa*, vol. 19, no. 1 (Hanover, NH, New York).

— (1974) 'Aish: Egypt's Growing Food Crisis', AUFS, Field Staff Reports, Northeast Africa Series, *Africa*, vol. 19, no. 3 (Hanover, NH, New York).

— (1975a) 'Chickens and Eggs: Egypt's Population Explosion Revisited', AUFS, Field Staff Reports, Northeast Africa Series, *Africa*, vol. 20, no. 1 (Hanover, NH, New York).

— (1975b) 'The Opening. Part I: Egypt's Economic New Look', AUFS, Field Staff Reports, Northeast Africa Series, *Africa*, vol. 20, no. 2 (Hanover, NH, New York).

— (1975c) 'The Opening. Part II: Luring Foreign Capital', AUFS, Field Staff Reports, Northeast Africa Series, *Africa*, vol. 20, no. 2 (Hanover, NH, New York).

— (1979) *Hydropolitics of the Nile* (Syracuse, NY).

— (1984) *The Egypt of Nasser and Sadat. The Political Economy of Two Regimes*, 2nd edn (Princeton, NJ).

Weheba, A. F. (1960) 'An Outline of the Economic Geography of Egypt during the Middle Age (640–1517 AD)', *Bull. de la Soc. de Géogr. d'Égypte*, vol. 33 (Cairo), pp. 219–40.

Weiss, D. (1964) *Wirtschaftliche Entwicklungsplanung in der Vereinigten Arabischen Republik. Analyse und Kritik der ägyptischen Wachtumspolitik* (Cologne, Opladen).

Wendorf, F., R. Schild and B. Issawi (1976) 'Prehistory of the Nile Valley', *Studies in Archaeology* (New York, San Francisco, CA, London).

White, H. G. E. (1935) *The Monasteries of the Wadi en Natrun* (New York).

Wickering, D. (1991) 'Experience and Expression: Life among Bedouin Women in South Sinai', *Cairo Papers in Social Science*, vol. 14, monograph 2 (Cairo).

Wiercinski, A. (1958) 'Introductory Remarks Concerning the Anthropology of Ancient Egypt', *Bull. de la Soc. de Géogr. d'Égypte*, vol. 31 (Cairo), pp. 73–84.

Wiet, G. (1964) *Cairo. City of Art and Commerce* (Norman, OK).

Wilber, D. (1969) 'Public Health and Welfare', in D. Wilber, *United Arab Republic – Egypt* (New Haven, CT).

Willcocks, W. (1913) *Egyptian Irrigation*, 3rd edn, 2 vols (London).

Wilms, A. (1985) *Zabalin. Die Müllmenschen von Mokkatam, Cairo* (Bremen).

Wilson, R. (1975) *Rural Employment and Land Tenure. An Egyptian Case Study* (Durham).

— (1983) *An Evaluation of Egypt's Attempts at Export Diversification*, Centre for Middle Eastern and Islamic Studies, Economic Research Paper no. 11 (Durham).

Wirth, E. (2000) *Die orientalische Stadt im islamischen Vorderasien und Nordafrika. Städtische Bausubstanz und räumliche Ordnung, Wirtschaftsleben und soziale Organisation* (Mainz).

Wirth, E., and H. Mensching (1989) *Nordafrika und Vorderasien* (Frankfurt).

Wolf, P. (1987) 'Melioration von Salz- und Alkaliböden', *Der Tropenlandwirt*, vol. 33 (Kassel).

Wolf, W. (1962) 'Kulturgeschichte des alten Ägypten', *Kröners Taschenausgabe* 321 (Stuttgart).

World Bank (2001) *World Development Report 2000/2001* (Washington, DC).

Wrage, W. (1965) 'Die sterbende Fellachenkultur Nubiens', *Geographische Rundschau*, vol. 17, no. 8 (Braunschweig), pp. 317–22.

Wurzel, U. G. (2000) *Ägyptische Privatisierungspolitik 1990 bis 1998* (Münster, Hamburg, London).

— (2001) '"Privatisierung am Nil": Eine gelungene Inszenierung', *inamo* 26, pp. 13–17.

Wüst, H. S. (1983) 'Assuan-Staudamm', in *Umschau*, vol. 25/26, pp. 764–8.

Yates, W. H. (1843) *The Modern History and Condition of Egypt. Its Climate, Diseases and Capabilities Exhibited in a Personal Narrative of Travels* (London).

Zaalouk, M.(1989) *Power, Class and Foreign Capital in Egypt. The Rise of the New Bourgeoisie* (London, Atlantic Highlands, NJ).

Zahran, M. A., and A. J. Willis (1992) *The Vegetation of Egypt* (Cambridge).

Zaied, M. K. S. (1968) *Der Assuan Hochdamm (Sadd-el-Ali) und seine wirtschaftliche Bedeutung für Ägypten (Landwirtschaft, Industrie, Elektrizität etc.)* (Graz).

Zaki, M. K. (1971) 'Nomadentum und Stammesbewußtsein in der Geschichte Ägyptens des 19. und 20. Jahrhunderts', *Internationales Afrika Forum*, vol. 7, no. 2 (Munich), pp. 114–20.

Zaki, R. (1993) *Troubling Cases* (in Arabic) (Cairo).

Zein al Din, S. (1983) *Exportstrategien für Ägypten* (Bochum).

Zimmermann, J. J. (1984) '*Neue Städte in Ägypten*', *Geographische Rundschau* vol. 36, no. 5, pp. 230–5.

Zimmermann, S. D. (1982a) *The Women of Kafr al Bahr* (Leiden).

— (1982b) *The Cheese-Makers of Kafr al Bahr: The Role of Egyptian Women in Animal Husbandry and Dairy Production* (Leiden).

Index